Preparation for IELTS General Training
For the 2009 Updated Syllabus

IELTS Target 5.0

Leading to IELTS Academic

Teacher's Book

Chris Gough

SLT

Garnet
EDUCATION

Published by
Garnet Publishing Ltd
8 Southern Court
South Street
Reading RG1 4QS, UK

Copyright © 2010 Garnet Publishing Ltd.

The right of Chris Gough to be identified as the author of this work has been asserted in accordance with the Copyright, Designs and Patents Act 1988.

This edition first published 2010.

ISBN 978 1 85964 577-2

British Library Cataloguing-in-Publication Data
A catalogue record for this book is available from the British Library.

Production
Project manager: Simone Davies
Project consultants: Fiona McGarry, Rod Webb
Editorial: Mary Coomer, Vale Dominguez, Sarah Mellowes
Design and layout: Neil Collier, Sarah Church

Audio recorded and produced by Matinée Sound & Vision Ltd.

Garnet Publishing wishes to thank Doug Mackie, Synergy Total Business Solutions and the staff of Saudi Development and Training (SDT) for their assistance in the development of this project.

The author and publisher would like to thank the following for permission to reproduce copyright material:
Photo of Roald Amundsen on page 68, photographed by Syahidah Osman Cawley, courtesy of the National Library of Australia (nla.pic-an23814274).
Article on page 76 adapted from article '15 Successful Entrepreneurs Who Didn't Need College' with kind permission of Bytestart.co.uk.
Article on page 105 produced with kind permission of British Mensa Limited. For more information on British Mensa the High IQ Society, please visit their website http://www.mensa.org.uk
Article on page 178 adapted from article 'How to reduce office waste and save money' with kind permission of Bytestart.co.uk
Dictionary extracts on page 232, copyright Longman Active Study Dictionary © Addison Wesley Longman 1998.
Information in Reading 2, sections A1 and B2 on page 240, copyright U.S. Geological Survey Department of the Interior/USGS U.S. Geological Survey.
Article on page 278 adapted from article 'A Dozen Guidelines for Using E-mail', http://www.businessknowhow.com
Article on page 295, 'Bullying and harassment at work: Guidance for employees', reproduced under the terms of the Click-Use Licence, with permission from ACAS, http://www.acas.org.uk
Article on page 320 reprinted with permission from go2 – British Columbia Canada's tourism human resource association, http://www.go2hr.ca
Permission to reproduce an adapted version of the article 'Why People Shop on the Web' from http://www.useit.com/alertbox/990207.html on page 324 granted by Jakob Nielsen, Nielsen Norman Group.
Article on page 336, 'Higher World Tobacco Use Expected by 2010', adapted with permission of the Food and Agriculture Organization of the United States.
Use of WV tobacco data on page 340 sourced from WV statistics brief, West Virginia Health Statistics Center, Bureau for Public Health © September 2000.
Article on page 346, 'The Developing World's New Burden: Obesity', adapted with permission of the Food and Agriculture Organization of the United States.
Article on page 350 sourced from article 'Waste Disposal and Waste Management', http://ezinearticles.com
Article on page 362 adapted from article 'Environmental Impact of Tourism', www.ecoholidaying.co.uk

Every effort has been made to trace the copyright holders and we apologize in advance for any unintentional omissions. We will be happy to insert the appropriate acknowledgements in any subsequent editions.

Printed and bound
in Lebanon by International Press: interpress@int-press.com

Contents

Book map

General Training

Unit 1	**Life**
Speaking	personal information
Vocabulary	family / stages of life
Listening	listening for specific information
Reading	skimming
Writing	organizing / types of letter / beginnings and endings / a personal letter

Unit 2	**Learning**
Speaking	looking back / answering questions about the past
Vocabulary	subjects at school / expressing preferences
Listening	listening for numbers and dates
Reading	scanning / short answers
Writing	structuring a letter / stating your purpose / closing a letter

Unit 3	**Work**
Speaking	talking about work and jobs / introduction to exam task 2
Vocabulary	work / jobs / liking and disliking a job
Listening	listening for gist
Reading	scanning for paraphrased language
Writing	register / a letter of application

Unit 4	**Achievements**
Speaking	talking about success / answering exam task 3 type questions / two-way discussion
Vocabulary	success and achievements
Listening	predicting content / listening for paraphrased language
Reading	making sure that information is given in the text / recognizing distracters
Writing	understanding the task / deciding what to say / organizing your points

Unit 5	**Thoughts**
Speaking	how people think / expressing opinions / using the right expression
Vocabulary	ways of thinking
Listening	understanding and labelling diagrams
Reading	guessing unknown words and phrases / understanding new words and phrases from words you already know
Writing	understanding instructions / presenting a balanced argument

Unit 6	**Place**
Speaking	describing where you live / talking about towns and cities / comparing places
Vocabulary	places / describing places
Listening	maps and plans / noticing how information is repeated
Reading	paragraphs / topic sentences
Writing	paragraphs and topic sentences / supporting sentences

Unit 7	**Movement**
Speaking	saying how often you do something / answering questions about travel / expressing opinions
Vocabulary	methods of transport / ways of travelling
Listening	completing a summary / making sure answers fit
Reading	recognizing facts and opinions
Writing	linking words

Unit 8	Time
Speaking	talking about time / questions and answers / answering the question
Vocabulary	time or no time / time expressions
Listening	completing a table
Reading	completing a summary with a choice of words / making sure answers fit
Writing	making a request

Unit 9	Money
Speaking	talking about money / shopping habits and preferences / expressing opinions / follow-up comments
Vocabulary	comparing time and money / words with opposite meaning
Listening	identifying key words that you don't know
Reading	understanding references
Writing	elements of a good composition / introducing opinions

Unit 10	Feelings
Speaking	saying how you feel / disagreeing politely
Vocabulary	situations and feelings / extreme adjectives
Listening	classifying
Reading	using topic sentences to predict
Writing	complaining and requesting / linking words

Unit 11	Health
Speaking	lifestyle / talking about health problems / telling stories
Vocabulary	typical health problems / accidents
Listening	flow charts
Reading	sentence completion
Writing	writing a discursive composition / nouns that add cohesion

Unit 12	Nature
Speaking	talking about climate, weather and temperature / answering the question properly
Vocabulary	climate / weather conditions
Listening	recognizing register / understanding formal and informal language
Reading	recognizing different text types
Writing	deciding what to say / writing the main part of a composition

Unit 13	Construction
Speaking	talking about home and neighbourhood / contrasting ideas
Vocabulary	describing your home / neighbourhood
Listening	spelling answers correctly
Reading	coping with longer texts
Writing	a letter of complaint / spelling and punctuation

Unit 14	Technology
Speaking	talking about technology / giving examples
Vocabulary	machines, appliances, devices and gadgets / effect verbs
Listening	understanding different accents
Reading	timing yourself / improving your reading speed
Writing	having enough to say / making sure you write enough

Unit 15	Society
Speaking	discussing social issues / fitting a punishment to a crime / explaining what you mean when you can't remember a word
Vocabulary	social issues / crime and punishment
Listening	transferring answers to the answer sheet
Reading	checking your answers on the answer sheet
Writing	choosing what to say and how to say it

Book map

Academic section

Unit 1	Life	
Reading	applying your reading skills to an academic text	
Writing	interpreting and describing bar charts	
Unit 2	Learning	
Reading	reading for gist / reading for detail / dealing with unknown vocabulary	
Writing	interpreting and describing pie charts	
Unit 3	Work	
Reading	recognizing paraphrased language / dealing with statistics	
Writing	interpreting and describing line graphs / linking a description together	
Unit 4	Achievements	
Reading	understanding references and linking	
Writing	describing a flow chart / using the passive to describe a process / linking a description of a process together	
Unit 5	Thoughts	
Reading	timing yourself / checking answers	
Writing	composition content (difference between General Training and Academic writing task 2) / improving compositions for the Academic exam	

Introduction

How this book works

IELTS Target 5.0 is aimed at the growing number of students who want to take the IELTS exam while they are studying at a pre-intermediate level. The aim is to prepare these students for the General Training exam rather than the Academic exam, though some additional practice is provided at the end of the course.

Scoring 5.0 in the General Training exam is more realistic than doing so in the Academic exam. The length and academic content of the reading passages in the Academic exam, together with the more challenging writing tasks, makes the Academic course far more demanding for students.

This book consists of 15 units (with an additional five units for the Academic section) and develops in terms of challenge, to take students from a strong elementary to intermediate level. The earlier units focus on basic skills and basic language, including sentence structure and spelling. The texts and recordings are short and simplified to guide students and give them confidence. By the end of the course, students will be tackling texts and working with language that is close to the level of what they will deal with in the exam.

Each unit consists of five modules, which are briefly summarized below.

Speaking and Vocabulary

The focus is on speaking exam practice and preparing students for the type of interaction they can expect with the examiner. There is frequent practice in understanding and answering appropriately the type of questions that the examiner is likely to ask students. The vocabulary selected is the vocabulary that students are most likely to need during the speaking exam. There are frequent reflective tasks that allow students to assess their progress and talk about concerns they may have.

Note that there is not a grammar syllabus. Grammar is dealt with mainly as revision, as it is assumed that most students will be studying grammar on a general English course at the same time as they work through this course. Some major grammar points are dealt with a little more thoroughly, but generally the aim is to develop the students' ability to use the grammar in order to communicate or to recognize it when they are reading. The grammar checks in each unit focus attention on key grammar points as they arise. The teacher can decide whether further grammar practice is necessary, depending on the sorts of difficulties students encounter.

The speaking section in each unit focuses attention on a key pronunciation point. Sometimes this involves practising difficult individual phonemes, and sometimes it involves working with stress and intonation. These points are there to help students improve their pronunciation in the Speaking Module of the exam.

Listening

The Listening Module is roughly divided into two parts. The first part aims to engage students in a topic, pre-teach vocabulary and then focus on a key skill or particular IELTS exam technique. The second part aims to practise the skill or technique, and then encourage students to reflect and develop. Each unit focuses on a different skill or technique, but those skills and techniques are revised as the course progresses. All listening tasks are just like the ones students will tackle in the exam.

Reading

The Reading Module is designed like the Listening Module. Earlier units focus on a number of short texts and general reading skills, while later units deal with longer texts and exam technique.

Both the Listening and Reading Modules end with a focus on key vocabulary in context. The aim here is to focus on the semi-formal vocabulary that is likely to occur in recordings and texts which make up the IELTS exam. Sometimes students are encouraged to select vocabulary from a text that they think will be particularly useful to them and they should record and revise.

Writing

The Writing Module focuses equally on the two parts of the writing exam. Earlier units focus more on correspondence tasks – letter and e-mailing writing – while later units focus on the more challenging discursive compositions. Each unit provides analysis of and practice with a particular writing skill or writing technique that is required for the exam. There is a focus on step-by-step guided writing, and there are model compositions for all of the writing tasks.

Consolidation and Exam Practice

This is divided into two parts. The first part revises the speaking focus and vocabulary presented in the first module. Occasionally, a speaking skill will be developed and there might be a new focus. The second part practises listening, reading or writing skills under something closer to exam conditions. The units in the first section of the book practise two skills with short tasks that students are able to manage. The units in the second two sections focus on one skill and provide fuller exam practice.

Exam tips and Question-type tips

These tips occur all the way through the course. They are there to help you know how to approach the various tasks that make up the exam, and to provide advice on how to go about getting the highest score possible in the exam. They also give advice that will help students to improve their all-round level of general English.

Reviews

There is a review at the end of each of the three sections. The aim is not simply to revise language that has been learnt, but to reflect on what has been achieved and what needs most work. There are tasks that encourage students to revise the vocabulary they have learnt independently and to reflect on which of it is most useful to them.

Mock tests

There are three mock tests provided as pamphlets in the book. The first two tests are designed to be slightly more challenging than the content of the course, but not quite as challenging as the actual exam. The third mock test is at the level you can expect from the exam. Students should do the tests once they have completed the relevant section of the Course Book, i.e., when they have completed the first section and so on.

Workbook

There are Workbook tasks for each of the four modules in the Course Book units. Students may complete these tasks in class if the teacher feels that they need further practice with a point, or complete them for homework. Direct reference is made to these Workbook tasks in the Course Book Reading Modules, as the tasks specifically focus on the content of the Reading Module.

As students work through the course, they will learn more about the exam and what they have to do in each module. By the end of the course, students will know everything about every part of the exam and what is expected of them. When they have finished the General Training course, they will be ready to either sit the General Training exam or to take a short course that will prepare them for the Academic exam.

IELTS Target 5.0 Academic

Some students are studying at a pre-intermediate or intermediate level, but need to pass the Academic IELTS exam in order to enter university or apply for a job. At the end of IELTS Target 5.0 General Training, there is a short course that provides practice specifically for the Academic exam.

IELTS Target 5.0 focuses on the reading and writing skills that students need to progress toward the Academic exam, and will prepare them to sit the exam within a few weeks. There is a longer introduction to IELTS 5.0 Academic and some introductory tasks for students to complete at the beginning of that section.

1 Life

Unit overview

The first unit is based around the topic of life. It is designed to give learners a general taste of what they can expect in the various sections of the IELTS exam, without stretching them too far or challenging them too much at this early stage.

Speaking and Vocabulary

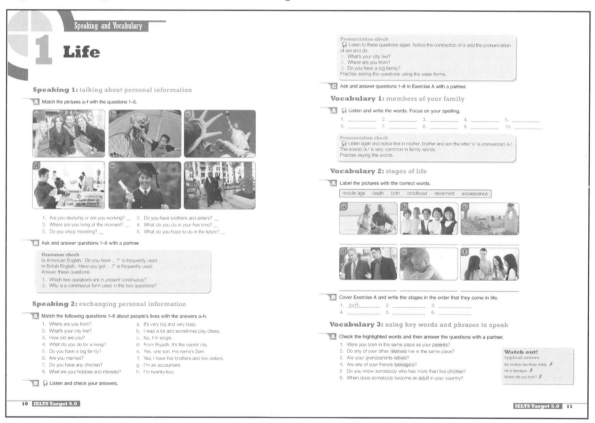

Objectives

- To introduce students to the first part of the IELTS Speaking Module, and practise some of the questions and answers that they will need for that part of the exam.

- To revise and check some basic vocabulary used to talk about stages of life, relationships and family members, and to present some typical IELTS vocabulary that will help students to talk more fluently about their lives.

Speaking 1

A Give students a minute or two to think about the pictures, and then allow them to work individually to match the questions with the pictures. Say the letter of each photo so that students can practise the questions. Drill questions if students' pronunciation is poor so that they are better prepared for Exercise B. They should then be given a few moments to think about answering the questions before talking to a partner.

Answers: a. 2 b. 4 c. 5 d. 1 e. 6 f. 3

B Listen to what students are saying, but avoid correction at this point. The aim is to introduce students to this type of exchange, and the focus should be on fluency. Set a time limit of six to eight minutes.

> **Grammar check**
>
> Students might have heard both '*Do you have ...?*' and '*Have you got ...?*' Check that they have understood both questions.
>
> Questions 1 and 3 are the present continuous. The tense is used because the question is about something temporary rather than something permanent. Note that question 5 is the present simple, and that 'travelling' is a gerund.

Speaking 2

A Students can work individually to match the two parts of the exchanges, but should then be given a moment to compare with a partner. There is no need to give feedback, as students will hear the exchanges in Exercise B.

B 🎧 Play the recording, and pause after each exchange. Drill the exchanges if students' pronunciation is poor so that they are better prepared for Exercise C. Focus on areas where there are problems with pronunciation.

Answers: 1. d   2. a   3. h   4. g   5. f
6. c   7. e   8. b

Tapescript 🎧 **1** (1 min, 29 secs)

B **Listen and check your answers.**

1
Examiner: Where are you from?
Student: From Riyadh. It's the capital city.

2
Examiner: What's your city like?
Student: It's very big and very busy.

3
Examiner: How old are you?
Student: I'm twenty-four.

4
Examiner: What do you do for a living?
Student: I'm an accountant.

5
Examiner: Do you have a big family?
Student: Yes, I have five brothers and two sisters.

6
Examiner: Are you married?
Student: No, I'm single.

7
Examiner: Do you have any children?
Student: Yes, one son. His name's Sam.

8
Examiner: What are your hobbies and interests?
Student: I read a lot and sometimes play chess.

> **Pronunciation check**
>
> Ask students what *are*, *do* and *have* are, and establish that they are auxiliary verbs (verbs that form tenses). Play the recording and ask students to reproduce the auxiliary verbs as they hear them. You could use phonetic script to show how the three verbs are produced weakly (i.e., when unstressed).
>
> are: /ɑː(r)/ do: /duː/ have: /hæv/
>
> Drill the examples, and then give students a moment to practise in pairs.

Tapescript 🎧 **2** (0 mins, 44 secs)

Pronunciation check

Listen to these questions again. Notice the contraction of *is* and the pronunciation of *are* and *do*.

1 What's your city like?

2 Where are you from?

3 Do you have a big family?

Practise asking the questions using the weak forms.

C Allow students to practise the exchanges. Listen for pronunciation, especially intonation. Students should sound 'interested', and they should use rising intonation to ask questions. Stronger students could be told to remember the questions rather than reading them directly from the page.

Vocabulary 1

A 🎧 Students are probably familiar with these words. This is a revision exercise that focuses on spelling. Play the recording, pausing after each word to give students time to write. To feed back, ask students to spell the words for you as you write them on the board.

Answers: 1. father   2. mother   3. brother   4. sister   5. grandfather   6. son   7. daughter   8. aunt   9. uncle   10. cousin

> **Tapescript** 🎧 3 (1 min, 1 sec)
>
> **A Listen and write the words. Focus on your spelling.**
>
> **1** father
>
> **2** mother
>
> **3** brother
>
> **4** sister
>
> **5** grandfather
>
> **6** son
>
> **7** daughter
>
> **8** aunt
>
> **9** uncle
>
> **10** cousin

Students may want to ask about other family members that are not included in this task (nephews, nieces, in-laws and so on). It is important that students learn the vocabulary that is most useful to them. You can teach any extra words they may need to talk about their families. However, at this level they can easily be overloaded with too much vocabulary, and you should avoid teaching lists of new words for the sake of it.

> **Pronunciation check**
>
> The sounds /ʌ/ and /ð/ are often difficult for students to produce. Draw attention to the box, and model the example words clearly. You might like to put the phonemes on the board, and ask students to add any other words they know under each phoneme. Ask a few students to reproduce the examples.

> **Tapescript** 🎧 4 (0 mins, 25 secs)
>
> *Pronunciation check*
>
> Listen again and notice that in *mother*, *brother* and *son* the letter 'o' is pronounced /ʌ/. The sound /ʌ/ is very common in family words. Practise saying the words.

Vocabulary 2

A Students will find these words more challenging. You can put them into pairs to complete the task or allow them time to work individually. Point out that some of the words are nouns, and are formed from words that students may already know, like 'child'/'childhood'. Remind them to match the words they know first, and then the meanings of any remaining may become clear.

During feedback, clarify anything that students are still not sure about. Give explanations and examples, such as the following:

middle age – this is the period from about 40 to 60. After 60, you are beginning to get old. Most of your parents are middle-aged.

Note that 'adolescence' is different from 'puberty', which is the physical change from childhood to adulthood.

Answers: a. retirement   b. childhood   c. death   d. middle age   e. birth   f. adolescence

B The aim of this activity is to consolidate and practise spelling. Make sure students cover Exercise A. Workbook Exercise C consolidates this language, and if students are having difficulties, it could be set at this point.

Answers: 1. birth   2. childhood   3. adolescence   4. middle age   5. retirement   6. death

Vocabulary 3

A Students can either work individually with dictionaries or talk to a partner to check the key words. Some will be known, and some are probably new. Set a time limit of about five minutes, and then give feedback. As you go through the words, refer to other parts of speech – for example, 'retire' is the verb and 'retirement' (learnt previously) is the noun, etc. Point out that 'children' is an irregular plural. Check the pronunciation of tricky words like 'marriage'. Allow another five minutes or so for students to ask and answer the questions.

Watch out!

Draw attention to this box, and tell students that the boxes are a feature of the course. They should look out for the boxes themselves as they work through the book. You can draw attention to the boxes if you think a particular point needs to be made.

Listening

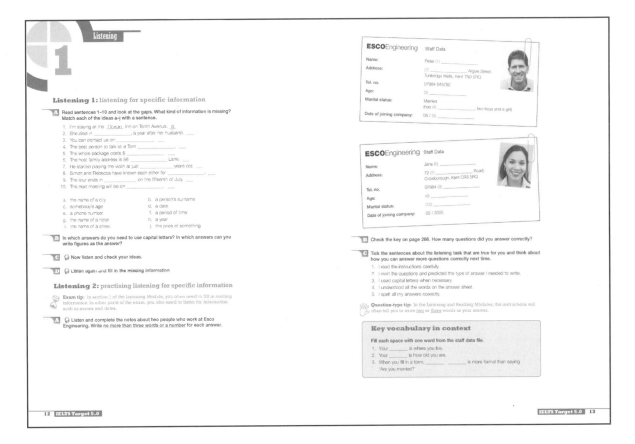

Objectives

- **To introduce students to the fact that listening for specific information is a common feature in the IELTS Listening Module, and that it is a part in which, at their level, they can score highly.**

- **To introduce the practice of looking at instructions carefully, and using instructions to make predictions.**

- **To introduce the practice of checking spelling, and checking that capital letters have been used appropriately.**

Listening 1

A Explain that names, dates and so on are what students are frequently listening for in an exam listening task. Tell students to look at the sentences 1–10 before looking at the ideas a–j. Work through the sentences and elicit ideas, but don't tell students at this point whether they are right or wrong. Then allow students three or four minutes to work individually to do the matching task. There is no need to give feedback, as students will listen to the answers in Exercise C.

B When students have finished the matching task, ask them quickly which answers need initial capital letters. At this point, you can say if they are right or not without giving the actual answers.

Answers:
Sentences 1, 4, 6 and 9 need initial capitals. Sentence 10 will need an initial capital if it is a day, i.e., Friday, or a month, i.e., July.

C 🎧 Tell students to put pens down, and play the recording once just to let students check their answers to Exercise A.

Tapescript 🎧 **5 (1 min, 45 secs)**

C **Now listen and check your ideas.**

1 Hi, is that Martin? Hi, I'm here in New York. I'm staying at the Ocean Inn on Tenth Avenue.

2 (fade in) ... and she died in 1984, a year after her husband.

3 (fade in) ... and, of course, you can contact us on 0207 389 152, twenty-four hours a day.

4 I'm not really sure. I think the best person to talk to is Tom Henderson.

5 (fade in) … and the whole package costs $320.

6 (fade in) … Yes, that's Bournemouth, and the host family address is 56 Green Lane.

7 (fade in) … and incredibly, he started playing the violin at just four years old.

8 Simon and Rebecca have known each other for twenty years.

9 (fade in) … and the tour ends in Manchester on the fifteenth of July.

10 (fade in) … so, I think that's everything. The next meeting will be on April the seventeenth.

D 🎧 Play the recording again, pausing after each sentence to allow time to write. Write the answers on the board as feedback. Point out the use of capital letters as you go.

Answers:
1. Ocean, g
2. 1984, h
3. 0207 389 152, e
4. Henderson, b
5. 320, j
6. Green, i
7. four / 4, c
8. twenty years / 20 years, f
9. Manchester, a
10. April 17 / April the seventeenth, d

Tapescript 🎧 6 (0 mins, 11 secs)

D Listen again and fill in the missing information.

[Play track 5 again]

Listening 2

A 🎧 Students are given a little more information about the situation here than they would get in the actual exam.

Read through the instructions with the students, making sure they know what to do. Ask them if it is acceptable to write two words as an answer (yes), and if it is OK to write four words (no). Tell

students that in the exam, they will have 30 seconds to look at the questions, but that in this exercise they can have a little longer. Allow about a minute to look through and answer any questions they have. Students might find it difficult to listen to the recording only once, but avoid playing it a second time. Students can discuss what difficulties they had, and then listen again later (see Exercises B and C).

Tapescript 🎧 7 (2 mins, 42 secs)

A **Listen and complete the notes about two people who work at Esco Engineering. Write no more than three words or a number for each answer.**

Greg: Oh, hi Maggie. It's Greg.

Maggie: Hi, Greg.

Greg: I'm phoning to check some information about some of the staff. I'm putting all the staff data into new files, and I notice that I don't have files for two people. I think you might have them.

Maggie: Oh, really? What are their names?

Greg: Peter Austin and Jane Moore.

Maggie: Let me have a look. Yes, I've got them here. Shall I send them to you?

Greg: No, you don't need to. Just give me the information now. I can write it on some new files. I don't really need the photos if you've got photos there.

Maggie: OK. Well, Peter Austin first.

Greg: Now, is that Austin with an 'i' or Austen with an 'e'?

Maggie: It's A-U-S-T-I-N, and his address is a hundred and ten Argyle Street, Tunbridge Wells, Kent TN3 5RQ.

Greg: A hundred and ten?

Maggie: Uh-huh.

Greg: And his phone number?

Maggie: It's 07984 645792.

Greg: OK – and how old is he?

Maggie: He's forty-seven.

Greg: Forty-seven. And what about his marital status?

Maggie: He's married. There's a note here that he has three children – two boys and a girl.

Greg: OK, and finally – when did he join the company?

Maggie:	He started with Esco in August two thousand and three.
Greg:	Thanks, Maggie. Now, what about Jane?
Maggie:	Her name's Jane Moore. That's M-O-O-R-E, and her address is 72 Cedar Road, Crowborough, Kent CR3 5RQ.
Greg:	CR3 and what, sorry?
Maggie:	CR3 5RQ.
Greg:	And how do you spell Cedar?
Maggie:	C-E-D-A-R. Her phone number is 07984 650396.
Greg:	07984 650396.
Maggie:	Yes. Now, she's twenty-two and she's single.
Greg:	OK.
Maggie:	And she started with Esco in 2005 – February 2005.
Greg:	Right, thanks, Maggie. That's very helpful. Goodbye now.
Maggie:	Goodbye.

Key vocabulary in context

Sometimes it is necessary to pre-teach vocabulary, and sometimes vocabulary is best learnt in context once it has been read or heard. Students can work individually or directly in pairs. Ask them to tell you the answers for feedback, as they will practise saying the words and you can check pronunciation.

Answers: 1. address   2. age
3. marital status

For further listening practice, tell students to complete the exercises on page 5 of the Workbook. Set as an extra activity or homework task.

B Checking answers and then reflecting on how many questions were answered correctly and why is a constant feature of the skills sections. Give students sufficient time to check and think about why they may have answered incorrectly, before moving on to Exercise C.

Answers:
1. Austin
2. 110
3. 47
4. three children / 3 children
5. 2003
6. Moore
7. Cedar
8. 650396
9. twenty-two / 22
10. single

C Students may not be familiar with this type of reflective process. Explain that identifying what they are doing well and not doing so well is a very good way of focusing on what they can do better next time. In this first unit, you might like to work through the task, asking various students to tell you how well they feel they did. Later, they can work on these tasks individually or with a partner. Play the recording again if necessary, and tell students to focus on why the correct answers are correct.

Reading

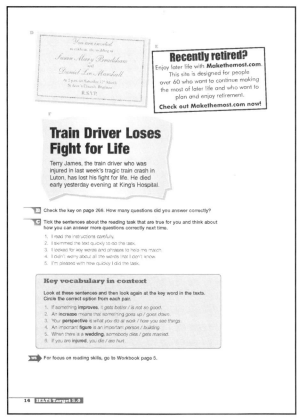

Objectives

- To introduce students to the concept of skimming, and to show them that recognizing the source and the purpose or function of what they read is very important.

- To introduce students to skimming a text before reading it more carefully.

- To show students that it is not essential to understand all the words in a text in order to complete a task.

Reading 1

Explain that 'source' means 'where something comes from'. The source of a text could be a magazine article or a leaflet given to you in the street. The presentation of language, and the type of language used in a text, will vary hugely depending on the source.

A Read through the possible sources 1–6 with the students, and check any words they don't know. A journal is generally a little more serious in terms of content than a magazine. Check the pronunciation of 'advertisement' with stress on the second syllable, since it is a word that students will meet many times in this course. You can either look at the example number 1 before looking through the other sources, or do it once you have looked through them all. Make sure students work individually now, as they will compare answers and discuss how they did the task in Exercise B. Don't give answers until students have completed Exercise D.

B Encourage students to discuss how they approached the task, and what they looked for in each extract. They should mention features such as the design and layout of the extract, the level of formality of language used, typically used introductions or endings, and key words and phrases that they quickly recognized. Mention these features and others that you feel are useful during feedback.

Answers: 1. e   2. a   3. b   4. f   5. d 6. c

C Read the exam tip with students, and make clear that the purpose or function of a text is what it is written for and what the reader is supposed to get from reading it. The task gives further skimming practice, and it is important to point out that students may not need to read all the texts again. You can either work through this text with the whole class or set it for individual completion, and then check.

Answers: 1. c   2. a   3. f   4. b   5. d 6. e

D Students complete the summary to reflect on what they have done. The task should reinforce the importance of skimming, and present some typical jargon words that you will probably want to use later in the course. Students should work individually. You can give feedback either by telling them the correct answers, or by asking one student (with clear pronunciation) to read the text with the correct options.

Answers: The correct options are: quickly / general / before / slowly

Reading 2

A Tell students that they are going to practise what they have just been focusing on. It would be a good idea to read through the source options 1–6 with them in case there are any words they don't know. 'Biography' is explained, but 'invitation' might be new. Allow sufficient time for students to complete the task properly – getting most answers correct will give them confidence.

B Checking their answers, and then reflecting on how many questions were answered correctly and why, is a constant feature of the skills sections. Give students sufficient time to check and think about why they may have answered incorrectly, before moving on to Exercise C.

Answers: 1. B   2. D   3. E   4. C   5. A 6. F

C Students will be more familiar with this type of reflective process having completed the listening section. Remind them that identifying what you are doing well and not doing so well is a very good way of focusing on what you can do better next time. You may like to close the task by asking how many students are happy with the number of correct matches they made, or even how many matched all correctly. You may also like to ask one student what he or she will do differently next time.

If there is time in the lesson, it would be good to work through the task in the Workbook now, or set it up for homework. The task gives further practice with reading for gist.

Key vocabulary in context

Remind students that an effective way of learning and remembering new vocabulary is to study it closely, once it has been presented in context. The vocabulary here appears to be unrelated, but that is because it appears in a series of unrelated extracts. These are all high-frequency, useful words. Students should work individually to complete the task. Remind them to check the words again in the extracts. For feedback, ask them for the correct options so they can practise saying them. Correct any errors of pronunciation, and model the words for them clearly.

Answers: 1. gets better   2. goes up
3. how you see things   4. person
5. gets married   6. are hurt

Writing

Objectives

- To introduce students to the basic concept of planning and organizing their writing.

- To introduce students to the different types of letters they will be required to write in the IELTS exam.

- To present and practise typical ways to start and end letters.

- To present and practise the typical content of an informal letter of introduction, and how such a letter should be organized.

Writing 1

A Read the exam tip with students, and then ask them to give you a few examples of what 'planning and organizing' means. Don't worry now about accepting or rejecting their ideas, as the task develops the idea. Students can work individually or in pairs to complete the ordering task.

Answers: 1. c 2. a 3. e 4. f 5. d 6. b

B Read the rubric with students and make sure they are clear about the time and word count. Put them into pairs and allow them sufficient time to work out their timings for each stage. Feeding back on this task could be very time-consuming if everyone wants to have a say. It is probably best to either ask one strong pair to read out their timings, or for you to put the timings below on the board as they work, and then ask them how their timings compare.

Answers: There is no correct answer, but a sensible breakdown would be:
1. 2 minutes   2. 3 minutes
3. 1 minute   4. 2 minutes
5. 10 minutes   6. 2 minutes

Writing 2

A Read the letter types 1–6 with students, and deal with any unknown words. Point out that 'complaint' is a noun derived from the verb 'complain', that 'request' is a formal way to say 'ask for', and that 'apology' is a noun related to 'apologize', which is a formal way to say one is sorry. Tell students that all of these are useful words to remember. Students should work individually to complete the task. The quickest way to give feedback will be simply to tell students the answers, as there is no benefit in discussing or comparing answers.

Answers: 1. D   2. F   3. E   4. A   5. B   6. C

B Students should do this task on their own, but tell them that they can highlight all the opening lines if they want. It would be a good idea to point out how frequently letters begin 'I am writing to …' Monitor students as they write their chosen sentence.

C Ask students if they know how to end letters in different ways before setting up the task. Students should work individually to complete the task. Tell students the answers to check the activity.

Answers:
Ending 1 can go with A and F (it is a little too friendly and positive for B)

Ending 2 goes with C

Ending 3 goes with D

Ending 4 goes with B (it is probably a little too cold for A and F)

Ending 5 goes with E

D Students can work in pairs as suggested, or you can approach this task as a whole-class discussion if time is short.

Answers:
1. when you start the letter with the name of the person you are writing to / when you start the letter 'Dear Sir' or 'Dear Madam'
2. when you know the person you are writing to well or have written to him or her a number of times
3. regards / kind regards / all the best / best for now / love / lots of love, etc.

Writing 3

A Read the rubric with students. Make sure they understand that there is not a correct answer to the task, but that some information is more likely to be included. Explain to students that they will be staying with a host family in order to improve their English. Encourage students to discuss and justify their ideas during pairwork. Set a time limit, as there is not necessarily a logical ending to the task. There is no need to give feedback or check answers, as the following task deals with that.

B Students should work individually, and write numbers against the points in Exercise A. Give them sufficient time to complete the task. You might like to write the answers below on the board as they work, as giving feedback orally here could become confusing. Make sure students understand that this is not the only order in which points could be made.

Answers:
your name 1
your age 2
where you live 3
your family 4
your hobbies and interests 5
your studies or job 6
your favourite music 7
your personality 8
why you're studying English 9

End the task by asking whether anyone included all the same points as Bruno.

C Students may try to do this before they begin Exercise B or as they are doing it. If not, you can either give them a couple of moments to choose individually how they want to start and end the letter, or ask the whole class.

Answers: The letter should start with 'Dear' and can end with either 'Best wishes' or 'Regards'.

Writing task

Writing tasks are found either in the Workbook or in the exam practice section at the end of the unit. For this unit, the task is in the Workbook.

You will know what you can expect from your students with this first writing task. Some of them may only be able to manage a string of short sentences at this stage, and will find it difficult to link ideas together more cohesively. Some stronger students may be able to link ideas, and write something more solid. The important thing here is that they learn from the process, and not worry too much yet about the product. Tell them that at this stage, the best approach is to more or less copy the model letter, substituting facts about their lives for the facts about Bruno's. Monitor as students work so that you can check obvious errors and offer alternatives, but don't worry too much about grammatical accuracy. Students could exchange letters when they have finished.

You could also build up a letter on the board with different ideas suggested by various students in the class. This will give students more confidence to do the writing task for homework.

If students do complete their own letters and you choose to collect them in, it would be better to use the process to get an idea of what they are capable of, rather than correct too heavily. At this stage, you may be correcting almost every line they write.

Consolidation

Speaking

A Talk with a partner. Answer these questions about the first part of the Speaking Module.

1. How long does the first part of the Speaking Module take?
2. Is it about a third or about half of the total Speaking Module?
3. What kind of questions will the examiner ask?

B Look at these possible questions. Tick them if you think they are easy to answer and cross them if they are difficult to answer. Then compare your thoughts with a partner.

1. What do you like doing in your free time?
2. Which part of the world would you most like to visit?
3. Why are you learning English?
4. How long have you lived there? (your hometown)
5. Who was your favourite teacher at school?
6. Tell me about a famous person that you admire?

C Walk around the class. Practise asking and answering the questions with other students.

Vocabulary

A Write one word to complete each sentence below.

1. Your mother and father are your _____.
2. Your father's father is your _____.
3. Your mother or father's brother is your _____.
4. Your mother or father's sister is your _____.
5. Your son's sister is your _____.
6. The children of your uncles and aunts are your _____.
7. All of the people in your family are your _____.

B Fill the gaps with a word made from the root words in the box.

1. What do you do for a _____living____?
2. One of my uncles has got ten _____.
3. I didn't have any brothers and sisters, but I had a very happy _____.
4. I want to be happily _____ before I'm thirty.
5. My father seems to be very happy in his _____.

live
child
child
marry
retire

C 🎧 Mark the main stress on these key words from the unit. Then listen and check. Practise saying the words.

1. interests 2. family 3. relatives 4. teenager 5. retirement 6. adolescence 7. improve

Errors

A There are errors in all of these sentences (sometimes more than one). Correct them.

1. He's from new york.
2. My father's engineer.
3. Have you brothers and sisters?
4. I have 22 years.
5. His name's alan murray.
6. I work for a company called friendly products.
7. Where was you born?
8. I write to apply for job in yesterday's newspaper.

IELTS Target 5.0 19

Speaking

A The aim of the first task is to clarify for students what they should expect in the speaking part of the exam. They will know the answers to some of the questions from what they practised in the first unit, and they may know answers to other questions from having read about the exam, or having spoken to people who have done it. Giving students some time to discuss the questions should ensure that they remember the information better than if you simply tell it to them. Students can either discuss the questions in pairs or small groups.

Answers:
1. 4–5 minutes
2. about a third
3. questions about the student's life (like those practised in the first part of this unit and in Exercise B that follows)

B The aim of this activity is to get students thinking about which questions they feel comfortable and confident with. They should work individually before comparing their ideas. You could feed back by asking a couple of students why they think one question is easy and another difficult, but avoid a long discussion.

C Students can work in pairs or you can ask different students for the answers. Set a time limit or allow each student to ask each question once only.

Vocabulary

A This task practises vocabulary that students have learnt in the unit. They should know the words, but may forget how to spell them. Set the task for individual completion. To feed back, you could ask students to come and write the words on the board, or to save time, you could write them on the board as students are working.

Answers: 1. parents 2. grandfather 3. uncle 4. aunt 5. daughter 6. cousins 7. relatives

To follow up this task, you could practise possessives by telling students to close their books and then asking students questions, like 'Who is your uncle?', and 'Who is your grandmother?'

B This task checks whether students remember words, and if so can spell them correctly. Refer students to the 'root' words in the box – they could think of some different forms before completing the activity. Students should work individually. Feedback could be approached as in Exercise A.

Answers: 1. living 2. children 3. childhood 4. married 5. retirement

C 🎧 Students might like to work in pairs so that they can say the words aloud to each other. Do the first item with them as an example, showing them how to either underline a syllable or put a stress mark before it. You will need to write the words on the board, and mark the stress as they listen to each.

Answers: interests   family   relatives   teenager   retirement   adolescence   improve

C Mark the main stress on these key words from the unit. Then listen and check. Practise saying the words.

1 interests

2 family

3 relatives

4 teenager

5 retirement

6 adolescence

7 improve

Errors

A Each unit ends with this type of task. It is very useful for students to be reminded of the types of errors they are likely to make. Tell students that errors are grammatical, lexical (a wrong word has been used) or to do with punctuation (e.g., capitalization of letters). There are no spelling errors. They can either complete the task individually or work in pairs. You could ask students to come and write the correct sentences on the board. You will need to write the correct versions of each on the board to clarify.

Answers:
1. He's from New York.
2. My father's an engineer.
3. Have you got any brothers and sisters?
4. I am 22 (years old).
5. His name's Alan Murray.
6. I work for a company called Friendly Products.
7. Where were you born?
8. I am writing to apply for the job in yesterday's newspaper.

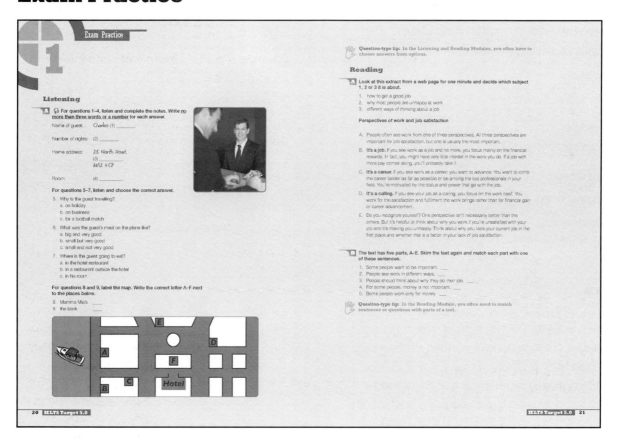

Listening

At this stage, the content of the exam practice section is less challenging than students will face in the actual exam. It is important now that they become familiar with the types of task they will need to complete, and gain confidence.

A 🎧 Tell students they will practise all parts of the Listening Module as the course progresses, and by the time they take the exam, they should hope to do as well as possible in all parts. The first part is the easiest, and at this level students should make sure that they score as highly as possible. Make sure students use the 30 seconds to read through the questions, and know what they have to do. At this stage, it is probably a good idea to deal with any words in the questions that they don't know, but tell them that they will not be able to do this in the exam, and they will need to get used to not understanding some words in the questions. Tell them they will hear the recording once only, and that for now they can write the answer in their books or in a notebook, but that in the exam they will have to transfer answers onto an answer sheet.

Students work individually as they listen to the recording.

Answers: 1. Hunt   2. two / 2   3. Manchester   4. 104   5. b   6. c   7. b   8. D   9. B

Tapescript 🎧 **9** (3 mins, 22 secs)

A   **For questions 1–4, listen and complete the notes. Write <u>no more than three words or a number</u> for each answer.**

Guest: Good evening.

Receptionist: Good evening. How can I help?

Guest: I have a reservation in the name of Hunt – a reservation for two nights. That's Charles Hunt.

Receptionist: Yes, Mr Hunt, let me see. Ah, here it is. Yes, two nights. I'll just need to photocopy your passport – do you have it?

Guest: Um, yes, of course – there you are.

Receptionist: Thank you. Could you just write your home address on the form here, while I copy the passport?

Guest: Yes, of course.

Receptionist:	Thank you. Oh, you're from Manchester. I was there two years ago for a football match. Manchester has a very good team.
Guest:	Yes, that's true. I'm actually more interested in rugby myself.
Receptionist:	Here's your key. You're in room one-oh-four – that's on the first floor. It's an interior room, so it should be very quiet. I think you asked for that.
Guest:	Oh yes, thank you. It's very important to sleep well when you have work to do. Can you tell me if the bill is already paid? I'm here for a conference and my company is paying the bill. Usually they pay it before I travel, but sometimes I have to pay and then claim expenses.
Receptionist:	Let me check. Don't worry, sir, the bill has been paid in full.
Guest:	Oh, good, that's one thing I don't need to worry about. Is the restaurant still open? I know it's late, but the meal on the plane was tiny – and not very tasty either.
Receptionist:	I'm sorry, sir – the restaurant closes at nine-thirty, but there are two or three very nice places near the hotel. They will be open for a while.
Guest:	Oh, good. I'll have a quick shower and then get something. Which restaurant do you recommend?
Receptionist:	Mamma Mia's is probably best. It's very close to the hotel, and it isn't at all expensive – the food is delicious. When you come out of the hotel, you go right and then take the first left. You'll come into a big square and you'll see Mamma Mia's on the right.
Guest:	That's sounds great. Oh, and one more thing – sorry – is there a cash machine nearby? I didn't have time to get any euros at the airport.
Receptionist:	Yes, the nearest bank is very close, too. Turn left out of the hotel and go down to the harbour. Turn left and you'll see the bank. There are two cash machines outside.
Guest:	Thank you very much.

Receptionist:	Not at all. I hope you enjoy your meal and your stay with us. Goodnight.

For questions 5–7, listen and choose the correct answer.

[Play track 9 again]

For questions 8 and 9, label the map. Write the correct letter A–F next to the places below.

[Play track 9 again]

Reading

The text is typical of the type of text that students will see in the second part of the Reading Module, but is considerably shorter than the texts they will have to read in the exam. Remember that they have already seen the title and first line of this text in Reading 2, and they have checked the meaning of 'perspective'. The first task is there to lead them into the text and remind them about the importance of skimming – though the first question in any part of the Reading Module might test their understanding of the whole text in this way.

Tell students that in the Reading Module they will write their answers directly onto an answer sheet, but for now, they can write in their book or notebook.

A Set the task for individual completion, and set a strict time limit. Give students the correct answer before moving on to the matching task. You can clarify the meaning of 'satisfaction' in the title now, but don't help with any more vocabulary from the text yet.

Answers: 3 is the correct answer.

B Make sure students look at the task before reading the text more carefully. You can either set a time limit or allow students the time they need. Perhaps you can end the task when half the students have completed it. Students who finish earlier can compare answers with a partner. Write the answers on the board in case students don't hear them properly.

Answers: 1. C   2. A   3. E   4. D   5. B

Unit 1 Workbook answers

Speaking and Vocabulary

A   1. David is Joe's father.
     2. Pauline is Joe's mother.
     3. Steve is Joe's brother.
     4. Jenny is Joe's sister.
     5. Arthur is Joe's grandfather.
     6. Liam is Joe's son.
     7. Katy is Joe's daughter.
     8. Christine is Joe's aunt.
     9. Malcolm is Joe's uncle.
     10. Tony is Joe's cousin.

B   Students' own ideas.

C   1. birth   2. childhood   3. adolescence
     4. middle age   5. retirement   6. death

Listening

A   Students' own answers.

Tapescript 🎧 10 (1 min, 3 secs)

A   **Listen and write answers to the questions. You don't need to write sentences.**

1   How old are you?
2   How many brothers and sisters do you have?
3   Are you a student or do you work?
4   Are you married?
5   Do you have any children?
6   What do you do in your free time?
7   How long have you studied English?
8   Which part of the world would you most like to visit?

B   1. 32   2. 58   3. 302   4. 19   5. 11   6. 30
     7. 100   8. 77   9. 85   10. 115

Tapescript 🎧 11 (1 min, 30 secs)

B   **Listen and write the numbers that you hear.**

1   Terry Hall lives at thirty-two Marshes Lane.
2   My father retired when he was fifty-eight years old.
3   Your lesson is in room three-oh-two this morning.
4   My brother got married when he was only nineteen.
5   One of my uncles has eleven children.
6   You have thirty seconds to read the questions.
7   I live about a hundred kilometres from the capital city of my country.
8   The average age to die in the United States is seventy-seven.
9   Many women in Japan have a life expectancy of eighty-five years.
10   A man in China claims to be a hundred and fifteen years old.

Reading

A   The correct summaries are 2, 3 and 6.

The parts of the text that provide the answers are underlined below. (Students may feel that supporting sentences also provide the answers.)

A new report says that people who have no control over their working lives and who never need to make decisions are more likely to die early than people in more important jobs who are making decisions all the time. People with the most boring jobs who do the same thing every day are unhappier and are more likely to have a lifestyle with more dangers to health. It seems that having a job with more meaning and having more control over what you do can lead to a longer life expectancy.

The report also says that having any job is better than having no job at all. Being unemployed has a negative affect on people's health and can increase the risk of dying early.

Writing

A   1. interests
     2. hobbies
     5. daughter
     7. parents
     8. relatives
    10. death
    11. address
    13. improve
    14. increase (the remaining words are spelt
        correctly)

B   The writing task is dealt with in the main section
     of the Teacher's Book.

2 Learning

Speaking and Vocabulary

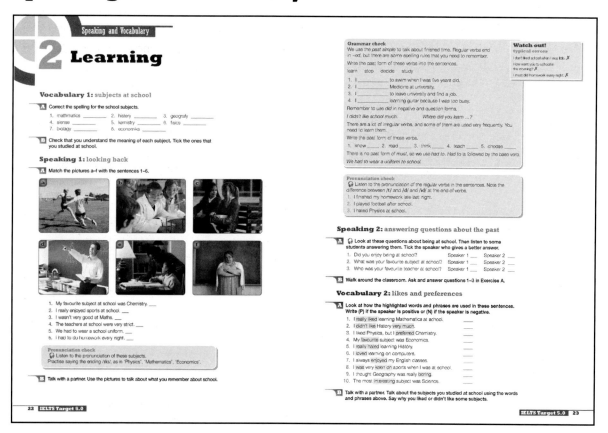

Objectives

- To give students further practice answering the type of questions they can expect in the first part of the IELTS Speaking Module.

- To revise and check some basic vocabulary used to talk about school and subjects at school, and to present and practise ways of expressing preference.

- To revise and practise the use of the past simple tense.

Vocabulary 1

A Brainstorm typical school subjects to introduce the lesson. Check students' pronunciation as they offer suggestions. Don't write subjects on the board now, as the task checks their spelling.

Students can work individually or in pairs to correct the spelling mistakes. You can either write the correct spellings on the board or ask students to come to the board.

Answers: 1. Mathematics   2. History
3. Geography   4. Science   5. Chemistry
6. Physics   7. Biology   8. Economics

B Check that students understand all subjects as they complete Exercise A. Otherwise, check as you give feedback to Exercise A when writing the correct spellings on the board. Give them a moment to tick the subjects they studied (probably all of them), and get a quick general consensus from the whole class.

Speaking 1

A The aim of the task is to trigger students' memories so that they are motivated to talk about their own school days. Check that students understand the meaning of 'strict'. Tell them to look at the pictures for a moment before they complete the matching task individually. Give feedback by asking them which sentence goes with a picture. In this way, they practise saying the typical sentences which they will need later. As you give feedback, check the pronunciation of 'favourite' (two syllables), which they will need to use frequently in speaking activities. Point out that you 'do' rather than 'make' homework, and that we say 'good at' rather than 'good in'.

Answers: 1. b   2. a   3. d   4. f   5. c   6. e

Pronunciation check

Point out the frequency of the /ɪks/ ending, and that it can be difficult to say because of the two final consonants coming together. Students should try to produce the sound, and then practise saying the names of the subjects that have the ending.

Tapescript 🎧 12 (0 mins, 19 secs)

Pronunciation check

Listen to the pronunciation of these subjects. Practise saying the ending /ɪks/, as in 'Physics', 'Mathematics', 'Economics'.

B Students can work in pairs or small groups. Remind them that this is the type of discussion that is common in the Speaking Module of the exam, and that they should make contributions without being asked direct questions. Monitor as students are talking, and correct basic errors. You could round up by asking one student to tell you one thing they especially remember about being at school, but avoid a lengthy feedback session as it will ultimately be a repetition of what they have just done.

Grammar check

The grammar focus in this unit is a little heavier than in some others, but you should have a time limit in mind for how long you are prepared to spend on this if students have difficulties. The aim of the grammar boxes is to remind students about a grammar point, and not to practise it rigorously. Time spent studying grammar will mean less time practising the skills that are more beneficial in terms of passing the exam. You might like to tell students to check a grammar point outside class if they are still finding it difficult to master.

You can either read through the grammar box summary with them and set each task as you come to it, or tell students to read through the whole grammar box, completing the tasks as they go. Checking the Watch out! box will probably tell you more about what students do and don't know than anything else. You could put them into pairs to correct the sentences in the Watch out! box.

Answers:
1. learned (add '~ed' when verb ends in consonant*)
   * note that the '~t' ending is more common in British English than other varieties.
2. studied (add '~ied' when verb ends in '~y')
3. decided (add only '~d' when verb ends in '~e')
4. stopped (double the consonant when the verb ends in a consonant after a short vowel)
   irregular verbs: knew / read / thought / taught / chose
   Corrections of typical errors: I didn't like school ... / How did you go to ... / I had to do ...

Pronunciation check

The important thing in this activity is that students don't produce all their past verbs with /t/ endings, which is very typical of students at this level. The /d/ and /ɪd/ endings tend to happen naturally because of the preceding consonant sound. Play the recording two or three times so that students can hear the endings, and then tell them to practise the sounds. You could put the phoneme endings on the board, and then ask students to add one or two more verbs to each column. Pay attention to the pronunciation of past forms when there are consonant clusters, as in 'stopped' and 'asked'.

Tapescript 🎧 **13** (0 mins, 42 secs)

Pronunciation check

Listen to the pronunciation of the regular verbs in the sentences. Note the difference between /t/ and /d/ and /ɪd/ at the end of verbs.

1   I finished my homework late last night.

2   I played football after school.

3   I hated Physics at school.

Speaking 2

A   Make sure students read the three questions and understand that they will hear two answers to each. Then play the recording. You might prefer to tell them just to listen the first time they hear the recording, and then to fill in answers the second time.

Tapescript 🎧 **14** (1 min, 30 secs)

A   **Look at these questions about being at school. Then listen to some students answering them. Tick the speaker who gives a better answer.**

1
Examiner: Did you enjoy being at school?
Speaker 1:   No, I didn't.
Examiner: Did you enjoy being at school?
Speaker 2:   Well, I enjoyed school when we studied the subjects I was good at, but I didn't really enjoy it when we studied Maths and Physics. I found those lessons very difficult.

2
Examiner: What was your favourite subject at school?
Speaker 1:   History. I was very good at remembering dates, and I loved learning about kings and queens.
Examiner: What was your favourite subject at school?
Speaker 2:   Maths. I liked my teacher of Maths.

3
Examiner: Who was your favourite teacher at school?
Speaker 1:   Mr Adams. But I also liked Mr Brown.
Examiner: Who was your favourite teacher at school?
Speaker 2:   I think it was Mr Lindsey. He was our English teacher. He made the lessons really interesting and wasn't strict like some of the other teachers.

Answers:
1. Speaker 2 gives the better answer
2. Speaker 1 gives the better answer
3. Speaker 2 gives the better answer

B   Students can work in groups. Tell students to ask each question to two students. Make sure the emphasis is on sounding interested and giving more than short functional answers.

Vocabulary 2

A   Allow students to get on with the task without going through and checking any of the highlighted phrases with them. You can't check the phrases without doing the task for them. It is better to let them get on and then concentrate on dealing with any phrases that are new to them during feedback. Students should work individually to complete the task. Ask students to tell you the positive phrases, and then the negative phrases as feedback. This way, they will practise saying the phrases, and you can check and correct pronunciation. 'be keen on' is the phrase that is most likely to be new, and you should make sure students remember it.

Answers: 1. P   2. N   3. P   4. P   5. N
6. P   7. P   8. P   9. N   10. P

B Monitor as students are talking, and encourage students to use the range of phrases they have just learnt.

For further speaking and vocabulary practice, tell students to complete the exercises on page 7 of the Workbook. Set as an extra activity or homework task.

Listening

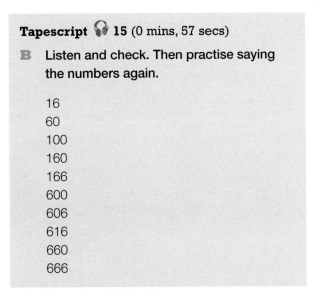

Objectives

- To introduce students to the fact that listening for numbers and dates is a common feature in the IELTS Listening Module.

- To practise listening carefully for specific information, especially numbers and dates.

- To revise the months of the year and ordinal numbers.

Listening 1

A You can either start by putting them into pairs as suggested, or conduct the initial phase as a whole-class activity. If you conduct this as pairwork, monitor so that you can hear students' pronunciation.

B 🎧 Play the recording, pausing between each number. Point out where the stress falls, and how the stress is different on 'sixty' and 'sixteen'. Then allow students the time they need to practise until they are happy with their production. Play the recording again if requested.

Tapescript 🎧 **15** (0 mins, 57 secs)

B Listen and check. Then practise saying the numbers again.

16
60
100
160
166
600
606
616
660
666

C 🎧 Tell students that they will hear some similar numbers. Play the recording without pausing, and see how well they do. Then play the recording again, and pause as you write the correct answers on the board.

Tapescript 🎧 16 (0 mins, 54 secs)

C Listen and write the numbers that you hear.

1 18
2 80
3 96
4 120
5 243
6 531
7 852
8 984

Answers: 1. 18 2. 80 3. 96 4. 120
5. 243 6. 531 7. 852 8. 984

D 🎧 Play the recording, pausing between each number. Then allow students the time they need to practise until they are happy with their production. Play the recording again if requested.

Tapescript 🎧 17 (0 mins, 47 secs)

D Listen and practice saying these bigger numbers.

1,000
10,000
100,000
1,100
1,500
1,550
1,555

E You could ask students how many months of the year they know before working through the task. Set the task for individual completion. Remind students to use initial capital letters. You will need to write the months on the board, or ask students to write the months on the board to clarify the correct spellings.

F Make sure students cover Exercise E, and that you clean the board. Students can work in pairs or individually.

Tell them to check the correct spelling themselves when they have completed the task.

G 🎧 You can pronounce the months yourself or play the recording. Then tell students to work in pairs to practise saying the months, as you monitor to check that pronunciation is accurate.

Tapescript 🎧 18 (1 min, 0 secs)

G Listen to the pronunciation of the months. Then practise saying them.

January
February
March
April
May
June
July
August
September
October
November
December

H Cardinal numbers are basic numbers (one, two, three, etc.). Every cardinal number has a corresponding ordinal number ('one' – 'first', 'two' – 'second' and so on). Write 'one' on the board and then label it 'cardinal number'. Ask students to provide the ordinal number – it doesn't matter if they don't understand. If somebody does provide 'first', write it next to 'one'. If nobody does, write 'first' yourself and then label it 'ordinal number'. Write 'two' under 'one' and ask students to provide the ordinal number again. Make sure they spell it correctly. Continue with 'three' and 'four', and then clean the board before students attempt the task in the book. Alternatively, continue with the task on the board instead of in the book. Doing the whole task in the book and then going through it on the board for feedback will be quite time-consuming, so you might like to ask students to come up and write the numbers on the board directly and copy them into their books as they go. The task that follows deals with pronunciation, but it would be a good idea to check this as you work through this task.

Answers: 1. first 2. second 3. third
4. fourth 5. fifth 6. sixth 7. seventh
8. eighth 9. ninth 10. tenth 11. twelfth
12. fifteenth 13. twentieth 14. twenty-fifth
15. thirtieth

I 🎧 Play the recording, pausing between each number. Drill any ordinals that students have difficulties with. Then give them some time to practise saying the ordinals in pairs.

Ｊ　🎧 Write the date from the book on the board, and ask a student to read it aloud. Then ask another couple of students, and see if they read it the same way. Play the recording, and get the two different ways of saying the date on the board. Drill it a few times before going on to the following practice task.

Ｋ　Allow students time to practise with a partner, and then get a correct version of each date from different students.

Ｌ　🎧 This task practises the way that students should write dates when they are part of a question in the Listening Module. Tell them that the easiest way to write dates is to simply write the month and number, and that they don't need to reproduce in writing what is said in spoken language.

Ⅿ　It doesn't matter if students don't know some of the dates. The aim is to practise saying dates accurately, and with the correct stress and intonation. Once they have practised in pairs, check each question with a different student. Ask students a few similar questions about important dates in your own country if you want to.

Listening 2

Read through the question-type tip with students.

Ａ　🎧 Read the instructions with the students. Tell them that the lead-in rubric tells them a little about what they are going to listen to. Give students about a minute to read through the questions and understand what they have to do before you play the recording. If you feel that students will still be unsure about what to do, you can ask questions to check. Students might find it difficult to listen to the recording only once, but avoid playing it a second time. Students can discuss what difficulties they had, and then listen again later if necessary (see Exercises B and C).

is an advanced course, for people who already know quite a lot about the subject.

Graham: Oh, I see. Well, I'm quite a keen photographer, but at the moment it's just a hobby. I want to learn more so that I might be able to do some work professionally at some time. I think the intermediate course would be a bit easy for me. Perhaps the advanced course would be best. When does it start?

Receptionist: The advanced course starts on September the eighteenth.

Graham: OK, just let me note that down – the eighteenth of September. And how long does the course run for?

Receptionist: It's a twelve-week course, but there's a week off in the middle for half-term. So, you do twelve lessons over thirteen weeks.

Graham: So, what's the date that the course finishes?

Receptionist: It finishes on the fourteenth of December.

Graham: The fourteenth – OK – that's quite near Christmas, isn't it? Can you tell me how much the course costs?

Receptionist: Yes, it's ninety-six pounds.

Graham: Ninety-six, that's not too bad.

Receptionist: That's paid in advance. And I'm afraid there's no refund if for any reason you can't complete the course.

Graham: Yes, of course. That's fair. How many people are there usually in the class? I've heard the groups are quite small.

Receptionist: Well, we can't say for sure, but there are usually between six and ten people in a group. On the last advanced course, there were seven participants.

Graham: Oh, good. That's sounds perfect. Can I enrol for the course now – on the phone?

Receptionist: Yes, of course. I'll take your details now, and you can pay by card now or send us a cheque if you prefer. So, first of all, what's your name?

Graham: It's Graham Merton – that's M-E-R-T-O-N.

Receptionist: And your address?

Graham: Flat three, a hundred and nine Chelsea Court. That's in Oxford.

Receptionist: OK, and how old are you? We like to know more or less the age of each group.

Graham: I'm twenty-eight.

Receptionist: OK, Graham. We'll send confirmation and some course information in the post. Now, how would you like to pay?

Graham: I'll pay with my card now.

Receptionist: OK, if you can … *(fade out)*

For questions 3–8, complete the man's notes. Write <u>no more than three words or a number</u> for each answer.

[Play track 22 again]

For questions 9–12, complete the booking form that the receptionist fills in.

[Play track 22 again]

B Give students sufficient time to check answers and think about why they may have answered incorrectly, before moving on to Exercise C.

Answers: 1. c   2. c   3. September 18   4. 12 / twelve   5. December 14   6. 96   7. 6   8. 7   9. Merton   10. 3   11. 109   12. 28

C Students will by now be a little more familiar with this type of reflective process, but note the questions are not the same as in the previous unit. Remind them that identifying what they are doing well and not doing so well is a very good way of focusing on what they can do better next time. Allow students time to reflect and complete the task, and then ask them if they are happy with the number of correct answers. Play the recording again if necessary, and tell students to focus on why the correct answers are correct.

Answers: 1. class / lesson   2. course
3. class

For further listening practice, tell students to complete the exercises on page 8 of the Workbook. Set as an extra activity or homework task.

Reading

Objectives

- To introduce students to the concept of scanning, and to show them that looking for specific information is a common requirement of the IELTS Reading Module.

- To contrast skimming with scanning, and make the distinction clear.

- To introduce students to the type of questions that involve scanning, and to practise scanning for specific information.

Reading 1

A Set the skimming task before focusing on the picture. The picture will give students an idea about what the text is about, and this will help them to anticipate the topic. Note also that Exercise B gives students the opportunity to talk about the topic. Set a time limit (perhaps 30 seconds) for the task, and then ask them to tell you the answer.

Answers: The extracts are all about learning to drive.

B Allow time for students to discuss the questions. Avoid going through each question again for feedback. You could round up by asking, 'So, how many people passed their driving test first time?' Read through the exam tip with students.

C Set the task for individual completion. Call time when four of five students have completed it, so that the need to improve reading speed is reinforced. Elicit the answers and write them on the board.

Answers: 1. 2 / two hours   2. 21   3. £38
4. 40 / forty minutes   5. an 'L' plate

Read through the question-type tip with students. Tell them that the instructions usually require them to write no more than two or three words for each answer.

D This is another type of task that usually involves scanning. In the actual exam, students will have a third option, 'not given', but at this stage 'true' or 'false' is enough. Don't mention the 'not given' option at this point, as it is introduced in Unit 4. Students will probably be familiar with true/false questions from previous studies, but make sure they understand that there must be evidence in the text to support their choice of true or false. Set the task for individual completion, and give oral feedback. You might need to explain where in the text an answer is provided.

Answers: 1. F   2. F   3. F   4. T

E Having completed the tasks, students should now understand what scanning is. The aim of this activity is to consolidate that. Give students a moment to read the options, and then ask them the answer.

Answers: 3 is the correct definition.

Reading 2

Tell students to work alone on the lesson. The text is shorter and less challenging than those they will tackle in the exam. The picture-matching gist task is there to practise further skim reading, and to give them confidence when answering the exam-type questions in Exercise B. It is not usual for students to match pictures to parts of a text in the Reading Module. Read through the exam tip with the students.

A Make sure students understand that they only need to skim to complete the task, and set a time limit of about a minute. Check answers before moving on to Exercise B.

Answers: 1. C   2. A   3. B

B Now simply tell students to complete the task. Set a time limit of about ten minutes, or end the task when about half the students have completed it.

C Checking answers and then reflecting on how many questions were answered correctly and why is a constant feature of the skills sections. Give students sufficient time to check and think about why they may have answered incorrectly, before moving on to Exercise D. Point out that answers 1 and 3 need an article.

Answers: 1. a professional   2. family and friends   3. a teaching certificate   4. goggles   5. plastic sandals   6. support

Read through the exam tip with students. This is an important piece of advice at this level. Students will probably have to use words they don't fully understand as answers in short-answer and note-completion tasks.

D Students will by now be more familiar with this type of reflective process, but note the questions are not the same as in the previous unit. Remind them that identifying what they are doing well and not doing so well is a very good way of focusing on what they can do better next time. Allow students time to reflect and complete the task, and then ask them if they are happy with the number of correct answers. You may like to ask one student what he or she will do differently next time.

If there is time in the lesson, now would be a good time to work through the Workbook reading task. It uses this text to introduce students to the concept of paraphrasing, which will be the focus of the Reading Module in the next unit.

Key vocabulary in context

This task focuses on key nouns from the text, used here in a slightly different context. Students should complete the task individually. Give feedback orally.

Answers: 1. advantage   2. support
3. professional   4. safety

Check to make sure the students have covered the reading text before completing this matching activity. Tell the students to refer to the text to check their answers.

Answers: 1. b   2. d   3. a   4. c

Writing

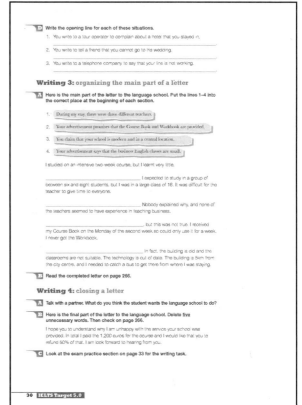

Objectives

- To introduce students to the basic concept of structuring a formal letter.

- To show students how to start a letter by stating their purpose, and end a letter by telling the reader what they want.

- To compare appropriate and inappropriate language in a formal letter.

- To practise writing a formal letter of complaint.

Writing 1

Ask students whether they have ever written a letter in English. Read through the exam tip with students.

A There are a few important words in the sentences that students might not know, and you will need to read through them with students. As you do so, it might be a good idea to put the sentences into the correct order together as a class. Alternatively, you can explain the words, and then give them a moment to work individually to put the sentences in order.

Answers:

2 Explain the situation and how it affects you (in what way it is good or bad for you).

3 Say what you want the other person to do.

1 State the purpose of your letter.

B There are not necessarily correct answers to these questions, but it will be beneficial for students to think about what is expected in a typical letter. Remind students that they will need to write 150 words. Put them into pairs to discuss the questions, or discuss these directly as a whole class.

Answers:

1. One or two sentences.
2. You will probably want to make three or four points, each of which will probably consist of one or two sentences. So, you will probably write between six and eight sentences.
3. Two or three sentences.

Writing 2

Read the exam tip, and clarify the meaning of 'purpose'. It is essential that students understand that everything they write in the IELTS exam must have a purpose.

A In Unit 1, you drew attention to the frequency of the phrase 'I am writing to ...' Refer students back to the appropriate page of Unit 1, and point this out to students again. Tell them that at their level, it is the safest way to begin a formal letter.

B It is very important that students understand the situation here, as the rest of the lesson revolves around it. Give students a moment to look at the advertisement and take in all the information. Then go through the questions in the rubric one at a time. Establish that the school offers English classes, and go through the claims the schools make. You will need to explain the meaning of 'highly qualified'. Then establish that the client was not happy, and check that students understand each of the reasons why.

C The aim here is to show students that stating your purpose must be done in an appropriate way. Even if you are unhappy about something, you do not use aggressive language, and the points you make must be relevant. Give students a moment to read through the options, and then to compare their correct option with a partner. As you check their answer, ask them to tell you why the other options are not appropriate.

Answers:
2 is the correct option.
1 is too direct and aggressive.
3 is too direct and gives information that you would expect to give later in the main part of the letter.
4 is too direct and begins with a demand that you would expect to find at the end of the letter.

D This task moves away from the central theme of the letter of complaint for a moment, so that students can practise writing opening lines which state a purpose. Go through each situation, and make sure students understand all the words. Students can work individually or in pairs to help each other. You should set a time limit, as this could be quite time-consuming. If you feel that time is short, or that three situations are too many for your students to cope with, divide the class into three, and give each group one of the situations. Write one good opening line for each situation on the board.

Answers:
1. I am writing to complain about a hotel I stayed in recently.
   I am writing about a hotel that your company arranged for me to stay in recently.
2. I am writing to tell you that I will not be able to come to your wedding.
3. I am writing to tell / inform you that my telephone line is not working properly.

Writing 3

A Make sure students understand that you are going back to the problem at the language school now. Remind them that you already have the opening line, and point out that the first line here, 'I studied on an intensive two-week course, but I learnt very little', is the second line of the opening paragraph. Tell them that they are now going to put together the main part of the letter. You probably don't need to read through sentences 1–4 with students, but make sure they know that they should read these first, and then put them into the spaces as they read the main part of the letter. If time is an issue, you can tell students simply to write the number of the sentence into the space, but it might be good practice for them to copy each sentence (see Exercise B below for feedback).

B For feedback, tell students to look at the model letter on page 266 of the Course Book (note that the final paragraph is missing from the first model, as students have not worked on that yet). The letter is reproduced below.

I am writing about a business English course I recently took at your school. I studied on an intensive two-week course, but I learnt very little.

Your advertisement says that the business English classes are small. I expected to study in a group of between six and eight students, but I was in a large class of 16. It was difficult for the teacher to give time to everyone.

During my stay, there were three different teachers. Nobody explained why, and none of the teachers seemed to have experience teaching business.

The advertisement promises that the Course Book and Workbook are provided, but this was not true. I received my Course Book on the Monday of the second week so could only use it for a week. I never got the Workbook.

You claim that your school is modern and in a central location. In fact, the building is old and the classrooms are not suitable. The technology is out of date. The building is 5km from the city centre, and I needed to catch a bus to get there from where I was staying.

Writing 4

A This can be done as pairwork, as suggested in the Course Book, or quickly as a whole-class discussion. Try to elicit 'refund', and point out that it can be both a noun and a verb.

B At this stage, writing the final paragraph will probably be too challenging for students, and so the aim here is to provide a model final paragraph with a task. The task aims to get students thinking about the types of mistakes they are likely to make, and to give them practice in correcting their work. They should work in pairs to identify and strike through the unnecessary words. For feedback, tell students to look at the complete model letter on page 266 of the Course Book. The final paragraph is reproduced below also.

I hope you understand why I am unhappy with the service your school provided. In total I paid 1,200 euros for the course and I would like you to refund 50% of that. I look forward to hearing from you.

C In this unit, the writing task can be found in the exam practice section at the end of the Course Book unit. See instructions for that section on page 45 of this book.

Consolidation

Speaking

A This task revises an important language point that is not rigorously practised in the first section of this unit. Students should work individually to complete the task. Play the recording in Exercise B to give feedback.

B 🎧 The aim of this activity is not only for students to check answers to Exercise A, but also to expose students to answers that sound interesting and extend beyond the purely functional one-word response. The first time you play the recording, focus on the question words. As you play the recording, write the question words on the board to clarify answers, as the words can sound similar if given only orally. If students have made mistakes, revise the basic rules ('who' for people, 'where' for place, 'when' for time, 'why' for reason, 'how' for manner).

B Listen and check.

1

Examiner: What was your favourite subject at school?

Student: I loved History because I was really good at it.

2

Examiner: Who was your best friend at school?

Student: His name was Marcus. He lived next door and we walked to school together.

3

Examiner: How did you get to school in the morning – did you walk or take a bus?

Student: Actually, my dad used to drive me to school.

4

Examiner: Why did you go to college instead of staying at school?

Student: Because the college had more subjects to choose from. I wanted to study Philosophy.

5

Examiner: Do you remember any school trips? Where did you go?

Student: I remember once we went to a museum in London. I think it was the Natural History Museum.

6

Examiner: In some countries, children learn languages from an early age. When did you start learning English?

Student: When I was eleven. We didn't do English at primary school.

Answers: 1. What   2. Who   3. How
4. Why   5. Where   6. When

C 🎧 Now tell students to listen to the full answers that students give, and play the recording again. You might like to pause between each one, and clarify any language that you think is worth focusing on. Point out that students give reasons for their answers, and note how 'actually' introduces an option that wasn't one of those suggested by the examiner.

Tapescript 🎧 **24** (0 mins, 14 secs)

C Listen again and notice how the second speaker answers each question.

[Play track 23 again]

D The aim here is for students to practise question forms, and their language should be accurate. Monitor as they write their questions, and correct any obvious errors. Encourage students to use different question words, rather than write five 'what' questions. Students can work in pairs if you prefer, but asking different students different questions is likely to be more enjoyable, and they may well know everything about the student they usually sit next to anyway. Tell students to ask each question to two students. Make sure the emphasis is on sounding interested, and giving more than short functional answers.

Vocabulary

A Point out that this is a good method of recording vocabulary that is related in this way. It can aid memory more efficiently than simply writing words in a list. The aim is also to check their spelling, so tell them not to look back in the unit. They can check their spelling when they have completed the task.

B The aim here is to practise verbs that are flexible but that students often confuse, and to practise using those verbs in the appropriate form. Tell students to decide which verb is used in which sentence first, and then to check which form of each verb is correct. Students should complete the task individually. Write the correct form of each verb on the board to give feedback.

Answers: 1. did   2. apply / have
3. passed   4. fail

C 🎧 All the words practised here are from the unit. Students can work in pairs and say the words aloud to one another. Show them how to mark stress, by underlining or putting a small

stress mark before the appropriate syllable (they have done this previously). As they are working, write the words on the board so that you or they can mark the stress during feedback. Then pronounce the words clearly for them as they check their answers. Finally, mark the stress on the board.

Tapescript 🎧 **25** (0 mins, 52 secs)

C Mark the main stress on these words. Then listen and check. Practise saying the words.

1 favourite
2 advantage
3 professional
4 safety
5 licence
6 certificate
7 support

Answers: <u>fa</u>vourite   ad<u>van</u>tage
pro<u>fes</u>sional   <u>safe</u>ty   <u>li</u>cence
cer<u>ti</u>ficate   su<u>pport</u>

Errors

A Students now know that each unit ends with this type of task. Remind them that it is very useful to notice and correct the types of errors they are likely to make. Point out that this time the errors are highlighted, so they simply have to correct them. They can either complete the task individually or work in pairs. You could ask students to come and write the correct sentences on the board. You will need to write the correct versions of each on the board to clarify.

Answers:
1. Did you do your homework last night?
2. I didn't like school. I had to do tests every week.
3. My father taught me to swim.
4. I didn't like Maths very much at school.
5. I was very keen on Geography.
6. I failed my driving test the first time I took it.

Exam Practice

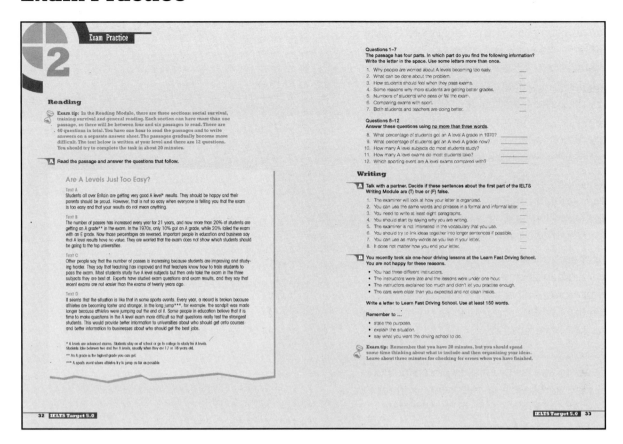

Reading

At this stage, the content of the exam practice section is somewhat less challenging than students will face in the actual exam. It is important now that they become familiar with the types of task they will need to complete, and gain confidence.

Read through the exam tip (which in this case is fairly lengthy information) carefully with students. Make sure they realize that they are being given a taste of what they will have to deal with in the exam, and that the exam passages will be longer and more challenging.

At this stage, we are calling paragraphs 'parts', as students will not yet understand the concept or function of a paragraph. Paragraphing is introduced in Unit 6.

Read through the instructions with students, and then allow them to do the task individually. After about a minute, check to see who is reading the text, and who is reading the questions. Tell students to stop, and ask them, 'Are you reading the text or reading the questions?' Remind them that they should have skimmed the text very quickly to get a general idea. Now they should be reading the questions carefully, so they know what to look for when they read more carefully. You might like to point out now that there is a small glossary to explain some cultural concepts, and that this is a usual feature of the reading section.

Now allow them 20 minutes to complete the practice task. Remind students that in the Reading Module, they will write their answers directly onto an answer sheet, but for now they can write in their book or notebook.

Students who finish earlier can compare answers with a partner. Write the answers on the board, so that students are clear about correct answers.

Answers: 1. B   2. D   3. A   4. C   5. B
6. D   7. C   8. 10%   9. 20%   10. 5   11. 3
12. the long jump

Writing

A   The aim of the first task is to revise what students have learnt so far about the Writing Module. The questions should be fairly easy to answer. If time is short, and you want to get on with the writing task, answer these questions as a whole class rather than in pairs.

Answers: 1. T   2. F   3. F   4. T   5. F
6. T   7. F   8. F

B   The instructions here give students a little more information than they can expect to be given in the actual exam. Make sure students read all the instructions and information carefully before they start writing. Tell them that their task is to open the letter, link the information (what they are not happy about) together in the main part of the letter, and then close the letter.

Read through the exam tip at the bottom of the page with them. Tell them to look back at the stages of writing they discussed in Unit 1, and to refer to the model letter from this unit.

Monitor as students work, but check closely that they are organizing their letters and making relevant points, rather than writing perfectly accurately. Students could exchange letters when they have finished.

If you collect students' letters to mark, it would be better to use the process to get an idea of what they are capable of, rather than correct too heavily. At this stage, you may be correcting almost every line they write!

For feedback, tell students to look at the complete model letter on page 266. The letter is reproduced below.

Dear Sir/Madam,

I am writing to complain about the driving lessons that I recently took with your driving school. There are a number of reasons why I am not happy.

Firstly, I had three different instructors, so it was difficult to build any kind of relationship with the person teaching me. Secondly, the lessons were supposed to be for one hour, but the instructors frequently ended lessons five minutes early.

In my opinion, the instructors were not very good either. They spent most of the time explaining what I should do, and did not give me the time I needed to practice.

Finally, I was unhappy that your cars were not very modern and sometimes not clean inside. They were not what I expected from a professional driving school.

I hope you understand why I am unhappy with the service your school provided. In total I paid 500 euros for the lessons and I would like you to refund 50% of that. I look forward to hearing from you.

Yours faithfully, Terry Black

Unit 2 Workbook answers

Speaking and Vocabulary

A   1. strict   2. lesson   3. uniform   4. test
5. revise   6. pass   7. university

B   1. wore   2. taught   3. thought   4. chose
5. met   6. knew, had   7. wrote   8. read

C   Students' own ideas.

Listening

A   Students' own answers.

> **Tapescript** 🎧 **26** (0 mins, 51 secs)
>
> A   **Listen and write answers to the questions.
> You don't need to write sentences.**
>
> 1   What was your favourite subject at school?
> 2   Which subject were you really good at?
> 3   What colour was your school uniform?
> 4   How far was school from your home?
> 5   How did you get to school in the morning?
> 6   How old were you when you left school?

B   1. August 3   2. November 23
3. October 16

> **Tapescript** 🎧 **27** (1 min, 32 secs)
>
> B   **Listen to the short dialogues and write
> the date that something is arranged.
> Just write the month and number.**
>
> **1**
> Customer: I'd like to book a table for two for
> next Saturday.
> Restaurant
> receptionist: Next Saturday. That's the third.
> What time is that?
> Customer: Oh, for eight-thirty.
> Restaurant
> receptionist: OK, that's a table for two on
> Saturday the third of August at
> eight-thirty. We'll see you then.
> Goodbye.

> **2**
> Hotel
> receptionist: Hello.
> Guest: Oh, hello. I'd like to book a room
> for the night of November the
> twenty-third. That's a Thursday.
> Hotel
> receptionist: The twenty-first – let me see ...
> Guest: No, the twenty-third.
> Hotel
> receptionist: Oh, I'm sorry. Yes, there are a few
> rooms free then. Would you like ...
> *(fade out)*
>
> **3**
> Chris: Hi, Martin.
> Martin: Oh, hi Chris.
> Chris: Listen, I'm having a party at my
> place in a couple of months. Do
> you think you'll be able to come?
> Martin: Do you mean in October?
> Chris: Yeah.
> Martin: I'm not sure. Let me check. What
> date is it?
> Chris::   It's the sixteenth – on the Saturday
> night.
> Martin: Uh-huh. Yeah, I'm free on the
> sixteenth. I should be able to come
> along. Thanks for calling.
> Chris: How are you, anyway ... *(fade out)*

Reading

A   This Workbook task introduces students to the
concept of paraphrasing, which is given a full
focus and explanation in Unit 3. For now, allow
students simply to take in what is here and to
complete the fairly simple matching/gap-fill task.

B   a. Learning to ski   b. Computers
c. good equipment

Writing

A   The writing task is in the Course Book. This is an
additional practice exercise that focuses on
typical spelling mistakes.

Correct spellings are:
birthday / licence / friends / lessons / too

Unit overview

The third unit is based around the theme of work, a topic that students will almost certainly need to talk about at some stage in the Speaking Module. The unit gives students a further taste of what they can expect in the various sections of the IELTS exam, focusing especially on how language in questions is paraphrased, and not usually exactly the same as what students hear or read.

Speaking and Vocabulary

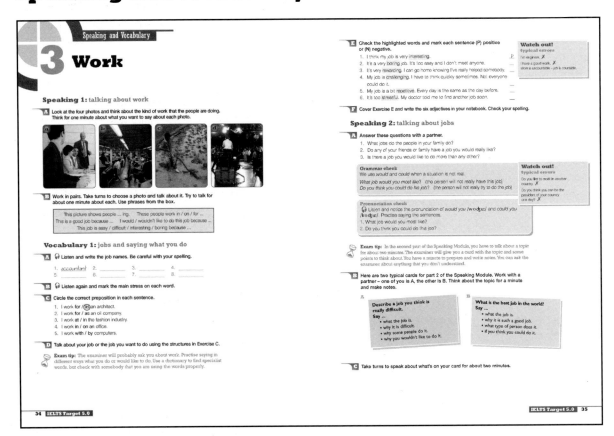

Objectives

- To give students further practice answering the type of questions they can expect in the first part of the IELTS Speaking Module.

- To introduce students to the task that they will meet in the second part of the IELTS Speaking Module, and to practise aspects of what they like or do not like about their work.

- To present and practise vocabulary connected with working life.

- To practise using 'would' and 'could' whilst talking hypothetically about working life.

Speaking 1

A and B   Start the lesson with this exercise, as any brainstorming or discussion will pre-empt what comes later in the lesson. Read through the sentence introductions in Exercise B with students, and then make sure they use the minute they have to think and prepare, and not to start talking straightaway. Tell students that you will tell them any key vocabulary that they want to use, but avoid pre-teaching vocabulary you think they might need, as there will be too much for them to take in. It is a good opportunity to show students how important it is to learn the words they need, and not the words somebody else decides to teach them. Monitor as students are talking, and note down any language that can go on the board, either because it is useful and well-expressed, or because it shows a typical error at this level.

Vocabulary 1

A   This is a revision exercise that focuses on spelling. If any words are unknown, you can quickly explain them as you go. Note that all of these words are difficult to spell, and students are bound to make mistakes. Use the example to show students what they should be doing and why. Play the recording, pausing after each word to give students time to write. To feed back, ask students to spell the words for you as you write them on the board. You could get them to come up and write the words on the board, but be aware that this would be time-consuming. Make sure you leave the words on the board for the next task.

Tapescript 28 (0 mins, 52 secs)

A   Listen and write the job names. Be careful with your spelling.

1   accountant

2   engineer

3   architect

4   lawyer

5   mechanic

6   electrician

7   manager

8   assistant

Answers:
1. a'ccountant
2. engi'neer
3. 'architect
4. 'lawyer
5. me'chanic
6. elec'trician
7. 'manager
8. as'sistant

B   Students will know how to mark stress now, but do the first one as an example, underlining or putting a stress mark before the stressed syllable. Then play the recording again, pausing between each word. You can either mark the stress on the words on the board, or wait until you have played the whole recording, and then go back.

Students may want to ask about other jobs that are not included in this task. It is important that students learn the vocabulary that is most useful to them. You can teach any extra words they may need to talk about their job, or jobs in general. However, at this level they can easily be overloaded with too much vocabulary, and you should avoid teaching lists of new words for the sake of it.

Tapescript 29 (0 mins, 12 secs)

B   Listen again and mark the main stress on each word.

[Play track 28 again]

C   Point out that many people talk about their job in terms of the field they work in, rather than by giving an exact job description, especially nowadays when job titles are more ambiguous. Students should work individually to complete the task. Write only the correct preposition on the board to make sure answers are clear.

Answers: 1. as   2. for   3. in   4. in
5. with

D Students should be able to use two or three of the structures to talk about the job they have or would like to have. You could provide further practice by telling them to talk about the line of work their friends and family members are in. Tell them not to simply use the job title, but to try to use the target language.

Read through the exam tip with students. If you are teaching students who all work in a closely-related area of business, you might like to brainstorm a few words and phrases that would be especially useful to learn.

Watch out!

Students should check these boxes themselves, but you might like to draw attention to how frequent mistakes with articles are made, when talking about work and jobs.

E The aim of this task is to provide students with some adjectives that they can use to talk about the job they do. It also gives practice understanding new words in context (the language surrounding the new words explains it to some extent). Most of the adjectives will be new, but avoid pre-teaching. Tell students to focus only on whether the context tells them that the word is positive or negative. They should work individually to complete the task. To feed back, use concept checks, like 'Give me an example of a really rewarding job', or 'Is working in a factory challenging or repetitive?'

Answers: 1. P   2. N   3. P   4. P   5. N
6. N

F This task checks that students have retained the new words, and that they can spell them. Monitor students, and point out spelling mistakes. Students can check their answers by looking back to the book.

Speaking 2

A The aim of this task is to prepare students for the more exam-oriented tasks later in the lesson. Give students three or four minutes to discuss the questions in pairs, and then ask for some feedback.

Ask students why the present simple is used in the first question, and 'would' in questions 2 and 3, as a way of leading into the grammar check box.

Grammar check

This is a complex grammar point at this level if presented or practised as a full second conditional with past verbs and so on. At this point, it is best to just focus on 'would' (especially with 'like') and 'could', and establish that they are used when the situation is not real. The 'Watch out!' box focuses on the same point, and you could quickly correct the sentences in the box with students if you want to. ('Would you like to work ...?' / 'Do you think you could be the president ...?')

Pronunciation check

The sentences here both practise pronunciation, and give some more natural examples of the type of conditionals that students might hear when talking about work. Play the recording, and if necessary get the sentences up on the board. Drill the sentences, and then allow a moment for students to say the sentences two or three times to a partner.

You can either read through the exam tip and then look at the discussion cards, or look at the discussion cards first, so that students have more of an idea about what the exam tip means.

Tapescript 🎧 30 (0 mins, 32 secs)
Pronunciation check

Listen and notice the pronunciation of *would you* and *could you*. Practise saying the sentences.

1   What job would you most like?

2   Do you think you could do his job?

B The discussion cards are designed so that students shouldn't need to check any words or phrases. Make sure students know who is A and who is B in their pair, and then tell them to read their card carefully. Check one more time that everyone understands all the points on their card and knows what to do, and then give them a minute to plan what to say. Tell them to make notes, but not to write full sentences that they then read. Some students might prefer not to write down their ideas.

C Tell students that you don't expect each of them to talk for an unbroken two minutes just yet, but they should talk for as long as possible. One student should talk, and then the other, as this will be closer to what they do in the actual exam. Monitor carefully, so that you can tell students what they did well and not so well. Later in the course, you might like to record (perhaps onto a camcorder) students working through this exam practice.

For further speaking and vocabulary practice, tell students to complete the exercises on page 9 of the Workbook. Set as an extra activity or homework task.

Listening

Objectives

- To introduce students to the concept of listening for gist, and to show how important it is to improve this skill.

- To encourage students to make predictions about what they will listen to.

- To show students that understanding the gist of a recording will help them understand detail.

- To practise listening for gist, and subsequently more detailed information.

Listening 1

A Allow students two or three minutes to look at the pictures, and discuss the situations. Then ask them to tell you about the pictures, and try to elicit or present key phrases, like 'it's an interview', 'commuters', 'colleagues in an office', 'people looking at job adverts'. Don't tell them too much about what is going on in any of the pictures, as it will pre-empt the listening task.

B 🎧 Tell students what they have to do, and play the whole recording. Ask students if they have made all the matches, and if not, play them the recording again. You might like to pause after each. Tell students the correct answers before they discuss how they accomplished the task.

Tapescript 🎧 31 (1 min, 54 secs)

B Listen to the four extracts and match them with the pictures. Write the number of the extract in the box.

1

Female voice: So, why do you want to leave the job you're doing now?

Male voice: Well, I don't really want to leave, but I need a new challenge. I need to try something I haven't done before. I've been at the same place for longer than I planned.

Female voice: So, would you say that you're ambitious?

2

Male voice: Take a look at this.

Female voice:	What is it?
Male voice:	It's the design for the new web page. Tony has just sent it through. What do you think?
Female voice:	Well, it looks good, but I'd need to ...

3

Female voice:	Steve – have you seen this job? It looks like what you're looking for.
Male voice:	Let me see. Oh, that's the one in Croydon, isn't it? The job looks quite interesting, but it's not very well paid, and travelling to Croydon every day would be so expensive.
Female voice::	What about this one? It's more local.
Male voice:	Yeah, I saw that one, too. I'm thinking about it, but the money's not great, is it?

4

Male voice 1:	Mike – hey, Mike!
Male voice 2:	Oh, hi Peter. I didn't know you worked in London. I haven't seen ...
Male voice 1:	No, I'm just going up for the day. I've got to see some people about a new project. So, do you do the journey every day? It must be a bit repetitive.
Male voice 2:	Oh, it's not too bad. It gives me thinking time, and I usually get some work done on the laptop ... *(fade out)*

Answers: a. 2   b. 4   c. 1   d. 3

C Students have already reflected on how they went about accomplishing a task in the skills sections, and so reflecting here should not be too unusual for them. Tell them to be specific about their answers, for example, 'The first picture helped to understand the dialogue that goes with it', or 'In the fourth dialogue, I heard somebody say "journey"'. If you feel that they are not really discussing the task in pairs, ask them to tell you, and guide them towards thinking about what they heard.

D Students complete the summary to reflect on what they have done. The task should

consolidate the importance of listening for gist, and present some typical jargon words that you will probably want to use later in the course. Students should work individually. You can give feedback either by telling them the correct answers, or by asking one student (with clear pronunciation) to read the completed text.

Answers: 1. topic   2. details   3. word 4. skimming

Read the exam tip with students, making sure they understand what 'prediction' means, and how important it is to predict when listening.

E The aim of this task is to practise predicting, as much as to practise listening skills. Tell students that they will only hear very short extracts, which come from longer exchanges or monologues. Tell students to look at the pictures carefully, and think about the type of language that is likely to occur. Point out that they are more likely to have visuals like these as support, than a photograph or drawing in the Listening Module. You can either tell students to work in pairs or conduct this as a whole-class discussion. Direct students towards being specific with their answers, for example, 'Somebody will give directions' rather than 'They will talk about a map'.

F 🎧 Play the recording as students match the images with the dialogues.

Tapescript 🎧 **32** (1 min, 41 secs)

F **Listen to the four extracts and match them with the images in Exercise E.**

Extract 1

Young male 1:	Have you applied for that job you saw in the paper last week? You said you were interested.
Young male 2:	Yeah, but I haven't heard anything yet. I really hope they give me an interview.

Extract 2

Receptionist:	Do you know where to find us? OK – well, when you come out of the station, take a left. Walk for about five minutes and then take a right into Wallingham Road. You'll see us there. It's a big red-brick building.

Extract 3

Male voice: So, what sort of day have you got today?

Female voice: Oh, don't ask! Really, really busy. I've gotta be at a meeting with Doug by nine, and then at eleven I'm supposed to be seeing Tim at ABC. I hope I get there in time. I'll be working on the Chicago project all afternoon … I've no idea what time I'll finish this evening. How about you?

Extract 4

Male voice: I'm pleased to say that the first half of this year is looking better than for the same period last year. March was an especially good month – sales hit ten thousand for the first time in nearly three years, and … *(fade out)*

Answers: 1. c   2. a   3. d   4. b

Listening 2

Read the exam tip with students.

A　🎧 The aim of the listening practice here is to show students how understanding the gist of a recording will help them understand detail. They will find it difficult to answer questions about specific details in the exam if they don't really understand what the recording is generally about.

In the exam, they will probably not have a task that involves matching pictures to extracts, and they certainly won't have gist questions followed by more detailed questions about the same extract. Make sure they understand that once they have answered the gist questions correctly, they will find the real exam-type practice questions much easier.

Give students a moment to look at the pictures and make predictions. Then play the recording. Go through the answers before moving on to Exercise B. Don't play the recording a second time for the gist task.

Tapescript 🎧 33 (3 mins, 42 secs)

A　Listen to the four extracts. For questions 1–4, match the extracts with the pictures. Write the number of the extract in the box.

Extract 1

Assistant manager: Oh, good morning. It's Toby, isn't it? Let me just finish this e-mail and I'll be with you. Sit down for a minute.

New staff member: Thanks.

Assistant manager: OK, that's done. Hello again, I met you when you came for the interview last month – I'm Julie. I'm Keith's assistant manager.

New staff member: Yes, I remember.

Assistant manager: I'm afraid Keith isn't here this morning, so I'm going to show you round. You're starting with us on Monday, aren't you?

New staff member: Yes, that's right.

Assistant manager: Well, thanks for coming in today. We always think it's good for people to have a good look round and meet some of the other staff before they start the job properly. Would you like a tea or coffee before we start?

New staff member: Um, no, thank you – I had a coffee on the train.

Assistant manager: OK, well, where shall we begin? First of all, this is the office I share with Keith. It can be very busy in here – people just come in and out when they like … *(fade out)*

Extract 2

Male speaker: OK, now I'm going to show you the plans for the new city-centre offices. Let me just turn this on … here we are. This is the ground-floor plan and, as you can see, the area surrounding the offices – the car park and gardens, and so on.

Male speaker: The entrance is here on West Street, and there's quite a large area here outside the front entrance. We'll probably have some bays here, where you can lock up bicycles. The car park is at the back, here – there are spaces for thirty cars. Now, I know that thirty spaces isn't nearly enough ... *(fade out)*

Extract 3

Female voice: Oh, hi Justin. Can I speak to Robert, please? Thanks. Hello, Robert, it's Debbie – listen, I'm afraid I'm going to be a bit late. There's trouble with signals or something. We haven't moved for ten minutes and I don't when it'll be clear again. I'm still seven stops from the office – I'm sorry, I should have left home earlier. Can you start the meeting, and then I'll ... *(fade out)*

Extract 4

Salesman: Good afternoon, madam.

Customer: Oh, hello.

Salesman: Did you see the catalogue I put through the door last week – Kleenhouse Products?

Customer: Oh, yes, I did have a quick look, but ...

Salesman: Well, today I'm here to show you some of the products. Have you got ten minutes?

Customer: Well, actually, I'm rather busy – I was in the middle of ...

Salesman: Five minutes, then. You won't find any of these kitchen and bathroom products at such low prices anywhere else.

Customer: No, I'm sorry, I said I was busy. I don't really need anything like this at the moment ... *(fade out)*

Read through the questions. Then listen to the extracts again. For questions 5–12, choose the correct answer a, b or c.

[Play track 33 again]

Answers: a. 3   b. 1   c. 2   d. 4

Read through the second rubric with students, and make sure they know what to do. Students might find it difficult to listen to the recording only once, but avoid playing it a second time. Students can discuss what difficulties they had, and then listen again later if necessary (see Exercises B and C).

Answers: 5. c   6. b   7. a   8. a   9. c   10. b   11. a   12. b

B   Give students sufficient time to check answers and think about why they may have answered incorrectly, before moving on to Exercise C.

C   Students will by now be more familiar with this type of reflective process, but note that the questions are not the same as in previous units. Remind them that identifying what they are doing well and not doing so well is a very good way of focusing on what they can do better next time. Allow students time to reflect and complete the task, and then ask them if they are happy with the number of correct answers. Play the recording again if necessary, and tell students to focus on why the correct answers are correct.

Key vocabulary in context

The key vocabulary here is related to the theme of work, and all the words are nouns. Students should work individually to complete the task. When they have finished, tell them to close their books. Read the definitions in a different order, and see if they can remember the key nouns. You could give the definitions, and tell them to write the words if you want to check spelling more rigorously.

Answers: 1. d   2. c   3. b   4. a

For further listening practice, tell students to complete the exercise on page 9 of the Workbook. Set as an extra activity or homework task.

Reading

Reading

3

Reading 1: scanning for paraphrased language

Exam tip: In the second part of the Reading Module, the texts will always be related to work. You might read a job application or a page of staff rules, for example.

A Look at the photos. Answer these questions with a partner.
1. What is each job?
2. What is good and not so good about each job?
3. Would you like to do any of the jobs?

B Use a dictionary to check these words and then match each with one of the photos.
a. farms ____   b. flights ____   c. pitch ____   d. tips ____

C Read the title of the passage on the next page. Will each person say good things or bad things about the job?

Exam tip: Always read the heading or title of a passage. It will help you predict what it is about.

D Read the four short texts and circle the job in each as quickly as possible.

E Scan the four texts and use the highlighted words to answer these questions. Write the letter of the text in the space. In which text does the writer say that ...
1. he or she was very tired?   ____
2. he or she got a lot of money from the job?   ____
3. he or she got no money for doing the job?   ____
4. he or she had free time to enjoy?   ____

Exam tip: In some scanning exercises, you need to look quickly for parts of the text that mean the same as the words and phrases in the question. You will not find the exact words and phrases from the question in the text.

F Scan the text again to answer these questions in the same way. Highlight the parts of the text that provide the answer. In which text does the writer say that ...
1. he or she enjoyed working outside.   ____
2. he or she met famous people.   ____
3. he or she doesn't do the job now.   ____
4. people don't think the job is interesting.   ____

38 IELTS Target 5.0

The Best Job I Ever Had

Text A
I had the best job in the world for three years and I didn't even get paid for it. From when I was 12 until when I was 15, I was a ball boy at Old Trafford. That's where Manchester United play their home matches. When the ball went off the pitch, I had to get it and give it back to one of the players as quickly as I could. I saw some great football matches and met footballers and football coaches from all round the world.

Text B
People think that being a waitress is boring and repetitive, but it's the best job I ever had. I worked in a very nice restaurant where all the customers had plenty of money. The restaurant didn't pay me very much, but I made a fortune from the huge tips that the customers gave me. I always did my job well because I knew that if the customers weren't happy, they wouldn't give me a tip.

Text C
The job I'm doing now pays very well, but it's quite boring and very stressful. I think I was happiest when I was picking fruit in France. My friends and I were students, and we travelled around France working on farms. We picked grapes and strawberries. We worked very long hours, and at the end of the day I was exhausted, but I was in the sunshine all day and I was working with the people I knew best.

Text D
These days, I stay at home and look after my two children, but for ten years I had the best job in the world. I was an air hostess working on international flights. I flew to Australia and South America. During the flights, I was very busy and the passengers were sometimes quite difficult, but I got three days off before the journey back. The airline put me in the best hotels and I had a great time. I saw some wonderful places in those ten years.

Reading 2: practise scanning for paraphrased language

A Look at the job titles in the advertisements on the next page and check that you understand them.

B Read the job advertisements and answer the questions. For questions 1–3, match each job advertisement with a description a–d. Write the letter of the description in the space. There is one description that you do not need.
1. advert A ____   2. advert B ____   3. advert C ____
a. You will deal with people who want to buy or who have already bought a product.
b. You will sell something.
c. You will design something.
d. You will work with money.

For questions 4–9, write the letter of the advertisement in the space. Which advertisement says that ...
4. you must know how to use a computer. ____
5. you will work closely with someone in a high position. ____
6. you will learn how to do the job when you start. ____
7. people are happy with the service provided by the company. ____
8. you will often talk to people directly. ____
9. you need to apply before a certain date. ____

Exam tip: When you are doing a reading exercise quickly, you might want to guess answers, and sometimes that's possible. However, you will feel more confident if you find the part of the text that provides the answer.

IELTS Target 5.0 **39**

A
ACCOUNTS DIRECTOR / FINANCIAL MANAGER
Up to £70,000 a year + company car.
A position managing our financial services and working directly with the chief executive. You should be a qualified accountant with experience in management.
Closing date for application: 11 March 09
Interviews: April 09

B
Our market is growing and we are looking for a
SALES EXECUTIVE
As part of our busy sales team, you will be ambitious. You will deal face-to-face with people regularly and must have excellent communication skills. You will be quick to understand new ideas and put them into practice.
You will receive full training and a good salary. For more information, please call 01456 554796.

C
Customer Service Administrator
Lewes, East Sussex
Good salary + benefits
We have more than a million satisfied customers in the UK, and we provide the highest quality service. To continue our success, we are looking for a full-time customer service administrator. The successful applicant must have previous experience and be computer-literate. He or she will need a friendly, professional telephone manner.
To apply, please send your CV to Sonya_Groves@Sureguard.co.uk

C Highlight the parts of the adverts that give the answers to questions 4–9. Then compare your ideas with a partner.

D Check the key on page 286. How many questions did you answer correctly?

E Tick the sentences about the reading task that are true for you and think about how you can answer more questions correctly next time.
1. I read the instructions for the questions carefully.
2. I skimmed the advertisements to answer questions 1–3.
3. I answered questions 1–3 quickly.
4. I read more carefully to answer questions 4–9.
5. It was quite easy to find the information I needed for questions 4–9.
6. I am happy with how many questions I answered correctly.

Key vocabulary in context
Circle the correct word from the three options. You can find the correct options in the job adverts.
1. A more formal word for job is position / protection / preparation.
2. If you do a job for a long time, you have experiment / experience / expression.
3. If you want to do well in a job, you are ambitious / amazing / absent.
4. Another way to say 'give' a service is prove / produce / provide.
5. If a company is doing well, it has surprise / success / support.

F Highlight words and phrases in the adverts that you think are useful.

Exam tip: It is not possible to learn all the new vocabulary from a text that you read, and usually it is not very helpful to try. Focus on words and phrases that are useful to you.

WB For more focus on reading skills, go to Workbook page 10.

40 IELTS Target 5.0

Objectives

- To further practise scanning a text for specific information.
- To help students to recognize language that is paraphrased.
- To practise recognizing paraphrased language in texts.

Reading 1

A The aim of this speaking task is both to provide some speaking practice, and to prepare students for the reading tasks that follow. Although students won't talk about pictures in the IELTS speaking exam, they will talk about the positive and negative aspects of various situations. This also provides a further focus on making predictions about the content of a text.

Answer the first questions with students to clarify the job titles, and then allow them to talk in pairs. The boy in the first picture is a 'ball boy' (note that in the past, there was only one ball, and ball boys around the ground had to run to get the ball and throw it back to a player when it went out of play. Nowadays, there are several balls so that the game flows more quickly). Teach them 'waiter' and 'waitress', and point out that '~ess' is a typical suffix to indicate that the person doing the job is female. We still use the term 'air hostess', but as more men do the job, the term 'flight attendant' is becoming more common. You can tell students that 'fruit picking' is a common seasonal job for students who travel around Europe.

Allow students three or four minutes to discuss questions 2 and 3. Avoid feedback that simply repeats what students have just done. Perhaps you could ask students which of the jobs they would most like to try, as a way to finish the task.

B Set this for individual completion, so that students get some practice using a dictionary with a clear purpose.

If not everyone has a dictionary, put them into pairs or small groups so that they can share dictionaries. Give feedback when a few students have completed the task. Don't tell students to read the text to check, as there are further preparation tasks.

Answers: a. 4   b. 3   c. 1   d. 2

C Read the question with the class and make sure they look only at the title. Establish that the title suggests that the speakers will talk about the positive aspects of a job.

The exam tip is very short and clear. Tell students to read it, and then close the book. Ask one student to tell you what the exam tip says.

D Read through the instructions with students and make sure they know what they have to do. Set a time limit of about a minute so that they don't read more than they need to. Check the answers orally.

Answers: A. ball boy   B. waitress
C. picking fruit   D. air hostess

E First, point out that parts of the text are highlighted, and that students will need to read these parts carefully to answer the questions. Tell them to read the questions first, and then to read the text as quickly as possible in order to answer them. End the task when about half the class have completed it. As students are reading, write 1–4 on the board so that you can give clear

feedback. Students can give you the letters for each number. Clarify some of the key expressions as you go, and emphasize how the questions have been paraphrased so that they don't repeat the exact words in the text.

Answers: 1. C   2. B   3. A   4. D

Read through the exam tip to consolidate what you have just shown the students.

F This task is more challenging, and students will need time to do it properly. At this stage, it is probably best to give them the time they need (you can tell them they will need to practise, and do it more quickly later). If students are having difficulties, you can stop them, and do one or two with them. Alternatively, you could put them into pairs. Give feedback as in Exercise E, but write the key part of the text that provides the answer on the board, too.

Answers:
1. C (I was in the sunshine all day)
2. A (and met footballers and football coaches from all round the world)
3. D (These days, I stay at home ... / but for ten years I had the best job in the world / I was an air hostess ...)
4. B (People think that being a waitress is boring and repetitive)

Reading 2

The aim is now to practise scanning and recognizing paraphrased language. Job advertisements are a fairly common source of text in the IELTS exam. The texts are far more challenging, and the aim is to give students something a bit closer to what they will have to deal with in the exam. Tell students that the advertisements contain some language that they will not understand, and that they only need to scan in order to answer the questions.

A In the exam, students will not have this kind of assistance, but for now it is better that they know something about each advertisement before they tackle the exam practice tasks. Go through the titles with them, making sure that what the job entails is clear, but try to avoid answering questions 1–3 in Exercise B. If you think it is impossible to explain the job titles without answering those questions, give them a couple of minutes to check any words (only in the job titles) they need in a dictionary.

B Make sure students read the questions carefully before they read the advertisements. You might like to read the instructions to the first three questions, so that you can point out that there is one more option than they need, and that this is a common feature of IELTS matching tasks. They should work individually. You can either set a time limit that you think your students can cope with, or end the task when about half the students say they have completed it.

When students have completed the task, read through the exam tip with them before they check their answers.

Ask them if they guessed any of the answers.

C Students will probably want the answers now, but it would be beneficial for them to reflect on whether they identified the right parts of the advertisements, or whether they guessed answers, and for you to check. As they compare with a partner, monitor, and ask students how they answered some of the questions (see answers below).

D Give students sufficient time to check and think about why they may have answered incorrectly, before moving on to Exercise E.

Answers:
1. advert A – d
2. advert B – b
3. advert C – a
4. C (be computer-literate)
5. A (working directly with the chief executive)
6. B (You will receive full training)
7. C (more than a million satisfied customers)
8. B (deal face-to-face with people regularly)
9. A (Closing date for application)

E By now, students will be familiar with this type of reflective process, but note the questions are not the same as in previous units. Remind them that identifying what they are doing well and not doing so well is a very good way of focusing on what they can do better next time. Allow students time to reflect and complete the task, and then ask them if they are happy with the number of correct answers. You may like to ask one student what he or she will do differently next time.

Key vocabulary in context

The rationale here is to contrast words that look similar. All the correct words are high-frequency words that students should retain. Students may or may not have to look back to the advertisements to choose the option in each case. Students can work individually or in pairs. When you give feedback, think about whether it is beneficial or not to talk about the meanings of all the distracters. It could be very time-consuming. Perhaps select words that you think your students might confuse.

Answers: 1. position   2. experience   3. ambitious   4. provide   5. success

F The important thing here is to show students that they should decide what vocabulary they need to retain, rather than simply learn what their teacher presents them with. Give them two minutes to highlight words and phrases they need. Monitor to check whether they are making sensible choices.

Read through the exam tip (which in this case is more of a general study tip) with students. You might like to then tell them to close their books, and see if somebody can tell you what it said.

The Workbook task for this unit is fairly extensive, and practises what students have been doing in this part of the lesson. Now would be good time to set it up as a homework task.

Writing

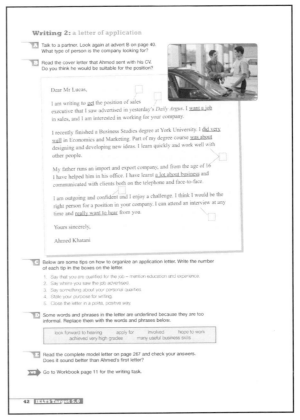

Objectives

- To introduce students to the basic concept of register.
- To recognize formal and informal use of written language, and to identify inappropriate use of informal language.
- To practise writing a formal job application.

Writing 1

A Previously, tasks of this type have come after the presentation and practice stages, but here the question would be too easy to answer retrospectively. You can either put students into pairs as suggested, or answer the question together as a class.

Answers: 4 is the correct definition.

B Students should work individually, and then compare with a partner. Give feedback orally. Point out that register is not determined simply by who you are writing to (whether you know

them or not), but also by the purpose or function – for example, if you are making a request or apologizing, the language you use is slightly more formal, regardless of who you are writing to.

Answers: 1. INF 2. VF 3. QF 4. VF
5. INF 6. QF 7. VF

Read the exam tip with students. Point out that it is their writing of formal letters that will need improving, especially before they take the exam.

C The aim of this activity is to contrast formal and informal language, as well as to present students with a number of high-frequency expressions that they can use in their letter writing. Students should work individually, and then compare with a partner. As they are working, write numbers 1–8 on the board so that you can be clear about answers during feedback. As you give feedback, point out features of style, such as contractions, colloquial words and so on.

Answers: 1. F 2. E 3. G 4. B 5. C
6. H 7. A 8. D

You could check what students have retained now. Tell them to cover the formal expressions. Then read out the informal expressions as they tell you the corresponding formal ones.

Read through the exam tip with students.

Writing 2

There is a model letter both at the back of the Course Book, and here in the Teacher's Book, but it would be a good idea to present the letter on an OHP transparency on the board, if possible. This would facilitate setting up tasks, and giving feedback.

A Tell students to look at the picture, and revise words like 'sell', 'selling', 'sales', 'salesman' and 'sales executive'. Refer students back to the appropriate advertisement on the appropriate page, and give them a moment to discuss the question. Then elicit ideas, and write a few key words on the board.

Answers: The company wants somebody who is ambitious, who has excellent communication skills and who is quick to understand.

B Explain a cover letter, and say that Ahmed has applied for the job they have been talking about. Make sure they understand that, for now, they are reading only to decide whether Ahmed is a suitable candidate. Tell them not to worry about the boxes and underlined words for now. Students can either talk in pairs for a moment or tell you directly what they think.

Answers: Yes, he would be suitable. The ad says that training will be provided.

C Remind students that organizing your compositions is essential. Go through the tips with students before they read the letter again more carefully. You might like to fill one box as an example, so that students know what to do. Students should work individually, and then compare with a partner. If you have the model on the board, either you or students can fill in the numbers for feedback. If not, you will have to give the answers orally for now, as looking at the model letter will allow students to see the answers for the next task as well.

Answers: See model letter after Exercise D.

D Read through the rubric with students, and then replace the first word 'get' with 'apply for' as an example. Students should work individually, and then compare with a partner. See Exercise E for feedback.

E Refer students to page 267 so that they can check their answers, and see the complete model letter (the same version is reproduced below). Tell students that they should use Ahmed's letter as a model when they write their own letter later.

Dear Mr Lucas, [4]

I am writing to apply for the position of sales [2] *executive that I saw advertised in yesterday's Daily Argus. I hope to work in sales, and I am interested in working for your company.*

I recently finished a Business Studies degree at York University. I achieved very high grades in Economics and Marketing. Part of my degree course involved designing and developing new ideas. I learn quickly and work well with other people. [1]

My father runs an import and export company, and from the age of 16 I have helped him in his office. I have learnt many useful business skills and communicated with clients both on the telephone and face-to-face. [3]

I am outgoing and confident and I enjoy a challenge. I think I would be the right person for a position in your company. I can attend an interview at any time and look forward to hearing from you.

Your sincerely, [5]

Ahmed Khatani

Writing task

The writing tasks are found either in the Workbook or in the exam practice section at the end of the unit. For this unit, the task is in the Workbook.

Read through the exam tip and remind students to use the model in the Course Book. Tell them not to worry if they copy complete phrases from the model, as the aim now is to learn those phrases so that they can use them when it comes to taking the exam.

A At this stage, it is still necessary for students to have a little assistance with preparation before attempting to write a complete letter. Give them a moment to discuss the question with a partner. You might need to help with key words in the advertisement (that they didn't worry about earlier) during the reading task.

B Monitor as students work, but check specifically that they are organizing their letters and making relevant points, rather than writing perfectly accurately. Students could exchange letters when they have finished.

If you collect students' letters to mark, it would be better to use the process to get an idea of what they are capable of, rather than correct too heavily. At this stage, you will still be correcting most of what they write.

No additional model is provided in this unit, as the model in the Course Book gives a very clear idea of what this type of letter should look like.

Consolidation

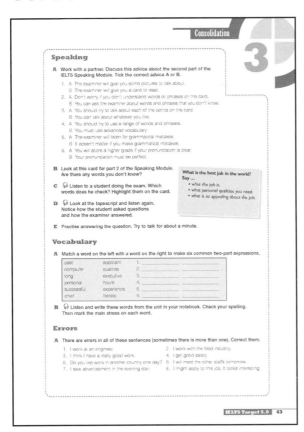

Speaking

A The aim of this activity is to consolidate what students have learnt about the second part of the IELTS speaking exam, before going on to practise another example of it. Students should discuss the options in pairs, and then tell you what they think.

> **Answers:** 1. B 2. B 3. A 4. A
> 5. A (basic mistakes at this level) 6. A

B The aim of this task is for students to learn how to check words and phrases on the card, and to feel confident about doing so. Tell them to look at the card and just think about the words and phrases they are not sure about.

C 🎧 Make sure students know they are going to listen to a student, and that the student is unsure about some of the words on the card. Make sure they know they should highlight or underline the words on the card as they listen. Play the recording.

Tapescript 🎧 **34** (1 min, 15 secs)

C Listen to a student doing the exam. Which words does he check? Highlight them on the card.

Student:	Can I check a few words on the card before I start to make my notes?
Examiner:	Yes, please do.
Student:	This word 'ideal' – does it mean something like 'perfect'?
Examiner:	Yes, it means more or less the same thing.
Student:	OK, and what about 'personal qualities'? I'm not sure I understand exactly what that means.
Examiner:	Your personal qualities are the things about you that make you good for the job – the right person for the job.
Student:	You mean, like if I'm hard-working or lazy?
Examiner:	Yes, those are good examples.
Student:	Thank you. Finally, I want to check 'appealing'. Does it mean 'what makes me want to do the job'? Is it a bit like 'attractive'?
Examiner:	Yes, that's right. Now, are you ready? You have a minute to plan what you want to say and make notes.

D 🎧 Give students sufficient time to read through the tapescript, and then play the recording again. There are some very useful examples of exchanges that students would be advised to learn.

Tapescript 🎧 **35** (0 mins, 18 secs)

D Look at the tapescript and listen again. Notice how the student asked questions and how the examiner answered.

[Play track 34 again]

E Students can talk with the same partner to practise the interaction. Tell them to take turns in being the student and examiner. Tell the examiner to time the student. Students should aim to get closer to two minutes of talking now.

Vocabulary

A This task revises vocabulary learnt in the unit. Students should complete the task individually. When they have finished, tell them to close the book and tell you which whole phrases they remember.

Answers: 1. past experience
2. computer literate   3. long hours
4. personal qualities   5. successful applicant
6. chief executive

B 🎧 This task revises vocabulary from the lesson, and checks spelling and pronunciation. Make sure students know what to do, and are ready to start writing before you play the recording. Pause after each word to give them time to write. Write the words on the board for them as you play the recording a second time.

Tapescript 🎧 **36** (1 min, 11 secs)

B Listen and write these words from the unit in your notebook. Check your spelling. Then mark the main stress on each word.

1 experience

2 successful

3 career

4 challenging

5 promotion

6 professional

7 financial

8 qualified

9 advertisement

10 applicant

Answers: 1. experience   2. successful
3. career   4. challenging   5. promotion
6. professional   7. financial   8. qualified
9. advertisement   10. applicant

Now the words are on the board, play the recording again as students mark the stress. They can do it in their notebook or come up to the board.

Answers: ex<u>pe</u>rience / suc<u>cess</u>ful / ca<u>reer</u> / <u>chall</u>enging / pro<u>mo</u>tion / pro<u>fess</u>ional / fi<u>nan</u>cial / <u>qual</u>ified / ad<u>ver</u>tisement / <u>app</u>licant

Errors

A Students now know that each unit ends with this type of task. Remind them that it is very useful to notice and correct common errors. Tell students that errors are grammatical, lexical (a wrong word has been used) or to do with punctuation (capitalization of letters). There are no spelling mistakes. They can either complete the task individually or work in pairs. You could ask students to come and write the correct sentences on the board, while others help from the floor. You will need to write the correct versions of each on the board to clarify.

Answers:
1. I work as an engineer.
2. I work in the food industry.
3. I think I have a really good job.
4. I get a good salary.
5. Would you like to work in another country one day?
6. I will meet the other staff tomorrow.
7. I saw the advertisement in *The Evening Star*.
8. I might apply for this job. It looks interesting.

Exam Practice

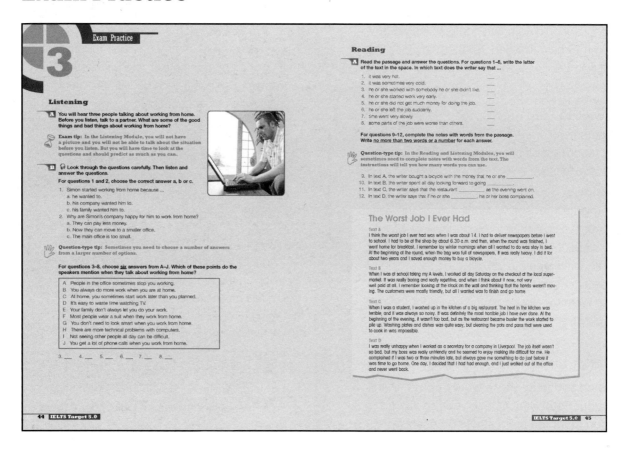

Listening

In this exam practice task, the recording is quite challenging, and is close to what they may hear in the exam. However, the tasks are a little less challenging, and again students are given preparation they will not be given in the exam.

A Tell students to look at the picture, and then read through the rubric with them. Elicit an example of a good thing and an example of a bad thing, and then give them three or four minutes to discuss the issue in pairs. Monitor, and write some of the students' ideas up on the board. Finish by working through what you have on the board, and tell students to refer to the ideas as they listen.

Read the exam tip with students, which repeats information that students have already been given.

B 🎧 Tell students to look through the questions carefully, and as they do so, make predictions. After a moment, stop them, and refer them to the question-type tip in the middle of the page. Read through it with students, and make sure they understand that there are two types of

multiple-choice tasks. Note that questions 3–8 are a little easier than they will be in the exam. Students will have a good chance of guessing answers when there are six correct choices out of ten. In the exam, there will be fewer correct answers. Tell them they will hear the recording once only. Tell them that for now they can write the answer in their book or in a notebook, but in the exam they will have to transfer answers onto an answer sheet. Students should work individually as they listen to the recording.

Tapescript 🎧 **37** (3 mins, 40 secs)

B **Look through the questions carefully. Then listen and answer the questions. For questions 1 and 2, choose the correct answer a, b or c.**

Female voice: So, Simon, I hear you're working from home, too, these days.

Male voice 1: Yeah, that's right. Well, I go into the office once a week, but I'm at home most of the time.

Female voice: Are you enjoying it?

Male voice 1: Well, there's good and bad, you know how it is. I didn't really choose to start working from

Male voice 2: home, and the rest of the family are not very happy about it – I'm always telling them to be quiet. The company decided that they had to close one of the offices. About twenty people had no office, and there wasn't enough space in the main office for twenty more people. So, they decided some of us would work at home.

Male voice 2: So, do you find that you get more work done?

Male voice 1: Well, yes and no. Sometimes, I really get a lot done in a very short time. In the office, there's always someone coming and asking a question, or starting a conversation about something. At home, you don't have that, of course. On the other hand, it's easy to get distracted by jobs around the house. You start cleaning or tidying up or mending something. When you're in the house all day, it's difficult to leave things alone. Sometimes it's midday before I really start work.

Female voice: Yeah, and I find that I often get distracted by the TV or surfing the net. When everyone is out of the house, I like to make a cup of coffee and watch the TV for ten minutes. I must admit, it's often more like an hour.

Male voice 2: My wife and the children don't really understand that I'm really working when I'm at home. You know – they think I have time to do jobs around the house as well. 'Jerry – could you fix the tap in the bathroom today?' 'Dad – can you drive me to football club this afternoon?' It makes me crazy.

Female voice: You just have to tell them you're at work. I have a friend who works from home and he puts his suit on in the morning. He says that it makes him feel like he's really at work.

Male voice 1: I must say that one thing I *do* like is not having to get ready for work in the morning. I can just put on a pair of jeans or shorts – and I don't need to shave for three days.

Female voice: So, has your company set you up with a new computer or given you a new laptop?

Male voice 1: That's a bit of a problem, actually. They've set me up with a new computer – it's really modern, and the Internet is really fast, but they say that I should only use it for work – you know – they don't want me using it for personal business. They want me to use my own computer for anything that's not connected with the job.

Male voice 2: So, you have two computers?

Male voice 1: Yeah, I don't really understand. So, do you two get a bit lonely working from home? I mean, don't you miss having other people around – discussing things and solving problems together?

Female voice: Yeah, I would like to spend more time with people. I had some good friends at work and I don't really see them much now.

Male voice 2: I'm always really pleased when somebody phones or e-mails me. You know – sometimes you go all day without speaking to anyone. My wife says that in the evening, I never stop talking.

Female voice: Well, I think more and more people will have to do it. Now that everyone has a computer at home and e-mailing is so fast, there's just no need for everyone to travel to work.

Male voice 1: Yes, I think you're right. In the future, it'll be … *(fade out)*

For questions 3–8, choose <u>six</u> answers from A–J. Which of these points do the speakers mention when they talk about working from home?

[Play track 37 again]

Answers: 1. b   2. c

The answers to questions 3–8 are in alphabetical order, but any order is fine as long as the correct six answers are chosen.

3. A   4. C   5. D   6. E   7. G   8. I

Reading

A   This text is shorter and less challenging than students will be given in the exam, but there is no preparation.

This would be a good time to allow students to work through the tasks with the minimum of help, and see how well they do. Read the question-type tip in the middle of the page with students first, so that they know how to answer questions 9–12. Tell them to follow the advice they have been given about tackling the Reading Module so far, and to apply it now. Then set a time limit of about 15 minutes. To give feedback, write the answers on the board so that they are clear. For questions 1–8, it would be a good idea to give students the lines that provide the answers, as they have been focusing on paraphrasing. Note that question 12 may be more difficult to answer than 9–11 because the two words used are separated by other words in the text.

Answers:

1. C (The heat in the kitchen was terrible)
2. A (icy winter mornings)
3. D (overall feel of extract)
4. A (I had to be at the shop by about 6.30 a.m.)
5. B (not very well paid)
6. D (One day ... I just walked out of the office and never went back)
7. B (looking at the clock on the wall and thinking that the hands weren't moving)
8. C (Washing plates and dishes was quite easy, but cleaning the pots and pans ... was impossible)
9. saved
10. home
11. became busier
12. was late

Unit 3 Workbook answers

Speaking and Vocabulary

A 1. What do you do for a living?
2. Do you enjoy what you do?
3. Is there a job you would really like?
4. What is the most difficult job you have done?

B Students' own answers.

C Students' own answers.

Listening

A a. getting promoted to a better job 3
b. getting a pay increase 1
c. applicants for a position 4
d. holidays 2
e. leaving a job 3

Tapescript 🎧 38 (1 min, 57 secs)

A Listen to the four extracts. Write the number of each extract against the topic below. There is one extra topic.

1

Man 1: Well, I'm hoping my salary will go up in September. I could certainly do with a bit more money.

Man 2: Yeah, I know what you mean. We got three per cent last year, but I don't expect that again this year.

2

Woman 1: I'm really bored with work at the moment. I need a break.

Woman 2: Can you take a week or two off soon?

Woman 1: Um, it's difficult. I've taken three weeks already, and I only get four for the whole year.

Woman 2: You should be a schoolteacher. They get the whole summer off!

3

Man 1: Did you hear that David Jones is leaving his position?

Man 2: Really? Is that good for you?

Man 1: Well, I hope so. I can't say the job's mine, but I'm the only person inside the company that could do it. They could advertise the position outside the company, of course.

Man 2: Would you enjoy all the responsibility?

Man 1: Well, yes. I need a new challenge, and the extra money would be good.

4

Man 1: So, I'm sure we'd all agree that this hasn't been easy, but we have a shortlist of three. I think all three are very strong and would all fit in very well here. Unfortunately, we can only choose one. I know what I think, but I'd like to hear your views first. Tony, why don't you start?

Man 2: Yeah ... OK ... well, I agree they're all strong, but for me, Matthew is the man for the job. Everything about him says ... *(fade out)*

Reading

Note that all the true/false questions are true. This doesn't matter, as the important thing is to identify the parts of the text that provide answers.

A 1. experts   2. overuse of gesture
3. detecting   4. clear signs
5. make the right impression

B 1. T   2. T   3. T

C 1. T (Not making eye contact ... sends out the wrong message)
2. T (A firm handshake and a friendly smile are probably more important)
3. T (The key is to make the interviewer feel that you will fit in.)

D See Exercise C.

Writing

The writing task is dealt with in the main section of the Teacher's Book.

4 Achievements

Speaking and Vocabulary

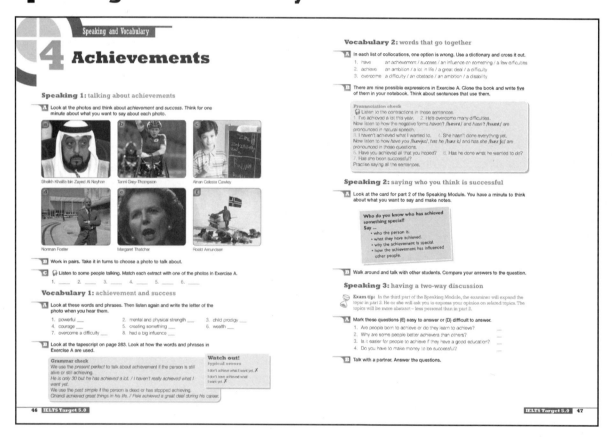

Objectives

- To give students further practice answering the type of questions they can expect in the second part of the IELTS Speaking Module.

- To practise talking about achievement and success, and to practise using the present perfect to talk about achievements.

- To introduce students to the task they will meet in the third part of the IELTS Speaking Module.

- To present and practise vocabulary, particularly collocations, connected with achievement and success.

Speaking 1

A Tell students that 'achieve' and 'succeed' are verbs, and that 'achievement' and 'success' are the related nouns. Say that 'achieve' is followed by an object so you achieve something (a goal or a desire), whereas 'succeed' is not followed by an object (if you succeed, you do well). Point out that 'achievement' is countable, and that 'success' is usually uncountable.

B Give students a few minutes to look at the photos, as you pronounce the names for them. Tell them that it doesn't matter if they don't know the people, as they will learn more about them afterwards, and for now they should use the images to guess what they have achieved. Don't tell students anything you know about the people yet. Then give them a further minute, and make sure they use it to prepare, and not to start talking straightaway. Tell them any key vocabulary that they want to use, but avoid pre-teaching vocabulary as there will be too much for them to take in. Give students sufficient time to talk properly. This will be a good opportunity to teach vocabulary that might occur later in the lesson. Monitor as students are talking, and note down any language that can go on the board, either because it is useful and well expressed or because it shows a typical error at the level. Tell students that they will hear these people described in Exercise C.

C 🎧 Make sure students know what to do, and play the recording. Check their answers, and then play the recording again, pausing after each extract. Clarify who each person is by writing their title / description on the board (Prime Minister / architect / sheikh / disabled athlete / explorer / child prodigy). Don't write any additional vocabulary at this point, as the following task focuses on that.

Tapescript 🎧 **39** (2 mins, 59 secs)

C **Listen to some people talking. Match each extract with one of the photos in Exercise A.**

Extract 1
Speaker 1: I want to talk about [BLEEP]. I don't like everything about her, but to become the Prime Minister of Britain at that time was incredible. Not only was she the first woman to become the Prime Minister, but she was from a normal background – you know, she didn't come from a rich family or anything like that. She had a very big influence on the twenty-first century – certainly in Britain.

Extract 2
Speaker 2: Real achievement means creating something – leaving something for people to see in the future. Writers, artists and film-makers are important, but I think architects are special. They leave something real – something that everyone can look at and use. [BLEEP] is probably the most important architect in the world at the moment. More people should know about him.

Extract 3
Speaker 3: [BLEEP] is the ruler of Abu Dhabi. He's one of the most powerful men in the Middle East and one of the richest in the world. He uses his wealth to help his country. He pays the best designers and architects to turn Abu Dhabi into a very important country.

Extract 4
Speaker 4: Well, here's someone who has really overcome difficulties to succeed. Her name's [BLEEP]. It's difficult for fully able people to succeed in sport – to do it when you have a physical disability like hers is just amazing. She's a superwoman.

Extract 5

Speaker 5: I'd like to say something about [BLEEP]. He's the only one who's no longer alive. I think he died in the nineteen-twenties. I think what he achieved shows true courage. He had the mental strength to achieve his dream and the physical strength to succeed in terrible conditions.

Extract 6

Speaker 6: This is a picture of the child prodigy, [BLEEP], from Singapore. I think he's only about six years old, but he's already passed exams. Now, he's studying Chemistry at a college. Achieving something like this at such a young age is just fantastic. What will he achieve by the time he's forty or fifty?

Answers: 1. e   2. d   3. a   4. b   5. f
6. c

Vocabulary 1

A and B The aim of these activities is to focus on some useful vocabulary, which occurs later in the lesson, as well as practising listening skills. Make sure students know what to do, and play the recording. You can then ask students to listen again and write the letter of the photo when they hear the extracts. Check answers, and practise the pronunciation of useful words.

Answers: 1. extract 3   2. extract 5
3. extract 6   4. extract 5   5. extract 2
6. extract 3   7. extract 4   8. extract 1

Grammar check

Students at this level will probably have difficulty distinguishing between past simple and present perfect. You might like to draw a timeline to illustrate the rules given. Remember that the aim of the grammar boxes is to remind students about a grammar point, and not to practise it rigorously. Time spent studying grammar will mean less time practising the skills that are more beneficial in terms of passing the exam. You might like to tell students to check a grammar point outside class if they are still finding it difficult to master. Students can look at the 'Watch out!' box if and when they need to.

Vocabulary 2

A Some of the collocations have already been presented in the lesson, others not. If you think that words going together like this is something completely new to students, show them a simple example – for example, you 'do' and not 'make' your homework, and talk about 'heavy' but not 'strong' rain. Encourage them to use dictionaries – students can work in pairs or small groups if there are not dictionaries for everyone. Give feedback orally, telling students which option is wrong.

Answers:
1. 'an achievement' is wrong
2. 'a difficulty' is wrong
3. 'an ambition' is wrong

B The aim of this activity is to check what students have retained. Make sure they close their books. They can write more than five of the collocations if they wish. Encourage them to write the collocations into a context if they can, for example, 'My grandfather has achieved a lot in life.'

Pronunciation check

These sentences practise pronunciation, and give some more natural examples of the type of present perfect structures that students will hear and want to use when talking about achievements. Play the recording, and drill the sentences. Then allow a moment for students to say the sentences two or three times to a partner.

Pronunciation check

Listen to the contractions in these sentences.

1 I've achieved a lot this year.

2 He's overcome many difficulties.

Now listen to how the negative forms *haven't* and *hasn't* are pronounced in natural speech.

3 I haven't achieved what I wanted to.

4 She hasn't done everything yet.

Now listen to how *have you*, *has he* and *has she* are pronounced in these questions.

5 Have you achieved all that you hoped?

6 Has he done what he wanted to do?

7 Has she been successful?

Practise saying all the sentences.

Speaking 2

A Students have practised this type of task before, and should know what to do now. They know that they can ask about any words and phrases they don't know, and have heard students doing that. Remind them they have a minute to plan what to say, and that they should write notes if they want to.

B Walking around like this means that students can practise the process three or five times. Tell them that saying the same thing each is fine, and that they should try to add ideas and speak for longer each time. Monitor students, and note errors that you want to pick up on, but don't interrupt what they are starting to correct.

Speaking 3

The aim of this activity is to introduce students to the third and most challenging part of the Speaking Module. The aim is not to provide rigorous practice, and it should not be expected that they will accomplish the practice task well. Later in the course, students will be given more guidance, and further practice with this part of the exam.

Read the exam tip, and make sure students understand 'abstract' (meaning 'more about ideas rather than facts').

A Tell students that questions in this part of the exam will be more challenging, but they will have to attempt to answer. Tell them these are examples of questions that they might find difficult. Give them time to think individually, and mark each question. When they have finished, ask them which questions they would find difficult and why.

B Monitor as students talk, and try to note down the difficulties they are having. Point these out to them when they have finished. Tell them that they will hear students answering questions like these, and they will feel far more confident by the time they take the exam.

For further speaking and vocabulary practice, tell students to complete the exercises on page 12 of the Workbook. Set as an extra activity or homework task.

Listening

Objectives

- To reinforce the importance of making predictions before listening to a recording.
- To guide students towards what they should try to predict before listening to a recording.
- To help students to recognize language that is paraphrased.

Listening 1

Students have already been given advice about making predictions before they listen and read. The aim now is to give them guidance and practice in doing that.

A Read through the listening task instructions with the students, and let them think about it for a moment. Answer the first question together as a class. The answer should clearly be 'yes', though some students might say that being told what the recording is about will make them nervous, and that they won't understand anything. Then answer question 2 together as a class. The answer here should be very general. The following task asks for more specific ideas.

Try to elicit something along the lines of 'the talk will be formal', 'the speaker will talk about intelligence', 'the speaker will talk about having a good teacher' and so on.

B Allow students four or five minutes to discuss ideas in pairs. Then get some ideas from the class, and write them in note form on the board. Reasons might include clever children, good teaching, small classes. Key words and phrases might include 'intelligent', 'intelligence', 'exam results', 'pass tests', etc.

Note that students will not actually listen to a recording about this topic, and you might want to tell them this. They will, however, read about it later in the reading section of this unit.

Read the exam tip with the students. It consolidates what they should have discovered from doing the tasks.

C It is important to see how this task, and the following Exercises D and E, work together before you continue with this next stage of the lesson. The aim is to show students how they can make predictions from looking at the introductory line, and then carefully reading questions.

Give students a minute to read the three introductory lines. Tell them to think about the content of the recording, but do not ask them to make any predictions.

D Tell students that they will have to answer this type of multiple-choice question in both the Listening and Reading Modules. Make sure they understand that the question relates to only one of the topics in Exercise C, and then give them half a minute to decide which one. Tell students not to call out the answer, as all students need to think about this. Ask students to tell you how they know what the correct answer is.

Answers: The correct topic is 2.

E The aim of this activity is to show students that it is possible to guess answers logically sometimes, but that it is only advisable if they really don't understand the recording. Some students may know that options B and C are not very likely because it wouldn't make business sense. Give students a moment to think about whether they could predict the correct answer, and ask them what they think. If any students make a confident prediction, ask them how they know. Don't give them any advice or the correct answer yet, as they will listen shortly.

Read the exam tip with students.

Listening 2

A new listening stage begins here because the focus moves on to recognizing paraphrased language, but students continue working around the topic of 'starting your own business'.

A Give students a moment to read the two options and make their choice. Ask students who chose 1 to put their hands up, and then those who chose 2. Tell them that the correct answer is 2, and then read through the exam tip. Remind students that they have looked at how language is paraphrased in the Reading Module, and tell them the Listening Module is the same.

B 🎧 Ask students to listen to the recording that answers the question about starting your own business, and focus on how language is

paraphrased. Get the students to choose an answer a, b or c, then tell them the correct answer, and ask how many students previously guessed it correctly.

Tapescript 🎧 **41** (0 mins, 51 secs)

B **Listen to this extract that provides an answer to the question in Listening 1D. Choose a, b or c.**

Male voice: *(fade in)* ... so, once you've got that, you then have to do your homework. Look through local directories or take a tour of the town. If other companies are providing a similar service, you should try to offer something a bit different. Of course, you must expect competition, but starting up a business in an area where everyone is trying to sell the same thing is dangerous. And don't just put your prices down. Customers are not always attracted to the provider who charges less than everyone else.

Answers:
The correct answer is a (at this point, don't explain why).

C 🎧 Play the recording again, pausing the audio at key points. Tell the students to write down words and phrases they hear that provide the answer. There is no need to check answers for feedback, as you can now refer then to the appropriate tapescript (it is reproduced on the following page). When they have compared what they noted down with what is in the tapescript, point out the paraphrasing (highlighted). You could also point out why the other options are wrong (b because it exaggerates what the recording says, and c because the recording states the opposite).

Tapescript 🎧 **42** (0 mins, 20 secs)

C **Listen again and identify the words and phrases that provide the answer and tell you that the other options are wrong. Then check the tapescript on page 284.**

[Play track 41 again]

(fade in) ... so, once you've got that, you then have to do your homework. Look through local directories or take a tour of the town. If other companies are providing a similar service, you should try to offer something a bit different. Of course, you must expect competition, but starting up a business in an area where everyone is trying to sell the same thing is dangerous. And don't just put your prices down. Customers are not always attracted to the provider who charges less than everyone else.

Listening 3

Students should be ready to be more independent now when working through the practice stage of the skills section. They know that they have time to read the questions, and they know how to predict. In this task, all the questions are multiple-choice ones, and they have practised those task types before. Once you have worked through Exercise A, which checks they understand a key phrase in the recording, they should proceed unaided.

A Give students a minute to look up the phrase and then give a definition of your own. Make sure everyone understands the phrase before commencing, as it is the key to making predictions and answering questions.

B 🎧 You might like to give students a little longer than 30 seconds to read through the questions, but make sure they understand that 30 seconds is what they will have in the exam. It is probably best to stop explaining words in questions now, as they will have to learn to cope with this problem.

Note again that the task that includes questions 5–9 is easier than it will be in the exam. They will need to choose fewer answers from a greater number of options.

Play the recording. Students might find it difficult to listen to the recording only once, but avoid playing it a second time. Students can discuss what difficulties they had, and then listen again later if necessary (see Exercises C and D).

Tapescript 🎧 **43** (5 mins, 46 secs)

B Listen to somebody giving a talk about how setting goals can help you achieve more. For questions 1–4, choose the correct letter a, b or c.

Male voice: Good evening, everyone. It's good to see that so many people managed to make it – an achievement in itself when I'm sure you're all so busy. This evening, I'm going to talk with you about setting goals, and how setting goals can help you understand what you really want to achieve. First, though, I'd like to start by saying what I think achievement actually means. I think some people think it's simply about being successful in a job or making money, but it certainly doesn't have to mean that. Achievement is simply accomplishing goals that you set for yourself – doing what you planned to do – and people might plan to do all sorts of different things.

Achievement is about realizing your dreams. I would also like to say that to achieve, you must have belief – belief that you can do whatever it is you want to do. There is more to achievement than simply wanting to do something. Anyone can say that they want something, but actually getting it is not so easy. To get it, you must believe that it is yours. Not having belief is the main reason that so many people do not achieve. If you really want something, you must talk and act like you already have it – then you have belief, and then you will achieve.

So, goal setting. Goal setting is about imagining the future, and then turning the dream into a reality. Setting goals helps you to be clear about what you really want, and helps you concentrate on getting what you want. Setting goals will help you see what is stopping you from knowing what's important. And because achieving goals makes you feel good, you will be more confident and succeed more easily. Goal setting is something that all achievers do, whether they are high-flyers in business or successful athletes.

B It is important that you set both long-term and short-term goals. First, you need to have an idea of what you want from life – I call this the 'big picture' – then, you break this down into a number of smaller goals that you need to achieve in order to achieve the overall goal. As I say, the first step is to see the big picture. Think about what you want in the next fifteen or twenty years – doing this will influence all the smaller goals that you set yourself. You need to think carefully about different areas of your life and how they influence each other. You should identify the important areas of your life, and try to set goals in each of those areas.

Here are the areas that most people want to focus on, but remember that everyone is different. First, think about your career – how important is your career to you? Do you want to be a manager or run your own business, or are you happy working for other people? Connected to this is the financial side of your life – what sort of income do you want to have? Is wealth important to you?

You need to think about long-term relationships – at what age do you hope to be married? Do you want to have children? How much time do you want to spend with the people you love?

You need to think about your health and how that could change what you can achieve. How will you stay healthy as you get older? Do you do anything that is not good for your health, and how will you try to do those things less or stop doing them completely?

Finally, you need to think about your free time – your hobbies and interests. How much time do you want to have to do what you really enjoy? It is difficult to achieve goals in one area if you feel that you don't have the time to do the things that really make you happy.

Now, when you have this overall picture, try to set yourself one goal for each area. Make sure the goals are what you really want, and not what you think other people want from you. Of course, in life, it is important to make the people around you happy, but you must focus on what you want.

Now, I will go on to talk about how to break your lifetime plan down into short-term goals. But first, does anyone have any questions about what I've said so far?

For questions 5–9, choose <u>five</u> answers from A–H. When the speaker talks about different areas of life, which of these does he mention?

[Play track 43 again]

For question 10, choose the correct letter a, b or c.

[Play track 43 again]

Answers: 1. C   2. B   3. A   4. B

The answers to questions 5–9 are in alphabetical order, but any order is fine as long as the correct five answers are chosen.

5. A   6. B   7. E   8. G   9. H   10. C

C Give students sufficient time to check answers and think about why they may have answered incorrectly, before moving on to Exercise D.

D Students will by now be familiar with this type of reflective process, but note the questions are not the same as in previous units. Remind them that identifying what they are doing well and not doing so well is a very good way of focusing on what they can do better next time. Allow students time to reflect and complete the task, and then ask them if they are happy with the number of correct answers. Play the recording again if necessary, and tell students to focus on why the correct answers are correct.

There is no vocabulary in context for this section of this unit. Most of the key language has been presented and practised earlier in the unit.

For further listening practice, tell students to complete the exercise on page 12 of the Workbook. Set as an extra activity or homework task.

Reading

Objectives

- To show the importance of checking that information is given in a text, and that questions are not answered quickly and carelessly.

- To show students that distracters can often trick them into giving wrong answers.

- To introduce students to the 'not given' option as an addition to the 'true'/'false' option they have already practised.

Reading 1

A Tell students to look at the picture, and ask them if they remember who the boy is before reading the rubric. Then read through the rubric with students so that they remember his name, and give them a few minutes to answer the questions.

Alternatively, answer question 1 as a whole class, and elicit the phrase 'child prodigy'. Then give them time to answer question 2. Students will probably not be familiar with asking their own questions of a text, but it is a very good way of motivating them to read with purpose. Ask students to give you a few questions that they would like answered about Ainan as feedback.

B This task reinforces the benefit of predicting and preparing before reading a text. Make sure students know that they are guessing answers, and that it doesn't matter if they are right or wrong. They can work individually or in pairs. Students will read the text to see if they are right.

C Read the rubric with students, and say that 'not given' means that they can't find the answer in the text (a full explanation is given in the exam tip after the reading task). Tell students to read the text, and write their answers alongside the guesses. Make sure they understand that this task is to check whether their guesses in Exercise B were correct or not. It is important that you don't give students the answers yet, as they need to work through Exercise D first.

Read the exam tip with students. Then give them a moment to decide if they are happy with their answers. Ask them whether they are sure the information is really given.

D The aim of this activity is to show students how easy it is to make mistakes with this type of task. They may have difficulty if they don't read carefully, and if they make assumptions and answer questions without checking that the text really provides the answer. Make sure they understand that these are comments made by a fictitious student, and that the student has made some mistakes. Their task is to identify which questions the student has answered correctly or incorrectly, and why the student has made mistakes.

The task is quite complex in terms of reading the student's comments, then looking back to the text and then comparing the student's comments with their own answers. Students should work in pairs, and they should be given around 10–12 minutes to complete the task properly.

E When students have finished, refer them to the page with the answers to Exercise B. Give them a moment to think about any answers they got wrong, and any decisions they made about the comments in Exercise D. Then go through the comments in D, and compare each with the real answer so that you explain the mistake that the fictitious student made (see below).

Answers to Exercises B and D:
1. T (the student in D is correct)
2. T (again, the student in D is correct)
3. NG (the student in D has made an assumption – the text does not give him that information)
4. F (the student in D is correct)
5. F (the student in D is wrong. The text says that some experts believe that not having a normal childhood can do long-lasting damage – it does not only say what the mother and father think)
6. T (the student in D is correct)
7. NG (the student in D is wrong – yes, the text only mentions one programme, but that does not tell us that Ainan doesn't watch other programmes)
8. F (the student in D is correct)

To finish the activity, ask students whether they made any of the same mistakes that the fictitious student made. Remind students that it is essential they check that information is given, and that distinguishing between false and not given answers can be difficult.

Reading 2

Tell students that 'distracters' are the options they have that are not correct answers. So, in a multiple-choice task, if A is the correct answer, B and C are distracters. Remind them that distracters will never be ridiculously wrong answers, and they will have to read carefully to make their choices. Read through the exam tip with them.

A The aim of this activity is to look more closely at the type of question that students can easily get wrong. Give students a moment to read the question and think about their answer. Then ask one student to explain.

Make sure you rephrase the answer so that everyone understands.

Answers:
The text says that he has already passed his Chemistry O level (not A level, so only one small detail is different), and that he is studying for his A level now (which could also lead the reader to conclude that he has passed his exam).

Reading 3

Tell students that the text is the type of text they will see in the second part of the Reading Module – survival training. Tell them that this text is a bit shorter and more manageable than the one they will see in the exam.

Note that they have been prepared for this text to an extent by talking about Ainan and his parents' desire for him to go to university.

A Students should be ready to be more independent now when working through the practice stage of the skills section, but the quick lead-in task will provide a little additional preparation and opportunity to talk. Tell students to look at the names and then to cover the text. Students can either talk in pairs for a minute or tell you directly what they know. Avoid a lengthy discussion about any of the people, and don't give away information that is tested in the questions.

B Students know by now that they should look at the title of all texts, skim the text and then read the questions before reading the text more carefully. They have practised the task types before, but point out the additional heading that is a distracter.

C Students will probably want the answers now, but it would be beneficial for them to compare how they chose their answers and to reinforce the importance of finding information in the text. Students should do this individually, and then compare with a partner. Monitor and ask various students how they arrived at some of their answers. Help with any key words, like 'revolutionized', but avoid teaching all unknown vocabulary from the text.

D Give students sufficient time to check and think about why they may have answered incorrectly, before moving on to Exercise D. The key is reproduced below, together with the parts of the text that provide answers.

Answers:
1. d   2. e   3. b   4. a
5. T (Parents and teachers spend much of their time emphasizing the need ...)
6. NG

7. F (there are plenty of entrepreneurs and high-fliers who dropped out of school)
8. F (He dropped out of school ... and started his first successful business venture, a magazine called *Student*)
9. NG   10. NG
11. T (he left Harvard College in 1975 to set up his own computer software company)
12. F (... doesn't mean that everyone can get to the top in business without a college or university degree)

Note that question 6 is the focus of analysis and practice in the Workbook.

E By now, students will be familiar with this type of reflective process, but note the questions are not the same as in previous units. Remind them that identifying what they are doing well and not doing so well is a very good way of focusing on what they can do better next time. Allow students time to reflect and complete the task, and then ask them if they are happy with the number of correct answers. You may like to ask one student what he or she will do differently next time.

Key vocabulary in context

The task further checks comprehension of vocabulary in the text, and focuses on words and phrases that students are likely to see in the second part of the Reading Module. The words and phrases are in the order in which they occur in the text. Students should work individually, and then compare answers with a partner. As feedback, you could tell students to close their books and then tell you what they remember, as you write the words in two columns under the correct heading on the board. Check specifically the spelling of the most useful words, like 'career', for example. Check the pronunciation of 'entrepreneur' and point out that it is a word from French, with the stress on the final syllable.

Answers: 1. degree (L)   2. career (W)
3. education (L)   4. best grades (L)
5. graduates (L)   6. entrepreneur (W)
7. business venture (W)   8. apprentice (W)
9. college dropout (L)

The Workbook task for this unit looks more closely at why it is difficult to distinguish between 'false' and 'not given' answers. It would probably be best for students to revisit this a little after completing the section. Now would be a good time to set it up as a homework task.

Writing

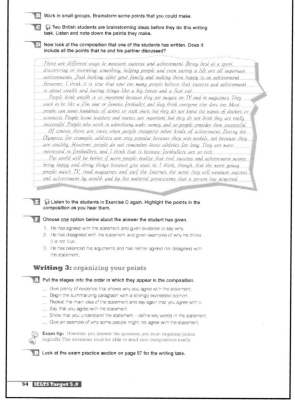

Objectives

- To introduce students to the second part of the IELTS Writing Module.

- To help students understand the instructions to a writing task, and what is expected of them in terms of an answer.

- To help students decide on the content of a discursive composition.

- To introduce students to the concept of basic organization of ideas in a discursive composition.

Writing 1

A The aim of the discussion stage is to get students thinking about what could form the content of the composition they will focus on later in the lesson. Tell them to look at the pictures, and then at the two questions. Then give them a minute to think about what they want to say before they start talking. After three or four minutes, get some ideas from the class. Try to elicit key vocabulary that will occur later in the lesson (being happy / wealth / winning medals, etc).

B The aim of Exercises B and C is to introduce students to the type of composition they will have to write in the second part of the exam, and to show them that instructions for this type of writing task can present difficulties. Tell students that they are going to focus on the second writing task, and give them a moment to look at the instructions. Tell them not to ask any questions yet.

C Tell students to tick one option in each sentence, and then compare with a partner. Get a general consensus about whether the task is manageable or difficult, and ask students who ticked the b options to explain why.

D The aim of this activity is to show students that not understanding words in the instructions may cause problems, and to explain the words so that they can later attempt the writing task. Note that students will not be able to look up words in the instructions in the exam, and you should tell them that they will need to improve their IELTS vocabulary.

Give students time to read the notes from the student, then ask them if they now understand the task better. Assure them that by the time they take the exam, they will be in a position to understand task instructions far more easily.

Writing 2

The aim of this part of the lesson is to tackle a problem that is often underestimated – whether students actually know what to say about an issue, regardless of the fact that they have to say it in a foreign language. It is often a good idea to ask students if they could answer the question in their own language. Students often admit that they wouldn't be able to. Students need a lot of guidance and practice in this area, and need to learn that simple ideas are perfectly acceptable. They are not expected to solve a complex social issue.

A Read through the rubric and the options with the students, and then let them tick the option they feel is the most true. Then have a class discussion following the points mentioned above.

Read the exam tip, which consolidates the points you have been discussing.

B Give the groups three or four minutes for brainstorming. Allow them to speak in their own language (if possible). The aim is to think of what you could say about the topic, not yet to say it in English. Monitor, and suggest a few points of your own. Feedback from students is not necessary, as they will now listen to some students discussing the writing task, and then compare ideas.

C 🎧 Explain what they are going to listen to. It is probably best to play the recording right through with pens down, and then play it again, pausing to allow students to make notes. They will not be able to make notes as they listen to the whole conversation. Note that students will listen to the conversation again after they have seen a model composition, so they don't need to worry if they miss some points. There is no need to get feedback from students, as they will now read a model composition that includes most of the points made in the conversation.

Tapescript 🎧 44 (3 mins, 23 secs)

C Two British students are brainstorming ideas before they do this writing task. Listen and note down the points they make.

Male voice: So, first of all, do you agree with the statement?

Female voice: Yes, I do. Too many people think that if you make a lot of money, you are successful. I don't think making money means that you are happy, and for me, being happy is the most important thing. Being happy is an achievement.

Male voice: Yes, I suppose so, but I don't think that you must be happy to say that you have achieved something. People like artists and scientists achieve great things, but that doesn't mean they are happy. Sometimes people like that are quite unhappy.

Female voice: Yes, that's true, but the important thing is that the people you mention – artists and scientists – achieve great things, but not only for the money. People should see that.

Male voice: Don't you think that people do recognize the achievements of people like that?

Female voice: No, not really. If you ask people to name a modern-day scientist, they will know one or two, but if you ask them to name actors or footballers, they will know hundreds. I think they know those people because they are rich and famous.

Male voice: Yes, I guess some people are even famous just because they are rich – like Paris Hilton.

Female voice: And I'm sure most people know Bill Gates because he was the richest man in the world – not because he was so brilliant.

Male voice: You mentioned footballers before. Don't you think that people in sport are considered successful because they win medals and prizes? They don't all make lots of money. Everyone likes Olympic athletes because they do something special.

Female voice: Yes, I agree, but most sportsmen are very rich – especially footballers, and they are the most famous. It seems that more and more of them are doing it for the money.

Male voice: OK, but what about ordinary people? Do you think that people who do important jobs, like nurses and teachers, think that they have achieved something?

Female voice: Maybe – but I'm not sure that most people think that nurses and teachers are real achievers. Images on TV and in magazines make people think they should make big money and live in beautiful houses and drive expensive cars. That's what they understand by success.

Male voice: Yes, people who work in advertising, for example, are considered successful, even though other people do more useful jobs. Perhaps we should think that real achievement is helping people and doing good for people – even saving somebody's life. If somebody goes to Africa to save children, people respect them – but I'm not sure that they really think that that person is successful.

Female voice: Yes, that's a very good point. Doing good for other people is an achievement, but I still think that being happy is the real aim of life. If you are happy and your family is happy, then you have really achieved something.

D Allow the students at least ten minutes to read through the composition, and check it against the notes they made while listening. Encourage them to ask you questions about any key vocabulary in the composition, but not to check every word.

E 🎧 Play the recording again, pausing at various points. Tell students to highlight or number points in the composition as they are made in the conversation. Going through each point with them during feedback will be laborious and time-consuming. Refer them to the tapescript on page 285, and give them another few minutes to compare that with the composition.

Tapescript 🎧 **45** (0 mins, 15 secs)

E **Listen to the students in Exercise C again. Highlight the points in the composition as you hear them.**

[Play track 44 again]

F The aim of this activity is to show students that there are different ways of responding to the statement in the task. Read through the three options with students, explaining 'evidence', and then give them a moment to make their choice. Students will look at more balanced compositions of this type later in the course.

Answers: The correct option is 1.

Point out that although the student has agreed with the statement, he has made points to take the opposite viewpoint into consideration.

Writing 3

The aim of this activity is to introduce students to the concept of organizing this type of composition. At this level it will be very challenging to write an accomplished composition of this type, and students will find organizing their ideas into a logical whole particularly difficult. However, the first thing the examiner will notice is the organization of a written piece of work, and it is an area students will have to work on. This aspect of all writing tasks is focused on rigorously later in the course.

A There is too much to read through with students, and they will lose concentration. Make sure they know what they have to do, and that they look back at the composition as they do it. Tell them to check any new words in the list of stages with you. Students should work individually, and then compare with a partner.

Give feedback orally, but write the numbers in the correct order down the board so that it is clear. Note that students will probably have found the task quite challenging, and will understand more about the organization of the composition from seeing the correct order now. Explain anything that is not clear during the course of this activity.

Answers:

3 Give plenty of evidence that shows why you agree with the statement.

5 Begin the summarizing paragraph with a strongly expressed opinion.

6 Repeat the main idea of the statement and say again that you agree with it.

2 Say that you agree with the statement.

1 Show that you understand the statement – define key words in the statement.

4 Give an example of why some people might not agree with the statement.

Read the exam tip with students.

Writing task

In this unit, the writing task can be found in the exam practice section at the end of the Course Book unit. See instructions for that section on page 85 of this book.

Consolidation

Speaking

The aim of the speaking section on this consolidation page is to revise what students should expect from the third part of the Speaking Module, and show them some examples of good and not very good answers.

A Students should work individually to revise what they know about the third part of the Speaking Module, and then compare with a partner. Ask them to give you the answers for feedback. Emphasize that students cannot be both fluent and perfectly grammatically correct at their level. Worrying too much about accuracy will stop them from saying what they want to say.

Answers: 1. F   2. T   3. F   4. T   5. T
6. F   7. T   8. F

B Give students a moment to think. They don't have to tell anyone what the answer to the question was.

C Read through the rubric with students, and make sure they know what to do. Play the recording straight through. You can pause after each speaker during the next task.

Tapescript 46 (1 min, 34 secs)

C **Listen to some students answering the question. Mark each speaker (G) good answer or (NG) not a good answer.**

Examiner:	... and do you think people are born to achieve or do they learn to achieve?
Speaker 1:	Yes, I think so.
Examiner:	... and do you think people are born to achieve or do they learn to achieve?
Speaker 2:	I don't know – maybe are born with this ability.
Examiner:	... and do you think people are born to achieve or do they learn to achieve?
Speaker 3:	Mm, I didn't think about it before. Some people is born very clever so maybe can achieve a lot. Other people is not so clever, but try and try and try – maybe that is learn to achieve.
Examiner:	... and do you think people are born to achieve or do they learn to achieve?
Speaker 4:	Mm, it's a good question. I guess some people are born to achieve. You know, like a genius or someone with an incredible talent, but some people learn to achieve. Maybe their parents teach them good things or they learn by mistakes.

Answers: 1. NG   2. NG   3. G   4. G

D Give students time to read through the questions so that they know what they are listening for. When they are ready, play the recording again, pausing after each speaker for a moment. To give feedback, play the recording a third time, giving them the answers as they listen.

Answers: a. speaker 3   b. speaker 2
c. speaker 1   d. speaker 4

E Give students time to read the questions and think about what they want to say. Tell them you don't expect perfect answers at this stage. It might be a good idea for them to answer each of the questions twice so that they gain confidence. Monitor, and choose a successful student to tell their answer to the rest of the class.

Vocabulary

A This task revises vocabulary learnt in the unit, and it emphasizes the need to learn the different forms of common words and checks spelling. Students should complete the task individually. For feedback, either you or students should write the answers on the board.

Answers: 1. successful   2. difficulties
3. ambitious   4. strength   5. powerful
6. education

B This task revises the collocations that students have learnt throughout the unit. Give them time to look through the list, and then tell you the one wrong phrase. Then give them time to use the phrases in contexts of their own. Dividing the phrases so that each half of the class has four or five each will save time.

Answers: The wrong phrase is 'have a failure'.

Errors

Students now know that each unit ends with this type of task. Remind them that it is very useful to notice and correct common errors. Tell students that there are no spelling mistakes (though one error might look like one). They can either complete the task individually or in pairs. Write the correct sentences on the board for clarity.

Answers:
1. James has had a lot of success in business.
2. I haven't achieved what I want yet.
3. He was taught Chemistry at school.
4. My father had an influence on my decision.

Exam Practice

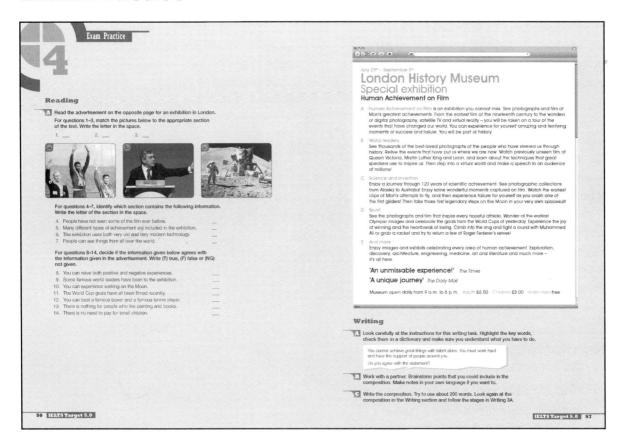

Reading

A Tell students that this type of advertisement is a common type of text in the first part of the Reading Module, and this text is approaching the level of challenge they will face in this part of the real exam. The first matching task is easier, though, and is designed to help them read for gist and to give them confidence. It is not usual to match pictures to parts of a text in the IELTS Reading Module.

Write the answers on the board so that they are clear. For questions 4–14, it would be a good idea to give students the lines that provide the answers.

Answers:
1. d   2. b   3. c
4. B (Watch previously unseen film)
5. E (images and exhibits celebrating every area of human achievement)
6. A (From the earliest film of the nineteenth century to the wonders of digital photography, satellite TV and virtual reality)
7. C (collections from Alaska to Australia!)
8. T (experience for yourself amazing and terrifying moments of success and failure)

9. NG
10. T (take those first legendary steps on the Moon in your very own spacesuit!)
11. F (celebrate the goals from the World Cups of yesterday)
12. T (Climb into the ring and fight a round with Muhammed Ali or grab a racket and try to return a few of Roger Federer's serves!)
13. F (art and literature)
14. T (Under-fives free)

Writing

A At this stage, students will need quite a lot of assistance with preparation before attempting to write a complete composition of this type. Tell them that the important thing now is to attempt the composition, make some valid points, and organize the points as well as they can.

Give students a minute or so to read the task instructions, and then allow them to ask questions about any words they don't know. They will want to check 'talent', and perhaps revise 'support'.

B This stage will be very important for students at this level. They can work in pairs as suggested, or in small groups. Give them at least ten minutes for this, and monitor, giving a few of your own ideas. Write some points up on the board so that everyone has some points they can include.

C Now allow them 40 minutes to complete the task (you might want to end earlier than that if students have managed all they can, and you think looking at the model will be more beneficial). Tell them to use the composition in the Writing Module as a model. Monitor as students work, but check specifically that they are organizing their ideas and making relevant points rather than writing accurately.

When students have completed the task, tell them to look at the model composition on page 267 of the Course Book. Put them into pairs to compare their composition against the model. The model is reproduced below.

If you collect students' compositions to mark, it would be better to use the process to get an idea of what they are capable of, rather than correct too heavily. At this stage, you will be correcting most of what they write.

Some people think that having great talent is enough to succeed in life. They see actors and artists and great sportsmen and think they are successful because they were born with talent. They forget that these people also worked very hard to get where they are.

In my opinion, talent can only take you so far. To reach the top you also need the desire to be the best and the discipline to work hard to be the best. You must also get the right advice and listen to it. You need the support of the people around you – your friends and family.

I think there are many talented people who are not successful because they are lazy. Some don't succeed because their parents or their teachers don't push them to do well. Some talented people are quite unusual and their friends and family don't take them seriously. Then they don't have the confidence to succeed.

My hero is the basketball player Michael Jordan. He had incredible natural talent, but he was the first player to arrive for training every day and the last player to leave. This desire to work hard and to practise is what made him the best.

To sum up, I want to say that talent, hard work and support from others must go together if somebody is successful. There are many people in top positions who have less natural talent than another person who has not achieved very much at all.

Unit 4 Workbook answers

Speaking and Vocabulary

A 1. achieved   2. succeeded   3. has
   4. influenced   5. overcome

B Students' own answers.

Listening

A 1. b   2. b   3. c

> **Tapescript** 🎧 **47** (1 min, 49 secs)
>
> A **Listen to people talking about sporting achievements and choose the correct answer a, b or c.**
>
> **Speaker 1:** Muhammed Ali called himself 'The Greatest', and for me, he really was the greatest sporting figure. Not only was he world heavyweight champion, but he was heavyweight champion three times. I think he was nearly forty when he won the title for the third time. Everyone thought he was finished, but he came back to be the champion. That's incredible.
>
> **Speaker 2:** Well, of course, I want to talk about a sportswoman. I think Martina Navratilova achieved something amazing. I don't know how many times she played at Wimbledon, but I know she was ladies' singles champion nine times – nine times, can you believe it? She won doubles titles and mixed-doubles titles, too. There will never be another tennis player like her again.
>
> **Speaker 3:** I can't say that Ayrton Senna was the greatest racing driver ever because, of course, he was killed before he had a chance to prove it. Michael Schumacher dominated Formula One for many years, but I think Ayrton Senna was the better

driver. The Brazilian people loved him – maybe even more than Pelé – and his early death was a terrible tragedy.

Reading

A 2 is the correct advice.
   Read through the exam tip with students.

B The correct answer is NG because they have been *trying* to reduce it. The sentence does not say that they have achieved that. It also does not say that they have not achieved it.

C Extract A 1. NG   2. T   3. F
   Extract B 1. F   2. T   3. NG

Writing

A Students refer to the composition in Course Book for correct version.

B Students' own ideas.

Thoughts

Unit overview

The fifth unit is based around the theme of intelligence and the way people think. There is an overall aim of giving students practice with dealing with unknown vocabulary, and they will meet some slightly more challenging language than previously. The unit gives students a further taste of what they can expect in the various sections of the IELTS exam.

Speaking and Vocabulary

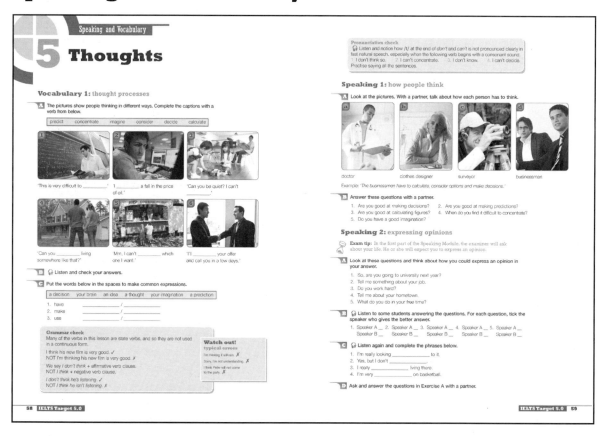

Objectives

- To practise expressing opinions in the context of the second and third parts of the IELTS Speaking Module.

- To encourage students to give fuller answers than a simple 'yes' or 'no' to questions.

- To present and practise vocabulary connected with thought-processes and intelligence.

- To present students with further examples of common collocations, and to show how important it is to learn collocations.

- To revise the use of state verbs, i.e., not used in a continuous form.

Vocabulary 1

A The aim of this activity is to present students with a range of verbs that will help them to be more specific, rather than just saying 'think'. Start the lesson by writing 'think' in the middle of the board and circle it. Then elicit different ways that people can think (you might need to give an example). Write sensible ideas around the headword on the board. Ask students to spell the words for you.

Do not go through the verbs in the task with students, as you would simply be doing the task yourself. Some may be verbs that students have previously suggested. Make sure they use the pictures as a context for each of the verbs. Students can work individually or in pairs. There is no need for feedback, as Listening Exercise B provides the answers.

B 🎧 Make sure students understand what they are listening to, and play the recording.

Tapescript 🎧 **48 (0 mins, 54 secs)**

B **Listen and check your answers.**

1 This is very difficult to calculate.

2 I predict a fall in the price of oil.

3 Can you be quiet? I can't concentrate.

4 Can you imagine living somewhere like that?

5 Mm, I can't decide which one I want.

6 I'll consider your offer and call you in a few days.

Answers: 1. calculate 2. predict
3. concentrate 4. imagine 5. decide
6. consider

C The aim of this activity is not only to present the six useful collocations, but also to show students the importance of learning collocations. Tell students that learning which words go together with words they already know is just as important as learning new words. Students should complete the task individually, and then compare with a partner. To give feedback, write the three verbs on the board and tell them to close their books. Then ask students to come and write the nouns in the correct place on the

board. Check their spelling and pronunciation as they do so.

Answers:
1. an idea / a thought
2. a decision / a prediction
3. your brain / your imagination

Grammar check

Write on the board 'I'm liking football', and the first two lines from the 'Watch out!' box ('I'm thinking it will rain' and 'I'm not understanding'). Ask students if the sentences are good, and see if they can explain why not. You will need to help them out, but thinking it through like this will be better than simply being told about it. Introduce the term 'state verbs', and read through the first part of the grammar check box with them.

Avoid lecturing with the following information as it will probably not help them. *State verbs* are verbs that describe a state rather than an action ('I like', 'I know', etc.). The agent does not actually do anything. *Dynamic verbs* ('run', 'jump', etc.) describe actions. The agent does something – performs an action. Most verbs of thinking ('think', 'understand', etc.) work in this way. Note that some verbs can be both state verbs and dynamic verbs when used in with different meaning ('I see what you mean' and 'I'm seeing him tomorrow'). Because state verbs are not really actions, they are not normally used in a continuous form. Then tell them to read the second part of the box, and to correct the third sentence in the 'Watch out!' box.

Answers: I don't think Peter will come to the party.

Pronunciation check

Write 'I don't think so' on the board, and then say it two or three times, illustrating how the final /t/ on 'don't' is not pronounced. Tell students to read the pronunciation check box, and then play the recording. Drill the sentences, and then allow a moment for students to say the sentences two or three times to a partner.

Tapescript 🎧 **49** (0 mins, 49 secs)

Pronunciation check

Listen and notice how *t* at the end of *don't* and *can't* is not pronounced clearly in fast natural speech, especially when the following verb begins with a consonant sound.

1   I don't think so.

2   I can't concentrate.

3   I don't know.

4   I can't decide.

Practise saying all the sentences.

Speaking 1

The aim of Exercises A and B here is to provide students with an opportunity to use the language they have learnt so far in the lesson.

A   Give students a moment to look at the pictures, and tell them to read the example. Give them a further minute to think about and plan what they want to say. Monitor to check that students are attempting to use language from the previous stages of the lesson.

B   Encourage students to give reasons and examples that support what they say, and not to just answer 'yes' or 'no'. Ask each of the questions to a different student to provide some feedback, and round off this speaking stage.

Speaking 2

The aim of this activity is to make students aware that giving blunt yes/no answers is not very communicative, and means the examiner is forced to ask more questions than he/she would like to. Read the exam tip with students.

A   Give students a moment to read through the questions and think about possible answers, but tell them they do not need to answer yet.

B   🎧 Make sure students know that they are listening to students answering exam-type questions, and are clear about what they have to do (tick one option A or B in each case). Play the recording, stopping after the first speaker, so that you can check the answer as an example. Then play the rest of the recording. Check answers before going on to Exercise B. They should tell you why one of the answers is better in each case.

Tapescript 🎧 **50** (2 mins, 17 secs)

B   **Listen to some students answering the questions. For each question, tick the speaker who gives the better answer.**

1 – Speaker A
Examiner: So, are you going to university next year?
Speaker A: Yes, I am.

1 – Speaker B
Examiner: So, are you going to university next year?
Speaker A: Yes, I'm really looking forward to it.

2 – Speaker A
Examiner: Tell me something about your job.
Speaker A: I'm a lawyer.

2 – Speaker B
Examiner: Tell me something about your job.
Speaker B: I'm a lawyer. It's quite challenging, but I really enjoy it.

3 – Speaker A
Examiner: Do you work hard?
Speaker A: Yes, but I don't mind. It's always interesting.

3 – Speaker B
Examiner: Do you work hard?
Speaker B: Yes, very hard.

4 – Speaker A
Examiner: Tell me about your hometown.
Speaker A: It's a very big town.

4 – Speaker B
Examiner: Tell me about your hometown.
Speaker B: Well, it's very big, but not too big. I really enjoy living there.

5 – Speaker A

Examiner: What do you do in your free time?

Speaker A: I'm very keen on basketball. I think it's the most exciting sport.

5 – Speaker B

Examiner: What do you do in your free time?

Speaker B: I play basketball on Fridays.

Answers: 1. Speaker B   2. Speaker B
3. Speaker A   4. Speaker B   5. Speaker A

C 🎧 Give students a moment to read through the sentences and understand what they have to do. You can either play the recording right through, or pause at the point the missing word occurs. Decide what your students can manage. Tell them to look at the tapescript on page 286 to check answers.

Tapescript 🎧 **51** (0 mins, 11 secs)

C **Listen again and complete the phrases below.**

[Play track 50 again]

Answers: 1. forward   2. mind   3. enjoy
4. keen

D Students can talk to a partner, or walk around asking various students the questions. Emphasize the need to give fuller answers that invite the other speaker to continue the conversation.

For further speaking and vocabulary practice, tell students to complete the exercises on page 14 of the Workbook. Set as an extra activity or homework task.

Listening

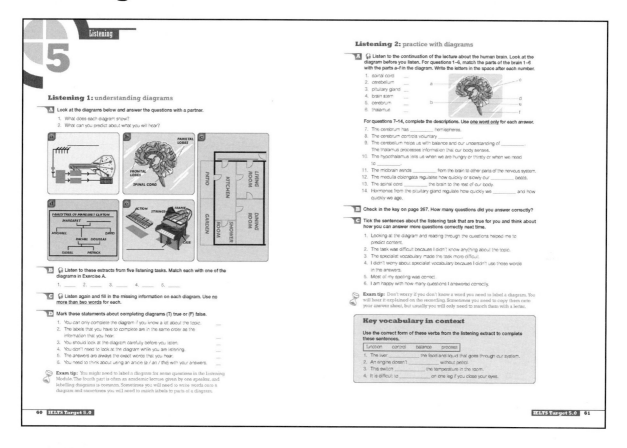

Objectives

- To practise listening in order to label diagrams.
- To show students that you do not need to know about a topic in order to complete a task successfully.
- To practise dealing with language related to a specific topic that you do not understand.
- To reinforce the need to make predictions before listening to a recording.

Listening 1

A Give students a moment to look at the diagrams, and answer the first question together as a class. Students can talk with a partner if you prefer. Write the answers on the board, as this will prepare students for what they will listen to and provide the basic key vocabulary they need. Then give them time to talk in pairs and make predictions about what they will hear in the recording. Students learnt about the importance of making predictions in the last lesson and should be able to do this fairly well now. Ask them to tell you what they might hear, and write

any useful vocabulary under the words on the board. However, only write words that they suggest, as giving them key words will make the listening task too easy.

Answers:

1. a. television reception   b. human brain
   c. plan of a house (ground floor)
   d. family tree   e. piano
2. (possible ideas – not necessarily in the recording)
   a. receive signals / sound / picture, etc.
   b. head / mind / parts / thinking, etc.
   c. rooms / kitchen / living room, etc.
   d. family / husband / wife / father, etc.
   e. instrument / pedals, etc.

B 🎧 Tell students that they will listen to the recording twice. Make sure that the first time they listen, they complete the task and don't try to label the diagrams. Play the whole recording.

> **Tapescript** 🎧 52 (2 mins, 50 secs)
>
> **B** Listen to these extracts from five listening tasks. Match each with one of the diagrams in Exercise A.

1

Estate agent: OK, here we are. This one is a little bit bigger than the last one we saw, as I guess you can see. The owners are out for the day, so I'll need the key. Here we are. Right, as we go in, you'll see we're in a fairly large entrance hall – plenty of room for bicycles and wet umbrellas. Now, through here is the hall itself – very large and ... *(fade out)*

2

Voice: Now, remember we said that the human brain is not a single mechanism. It is, in fact, made up of a number of different parts. Each part controls a different function. Think of your brain as an orchestra, with many musicians playing an important part. First, we will look at this top view of the brain. As you can see, the frontal lobes are located just behind the forehead. It is the frontal lobes that are responsible for complex thinking, like imagining and planning. Behind the frontal lobes are the parietal lobes, and they ... *(fade out)*

3

Voice: Now, as most of you will already know, from the fifteenth century until 1956, the house was owned by the Clifton family – then, of course, it was bought by the Trust. I'd like to stop in the hallway here to take a look at the Clifton family tree. Right at the top here, you can see Charles Clifton, the original owner, and his wife, Margaret. They bought the property ... *(fade out)*

4

Voice: And down here, of course, we have the pedals. Most pianos have two or three pedals. They sustain or soften the sound as the instrument is played. They are connected to the action by levers. Like all other parts ... *(fade out)*

5

Voice: With an old-style cathode-ray tube, the TV set takes the incoming signal and breaks it into its separate audio (sound) and video (picture) components. The aerial on the roof of the house picks up waves from the transmitter. The audio part feeds into an audio ... *(fade out)*

Answers: 1. c   2. b   3. d   4. e   5. a

C 🎧 Read through the instructions with students. Tell them that they might need to use words they don't know, and that they will have to write what they think they hear. Point out that the diagram of the brain does not need labelling in this task. Play the whole recording once with pens down so that students can just absorb the language on the recording. They can then listen a second time to complete the task. Pause between each extract to give students time to write answers. Students should tell you the answers, and how to spell the words they have written (spelling will be an important issue for these students in the Listening Module). Pay particular attention to the words they won't know, like 'pedals' and 'aerial', and see if they can guess spelling.

Tapescript 🎧 **53** (0 mins, 16 secs)

C Listen again and fill in the missing information on each diagram. Use <u>no more than two words</u> for each.

[Play track 52 again]

Answers:
diagram a: aerial
diagram c: entrance hall
diagram d: Charles
diagram e: pedals

D The aim of this activity is for students to reflect on what they have just done, and to identify any difficulties they had. Students should work individually, and then discuss their answers with a partner. Give answers orally.

Answers:

1. F (Even if the topic is one that most people don't know much about, answering questions will not depend on the comprehension of topic-specific vocabulary)
2. F (Sometimes they will be, but not always – they were not in the task students have just done)
3. T
4. F
5. T (Answers in this type of listening task are always words from the recording)
6. T (Questions are not usually designed so that articles are an issue, but some answers would be incorrect without an article. Note, though, that students must check that using an article doesn't take them over the number of words allowed)

Read the exam tip with students. The next practice task focuses on matching labels to parts of a diagram rather than completing labels.

Listening 2

The aim of this part is to provide practice with diagrams and to show students that they can complete a task successfully without having to know a lot about a topic beforehand.

A 🎧 Students should be ready to be more independent now when working through the practice stage of the skills section. They know that they have time to read the questions, and they know how to predict. However, the nature of the topic and the topic-specific vocabulary means that students will need some guidance, and it would be best to work on the two parts of the practice stage separately. Give the students a moment to look at the diagram first, and then at the list of brain parts. Tell them that their task is to complete the diagram, and not to understand exactly what all the parts of the brain are.

If you want to, show them a simple task with invented words. Draw a square divided into four smaller squares on the board. Then tell them to copy it in their notebooks, and write four invented words on the board. Tell them to listen to you, and label each square within the square. Say 'the small square in the top right of the main square is *****. The square in the bottom left corner of the main square is *****', and so on. Students will easily complete the task and see that knowing the words is irrelevant.

Play the first part of the whole recording, and ask students how well they think they have done. Play the recording again if necessary, but tell students you will not pause, otherwise it would turn into a dictation.

Go on to questions 7–14 now, before allowing students to check answers to 1–6. Give students time to read through the instructions and the questions. Show them how the words they need to use are everyday words and not specialist words.

Play the recording once only. Students might find it difficult to listen only once, but avoid playing it a second time. Students can discuss what difficulties they had, and then listen again later if necessary (see Exercises B and C).

Tapescript 🎧 **54** (4 mins, 48 secs)

A **Listen to the continuation of the lecture about the human brain. Look at the diagram before you listen. For questions 1–6, match the parts of the brain 1–6 with the parts a–f in the diagram. Write the letters in the space after each number.**

Voice: OK, we have looked at the top view of the brain and seen how it is divided into lobes. Now, we are going to look at a more complex diagram of the centre of the brain. I will briefly go through some of the important parts that make up the brain, and then talk more about what each does. First of all, you can see that by far the largest part of the brain is the cerebrum, and it is made up of the three lobes we have already talked about. The lobe below, coloured yellow on the diagram here, is the cerebellum. Right in the centre of the brain, here, is the thalamus. The hypothalamus is part of it, but it has a slightly different function. Now, here, running down from the centre of the brain, is the brain stem. It is made up of the midbrain, the pons and the medulla oblongata, and is connected to the spinal cord, which you can see here at the bottom of the diagram. Now, finally, this little gland just to the left of the midbrain – it looks like a little tail – is the pituitary gland.

OK, let's go back and say something about the function of the various parts of the brain. The cerebrum – the largest part, as we have said – has two halves or hemispheres. I will talk more about the difference between the two hemispheres later. The cerebrum is the part of the brain that is really our intelligence. It controls voluntary movement – that is, movement that we are in control of – speaking, for example – but it is also responsible for our emotional thinking and memory. The cerebellum is responsible for fine movement and coordination. It helps us with balance, for example, and to understand where we are ... in relation to space around us. The thalamus, here in the centre, processes what we feel with our body – touch and temperature, for example – and controls how we react to those senses. The hypothalamus has a similar function, but regulates bodily needs such as hunger and thirst, and tells us when we need sleep. Now, at the top of the brain-stem is the midbrain. This is a sort of switchboard – a very complex switchboard. It sends messages which help the brain communicate with other parts of the nervous system. The pons, in the middle of the brain stem, here, sends messages from the cerebrum to the cerebellum and spinal cord. The medulla oblongata is here, just above the spinal cord. It regulates essential bodily functions, like breathing and the rate of our heartbeat. The spinal cord is part of the central nervous system and runs down inside the spinal column. It connects the brain to nerves that go to the rest of the body. Now, the pituitary gland – this little gland – has a hugely important function. It releases hormones to the body that regulate all sorts of things – how quickly we grow and the size we grow to, the rate at which we age ... It also regulates whether we have a slow or fast metabolism and how we relate to stress. Now, I am going to show you a model of the human brain and I want you to identify ... *(fade out)*

For questions 7–14, complete the descriptions. Use <u>one word only</u> for each answer.

[Play track 54 again]

Answers:
1. f   2. e   3. d   4. b   5. a   6. c   7. two
8. movement   9. space   10. sleep
11. messages   12. heart   13. connects
14. grow

B Give students sufficient time to check answers and think about why they may have answered incorrectly, before moving on to Exercise C.

C Students will by now be familiar with this type of reflective process, but note the questions are not the same as in previous units. Remind them that identifying what they are doing well and not doing so well is a very good way of focusing on what they can do better next time. Allow students time to reflect and complete the task. This would be a good time to emphasize the importance of correctly spelling their answers. Ask them whether they are happy with the number of correct answers. Play the recording again if necessary, and tell students to focus on why the correct answers are correct.

Read the exam tip with students.

Key vocabulary in context

The aim of this activity is to reinforce the need to learn the various forms that words can have. In this case, the nouns have the same form as the verbs. Give students a moment to read the examples, and check anything they are not sure about. Students should work individually to complete the task, and then compare with a partner. They should realize that they will need to use a singular form sometimes, but you may tell them. Write the answers on the board.

Answers: 1. processes   2. function
3. controls   4. balance

For further listening practice, tell students to complete the exercise on page 15 of the Workbook. Set as an extra activity or homework task.

Reading

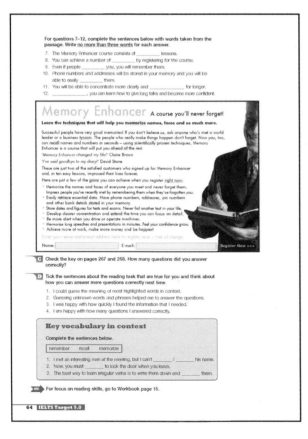

Objectives

- To practise dealing with unknown vocabulary in context.

- To help students use words they already know and to understand related new words.

- To practise a typical task from the IELTS Reading Module.

Reading 1

Start the lesson by asking students what they find difficult when they read, and bring the discussion around to vocabulary. Ask them what they do if they don't know a word or phrase in a text.

A Make sure students look only at the two highlighted items in the extract. They will almost certainly not know either of them.

B Tell students that the aim of reading the extract is to be able to understand the two highlighted items in context. Give them a minute or two to read, and then talk with a partner. Don't tell them what the items mean yet.

C Tell them to look at the definition and options, and choose the one they think is correct in each case. They can do this with the partner they have been talking to.

Answers: 1. b 2. d

Read the exam tip with students.

D The aim of this task is to practise what students have just prepared for, and to practise using clues around the unknown word or phrase to guess its meaning. Note that the aim is not to learn these particular words, though students might want to. Go through the highlighted words with them, and ask whether they know them or not. Do not explain any meanings now. Students should work individually to choose the definition options, and then compare with a partner. Ask students to tell you the answers as feedback.

Answers: 1. a 2. a 3. c

Reading 2

Students continue to work on guessing the meaning of new vocabulary, but now from the form of the new word, or the other parts of the phrase the new word occurs in. The context in which the new item occurs, however, is still very important.

Read the exam tip with students.

A Give students a minute or two to think individually, and then another two or three to discuss meanings with a partner.

B Work through this task as with Exercise D above.

Answers:
1. very clever
2. stupid
3. not concentrating
4. don't understand it at all
5. you can't make a decision

C This task gives students an opportunity to use the new phrases to talk about their own lives. They will need a few minutes to think and complete the sentences. Allow them to compare, and then get a couple of answers to each sentence from different students.

Reading 3

Tell students that the text is of the type they will be given in the first, and possibly second, part of the Reading Module. The text is probably a little shorter than the one they will see in the exam, but it is approaching the level of challenge they will face.

Unlike in the exam, however, here students are given guidance with the words and phrases that they will need to know or guess, in order to answer questions.

Students should be ready to be more independent now when working through the practice stage of the skills section. They know that they should look at the title and skim the text first, and then read the questions before reading the text more carefully. Once you have read through Exercise A with them, they should be left to work on their own.

A Read through the rubric with students, and give them a minute to look at all the highlighted words.

B Set a time limit of about 15 minutes.

C Give students sufficient time to check and think about why they may have answered incorrectly, before moving on to Exercise D. The answers are reproduced below, together with the parts of the text that provide answers.

Answers:
1. T (techniques that will help you memorize names, faces …)
2. NG (Although probably false, the text doesn't provide an answer)
3. T (people who really make things happen don't forget)
4. F (using scientifically proven techniques)
5. F (will put you ahead of the rest)
6. NG
7. ten / 10 8. gains 9. forget 10. retrieve
11. focus on detail 12. In minutes

D By now, students will be familiar with this type of reflective process, but note that the questions are not the same as in previous units. Remind them that identifying what they are doing well and not doing so well is a very good way of focusing on what they can do better next time. Allow students time to reflect and complete the task, and then ask them if they are happy with the number of correct answers. You may like to ask one student what he or she will do differently next time.

Key vocabulary in context

This task focuses on words that are easily confused, all of which come from the text students have just read. Students can work individually or in pairs. Write the answers on the board. Explain that 'recall' means 'to look back', while 'remember' can mean that, but it also means to not 'forget'.

Answers: 1. remember / recall   2. remember
3. memorize

The Workbook task for this unit gives further practice with guessing the meaning of new words and phrases in order to answer questions. Now would be a good time to set it up as a homework task.

Writing

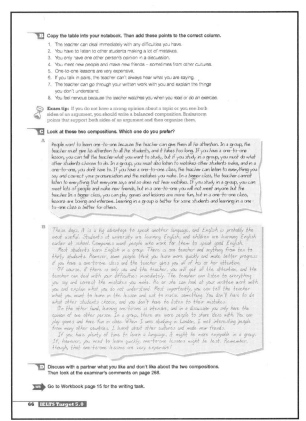

Objectives

- **To provide further practice with the second part of the IELTS Writing Module.**

- **To understand the instructions to a writing task, and what is expected of students in terms of an answer.**

- **To introduce students to the concept of a balanced discursive composition.**

- **To further help students decide on the content of a discursive composition.**

Writing 1

A The aim of the discussion stage is to get students thinking about what could form the content of the composition they will focus on later in the lesson. Tell them to look at the pictures and then at the questions.

Then give them a minute to think about what they want to say before they start talking. After three or four minutes, get some ideas from the class.

B In the previous lesson, students saw the type of composition they will have to write in the second part of the exam and focused on new words in the task description. Now they focus on what they might not know in the actual instructions. It is essential that students learn and retain these words, as they will see the same instructions each time they do this type of task.

Give students time to look at and absorb the task, and then think about the question. Go around the class getting an answer from a number of students.

C Read through the rubric with students. Give them two or three minutes to look at the new task instructions, and to absorb the notes the student has made. Go around the class again, getting an answer from a number of students.

Read through the exam tip with students. Then give them a couple of minutes to check any words they want to in a dictionary. Note that students will see these instructions several more times in this book and will understand them by the time they take the exam.

Writing 2

In the last unit, students saw how a student agreed with the statement in this type of writing task. Now the aim is to show students how they can balance an argument, and express both sides of an opinion. At this stage, remember that there is still the need to guide students generally towards having something to say about an argument of this type.

A Make sure students understand that they are still thinking about the writing task in Exercise B. Give them a moment to look at the student's notebook, and then run through the columns with them. Make sure that they understand what the '+' and '−' signs mean.

B Give students a moment to copy the table, making sure there is plenty of room to add notes. It will obviously be much quicker to simply write the numbers of the points into the columns, but it would be beneficial for students to copy the points out so that they stick in their minds. You can decide which option to take. Students should work individually, and then compare with a partner. To give feedback, copy the table onto the board as students are comparing ideas, and then add the numbers to the appropriate column with them.

Answers:

1. one-to-one +   2. group lesson −
3. one-to-one −   4. group lesson +
5. one-to-one −   6. group lesson −
7. one-to-one +   8. one-to-one −

Read the exam tip with students.

C You will need to give students sufficient time to read the two compositions properly. You can either set a time limit of about ten minutes, or go on to the discussion at Exercise D, when most students seem to be happy that they are ready. Tell students that there are no grammatical or spelling mistakes. The focus is on content and organization.

D It would be a good idea to ask the class which composition they think is better before students discuss them in detail. If students are unsure about which is better, there might not be much benefit in discussing them. Try to arrive at a general consensus that B is the better

composition. If students want to disagree now, they can. Students can work in pairs as suggested, or in small groups. Monitor, and offer some of your own opinions.

Students will probably want to see what the examiner says more than discuss it themselves. Refer them to page 268, and give them sufficient time to take in the points the examiner makes. The examiner's notes on each composition are reproduced here. Note that some points mentioned deal with issues that students have not yet looked at. Tell them not to worry now, and that these points will be covered later.

First composition: Points are relevant and well balanced – arguments that support both points of view. / Points not planned or organized. It seems like the writer is making points as he or she thinks of them. / Not organized into paragraphs so not easy to follow. / No introduction – writer goes straight into argument. / Some points are made in a repetitive way. Writer explains what the reader can understand from what has already been said. / Ideas not linked with typical linking words or phrases. / Vocabulary is used properly, but quite simple.

Second composition: All points are relevant and argument is well balanced. / Very good introduction – shows he or she understands question. / Very easy to follow – organized into paragraphs. / Points are planned and organized, and linked together with linking words and phrases. / Good range of vocabulary used to make points more interesting to read.

Writing task

The writing tasks are found either in the Workbook or in the exam practice section at the end of the unit. For this unit, the task is in the Workbook. Note that the teacher's instructions are almost exactly as they are for the last unit. Consider anything that you feel didn't work as well as you hoped the last time students wrote the composition, and try to work with that now.

A At this stage, students will need quite a lot of assistance with preparation, before attempting to write a complete composition of this type. Tell them that the important thing now is to attempt the composition, to make some valid points, and to organize the points as well as they can.

Give students a minute or so to read the task instructions, and then allow them to ask questions about any words they don't know. They will want to check 'absorbs', and perhaps clarify 'experience of life'.

This stage will be vital for students at this level. They can work in pairs as suggested, or in small groups. Give them at least ten minutes, and monitor, giving a few of your own ideas. Get some points up on the board so that everyone has some points they can include.

B Once students are ready to start writing, set a time limit of 40 minutes (you might want to end the task earlier than that if students have managed all they can, and you think looking at the model will be more beneficial). Tell them to use the second composition in the Writing Module as a model. Monitor as students work, but check specifically that they are organizing their ideas and making relevant points, rather than writing accurately.

When students have completed the task, tell them to look at the model composition on page 268 of the Course Book. Put them into pairs to compare their composition against the model. The model is reproduced below.

If you collect students' compositions to mark, it would be better to use the process to get an idea of what they are capable of, rather than correct too heavily. At this stage, you will be correcting most of what they write.

I have heard many people say that it is easier to learn new things when you are young than it is when you are old. I think they say this because children learn naturally and seem to absorb things without trying. However, I think it probably depends what you are learning and how much you really want to learn.

I know that I learnt how to use a computer very quickly when I was only about six years old, while my mother still finds it difficult. I think it was easy for me because I did not really realize I was learning something, and I just wanted to play the

games. My mother does not like technology, and she was nervous about learning something she did not really want to.

People say that children learn languages more quickly than adults, but I am not sure this is true. It takes a child ten years to learn to speak their language properly, but an adult can learn a foreign language if they live in another country in only two or three years. Because they have more experience of life they can apply it to translate and learn grammar rules. I think older people can learn just as quickly if they really need to.

I think young people can learn things like swimming much more quickly than older people. My father really wants to be good at golf and he practises a lot, but he does not get any better. My cousin started playing when he was ten and soon he was very good. However, some children want to learn a sport, but are not good at all. My answer to the question is, it depends what you are learning, and it is not always easier for young people.

Consolidation

Speaking

The aim of the speaking section of this consolidation page is to encourage students to use a wider range of vocabulary when they answer questions in the speaking exam.

A Give students a moment to read the options and choose their answer. Ask them which they think the correct answer is and why.

Answers: The correct answer is 2.

B Give students time to read through the questions and think about their answers. Tell them they don't need to answer the questions yet.

C Give students time to read through the questions and answers. Then give them two or three minutes to discuss the answer with a partner. Note that the vocabulary the students use to give the better answers is all the vocabulary learnt in the unit. Discuss answers with the students.

Answers: 1. B 2. B 3. A

D Students should answer the questions with answers that are true for them, rather than simply repeat the answers in the examples.

Vocabulary

A This task revises spelling of words from the unit. Students should work individually to identify and correct errors. Write the correct spellings on the board. Leave the words there for Exercise B.

Answers: 1. consider   2. prediction
3. imagination   4. concentrate   5. decision
6. memory

B 🎧 Students know how to mark stress now. They should work with a partner, and say the words aloud as they mark the stress. You or they can mark the stress on the words on the board.

Tapescript 🎧 55 (0 mins, 42 secs)

B **Listen and mark the main stress on the words in Exercise A above.**

1 consider

2 prediction

3 imagination

4 concentrate

5 decision

6 memory

Answers: 1. con**si**der   2. pre**di**ction
3. imagi**na**tion   4. **con**centrate   5. de**ci**sion
6. **me**mory

C This task revises vocabulary learnt in the unit, emphasizes the need to learn the different forms of common words and checks spelling. Students could think of different forms of the 'root' words in the box before completing the task individually. For feedback, either you or students should write the answers on the board.

Answers: 1. concentration   2. imagination
3. judgement   4. creative   5. creatively

Errors

A   Students now know that each unit ends with this type of task. Remind them that it is very useful to notice and correct the types of errors they are likely to make. Most examples here are wrong-word errors. Tell students that there are no spelling mistakes. They can either complete the task individually or in pairs. Write the correct sentences on the board for clarity.

Answers:
1. I'm sorry. I haven't made a decision yet.
2. Sorry, I don't remember your name.
3. I don't think I will pass this test.
4. Are you sure you remembered to close all the windows?
5. I'm looking forward to the weekend.

Exam Practice

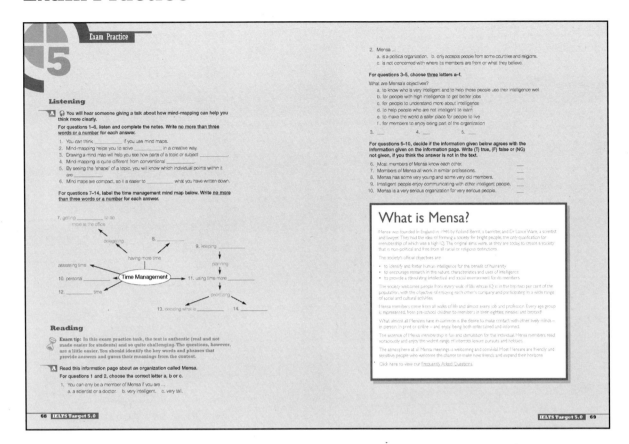

Listening

Exam practising is what students focused on in the Listening Module in the unit. The recording and degree of challenge in the task is close to what they will deal with in the exam. Students are not given preparation, and are left on their own more to get some experience of more realistic exam practice.

A 🎧 Read through the task introduction with students, and tell them that 'mind-mapping' is the theme of the recording, and that it will be explained. Allow students to read the question instructions themselves. Give them a minute to do this (though they will only have 30 seconds in the exam), and look at the map that needs labelling. Tell students that in the labelling part of the task, the information is not given in the same order as it is numerically.

You should play the whole recording once only, though if you really feel your students are not ready for that, pause after the first part (at the end of question 6), and give them a moment to write and check answers.

Tapescript 🎧 56 (6 mins, 29 secs)

A **You will hear someone giving a talk about how mind-mapping can help you think more clearly. For questions 1–6, listen and complete the notes. Write <u>no more than three words or a number</u> for each answer.**

Female voice: Good morning. I'm really pleased that so many of you are here. I know you are all busy. In some ways, that is what I'm going to talk about today – managing time, so that you feel more is getting done, that you are achieving more. I'm sure you have all heard something about mind-mapping, but most people I meet don't really know much about it. Mind-mapping is really a technique that helps you to think more clearly. It improves the way you solve problems and encourages you to solve problems creatively. Mind maps help you to understand the various parts of a topic or subject, and to then see how those parts fit together. The way you write down your ideas on a mind map means that information is easy to retrieve and to review. So, how is mind-mapping different from conventional note-taking? By conventional note-taking, I mean simply listing points on a page, as you probably do now. Well, mind maps are more two-dimensional – they allow you to see the shape of a topic, and make it easier to see what's important. Mind maps generally fit on a single side of paper – they are more compact – and that also helps you to go back and review.

So, now I'm going to show an example of a mind map, and I hope it will make clear what I've been saying. Let me just switch on the projector. OK, here we are. Now, this is a mind map for time management – a mind map designed to help you manage your time better, and see where you are wasting time and where you could save time. Remember – this is only a very simple example. Your mind maps can be bigger.

Now, first, you need to write the topic in large letters in the middle of your page – in this case, 'time management'. Put a circle or a box around it, if you like. Then, draw lines out to the main subheadings – the main points that you want to consider as parts of the topic. In this case, the major subheadings are red. Put general ideas on the left. In this case, there are three general points that the author wants to keep in mind: assessing time – how much time he has. Personal performance – by personal performance, he means how well he thinks he uses his time. And wasting time – how much of his time he thinks he uses badly – how much of his time is wasted. Above the main heading, the author

thinks about having more time and how perhaps he could have more time. His mind map has branched out, and he puts examples of having more time in another colour – in this case, blue.

He thinks about two ways that he could have more time. Firstly, delegating, and secondly, getting up earlier. Of course, if you get up earlier, the day is longer and you have more time! Above delegating, he gives an example of how he could delegate. He makes this another subheading and uses another colour – this time green. When he looks back at his mind map, he will see that one way that he could delegate is to get other people to do more around the office – perhaps he does too much himself at the moment.

Now, on the right, the author thinks about how he can use time more effectively – note again that this is one of his main subheadings, so it is written in red. As subheadings of that, he gives examples of how he could use time more effectively.

At the bottom, he thinks about prioritizing, and then he gives two examples of how he wants to prioritize – firstly, he explains what he means by prioritize – he must decide what is most important. Then, he notes how he can prioritize – by setting goals. The mind map will help him to remember that he must always have a clear idea of what is important, and that by setting goals, he can achieve more.

Finally, he decides that planning is important, and that is another subheading. He notes that keeping a diary is one good way to plan ahead and so use time more effectively. Perhaps he doesn't keep one at the moment, but he will start keeping one now he has his mind map.

Now, as I say, the author will probably add more ideas – each time you review a mind map, you can add points or delete them. Of course, time management is only one area in which mind-mapping can be a help. Now, I'm going to talk about other areas of your life where mind-mapping can ...
(fade out)

For questions 7–14, label the time management mind map below. Write <u>no more than three words or a number</u> for each answer.

[Play track 56 again]

Answers:
1. (more) clearly   2. problems
3. fit together   4. note-taking   5. important
6. review   7. other people
8. getting up earlier   9. a diary
10. performance   11. effectively   12. wasting
13. most important   14. setting goals

Once you have given the answers, you might like to play the recording again, if time permits.

Reading

Read the exam tip with students, which gives some information about the challenge of the task. The authenticity of the text might be a little daunting. Remind students that this type of advertisement is a common type of text in the first part of the Reading Module. Though the text itself is more challenging, students should be able to cope with the minimum of help. They know the procedure for tackling a reading task, and have practised all these task types.

A Before doing this task, you might like to do Workbook speaking and vocabulary Exercise D, which pre-teaches some of the vocabulary in this text.

Read the introductory line with them, but don't tell them anything about the organization. Set a time limit of about 15 minutes.

Write the answers on the board so that they are clear. It would be a good idea to give students the lines that provide the answers.

Answers:
1. b (a society for bright people, the only qualification for membership of which was a high IQ)
2. c (non-political and free from all racial or religious distinctions)

Note that letters in 3–5 can be in any order as long as the correct three letters are used. The answers here are in alphabetical order.

3. a (to identify and foster human intelligence)
4. c (to encourage research in the nature, characteristics and uses of intelligence)
5. f (to provide a stimulating intellectual and social environment for its members)
6. NG
7. F (people from every walk of life)
8. T (from pre-school children to members in their eighties, nineties and beyond!)
9. T (the desire to make contact with other lively minds ...)
10. F (The essence of Mensa membership is fun ... / The atmosphere at all Mensa meetings is welcoming and convivial. Most Mensans are friendly ...)

Unit 5 Workbook answers

Speaking and Vocabulary

A Students' own answers.

B 1. I had a fantastic time.
2. It's the best car I ever had.
3. It's very exciting and I really enjoy it.
4. It will be hard work, but I'm looking forward to it.

Tapescript 🎧 57 (1 min, 8 secs)

B Listen to some students answering the questions. Are their answers similar to yours?

1

Teacher: Have you been on holiday yet this year?

Student: Yes, I went to Spain with some friends. I had a fantastic time.

2

Teacher: Have you got a car?

Student: Yes, I drive a BMW. It's the best car I've ever had.

3

Teacher: Do you play any particular sports?

Student: Yes, I play indoor football. It's very exciting and I really enjoy it.

4

Teacher: What will you do when you leave university?

Student: I'm going to work for my uncle's company. It will be hard work, but I'm looking forward to it.

C 1. decided   2. concentrate
3. consider   4. thought
5. imagine   6. predict

D 1. I   2. U   3. I   4. U   5. I   6. U

Listening

A

Tapescript 🎧 58 (1 min, 49 secs)

A Listen and match each extract to a type of diagram below. Write the number of the extract in the space.

1

Voice 1: When the lorries arrive at the warehouse, they pull into the loading bays – you can see that there are ten bays, each with its own entrance to the warehouse. The goods are loaded onto the lorries with a forklift truck, but before that happens, there are ... *(fade out)*

2

Voice 2: Here, you can clearly see that thirty years ago, average temperatures for the summer months were much higher than they have been over the last decade.

3

Voice 3: The railway station is this large building to the left of Warrior Square. You can see that there's a car park at the back of the station – the main entrance to it is in Lincoln Street.

4

Voice 4: Now, the tube or pipe, if you like, which takes air from the nose and mouth down to the lungs and vice versa, is the trachea – that's T-R-A-C-H-E-A. It is also more commonly known as the windpipe.

5

Voice 5: Now, at the front of the drill here is the chuck – that's C-H-U-C-K, chuck. The bits are fitted into the chuck and the chuck can be tightened or loosened, depending on the bit size that is used.

Answers: map 3   graph 2   machine 5
process 1   human body 4

Reading

A 1. T (psychologists have needed to design ...
        to understand their brain capacity)
   2. NG
   3. F (whole extract tells us that the tests are to
        understand babies' brains)

B 1. flashing   2. stimuli   3. ingenious
   4. expressing a preference   5. response

Writing

The writing task is dealt with in the main section of
the Teacher's Book.

Review 1

Speaking and Vocabulary

A Talk with a partner. Answer these questions about the Speaking Module of the IELTS exam.

1. How many parts are there in the Speaking Module?
2. How long does each part last?
3. What happens in each part? How are the parts different from one another?

B Look at some comments made by students who are studying for the IELTS exam. Tick the ones that you most agree with.

☐ 'I think the first part of the speaking exam, when the examiner asks about your life, is quite easy. It's more difficult to think about what to say when you have to read a card.'

☐ 'I prefer the second part of the speaking because reading the card gives you ideas and you have time to plan what to say.'

☐ 'I don't like the third part of the speaking exam. You have to think quickly and you don't always have the words to express your opinion.'

☐ 'The third part of the Speaking Module is the most challenging but the most interesting. I can tell the examiner what I think – not just give him facts.'

☐ 'I try to learn as much vocabulary as I can – especially very common expressions. I think having the words is more important than being perfectly accurate in the speaking exam.'

☐ 'When I learn new words, I make sure I can pronounce them correctly. If the examiner can't understand what I say, he will get bored and give me a low grade.'

☐ 'It's important that you keep it simple. You should only say what you know you can say. If you don't know how to use the present perfect continuous, you shouldn't try to.'

C Write two comments of your own. Then compare with a partner.

D Write important words and phrases that you have learnt so far under each heading.

family and friends

stages of life

learning

expressing a preference

(my words and phrases)

work and jobs

achievement and success

thinking

Listening

A Answer these questions with a partner.

1. How many parts are there in the Listening Module of the IELTS exam?
2. How many questions do you think there are in total?
3. How are the various parts of the Listening Module different from one another?
4. Does the Listening Module gradually become more challenging?
5. What type of tasks have you practised so far?

B Tick the statement about listening in each pair that is true for you.

1. A I often understand the gist of a talk or conversation but not the details.
   B I can often hear details, but don't really understand what the people are talking about.
2. A It's easier to listen to just one person giving a talk.
   B I prefer listening to a conversation between two or more people. The context is clearer.
3. A I don't like writing when I'm trying to listen. I prefer it when I need to circle a letter or tick a box.
   B I don't mind writing when I'm listening if it's just a number or a name that is spelt for me.
4. A It's difficult to catch the words when I have to listen and complete notes.
   B I can usually catch the words I need, but then I don't have time to write them.
5. A I don't like looking at maps or diagrams when I'm trying to listen.
   B I like tasks with a map or diagram because the context is clearer.
6. A My listening has improved, and now I answer more questions correctly.
   B My listening is not really improving. I still answer a lot of questions incorrectly.

Reading

A Answer these questions with a partner.

1. How many sections are there in the Reading Module?
2. How many passages will you have to read?
3. How many questions are there in total?
4. How long do you have to answer all the questions?
5. How are the texts in the Reading Module different from one another?
6. Do the texts gradually become more challenging?

B Answer these questions with the same partner.

1. What is the difference between **skimming** and **scanning**? Give an example of each.
2. What is the **source** of a text? Give an example.
3. What is the **function** of a text? Give an example.
4. What is **paraphrasing**? How could you paraphrase 'the question isn't so easy'?
5. What do we mean when we say 'understand a new word or phrase **in context**'?

C Give yourself a score out of five for the progress you are making with each of these reading skills.

skimming / reading for gist ____
scanning / reading for specific information ____
general reading speed ____
understanding new words and phrases in context ____
recognizing paraphrased language ____

D Tick the statement below that is true for you.

A I am happy that my reading has improved since I started this course.
B I don't think my reading has improved since I started this course.

📝 **Task-type tip:** There are some listening and reading tasks that you haven't practised yet.

Writing

A Circle the correct option in these statements about the Writing Module of the IELTS exam.

1. You will have to write one / two / three compositions.
2. You have 30 minutes / one hour / two hours to write the compositions.
3. In the first part of the Writing Module, you will have to describe charts and graphs / write a story / write a letter.
4. For the first part of the Writing Module, you must write 100 / 150 / 200 words.
5. In the second part of the Writing Module, you will have to present an argument or express an opinion / describe a person or place / write a report.
6. For the second part of the Writing Module, you must write 150 / 200 / 250 words.

B When you write, you must consider all of the points below. For now, which two points are most important? Tick them.

1. You must answer the question and make points that are relevant to the question.
2. You must make sure that what you write is grammatically correct.
3. You must use a range of vocabulary and choose the right words and phrases.
4. You must organize your composition so that the examiner can read it easily and understand what you want to say.
5. You must use the right number of paragraphs and the right linking words.
6. You must use the right register – your writing must be appropriately formal or informal.
7. You must make sure that all your spelling is correct.
8. You must make sure that all your punctuation is correct.

C Answer these questions with a partner.

1. Which of the two compositions is easier for you to write?
2. How long will you spend writing the first composition?
3. How long will you spend writing the second composition?
4. Do you write too much or not enough for the first composition? Why?
5. Do you write too much or not enough for the second composition? Why?
6. Is your writing improving? Tick the aspects of your writing that have improved recently.

☐ understanding the question and knowing what to write
☐ planning and noting down ideas
☐ organizing ideas
☐ using paragraphs
☐ linking ideas together
☐ using the right register
☐ using a wider range of vocabulary
☐ spelling
☐ punctuation

What next?

You've only completed a third of the course, so don't worry if you haven't improved all aspects of your English. There is plenty of time to learn more and practise the skills and tasks that you find difficult. Here are some things that you should do now. Decide which ones you'd like to do first. Number them.

☐ Find as many opportunities to speak English as you can. If you have friends or relatives who speak good English, practise with them once or twice a week. Practise with other students in your class when you have a break or after the lesson. Practise talking about the topics that you will have to talk about in the exam.

☐ If listening is difficult, ask to borrow CDs and listen at home or on the bus or train. Listen to English that is at your level to give you confidence, and listen to English that is a little more challenging so that you know what to expect in the exam. Listen to extracts which have a tapescript so that, after you listen, you can read and check what you didn't understand and why you didn't understand it.

☐ Read as much as you can. Borrow books from a library and read articles in magazines and newspapers. Try to read any letters or documents in English that are related to your job. Read texts that are at your level to give you confidence, and read texts that are a little more challenging so that you know what to expect in the exam. When you read, notice how the text is organized. Look at how paragraphs and topic sentences are used and how words and phrases are used to introduce ideas. Practise reading without a dictionary so that you can guess the meaning of new words and phrases in context.

☐ Note down new vocabulary and make sure you revise it. Note down words and phrases that will help you talk about what is important to you. Note down words and phrases that will help you in the reading and listening modules and words and phrases that you can use when you write. Check the word and phrase list for each of the units you have studied in the Course Book.

☐ Practise writing sentences and short paragraphs to improve your grammatical accuracy, spelling and punctuation. Write complete compositions to practise organizing and linking. Do the writing tasks in the Course Book and Workbook, and ask your teacher to give you more writing tasks if you need more practice. Look at model answers to exam questions and notice how students answer questions. When you learn important new words and phrases, make sure you remember how to spell them.

Go on to the next section of the Course Book. Make sure you practise all aspects of your English, but focus on what you are having problems with. Don't worry if you don't make progress in all areas at the same time. It is much easier to learn English if you enjoy it!

Overview

The review units are very much reviews rather than revision units. The aim is for students to consolidate what they have learnt about the IELTS exam, and how to go about getting the grade they require. There are tasks which are designed purely to encourage students to reflect and discuss, and there are tasks which consolidate and have correct answers. The instructions given to teachers for the review sections are brief, as the aims and procedure for each task are fairly self-explanatory.

Speaking and Vocabulary

A Give students three or four minutes to discuss, and then go over answers as a class.

Answers:
1. three
2. part 1: 4–5 minutes / part 2: 3–4 minutes / part 3: 4–5 minutes
3. part 1: The examiner asks questions and invites students to talk about their own lives.
   part 2: The examiner will give the student a card, and the student will talk about the topic on the card for about two minutes.
   The examiner will ask one or two round-up questions.
   part 3: The examiner will ask the student more abstract questions, and ask for the student's opinion about issues related to the topic on the card in part 2.

B Give students ten minutes to read the comments and decide what they agree with most. Tell them to tick between two and four comments, even if they agree with most of them. You can discuss the comments as a whole class, or tell students to talk in pairs. This should take about ten minutes.

C Give students four or five minutes to write their own advice, and then another three or four to talk about them.

D Give students a moment to look at the web and then read through the headings with them. You could start by telling them not to look back at the units in the Course Book and see what they have retained. After five minutes, allow them to look back, adding words and phrases from the unit. Try to encourage them to do this in order to store new language, rather than simply to fulfil a task.

Listening

A As Exercise A in Speaking and Vocabulary.

Answers:
1. four
2. 40
3. The first is two speakers in a social situation, the second is one speaker in a non-academic situation, the third is up to four speakers talking about an academic topic, and the fourth is one speaker giving an academic lecture and is the longest extract.
4. yes
5. completing notes / completing sentences / multiple choice / matching labels to diagrams / labelling diagrams

B Give students around ten minutes to read and make their choices, and another ten to discuss them. It would be better to discuss this in a pair so that everyone can talk about their strengths and weaknesses. The benefit here is in identifying strengths and weaknesses, and discussing them. No solutions can be offered to each student right now.

Reading

A As Exercise A in Speaking and Vocabulary.

Answers:
1. three
2. probably five (but possibly six)
3. 40
4. One hour
5. In section 1, the texts are short, but contain a lot of information. They are usually public information texts – advertisements, leaflets,

etc. In section 2, there are two texts giving information related to college or university. In section 3, there is one longer text, usually an article, about any subject.

6. yes

B   As Exercise A in Speaking and Vocabulary.

Answers:

1. 'Skimming' is reading quickly to get a general idea of what a text is about. 'Scanning' is searching for specific information in a text.
2. The source is where it comes from – a catalogue or brochure, for example.
3. The function is what the text aims to do and how it aims to affect the reader, to persuade or complain, for example.
4. 'Paraphrasing' is saying something in another way, using different words. 'This question isn't so easy' could be paraphrased as 'this question is quite difficult'.
5. We mean understand from what we know about the text it occurs in, and the language that surrounds it.

C and D   Give students six or seven minutes to reflect, and then get some feedback from the class. Read through the task-type tip with students.

Writing

A   As Exercise A in Speaking and Vocabulary.

Answers:

1. two
2. one hour
3. write a letter
4. 150
5. present an argument or express an opinion
6. 250

B   Give students around six or seven minutes to read and make their choices, and then get answers from the floor. Try to arrive at a consensus, and then tell them the correct answer.

Answers:

1 and 4 are the most important points.

C   As Listening B above.

What next?

You might like to tell students to read this at home. You can check by asking questions or by having a brief feedback session. If there is time to read it in class, it might be better to read through one section at a time and getting some feedback, rather than reading it right through in one go.

Now instruct students to complete mock test 1.

6 Place

Unit overview

The sixth unit is based around the theme of place. Students talk about where they live, and where they would like to live, and compare city and country lifestyles. Students learn about how texts are organized into paragraphs, and learn the concept of topic sentences for the first time. The unit gives students a further taste of what they can expect in the various sections of the IELTS exam.

Speaking and Vocabulary

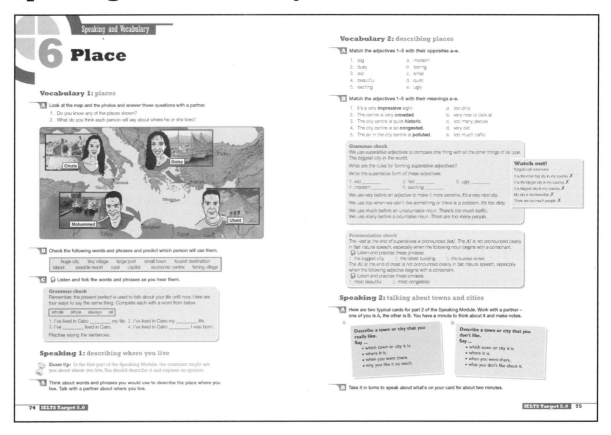

Objectives

- To give students further practice answering the type of questions they can expect in the first part of the IELTS Speaking Module.

- To practise talking about hometowns / cities and lifestyle in relation to where students live.

- To revise superlative forms in relation to talking about towns and cities.

Vocabulary 1

The aim of the first vocabulary section is to present words and phrases that students can use to talk generally about where they live.

A   Tell students to look at the map and the people in the pictures for a couple of minutes, and then read through the two questions with them. Make sure they understand that the second question is a prediction task. You could give an example, like 'Ubaid will say that he lives in a very big city'. There is no need to get feedback, as the following task develops the prediction.

B Go through the vocabulary with students, explaining any words that are completely new. If you prefer, you can tell students to use a dictionary as they complete the task. Students should work individually, and then compare ideas with a partner. There is no need to check answers, as their predictions are checked in Exercise C.

C 🎧 Tell students that they will hear each of the people in the pictures speak, and that the aim is to check their predictions from Exercise B. Students can either simply tick the words and phrases as suggested, or write the initial of the name of each speaker against each word or phrase in their notebooks.

Give students a couple of minutes to check the tapescript, and point out that describing where you live is usually necessary in the first part of the speaking exam.

Tapescript 🎧 **59** (1 min, 51 secs)

C **Listen and tick the words and phrases as you hear them.**

1
Voice: Hello, I'm Ubaid. I come from Cairo, which, as you probably know, is the capital of my country – Egypt. It's a huge city – one of the biggest and busiest in the world. I have lived here all my life and I love it. Some of the most famous attractions in the world are in Cairo, and it is a very popular tourist destination.

2
Voice: Hi. My name's Gulay, and I come from a small town on the south coast of Turkey called Fethiye. Not long ago, Fethiye was a little fishing village, but now it is a popular seaside resort. During the summer months, hundreds of thousands of tourists visit and it is very lively.

3
Voice: Hello. My name is Cinzia. I live in a tiny village called Savoca. It is in Sicily, which is an island off the south coast of Italy. Savoca is in the mountains and it's very rural – most people are farmers. It is quiet, but very beautiful.

4
Voice: Hello there. I'm Mohammed, and I'm from Libya. I live in Benghazi, which is a large port on the north coast. Benghazi is Libya's second city, and it is an important economic centre. It is growing bigger all the time, but it is a very exciting place to live.

Answers:
Ubaid – capital, huge city, tourist destination
Gulay – small town, fishing village, seaside resort
Cinzia – tiny village, island, rural
Mohammed – large port, economic centre

Grammar check

Although this is a grammar check, the focus is very much on learning some common fixed expressions. You could draw a timeline to quickly revise this use of the present perfect, but avoid long explanations about how and when the present perfect is used. Note that 'since' is used with a specific point in time, while 'for' is used with a period of time. It is possible to say 'for all my life', but speakers generally don't use the preposition. Drill the sentences before allowing students a few minutes to practice them.

Answers: 1. all   2. whole   3. always
4. since

Speaking 1

A The aim of this activity is to provide students with an opportunity to use the language they have learnt so far in the lesson. Read the exam tip, and then give them a moment to plan what they want to say. Encourage them to use any new vocabulary that relates to their own situation.

Vocabulary 2

The aim of this task is to provide students with further vocabulary to describe where they live, as well as go over a couple of grammar points, with which students at this level frequently make mistakes.

A The first task revises basic vocabulary that students should be familiar with. Give students a minute or so to work individually to match the opposites, and then check the task together. Focus on correct pronunciation as you give feedback. Point out also that the opposite of 'old' can be 'new' or 'young', but that parts of a town or city are usually described as 'modern'.

Answers: 1. c   2. d   3. a   4. e   5. b

B Tell students to work in pairs, and to use a dictionary if possible. To give feedback, tell them to close their books, and then read the definitions a–e as students give you the answers from memory. Concentrate on pronunciation, and clarify any queries. Finally, ask students to explain the difference between 'very' and 'too' before looking at the grammar check box.

Answers: 1. b   2. c   3. d   4. e   5. a

Grammar check

Read through the first line with students, and then give them five minutes to discuss the rules with a partner. Remember that the aim of the grammar boxes is to remind students about a grammar point, and not to practise it rigorously. Time spent studying grammar will mean less time practising the skills that are more beneficial in terms of passing the exam. You might like to tell students to check a grammar point outside class if they need to.

Answers: 1. oldest   2. hottest   3. ugliest
4. most modern   5. most exciting

Read through the second part of the grammar check box, and point out why 'very' and 'too' are used in the definitions a–e in Exercise B. Students can check the Watch out! box in their own time.

Pronunciation check

Tell students to read the pronunciation check box, and then play the recording. Drill the phrases, and then allow a moment for students to say the sentences two or three times to a partner.

Tapescript 🎧 60 (1 min, 10 secs)

Pronunciation check

The ~*est* at the end of superlatives is pronounced /ɪst/. The /t/ is not pronounced clearly in fast natural speech, especially when the following noun begins with a consonant.

Listen and practise these phrases.

1 the biggest city

2 the tallest building

3 the busiest street

The /t/ at the end of *most* is not pronounced clearly in fast natural speech, especially when the following adjective begins with a consonant.

Listen and practise these phrases.

1 most beautiful

2 most congested

Speaking 2

A and B By now, students know how to work through this type of task. Read the rubric with them, and then allow them to practise. Monitor to check that students are saying the right kind of thing, and are generally improving with this type of task.

For further speaking and vocabulary practice, tell students to complete the exercises on page 17 of the Workbook. Set as an extra activity or homework task.

Listening

Objectives

- To practise listening to information related to maps and plans.

- To further practise listening for specific information.

- To show students how key information is often repeated to help with spelling.

Listening 1

The aim of this task is to familiarize students with the type of maps and plans they might have to work with in the Listening Module of the exam. They are also exposed to different recording types, and different registers with different functions.

A   Give students a minute or so to look at the maps. Do not tell them anything about the places, as they will hear that on the recording. Make sure students understand that the first time they listen, they are simply matching the maps to the extracts, and not filling anything in. Play the whole recording once. When you check answers, you can also check the function or purpose of each extract ('Which extract is telling

people about something they might buy?', 'Which is the most formal / informal?' or 'Which dialogue is between friends?').

Tapescript 🎧 61 (4 mins, 12 secs)

A   **Listen and match the extracts with the maps.**

1

Voice: The south of England is a very popular part of the world for students to come to learn English. London is, of course, the most popular destination. Hundreds of thousands of students study at one of the capital's many language schools every year. Brighton is a busy city on the south coast. It, too, has a large number of schools, and many attractions that young visitors can enjoy. Brighton is about an hour away from London by train. Eastbourne and Hastings are smaller seaside towns to the east of Brighton. Hastings is the larger of the two, and has a few more study options. Another seaside resort – this time further west, in Hampshire – is Bournemouth. Bournemouth is a large town with several popular schools, and a busy student scene. For a quieter stay, students come to the Isle of Wight, an island just off the south coast. A ferry service connects the island with the mainland. Inland, the best option is Tunbridge Wells, a small but historic town between the coast and London. Students like to stay in Tunbridge Wells because it is quieter than London, but close enough to London to visit easily.

2

Voice: Andalusia is the largest region in Spain, stretching from the border with Portugal in the west, to the south-east coast of Almeria. Most tourists come to Andalusia for the sandy beaches and nightlife, and know very little about the fantastic sights that the region offers. Seville and Cordoba are both historic cities with much to see, but Granada is perhaps the most impressive of the bigger cities. It is only an hour from the coast, and is the home of the Alhambra Palace, one of the most famous buildings in Europe. The palace was built over 800 years ago, but remains largely in one piece. Ronda is a smaller town, but the Roman Aqueduct brings visitors from all over the world. Ronda is a pretty town, and the viaduct is one of the most important examples of Roman architecture in Spain. Andalusia also offers other forms of relaxation and adventure. South of Granada is the Sierra Nevada, a mountain range that offers some of the best skiing in western Europe. Many skiers stay in Granada and drive up into the mountains each day, but the mountain range now has a number of resorts with excellent accommodation. Much of the north of Andalusia is forest, and much of that is national park. The area also has some of the largest lakes in the country. Cazorla is probably the most popular village from which you can explore the forest and lakes by car or on foot.

3

Voice: Hi, Leo speaking. Hi, Tony. Didn't you bring a map with you? Oh, well, never mind – it's very easy. Come out of the station and walk straight down Queen's Road. Yeah, straight down – don't turn left or right. Walk past the cinema on the right, and then after three or four minutes, you'll come to a crossroads with a small clock tower in the middle of it. Turn right at the clock tower and walk up the hill. Take the third on the left – there's a taxi rank on the corner. No, on the left – the third turning. My apartment is on the right, about a hundred metres up the road.

Answers:
speaker 1 is map 2   speaker 2 is map 3
speaker 3 is map 1

B, C and D 🎧 Students will hear one extract at a time, and complete a different task for each. Give them time to read questions, and look at the appropriate map for each extract. Then play the recording. At this stage, if students want to listen to an extract a second time, they should be able to. Students can compare answers with a partner, or you can give direct feedback after each task.

Tapescript 🎧 **62** (0 mins, 13 secs)

B Listen to the first extract and match the letters on the map with the places below.

[Play track 61 again]

Answers: 1. Hastings, a   2. Isle of Wight, b
3. Brighton, c   4. Bournemouth, d
5. Tunbridge Wells, e   6. Eastbourne, f

Tapescript 🎧 **63** (0 mins, 12 secs)

C Listen to the second extract and complete each space with <u>one</u> word.

[Play track 61 again]

Answers: 1. Palace   2. Roman   3. mountain
4. forest / lakes

D Listen to the third extract and circle Leo's apartment on the map.

[Play track 61 again]

Answers: Leo's apartment is C.

Listening 2

Read the exam tip with students. Point out that repeating very specific information will often mean spelling it out.

A 🎧 Play the whole recording one more time, and then ask students if they remembered what was repeated.

Tapescript 🎧 65 (0 mins, 13 secs)

A Listen again. Notice examples of a speaker repeating information.

[Play track 61 again]

B Give them a few minutes to read the tapescript and check.

Listening 3

The aim of this activity is to provide listening practice with maps. Note, though, that the first task is not connected with the map. This makes the task more authentic, as in the exam there will rarely be more than one task related directly to the map.

A 🎧 Students should be more independent now when working through the practice stage of the skills section. They know that they have time to read the questions, they know how to predict, and they have practised all the task types. Read through the introductory line, give them a minute to read the questions, and then play the whole recording. Students might find it difficult to listen to the recording only once, but avoid playing it a second time. Students can discuss what difficulties they had, and then listen again later if necessary (see Exercises B and C).

Tapescript 🎧 66 (5 mins, 21 secs)

A Listen to a man talking to a group of people at a weekend work conference in a hotel. For questions 1–4, choose <u>four</u> correct statements from A–H.

Speaker: OK, can everyone listen again now, please? Now you know how much of the weekend will be work, and what some of the meetings and sessions are about, I'd like to tell you something about how you can spend some of the free time you have over the weekend – both inside the hotel, and outside in the town centre. As I've said, you'll be free from around five today and on Saturday, and from lunchtime on Sunday, and there's plenty to do. This is the first time we've had the conference at the Royal Spa Hotel, and I'm sure you'll agree it's a very nice place – really, there's no need to leave the hotel at all if you don't want to, but I'm sure some of you will want to get out for a change of environment.

OK – first, restaurants and bars. I'm sure you all saw that there was a bar near the entrance as you came into the hotel, but there are actually two more bars. One is also on the ground floor behind the main restaurant, and the other is on the top floor. That one has a very nice terrace where you can sit outside and enjoy the view. That bar is for hotel guests only, and is usually a bit quieter. As I say, the main restaurant is on the ground floor – we will have breakfast and lunch there, so you will get to know it well. There is also a smaller restaurant for coffee, sandwiches and snacks on the third floor, and that is also only for hotel guests. There is a gym and health club in the basement – the gym has a good range of equipment, and is open from seven a.m. I know some of you were talking about a swimming pool, but unfortunately there is no swimming pool. I will tell you where there is a pool close to the hotel in a moment. The health club has a sauna, which is open from ten a.m., but is not open on Sunday. There is a charge of four dollars for the sauna.

Now, I hope to see some of you around the hotel over the weekend, but I'm sure you will want to get out and see the town at some point. If you'd like to look at the map on the screen, I'll show the area around the hotel. There is a map of the town centre in your welcome pack, too. OK, you can see the hotel, here, in the middle of the map, and the main entrance, here, at the top in Carlisle Street. OK, that swimming pool I promised to tell you about is here in Cromwell Road. If you turn right out of the hotel, it's about ten minutes up the road, in the third street on the left. It's open until seven p.m., and until five on Sunday. There's a very nice park here to the north – again, about ten minutes away. In the middle of the park is a boating lake, so if the weather's good on Sunday, it might be a nice way to relax. If you want to see a movie this evening or on Saturday night, the cinema is here in the high street.

Come out of the hotel and turn left. The High Street, is only three minutes away. The cinema is here at the top of the street, next to a fairly large car park. Now, restaurants. There is a good Chinese restaurant in the middle of the high street, here, on the right. It's directly opposite the Town Hall. It's called the White Orchid. Another very nice restaurant is Leonardo's. It does Spanish and Mexican food. It's here at the bottom of the High Street. So, turn left at the end of Carlisle Street, walk down for five minutes, and you'll see it on the other side of the road. I went to Leonardo's last time I was here, so I can recommend it. Now, if anyone wants to see some live music, there is always a jazz band playing at the Pink Coconut. Yeah, that's right – the Pink Coconut. That's here in a little street behind the hotel. The street name is not on the map, but it's easy to find. Turn right out of the main entrance, and then take the first right to go back round to the back of the hotel. So, I think that's everything – please ask me if ... *(fade out)*

For questions 5–10, match the places with the letters on the map. You do not need to use all the letters on the map.

[Play track 66 again]

Answers:
Note that letters in 1–4 can be in any order, as long as the correct three letters are used. The answers here are in alphabetical order.

1. A   2. B   3. D   4. H   5. D   6. F   7. A
8. H   9. I   10. C

B Give students sufficient time to check answers and think about why they may have answered incorrectly, before moving on to Exercise D.

C Students will by now be familiar with this type of reflective process, but note the questions are not the same as in previous units. Remind them that identifying what they are doing well and not doing so well is a very good way of focusing on what they can do better next time. Allow students time to reflect and complete the task. Ask them if they are happy with the number of correct answers. Play the recording again if necessary, and tell students to focus on why the correct answers are correct.

Key vocabulary in context

The aim of this task is to revise the use of simple prepositions of place. Students can work individually and compare with a partner. Check the 'Watch out!' box with students to remind them that 'opposite' is a preposition on its own.

Answers: 1. in   2. on   3. off   4. on   5. to   6. on   7. in   8. at

For further listening practice, tell students to complete the exercises on page 18 of the Workbook. Set as an extra activity or homework task.

Reading

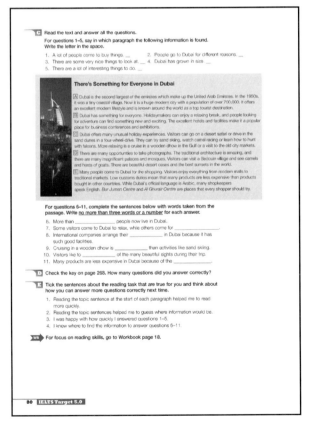

Objectives

- To introduce students to the concept and function of paragraphs in a text.

- To practise using paragraphs and topic sentences to read more quickly and effectively.

- To introduce students to the concept and function of a topic sentence.

Reading 1

In this book so far, paragraphs have been referred to as parts or sections of a text. Students may well be aware of paragraphs from previous studies, or from a general English course that they are studying in conjunction with this IELTS course. The aim of this first reading section is to introduce the concept of paragraphing as a way of dividing a text into manageable parts.

A and B This can be conducted as pairwork or as a whole-class discussion. If you think that only one or two students have been to each of the places, it might be better to talk as a class.

C Read through the rubric and question with students. Give them a few minutes to talk in pairs or small groups. Even if they have never been to Barcelona, they probably know something about the buildings and the football team. If you know a few students have been there, they can tell the class what they know.

D Tell students to skim read the text in order to see if any points they have mentioned are included. When they have read it, you can quickly compare what they mentioned with what is in the text.

E Give students four or five minutes to discuss the questions in pairs. There is no need to go into detail with feedback to the second question, as the next task provides answers.

Answers: 1. four 2. dealt with in next task

F Allow students three or four minutes to choose the correct option, and then another three or four to talk with a partner. Go through the answers, adding any comments you want to make. Don't go into much detail about question 6, as the topic sentences are the focus of tasks later in the lesson.

Answers:
1. give a text logical structure
2. easier
3. one subject
4. change the subject or make a new point
5. can be different lengths
6. the most important

G Read through the instructions, and make sure that the purpose of reading the text again is clear. Students should just read now, as any further explanation or analysis might confuse them. The Workbook task focuses on how texts are organized into paragraphs. You could consider working through it at this point if you feel it would be beneficial, before moving on to topic sentences.

Reading 2

Although students don't ever have to identify topic sentences in an IELTS task, they are frequently mentioned in both reading and writing IELTS practice. At this level, a basic understanding of what a topic sentence does is sufficient. Note that using topic sentences is also the focus of the Writing Module in this unit.

Pre-teach key vocabulary ('lagoon', 'canal', 'mainland', 'pedestrians', 'oar', 'festival', 'lace', 'sink (v)', 'flood (v)', for example), so that students can focus more on the organization of the text, and how topic sentences are used. Start by telling students to look at the picture, and then remind the class of who has been to Venice and what the class know about it. If possible, students should work individually to check new words in dictionaries, and then explain them to a partner. Tell them to use what they can see in the picture as they do so. Ask students questions so that they can answer with the appropriate word, rather than ask them for long definitions – 'What is the word for people who are walking and not driving?', 'What is this on the board?' (draw a picture of a small boat and an oar).

A Read through each of the topic sentences (don't tell students what the sentences are yet), and ask if they already knew that information. Even if students don't know much about Venice, they will probably know that some of this information is true. Set the task by looking at the example together. Give students about ten minutes to work individually, and then a minute or two to compare with a partner. To check answers, write the numbers in order on the board.

Answers: 2 / 5 / 3 / 4 / 1

B Give students a minute to choose the correct statement.

Answers: 1 is the correct statement.

Read the exam tip with students. Illustrate the advice with a simple diagram on the board. Draw a line in one colour, labelled 'topic sentence', and then three lines in another colour, labelled 'supporting sentences'.

Reading 3

Read the exam tip with students. Tell them that they are now going to practise using topic sentences to read more quickly, and to identify where information can be found.

A Although students should now be more independent when working through the practice stage of the skills section, the important thing here is to practise using the topic sentences. You might like to write the five topic sentences up on the board, so that students can read only them. Alternatively, tell them to read them in the book, but set a time limit of about two minutes. Then tell them to close their books.

B Students should now read the questions in Exercise C, and decide from the topic sentences in which paragraph the answers are probably to be found. Note that if the topic sentences are on the board, the focus is clearer, and students are not tempted to read more than they should. They should work individually, and then compare with a partner, giving their reasons. Ask them for answers so that you can check how useful looking at only the topic sentences has been, but don't tell them if they are right or wrong.

C Students should now work through the whole practice stage. Before doing so, tell them this text is the type of text they will see in the first part of the reading exam. Remind them that part of the aim for the first task (questions 1–5) is to check their ideas in Exercise B. Note that the first task should be quite easy, having done all the preparation. Set a time limit of about 15 minutes.

D Give students sufficient time to check and think about why they may have answered incorrectly, before moving on to Exercise E.

Answers:
1. E   2. B   3. D   4. A   5. C
6. 700,000 (Now it is a huge modern city with a population of over 700,000)
7. adventure (Holidaymakers can enjoy a relaxing break, and people looking for adventure can ...)
8. business conferences (The excellent hotels and facilities make it a popular place for business conferences and exhibitions)

9. more relaxing (More relaxing is a cruise in a wooden dhow ...)
10. take photographs (... many opportunities to take photographs. The traditional architecture is amazing, and ... magnificent palaces and mosques.)
11. low customs duties (Low customs duties mean that many products are less expensive)

E By now, students will be familiar with this type of reflective process, but note the questions are not the same as in previous units. Remind them that identifying what they are doing well and not doing so well is a very good way of focusing on what they can do better next time. Allow students time to reflect and complete the task, and then ask them if they are happy with the number of correct answers. You may like to ask one student what he or she will do differently next time.

The Workbook task for this unit practices ordering a text like those in the unit. As previously suggested, it could be done after completing Reading 1. Alternatively, it could be set up now as a homework task.

Writing

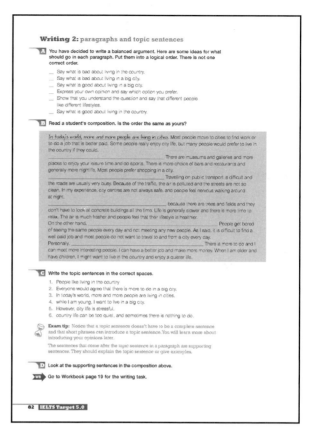

Objectives

- To provide further practice with the second part of the IELTS Writing Module.

- To give further guidance and practice on deciding what to say in a discursive composition.

- To practise paragraphing in a discursive composition.

- To introduce the basic concept of using topic sentences to introduce the paragraphs of a composition.

Writing 1

The aim of the first stage (Exercises A, B, C and D) is to get students thinking about what could form the content of the composition they will focus on later in the lesson.

A Tell students to look at the pictures, and elicit the phrases 'city life' and 'country life'. You could also introduce the alternative phrases 'urban life' and 'rural life'. Give students an example, 'The picture here tells me that cities are crowded, and that there isn't much space'. Then give students five minutes to talk in pairs. It is not necessary to record ideas, as the following task develops the topic.

B Make sure students understand what they have to do, and encourage dictionary use. They can pass dictionaries to each other or work in small groups to complete the task. Go over the task, dealing with any key words and phrases that are still not clear.

Answers: 1. CL   2. CO   3. CL   4. CO   5. CL   6. CO   7. CL   8. CO

C Having checked the meanings of the key words and phrases, this task should be easy, and you could correct it quickly as a class.

Answers: 1. P   2. P   3. N   4. N   5. P   6. P   7. N   8. N

D The aim of this activity is to provide some typical exam speaking practice. Give students two or three minutes to talk. If students come from various places, get a general consensus about who thinks they have an urban and who has a rural lifestyle.

E Tell students to look at the instructions for the writing task, and highlight the key words or anything they don't understand, as in previous units. Go through the instructions with them, and make sure they understand everything before answering the two questions. Give students three or four minutes to answer the questions, and then get feedback from various students. Try to guide students towards deciding that a balanced composition might be the right approach here (there would probably be more to say), but accept that some students might find it easier to say they love living in a city.

Writing 2

Students have focused on paragraphing and using topic sentences in the Reading Module, and now the aim is to get them thinking about the same thing in terms of their writing. Point out that the composition on the page is divided into paragraphs, and that although there is not one correct way of organizing and ordering points made in a composition, a simple exam composition will usually follow a pattern.

A Remind students of the meaning of 'balanced'. Give them six or seven minutes to read and order the points. Students should work individually to complete the task. Deal with any words they don't know as they work. Give them a further five minutes to compare with a partner, and discuss any differences of opinion. Get some feedback from students (or monitor closely), so that you can check they are on task, but don't give a solution, as students will compare their order with that in the model now.

B Tell students that the topic sentences are missing from the composition, and not to worry about that for now. Make sure they understand that they are reading simply to check the order in which points are made.

C Tell students that they will now need to read more carefully, and set about ten minutes to complete the task individually. This could, of course, be done quickly by writing just the numbers into the spaces in the composition, but students will benefit from copying the sentences out. They can compare answers if they finish early.

Answers:
Paragraph 1 – (3) In today's world, more and more people are living in cities.

Paragraph 2 – (2) Everyone would agree that there is more to do in a big city.

Paragraph 3 – (5) However, city life is stressful.

Paragraph 4 – (1) People like living in the country

Paragraph 5 – (6) country life can be too quiet, and sometimes there is nothing to do.

Paragraph 6 – (4) while I am young, I want to live in a big city.

Read both exam tips with the students. You can refer to examples that illustrate the first point if necessary.

D Give students a few minutes to read again. Then use the second paragraph to show how three simple sentences support the topic sentence.

Writing task

The writing tasks are found in the Workbook at the end of the unit. Note that the teacher's instructions are almost exactly as they are for the last two units. Consider anything that you feel didn't work as well as you hoped last time, and try to work on that now.

A Students will still need quite a lot of assistance with preparation before attempting to write a complete composition of this type. Tell them that the important thing is to attempt the composition, to make some valid points, and to organize the points as well as they can.

Give students a minute or so to read the task instructions, and then allow them to ask questions about any words they don't know. Check that they really understand 'experience life', and give some examples.

B This stage will be very important for students at this level. They can work in pairs as suggested, or in small groups. Give them at least ten minutes for this, and monitor, giving a few of your own ideas. Get some points up on the board so that everyone has some points they can include.

Once students are ready to start writing, set a time limit of 40 minutes (you might want to end the task earlier than that if students have managed all they can, and you think looking at the model will be more beneficial). Tell them to use the composition in the Writing Module as a model. Monitor as students work, but check specifically that they are organizing their ideas, and making relevant points, rather than writing accurately.

When students have completed the task, tell them to look at the model composition on page 268 of the Course Book. Put them into pairs to compare their composition against the model. The model is reproduced below.

If you collect students' compositions to mark, it would be better to use the process to get an idea of what they are capable of, rather than correct too heavily. At this stage, you will be correcting most of what they write.

In most countries these days, most young people go to university when they leave school. In some countries, it is usual to apply to the university which is closest to your hometown, so that you can continue to live with your family. In other countries, young people want to move away to a more exciting place where they can begin a new life. Moving is part of the university experience.

Many young people choose to move away from home because they want an adventure. They can live in a university residence or rent an apartment with other students. They are free from their parents' rules for the first time.

Moving away from home has disadvantages, however. Students can become homesick if they do not make new friends, and they can miss their friends from school and their brothers and sisters. Some young people do not know how to cook and are not very good with money, so they need their parents' support.

If students go to university near their home, they can live at home and have the support of their

family. It will also be much cheaper because they do not have to pay for accommodation or travel home at the weekend or during holidays. My brother and two of my cousins go to university in our city and are happy that they can live at home.

Some students who live at home feel that they miss the fun that some of the other students are having. They see other students living in a big house with lots of other young people and feel a bit envious.

Personally, I would prefer to live at home when I study, and I think I will do that. The university in my city has a good reputation, so there is no need to move away. I think I can concentrate on my studies better if I don't have to think about looking after myself and making friends.

Consolidation

Speaking

The aim of the speaking section here is to show students how the third part of the exam will follow on from the second, the type of questions the examiner might ask and how students can answer appropriately.

A Give students a moment to look back. Tell them to remember just the answers they gave (they don't have to answer the questions again).

B Some of the questions are still quite personal, and others much more abstract. Give them time to read through the questions, and mark each as instructed. Make sure students know they are not to answer the questions yet. Ask them to tell you what they think about each question, and encourage them to give reasons.

C Tell students to notice the way in which students explain the answers they have given. Play the whole recording with pens down.

Tapescript 67 (1 min, 38 secs)

C Listen to some students giving good answers to the questions.

1

Examiner: Which city in the world would you most like to visit?

Student: I'd really like to go to Beijing and see the Forbidden City. I can imagine China is a very exciting place to visit.

2

Examiner: So, why do so many people live in cities?

Student: I think they have to live in cities because of their job. In Thailand, people leave the country and come to Bangkok because it is the best place to find work.

3

Examiner: Are some cities becoming too big?

Student: Yes, I think so. I don't know the biggest city, but Mexico City and Shanghai are huge. There are a lot of poor people and pollution is a problem. The capital of my country is Istanbul. It is very crowded, and it is very expensive to buy or rent an apartment.

4

Examiner: Do you enjoy city life or would you like to live somewhere quieter?

Student: I really enjoy living in Tehran. The university is the best in Iran, and I meet people from all over the country. There is much more to do in Tehran than there is in my hometown.

D Play the recording again, pausing after each extract so that students can write answers. Note that this provides good listening exam practice, as well as preparing them to speak. You might need to play each extract a couple of times. To give feedback, tell students to look at the tapescript on page 290.

D   **Read the answers below. Then listen
    again and fill in the missing words.**

[Play track 67 again]

Answers:
1. can imagine
2. leave the country / best place
3. poor people / buy or rent
4. my hometown

E   Give students four or five minutes to answer the
    questions now. Tell them to answer the
    questions so that the answers are true for them
    (not to repeat the answers in the examples).
    Monitor to see how well students are doing.

Vocabulary

A   Students have not practised a task like this one
    yet. Treat it as a little test or competition. Set a
    time limit, and see how many questions students
    can answer in pairs without looking back in the
    unit. You or they can write the answers on the
    board to check spelling.

    Answers: 1. capital   2. village   3. island
    4. resort   5. ugly   6. sink

B   This task revises vocabulary learnt in the unit,
    emphasizes the need to learn the different forms
    of common words and checks spelling. Refer
    students to the 'root' words in the box – they
    could think of different forms of the words to
    help with the activity. Tell students to complete
    the task individually. Remind them to use capital
    letters at the beginning of a sentence. For
    feedback, either you or students should write
    the answers on the board.

    Answers: 1. historic   2. Pollution
    3. impressive   4. tourists   5. Tourism

Errors

A   Students now know that each unit ends with this
    type of task. Remind them that it is very useful to
    notice and correct common errors. Tell students
    that there are no spelling mistakes. They can
    either complete the task individually or work in
    pairs. Write the correct sentences on the board
    to clarify corrections.

    Answers:
    1. I have lived in this city all my life.
    2. London is the biggest city in England.
    3. Venice is the most beautiful city in Italy.
    4. There are too many people in most cities.
    5. There is too much traffic in my city.
    6. The college is opposite the park.

Exam Practice

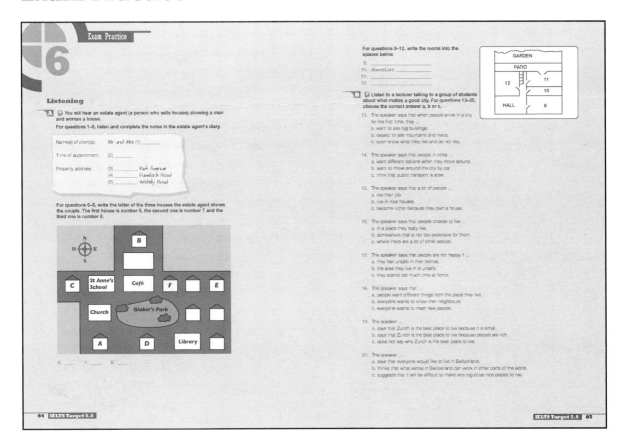

Listening

A and B 🎧 Apart from the final unit, students practise only one skill in each of the exam practice sections from now on. Note that questions make up the two parts of the practice in the same way that they do in the exam. Show students that there are two completely different parts in this activity, but that the first part is divided into three tasks.

Tell students that these recordings are what they can expect from the first and fourth parts of the exam.

The recording and degree of challenge in the task is close to what they will deal with in the exam. Students are not given preparation, and are left on their own a little to get some experience of more realistic exam practice.

Read through both the task introductions with students. 'Estate agent' is explained in the rubric, but make sure they know what it means. Allow students to read the question instructions themselves. Give them a minute for each, as there is quite a lot to read through. Remember, they will only have 30 seconds in the exam.

You should play the whole recording once only, though if you really feel your students are not ready for that, pause after the first part, and give them a moment to write and check answers. Write all answers on the board.

Tapescript 🎧 **69** (5 mins, 34 secs)

A **You will hear an estate agent (a person who sells houses) showing a man and woman a house. For questions 1–5, listen and complete the notes in the estate agent's diary.**

Estate agent: Good morning. You must be Mr and Mrs Clarke.

Man: Yes, that's right. Good morning.

Woman: Good morning.

Estate agent: So, is it Clarke with an E, or Clarke without an E? I wrote it in my diary, but I wasn't sure if I spelt it correctly.

Man: It's with an E. C-L-A-R-K-E.

Estate agent: Yes, that's what I thought.

Man: Anyway, please call me Andy.

Woman: And I'm Laura.

Estate agent: And I'm Ian. Thanks for coming over to the office. I hope this time is convenient for you. Nine o'clock is a bit early for some people, but I like to make an early start if I can. I've got three houses that I want you to see today.

Man: Nine o'clock is fine. I have to go into work when we've seen all the properties.

Estate agent: OK, well let me show you on the map where the three houses are. They're all quite close together near Blaker's Park. Do you know Blaker's Park?

Woman: Yes, we know it really well. It's a nice area.

Estate agent: Well, the first one I'll show you is the closest to the park. It's actually on the road that runs around the park, Park Avenue, just here on the right – number 14, I think. Yes, number 14.

Man: So, you get a view of the park from the front windows?

Estate agent: Oh, yes, the view of the park is fantastic. The second house is here – on the left side – that's the west side of the park – in Havelock Road. That's number 35. It's right next door to St Anne's School. Do you have school-age children?

Woman: Well, we have a boy of three, so near the school would be very nice in a couple of years.

Estate agent: Well, all three houses are pretty near the school, as you can see. Now, the third property – that's actually the furthest from the park, up here on the north side – that's Whitely Road, number 62. It's still only a few minutes' walk to the park, though.

Man: Number 62 – that's the number we live at now.

Estate agent: Oh, really? So, shall we go and have a look? I'll drive and you can collect your car when we come back.

Man: OK, that sounds fine.

Estate agent: OK, here we are. As you can see, the front of the house is very nice. It's been painted recently. The front garden is small, but very pretty.

Woman: Oh, yes, it's a lovely little garden.

Estate agent: Shall we go in?

Man: Yes, I'm looking forward to seeing inside.

Estate agent: So, this is the hall. It's quite a good size – room for a buggy. The first room, here on the right, is the living room.

Woman: Oh, this is very nice.

Man: Yes, it's big, isn't it?

Estate agent: Yes, it is a big room. Do you like the natural fireplace?

Man: Yes, very much. In fact, I like the whole room. I can imagine it's very relaxing.

Woman: Mm, well, let's see some more.

Estate agent: OK, next door here is a downstairs bathroom. There's a bigger family bathroom upstairs. This one is sandwiched between the living room and dining room.

Man: Oh, this is quite big for a second bathroom.

Woman: Yes, it'll be good to have two bathrooms. We only have one where we are now.

Estate agent: OK, next door here is the dining room.

Man: Oh, I like a separate dining room – it's quite big, too.

Estate agent: Yes, a bit smaller than the living room, but still a good size. There are doors here out to the patio.

Woman: Oh, how lovely – it's a nice patio – and the garden looks nice from what I can see from here.

Estate agent: Yes, I'll show you the garden, but first let's see the kitchen. That's out of the dining room and to the left. You can see that the kitchen is to the right of the back of the house. There's a window here on the left looking over the patio, and another one here looking out onto the garden.

Man: It's not the biggest kitchen, is it? I like a kitchen to be a bit bigger than this.

Estate agent: Well, it's not a bad size. Don't forget, you'll be able to eat in the dining room, so the kitchen is only for cooking.

Man: Yes, I suppose so.

Estate agent: So, shall we go out and see the garden or would you like to see upstairs first?

Man: I think we should … *(fade out)*

For questions 6–8, write the letter of the three houses the estate agent shows the couple. The first house is number 6, the second one is number 7 and the third one is number 8.

[Play track 69 again]

For questions 9–12, write the rooms into the spaces below.

[Play track 69 again]

Tapescript 🎧 **70** (4 mins, 23 secs)

B **Listen to a lecturer talking to a group of students about what makes a good city. For questions 13–20, choose the correct answer a, b or c.**

Speaker: *(fade in)* … now, in the future, some of you will probably be working as architects, some of you as interior designers, and some of you in town planning. For all of you, what I'm going to talk about is very important, and you should certainly know what it is about a city that attracts somebody or drives somebody away. Now, environment. What is environment, and what makes people like an environment? When people arrive in a city for the first time, the thing that they notice is the environment. People notice the buildings and the space between the buildings. They appreciate the way a city works with the natural features around it – the hills and mountains, the trees and the rivers. People quickly have a sense of what is beautiful or ugly about a city. People notice that the air is clean or unclean, they notice noise and smells. People know whether they can travel easily around the city – if

interesting places are within walking distance, if it is possible to drive, and if the public transport system is good. All of these first impressions can make people want to stay in a city or go somewhere else.

Another important aspect of a city's character is its economy. For many people, the choice of where to live is influenced by economy. During their working lives, people go where there is work. If that work is well paid and satisfying, people feel good about where they live. Homes are often a person's biggest investment – the value of a person's home increases, and affects his or her wealth. People like living in towns and cities where the value of their home is growing. Remember that people choose to live where they can afford to live – and they are unhappy if what they can afford is unpleasant. People hope that wherever they live, they will enjoy the same services and quality of life as everyone else.

Now, people often decide that they like or don't like a city because of its society. By society, I mean the people in the city, and how these people relate to one another. If people feel safe, they will like a place – if they feel unsafe, they won't. People are not happy if they think that where they live is dangerous – where they are afraid to leave their home. Some people want to feel that they are part of a community – they want to know the people around them. They want to talk to the neighbours – whether that is at the local shop or waiting at the school gates. Other people don't want that at all. They like the fact that in a big city they can get lost in the crowd. They enjoy the excitement, and want to meet new people all the time.

So, does the perfect city exist? Well, of course, the answer is no. As we go into the 21st century, cities are getting bigger and bigger, and people seem to be less happy with the cities they live in. You may be interested to know that for the last two years, Zurich, in Switzerland, has been identified as the best city in the world to live in. However, Switzerland is a rich country and the population is small. Is it possible to take what has worked in Zurich and try to make that work in Asia or South America or Africa, in cities with twenty or thirty million people? As planners and designers, this is a problem you must think about. You can help to shape the future. Now, I wonder if anyone would ... *(fade out)*

Answers: 1. Clarke   2. 9 / nine o'clock
3. 14   4. 35   5. 62   6. F   7. C   8. B
9. living room   10. downstairs bathroom
11. dining room   12. kitchen   13. c
14. a   15. c   16. b   17. b   18. a
19. c   20. c

Once you have given students the answers, and if there is time, you might like to play the recording again as students read the tapescript. Pause to point out why some answers are incorrect if students are still unsure.

Unit 6 Workbook answers

Speaking and Vocabulary

A Students' own answers.

B 1. crowded   2. congested   3. polluted
4. rural   5. tiny   6. huge   7. historic
8. impressive

C Students' own answers.

Listening

A Students' own answers.

Tapescript 🎧 **71** (0 mins, 58 secs)

A **Listen and write answers to the questions. You don't need to write sentences.**

1 What is the name of the town or city that you live in?
2 How long have you lived there?
3 Which city in your country has the biggest population?
4 Which city in your country do most people want to visit?
5 What is the most interesting city you have visited?
6 Which city in the world would you most like to visit?

B 1. Stockholm   2. Edinburgh   3. Casablanca
4. Amsterdam   5. Algiers   6. Warsaw

Tapescript 🎧 **72** (1 min, 48 secs)

B **Listen and write the names of these important cities.**

1 The capital of Sweden is Stockholm – that's S-T-O-C-K-H-O-L-M.
2 People often spell the capital of Scotland wrongly – it's E-D-I-N-B-U-R-G-H, Edinburgh.
3 Casablanca means 'white house'. That's C-A-S-A-B-L-A-N-C-A.

4 Holland's capital is Amsterdam. That's A-M-S-T-E-R-D-A-M.
5 The country is Algeria – that's A-L-G-E-R-I-A, and the capital city is Algiers. That's A-L-G-I-E-R-S.
6 This year's conference is in Warsaw, in Poland. Warsaw – W-A-R-S-A-W.

Reading

A Paragraph 1 – B
Paragraph 2 – D
Paragraph 3 – C
Paragraph 4 – A

Writing

A, B and C The writing task is dealt with in the main section of the Teacher's Book.

7

Movement

Unit overview

The seventh unit is based around the theme of transport. It revises and develops some of the themes from the previous unit. Students talk again about where they live, and how they travel around. There is an emphasis on talking about frequency, and expressing opinion. The unit gives students a better idea of what they can expect in the various sections of the IELTS exam.

Speaking and Vocabulary

Objectives

- To give students further practice with answering the type of questions they can expect in the first and third parts of the IELTS Speaking Module.

- To present and practise different ways of saying how often something happens.

- To practise expressing opinions about both personal and more abstract issues.

Vocabulary 1

A The aim of the first vocabulary task is to revise basic methods of transport. Students learn the verbs and verb phrases that they are most likely to need in order to talk about their own lives.

Students should work individually to match. For feedback, tell them to cover the words, and then read the number of each picture to see if they remember the verb or verb phrase.

Speaking 1

The first speaking section presents and practises ways of expressing frequency. You might like to start the lesson by eliciting the adverbs of frequency. Draw a line on the board with 'always' at the end, on the left. Ask them what goes on the other end ('never'). Then elicit the adverbs that come between.

A This task will be easier if you start the lesson as suggested above. Note that 'sometimes' is not included in the task, but as in one of the explanations, the assumption is that students will know 'sometimes', and can use it to learn the words they might not know. Students should work individually, and then compare with a partner. For feedback, write the numbers and letters on the board to clarify answers.

Answers: 1. e   2. d   3. b   4. c   5. f   6. a

B Students should work in pairs to discuss this. Different people have different views about what is frequent and what is not, but you could work through one of the examples below to give them an idea of how to approach the task. Make sure they know there is not a correct answer. See whether students agree on answers for feedback.

Suggested answers: 'Three times a week' is 'very often' if you are talking about playing tennis. It is 'not very often' if you are talking about brushing your teeth.

'Once a month' is 'occasionally', 'rarely' or 'not very often' if you are talking about eating fruit. It is 'very often' if you are talking about going to watch a football match.

'Every day' is like 'always', (but point out that 'I always take a taxi' doesn't mean anything unless you give more information – e.g., 'I always take a taxi to work'; see 'Grammar check' box).

'Twice a year' is 'rarely' if you are talking about going out to eat, but 'often' if you are talking about scuba-diving. Point out that 'occasionally' has a more positive connotation than 'rarely'.

Grammar check

The grammar check here reinforces what students have seen from doing the tasks. Either read through the points with them, or give them a minute or two to read to themselves.

Pronunciation check

Tell students to read the pronunciation check box, and then play the recording for students to listen and practise.

Tapescript 🎧 73 (0 mins, 40 secs)

Pronunciation check

Notice that *usually* has three syllables. It is pronounced /ˈjuːʒuəli/. *Occasionally* has four syllables. It is pronounced /əˈkeɪʒnəli/.

1   usually

2   occasionally

Listen and practise.

C Give students two or three minutes to plan what they want to say before they speak. Encourage them to use a range of words and phrases learnt in the lesson so far. Get some answers from individual students, and then discuss the question in Exercise D together as a whole class.

D See Exercise C above. Write any new methods of transport on the board.

Vocabulary 2

A The aim of this activity is to learn some useful words and phrases, as well as prepare students for the listening part of the speaking focus. Students can share dictionaries if necessary, and work in pairs or small groups. Ask various students for ideas so that you can check they have understood the words and their pronunciation. Make sure they understand that 'journey' is a very useful word, as it is used in all of these situations.

Answers:
1, 2, 3, 4, 5, 6, 7 – journey
3, 5, 6, 7 – wait in a queue
4, 7 – motorway
1 – get seasick, travel by boat
2 – economical
3 – take off, land, fly

Speaking 2

A Give students a minute or two to read through the questions. Make sure they know they don't have to answer them yet.

Students can look at the 'Watch out!' box in their own time.

B 🎧 Play the whole recording as students match. Play the recording again to go over answers.

Tapescript 🎧 74 (1 min, 32 secs)

B Listen to some students answering the questions. Match each speaker with a question.

A No, not really. I get quite nervous – especially when the plane is taking off and landing. I hate waiting for my bags at the airport, too.

B Yes, especially young people. It's very economical. I think older people are cycling more, too – petrol is becoming so expensive, and cycling keeps you fit.

C Well, I have a Lamborghini, so of course, the answer is yes. I love to get onto the motorway and really put my foot down.

D Yes, when I was in Greece I travelled from Athens to an island near Turkey. It was an eight-hour journey. I got really seasick. I don't really like being at sea at all.

E Yes, I take a bus to and from college every day. In the morning, I always have to wait in a queue. When the buses come, they are sometimes full, and I have to wait for the next one.

Answers: 1. speaker C   2. speaker A   3. speaker E   4. speaker B   5. speaker D

C Encourage students to answer the questions in a similar way to the students on the recording.

Speaking 3

A Read the rubric with students. Then give them a minute or two to read the questions. Make sure they know they don't have to answer yet. Ask them which they think are difficult to answer and why.

B 🎧 Make sure students know to now complete the second column, and play the whole recording. Play the recording to go over answers, pausing to clarify anything necessary.

Tapescript 🎧 75 (1 min, 30 secs)

B Listen to some students answering the questions. In the second column, match each speaker with a question.

A Yes, I think so. There are lots of companies that offer cheap flights these days. Planes use a lot of petrol, and it is not good for the environment.

B Yes, I think so. The trains are modern and comfortable, and very fast. We have small buses that are clean and comfortable. You only have to wait ten minutes.

C That's a good question. Perhaps wealthy people will travel more in small planes, or even have their own little flying machines.

D Yes, people should use buses and trains or the underground in very big cities. More streets can be used only for people walking, and the air will be cleaner.

E We can make public transport cheaper and nicer to use – you know, more modern trains and buses. We can also ban cars in city centres, or make people pay to take their car into the city centre.

Answers: 1. speaker B   2. speaker E
3. speaker D   4. speaker A   5. speaker C

Read through the exam tip with students. This is an important point, and the aim is to make students *feel less worried* by these abstract questions.

C Tell students to concentrate on how simple the answers are, in terms of the ideas they express.

D Walking around and talking to different students makes a welcome change from always talking to the same partner. Tell students to ask each question to a different classmate. They can ask more than one person a question if they want to. Monitor, and note who gives good answers to each question. To get feedback, ask a successful student to repeat the answer for the benefit of the class.

For further speaking and vocabulary practice, tell students to complete the exercises on page 20 of the Workbook. Set as an extra activity or homework task.

Listening

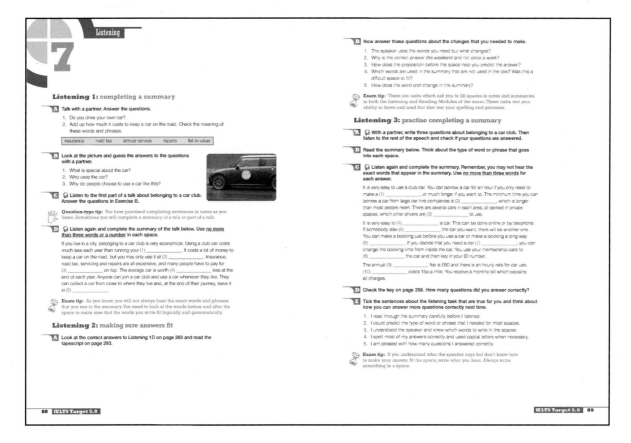

Objectives

- To introduce the concept of a summary completion.

- To show students that words used to complete a summary must fit grammatically, as well as logically.

- To practise completing a summary.

Sometimes the Listening Modules practise a particular listening skill, like listening for gist or recognizing key vocabulary. As the course progresses, the focus will be as much on particular task types, and helping students to approach that type of task.

Listening 1

A The aim of this speaking task is to provide some speaking practice, as well as prepare students for the listening tasks that follow. Ask the first question to the whole class, and see how many of them drive. Write 'keep a car on the road' on the board, and explain what it means. Go through the words and phrases with students, explaining each. Then give them a few minutes to add up the cost of keeping their car on the road. Give them a further minute or two to compare with a partner.

B You can either conduct this as pairwork as suggested, or discuss the questions as a class. Don't give answers, as students will listen to check in a moment.

C 🎧 Make sure students know they are answering the three questions in Exercise B, and play the whole recording. Get answers from the class, and write them in note form on the board.

Tapescript 🎧 76 (2 mins, 1 sec)

C **Listen to the first part of a talk about belonging to a car club. Answer the questions in Exercise B.**

Voice: More and more people in cities are joining car clubs. They are doing this because belonging to a car club, and using a car club car, is much more economical than running a car of their own. People in cities use public transport to get work. They walk their children to school and they walk to the supermarket. They may only use their car once or twice a week – perhaps only at the weekend. Why pay so much to keep a car on the road when you so rarely use it? If you add up the cost of keeping a car on the road, it is frightening. There is insurance and road tax, which goes up every year. Then, there is the cost of a yearly service – expensive, even if your car is new. If you drive an older car, of course, you will have to pay for repairs and new parts, too. For many people, there is the additional cost of parking. Finally, there is the fall in the value of your car – the average car falls in value by £2,000 a year. People who belong to a car club don't need to worry about any of this. They can use a car club car twenty-four hours a day, seven days a week. They can pick up a car from close to their home and leave it in the same place when they end their journey. Anyone can belong to a car club and save thousands of pounds every year ... *(fade out)*

Answers:
1. It is a car club car.
2. Members of the car club (anyone can join).
3. It is more economical than running their own car.

The question-type tip introduces the task students will now attempt. Read it through with students.

D 🎧 Give students time to read through the summary (a little longer than they will get in the exam), so that they know what to listen for. Tell students that you will pause the recording twice, so that they have time to write answers. Tell them not to call answers out. Play the recording, pausing where you think necessary. Play the whole recording through if you think your students can manage.

Tapescript 🎧 **77** (0 mins, 17 secs)

D **Listen again and complete the summary of the talk below. Use <u>no more than three words or a number</u> in each space.**

[Play track 76 again]

Read through the exam tip with students. Emphasize that the summary is short, and so language must be paraphrased in order to reduce it. Tell students that the words they use in the spaces are always words that they hear in the recording (it is the language around the spaces that changes).

Give students time to compare, focusing on whether the answers they have given fit logically and grammatically into the summary. Encourage them to discuss differences between what they and their partner have as answers. Play the recording one more time. You can either write the answers on the board or refer students to the tapescript on page 293, as suggested in the Course Book.

Listening 2

A Give students a few minutes to check their answers.

Answers: 1. own car   2. the weekend
3. parking   4. £2,000 / 2,000 pounds
5. the same place

B Tell students to analyze the answers in order to learn more about how to answer gap-fill questions. Note that this will apply in sentence completion, as well as note completion. The questions relate to the gap in the summary, so question 1 relates to the first gap. Give students five minutes to discuss this in pairs. Give clear answers, and check that students follow. Repeat answers if necessary.

Answers:
1. The order of the words, and the possessive from 'their' to 'your'.
2. Because the preposition 'at' before the gap doesn't fit with 'once a week'.
3. You know it will be a noun or a verb form with '~ing' (note that questions 2, 3 and 6 all have prepositions before the gap).

4. 'Be worth' is used in the summary, while 'fall in value' is used in the recording. Students might find this difficult because they don't know 'be worth'. However, there are clues to suggest that an amount of money is the answer.

5. It becomes a noun rather than a verb.

Listening 3

The aim of this activity is to provide listening practice with a summary completion. Note that the summary is a little longer than a summary will be in the exam. This is in order to fully practise the techniques that have been the focus of the unit.

Although students will be more independent now when working through the practice stage of the skills section, completing summaries is a new skill, and they have been given a little preparation and guidance to make the task more manageable.

A 🎧 This task provides some useful speaking practice, as well as preparing students for the listening. Students should discuss the questions in pairs so that everyone gets the opportunity to express a view. Writing your own questions as a way of predicting the content of a recording is motivating. Listening to see if those questions are answered is more so. Give students seven or eight minutes for the task, and then check both their views about the car club, and the questions they have written. Write three questions on the board. Make sure students understand that the first time they listen, they are listening to see whether their questions are answered. Finish by asking if any pair had all three of their questions answered.

Tapescript 🎧 **78** (3 mins, 19 secs)

A **With a partner, write three questions about belonging to a car club. Then listen to the rest of the speech and check if your questions are answered.**

Voice: Using a car club car is easier and more convenient than hiring a car from a large car hire company. Firstly, you can use a car club car for as long as you like. You can take it for an hour, or you can take it for a month. Being able to use a car for very short journeys is a huge advantage of a car club – a car hire company will always have a minimum twenty-four hour rental time. Most car club members use the cars for day trips and have the car back by the evening. They don't need to have it for twenty-four hours. Secondly, there are cars all around the city, so you will never have to walk more than ten minutes to pick up a car. The cars are parked in private car club parking spaces, which no other driver is allowed to use. When you bring the car back, the space will be waiting for you. Parking is never a problem.

Booking the car is very simple. You can book online, or you can book by telephone. Booking online couldn't be easier. You simply go onto the car club site and follow the instructions to make your booking. If the car you want is free, you can pick it up five minutes later. If another member is using the car you want, there will be another car nearby that you can use instead. If you want to book a car a month or two in advance, that is also possible. When you are in the car, you can extend your booking time if you need the car for longer. When you get to the car, you open it with your car club membership card, key in your identification number and then use the car keys, which you will find in the glove compartment.

So, how much does it all cost? Car club membership costs £60 a year. You then pay an hourly rate of between £2.50 and £3 to use the car – the cars with a bigger engine are a little more expensive than the smaller cars. You then have to pay fifteen pence a mile for petrol. Each month, your bill shows exactly what you have been charged for. If you need to fill the car with petrol at any time, you use the car club debit card, which you will find in the car. As I said before, it is all very reasonable. You would have to use a car club car very often for it to cost anything like it costs to keep your own car on the road. Now, with me I have ... (fade out)

B Students have heard the recording, so make sure they don't try to fill in any gaps from memory. Give them about a minute to read through the summary before they listen again.

C Play the whole recording. Students might find it difficult to listen only once more, but avoid playing it a third time. Students can discuss what difficulties they had, and then listen again later if necessary (see Exercise E).

Tapescript 79 (0 mins, 21 secs)

C Listen again and complete the summary. Remember, you may not hear the exact words that appear in the summary. Use <u>no more than three words</u> for each answer.

[Play track 78 again]

Answers: 1. short journey
2. 24 / twenty-four hours   3. allowed to
4. book   5. is using   6. in advance
7. for longer   8. open   9. membership
10. Petrol

D Give students sufficient time to check answers 1–10, and think about why they may have answered incorrectly, before moving on to Exercise E.

E Students will by now be familiar with this type of reflective process, but note the questions here are more specific to summary completion. Remind them that identifying what they are doing well and not doing so well is a very good way of focusing on what they can do better next time. Allow students time to reflect and complete the task. You might like to get some feedback from students to see what they have learnt from the practice.

Now would be a good time to reinforce the need for correct spelling of answers. Ask them if they are happy with the number of correct answers. Allow students to listen again and tell them to focus on why the correct answers are correct.

Read through the exam tip with students.

For further listening practice, tell students to complete the exercise on page 20 of the Workbook. Set as an extra activity or homework task.

Reading

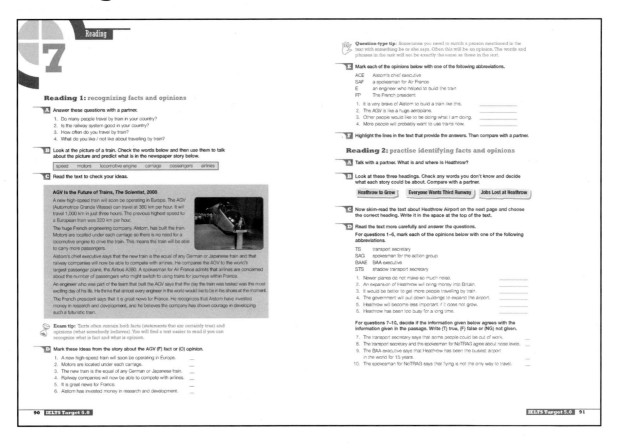

Objectives

- To help students recognize the difference between what is fact and what is opinion in a text.

- To practise reading a more formal text that is typical of the third section of the Reading Module.

- To introduce students to two further IELTS exam task types.

Reading 1

It will be easier to give feedback in this lesson if you have the text on an OHP transparency.

The aim of the first two tasks is to provide an opportunity for some speaking practice, as well as to prepare students for the reading tasks that follow.

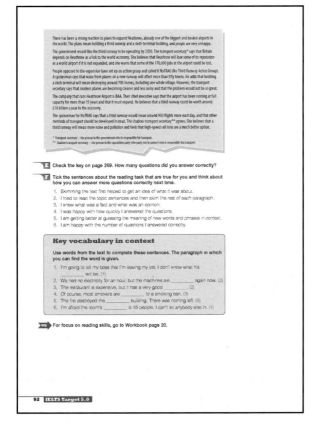

A Students will answer the questions in a different way, depending on whether they all come from the same country or from different countries. If they are from the same country, see if they can agree about questions 1 and 2. Give students five minutes to discuss the questions, and then discuss each point very briefly as a class.

B   Tell students to look at the picture and quickly ask them what they think. Do they like the design? What country do they think it was built in? Then tell them to look up the words in the box in a dictionary, as they discuss how the words might relate to the story. Pre-teaching the words yourself will be less motivating, and they should practise using dictionaries with a concrete goal. Students can work in small groups if there are not enough dictionaries for everyone. Do one as an example with them, 'I think speed will be in the story because this train is very fast – maybe it will tell us the top speed.' Monitor, as students talk to check their ideas (feedback will not be necessary, as students will read to check their ideas in a moment).

C   Make sure students know that they are reading now to check their ideas in Exercise B. Finish by asking students if they predicted how any of the words would be used correctly, but don't go through each word, as it will take time and not be beneficial.

Read through the exam tip with students. Ask them for one example of an opinion in the text.

D   Students will need sufficient time for this. Give them about six or seven minutes to work individually, and then a further three or four to compare ideas with partner. Give feedback orally, and be prepared to explain any difficulties. An OHP transparency would be very helpful here.

Answers:
1. F   2. F
3. O (Alstom's chief executive says that ...)
4. O (part of the same opinion as in 3)
5. O (The French president says ...)
6. F ('recognizes' suggests that this is true, and not his opinion)

The question-type tip introduces the task that follows (see below).

E   Read through the question-type tip as students look at the task. Note that in the exam, there may be more speakers than opinions, or vice versa – tell students this if you wish. Give students five or six minutes to work individually, and then a further two or three to compare ideas with a

partner. Check their answers, and write the correct answers on the board. Don't explain any difficulties yet, as they will identify the parts of the text that provide the answers.

Answers: 1. FP   2. ACE   3. E   4. SAF

F   Now that students have the answers, they will benefit from analyzing the paraphrasing here. Give them a few minutes to work individually, and then the same to compare. Write these answers on the board as they work (it may be better to highlight the answers on the text if using the OHP transparency).

Answers:
1. ... he believes the company has shown courage ...
2. He compares the AGV with the world's largest passenger plane, the Airbus A380.
3. ... every engineer in the world would like to be in his shoes ...
4. ... airlines are concerned about the number of passengers who might switch to using trains ...

Reading 2

As this is the first time students have practised this type of task, they will probably need a little background knowledge before reading a text that focuses on a particular social issue like this. Exercises A, B and C are designed to prepare students for the exam practice that follows.

A   This can be conducted as pairwork as suggested, or as a whole-class discussion. Pronounce 'Heathrow' for them, and then answer the question.

Answers: An airport (the biggest in the UK), 22km west of central London.

B   The aim here is to provide some speaking practice, and encourage prediction. Note, though, that two of the headings are distracters, so students shouldn't spend too much time discussing the possible stories. Encourage students to use dictionaries as they discuss the stories. You might like to work through one with them (choose one of the distracters) – 'Jobs lost at Heathrow', could be about workers losing their jobs because of technology, for example. Monitor as students talk, and get some ideas from them before moving on. Make sure the meaning of 'runway' is clear.

C Make sure students know that the aim here is simply to choose the correct heading, and thus to check their own ideas from Exercise B. Set a time limit of about three minutes. Give them the answer before moving on to the exam practice. Point out that the second heading is wrong because a lot of people don't want a third runway.

Answers: The correct heading is 'Heathrow to Grow'.

D Before working through the whole practice stage, tell students that this text is the type of text they might see in the third part of the reading exam. Note that the preparation work will mean they have a better general comprehension of the text, but this will not necessarily make the actual tasks easier. Tell them that answers will not be in the same order as they appear in the text, as this is a matching task. Set a time limit of about 15 minutes.

E Give students sufficient time to check questions 1–10, and think about why they may have answered incorrectly, before moving on to Exercise F. The answers are reproduced below, together with the parts of the text that provide answers.

Answers:
1. TS (... the transport secretary says that modern planes are ... less noisy ...)
2. BAAE (... believes that a third runway could be worth around £10 billion a year to the economy.)
3. STS (... feels that high-speed rail links are a much better option.)
4. SAG (... adds ... will mean destroying around 700 homes ...)
5. TS (believes that Heathrow will lose some of its reputation ... if it is not expanded)
6. BAAE (... says that the airport has been running at full capacity for more than 15 years)
7. T (she warns that some of the 170,000 jobs at the airport could be lost.)
8. F (spokesman says that noise from planes on a new runway will affect more than fifty towns ... However, the transport secretary says that modern planes are becoming ... less noisy)

9. NG ('he doesn't say 'the busiest in the world')
10. T (other methods of transport should be developed instead)

F By now, students will be familiar with this type of reflective process, but note questions 1–6 are not the same as in previous units. Remind them that identifying what they are doing well and not doing so well in both reading tasks is a very good way of focusing on what they can do better next time. Allow students time to reflect and complete the task, and then ask them if they are happy with the number of correct answers. You may like to ask one student what he or she will do differently next time.

Key vocabulary in context

This task is a little more challenging than previous vocabulary tasks, as students need to read again to identify the appropriate words. The aim is to consolidate useful vocabulary, as well as practise an important reading skill. Do the first one with them as an example, and then set it for pairwork. End the task when about half the class have completed it. Write answers on the board.

Answers: 1. reaction 2. operating
3. reputation 4. opposed 5. whole
6. capacity

The Workbook task for this unit provides further practice identifying fact and opinion. Now would be a good time to either work through it, or set it up as a homework task.

Writing

Objectives

- To practise writing a letter of complaint.
- To present and practise simple grammatical linking words.
- To revise and practise the use of relative clauses in a formal letter.

Writing 1

A The aim of this activity is to get students thinking about what could form the content of the composition they will focus on later in the lesson. Students can talk in pairs or as a whole class. Elicit key words and phrases, like 'passengers', 'flight', 'delay', 'be delayed'. If students have experienced a delay at an airport, ask them how the airline dealt with it, and if they were given a free meal or drink in compensation.

B Read the rubric with students, and set them three or four minutes to read through the notes. Then look at the link words below the notes, and the example. Show how the example isn't a complete sentence, and say that for the moment, students should link ideas simply, like this. Set a time limit, as students shouldn't spend too long trying to do this if any of the examples are difficult. It is best to monitor and give help as required. Don't give any answers, as students will see the sentences used in the model letter shortly.

C Tell students to read the whole letter before attempting the task. Then give them time to read again to focus on the linking words. They should work individually, and then compare with a partner.

Answers: 1. which   2. but   3. but
4. who   5. because   6. and   7. Although
8. When   9. so   10. which   11. Although
12. and

D Go over answers orally, but be prepared to deal with any difficulties.

Grammar check

Students will not be accustomed to focusing on grammar in the Writing Module of this book, but here it is necessary to revise and clarify a number of points. Mistakes with these grammar points are more likely to occur (or at least be noticed) in their written work. Note that Writing 2 is a simple writing practice activity this time.

There is quite a lot for students to take in, so read through the advice slowly, one step at a time. The advice about which pronoun to use should be fairly easy to grasp, but the advice about defining and non-defining clauses will probably be less clear. Remember that explaining this type of point is often not beneficial, and students will understand more from attempting the practice task. It might be a good idea to leave the advice about the different uses of 'so' until after practising the linking devices (Writing 2).

The advice about 'so' has its own little practice task. You can either work through this as you read the grammar check, or go back to it after Writing task 2, as suggested above.

Answers:

We use 'so' with adjectives, and 'such' with nouns and noun phrases.

1. so   2. such   3. so   4. such

Writing 2

You can either work through the task or do each question, and then get feedback. This stop-start approach might not appeal to all students, but checking answers as they go will probably give them confidence. Finding out you have got all your answers wrong after completing a task is a little soul-destroying. Point out students will need to delete some words, and use capital letters in their answers. Tell the students to work individually. Write the complete correct sentences on the board.

Answers:

1. I was late because there was a delay at the airport.
2. It was raining, so we decided not to play football.
3. Although it was raining, we played football.
4. There's the man who works in the local shop.

5. I worked until 9 p.m., which made me very tired.
6. When I arrived at the airport, all the taxis had gone.

Writing task

The writing tasks are found either in the Workbook or in the exam practice section at the end of the unit. For this unit, the task is in the Workbook.

A Students should be more confident about writing letters by now, but will still need preparation. The task here gives them more guidance than they will get in the exam. In many respects, they simply have to link all the problems together. Read through the first line of the rubric, and check students understand. You might like to draw a simple map on the board to clarify the concept of changing trains on route. Then read through each of the problems that occurred, referring to the map if it helps. Ask questions to check comprehension as you go – 'Why did you decide to take a taxi?' for example.

Read through the checklist with students, revising the three stages (remember they haven't worked on a letter for a couple of units now).

Read the exam tip at the bottom of the page. This is important and students should consider the alternatives they have. It largely depends on how confident they feel about the second writing task.

Monitor as students work, but check specifically that they are organizing their letters and making relevant points. There should be a little more accuracy now, particularly with linking devices and clauses. Students could exchange letters if they finish early.

Tell students to look at the model composition on page 269 of the Course Book. The model is reproduced on the following page. Put them into pairs to compare their composition against the model.

If you collect students' letters to mark, you should still be using the process to get an idea of what they are capable of, and to give constructive feedback, though you should correct mistakes that are below their level.

Dear Sir/Madam,

I am writing to complain about a train journey that I took recently with your company. There was a serious delay, which meant that I arrived at a wedding later than I planned.

I was travelling from Brighton to London, and needed to change at Croydon. However, because the train from Brighton was delayed for 20 minutes, I missed the connection. The next train to London was then cancelled, and there was not another for nearly an hour.

I knew I would be late, so had to take a taxi instead. This cost £35. I am angry that I had to spend this money when I had already paid for the train journey.

I had planned to arrive some time before the wedding, but I arrived just as it started. The journey was very stressful, and I could not enjoy the wedding as I hoped.

I hope you understand why I am unhappy with the service you provided. I would like a refund of the £35 taxi charge. I look forward to hearing from you.

Yours faithfully,

Monica Hart

Consolidation

Consolidation

Speaking

A Complete each sentence about your free-time activities.

1. I always _____ before I go to bed.
2. I usually _____ at the weekend.
3. I very often _____
4. I occasionally _____
5. I don't very often _____
6. I rarely _____
7. I never _____
8. I _____ three or four times a week.
9. I _____ once a month.
10. I _____ every day.

B Here are two typical cards for part 2 of the Speaking Module. Work with a partner – one of you is A, the other is B. You have a minute to think and make notes.

A
Describe the method of transport that you use most often.
Say ...
• what the method of transport is.
• what you use it for and how often.
• why it is better than other methods of transport.
• what the disadvantages are.

B
Describe a method of transport that you do not like using.
Say ...
• what the method of transport is.
• what you use it for and how often.
• what you don't like about it.
• how it could improve.

C Take turns to speak about what's on your card for about two minutes.

Vocabulary

A Fill the gaps with a word made from the root words in the box.

1. People often ride a bicycle because it is _____
2. If you are a young driver, _____ will cost more.
3. The _____ of Heathrow is not popular with everyone.
4. There is a _____ charge of £300.
5. I was quite surprised by Paul's _____
6. A lot of our profit goes into research and _____

economy
insure
expand
year
react
develop

Errors

A Correct the spelling mistakes.

1. occasionaly _____   2. usually _____   3. jurney _____
4. kue _____   5. passngers _____   6. engin _____

B There are errors in all of these sentences. Correct them.

1. I ride often my bicycle.   2. I go every week to the gym.
3. Have you ever done a long journey by boat?   4. I didn't know that Manchester was so big city.
5. That's the man which told me.   6. There was a delay on the train which made me late.
7. Who's going to pay the tickets?   8. Do you belong for any clubs?

IELTS Target 5.0   95

Students should complete the task individually, using forms of the words in the box. For feedback, either you or students should write the answers on the board.

Answers: 1. economical 2. insurance 3. expansion 4. yearly 5. reaction 6. development

Errors

A and B Students now know that each unit ends with an error-correction task. Here, there is an additional spelling focus. Remind them that it is very useful to notice and correct common errors. Tell them that one mistake is in punctuation. They can either complete the task individually or in pairs. Write the correct sentences on the board to clarify corrections.

Answers:

A 1. occasionally   2. usually   3. journey
4. queue   5. passengers   6. engine

B 1. I often ride my bicycle.
2. I go to the gym every week.
3. Have you ever made a long journey by boat?
4. I didn't know that Manchester was such a big city.
5. That's the man who told me.
6. There was a delay on the train, which made me late.
7. Who's going to pay for the tickets?
8. Do you belong to any clubs?

Speaking

A The aim here is to revise the different ways of talking about frequency presented the first module. Give students some examples for the first sentence – 'brush my teeth', 'have a shower', for example. Give them ten minutes to complete the task. Monitor to check grammatical and spelling mistakes. Give pairs five minutes to compare. Monitor to give feedback.

B and C By now, students know how to work through this type of task. Read through the rubric with them, and then allow them time to practise. Monitor to check that students are saying the right kind of thing, and generally improving with this type of task.

Vocabulary

A Students are now familiar with this type of task. It revises vocabulary learnt in the unit, emphasizes the need to learn the different forms of common words and checks spelling.

Exam Practice

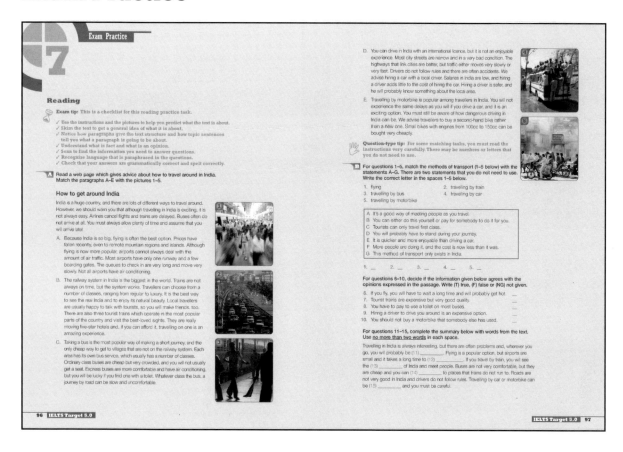

Reading

The aim of the exam tip is to revise the reading skills and exam techniques that students have focused on up until now. Either read the list of skills with students, checking each as you go, or give them five minutes to read through individually. Encourage them to go back at the end of the lesson and check they have used each skill to help them accomplish the task.

Students should be more independent with the exam practice, but the text is a little longer than they have read so far, and there are three separate tasks, one of which they have not practised yet. The picture-matching task should prepare them and give them confidence, though it is not a task they will see in the exam.

A   Read the first part of the introductory line, and ask students if any of them have been to India. If anyone has, ask the student to quickly tell the class what he or she most remembers. Tell students to look at the pictures, and then ask the student(s) who have been to India how they travelled around, and if that was memorable. If nobody has been there, tell them to look at the pictures and say what they see about India.

Tell students to skim the text to complete the matching task. Students must match each paragraph with the pictures labelled 1–5. Set a time limit of about three minutes. Give the answers before going on to the exam practice.

Answers: A. picture 1   B. picture 3
C. picture 4   D. picture 2   E. picture 5

B   The question-type tip above Exercise B introduces the task. Read it with students, and give them a minute or so to look at the first task.

Students should be ready to work through the exam practice tasks. Set a time limit of about 20 minutes. Remind them to follow the points revised in the skills checklist on page 96.

Write the answers on the board so that they are clear. It would be a good idea to give students the lines that provide the answers to some questions.

Answers:

1. F (... flying is now more popular / Prices have fallen recently, ...)

2. A (Local travellers are usually happy to talk with tourists, so you will make friends, too.)
3. D (and you will not usually get a seat.)
4. B (whole paragraph provides the answer)
5. E (... not experience the same delays as you will if you drive a car, and it is an exciting option.)
6. T (... queues to check in are very long and move very slowly. Not all airports have air conditioning.)
7. T (... are really moving five-star hotels and, if you can afford it, ...)
8. NG
9. F (hiring a driver adds little to the cost of hiring the car.)
10. F (We advise travellers to buy a second-hand bike)
11. late   12. check in   13. (natural) beauty
14. get   15. dangerous

Unit 7 Workbook answers

Speaking and Vocabulary

A flying: runway / take off / land / check in
driving: motorway /driving licence / road tax / parking
travelling by train: station / railway / carriage / platform

B Students' own answers.

Listening

A

> **Tapescript** 🎧 **80** (1 min, 47 secs)
>
> **A** **Listen and match each extract to a situation below. Write the number of the extract in the space.**
>
> **1**
> **Voice:** The next train from platform 6 will be the seven twenty-five to Worthing. Change at Gatwick Airport for connections to Littlehampton and Bognor.
>
> **2**
> **Woman:** We had a fantastic time. The cabin was lovely, and all the other passengers were really friendly. We sat at the captain's table for dinner one evening. David got a bit seasick at first, but he was OK after a few days.
>
> **3**
> **Man 1:** You look a bit red in the face.
> **Man 2:** Yeah – I've just cycled in. It's not the easiest journey – that hill coming up by the station is a killer!
> **Man 1:** Did you cycle it? Most people get off and walk there.
> **Man 2:** No, not me.
>
> **4**
> **Pilot:** Good morning, ladies and gentlemen. I'm your pilot today, and I'd like to welcome you aboard this British

> Airways flight to Copenhagen. I'm sorry that take-off is a little later than planned, but weather ... *(fade out)*
>
> **5**
> **Man:** Oh, no – I think I've gone past the junction we needed. Blast.
> **Woman:** Don't worry. I'm sure it's not far to a place where we can turn round and go back.
> **Man:** I'm not so sure – I bet there's not another junction for miles.

Answers: riding a bike, 3   flying, 4   driving, 5   travelling by train, 1   travelling by ship, 2

Reading

A reading task

B 1. F   2. O   3. F   4. F   5. O   6. O

Writing

A The writing task is dealt with in the main section of the Teacher's Book.

8 Time

Unit overview

The eighth unit is based around the theme of time. Students will talk about how they spend time, and focus on related abstract concepts, like history and time travel. They will learn how to complete tables, and there is a further focus on summary completion.

Speaking and Vocabulary

Objectives

- To give students further practice answering the type of questions they can expect in the first part of the speaking exam, and the follow-up questions that the examiner might ask.

- To present and practise different ways of talking about using time and the passing of time.

- To practise listening carefully to the examiner's questions, and making sure that the questions are answered.

Speaking 1

A The aim of the first speaking task is to get students thinking about how people see time, as well as prepare them for what follows in the module. This can be conducted as pairwork as suggested, or as a whole-class discussion.

The first stage can be quite brief, as the vocabulary task develops the theme, and presents expressions that students can use. There is no need to ask for feedback if you elect to put them into pairs.

Vocabulary 1

A Students can either check all the words and phrases individually, and then use them to talk, or check them as they talk. They should use dictionaries if possible, as it will be difficult for you to pre-teach without doing the task yourself. Give feedback by telling them to cover this task, and look at the pictures again. Ask them which expressions they remember for each picture.

Answers: The businessman is short of time / is always in a hurry / doesn't want to waste time.

The old people have plenty of time / like to take time to do things.

Vocabulary 2

The aim of this activity is to learn a range of typical ways to talk about how time is spent, and the duration of time. The focus is on fixed expressions, and collocation is important.

A Before students look at the task, write 'time' in the middle of the board, and circle it. Draw a line from the circle, and write 'spend'. Then spend two minutes brainstorming the verbs that collocate with time. Write any appropriate suggestions on the board. Students should then complete the task individually. They can read the sentences out to check answers. Point out the third-person verb form in 6.

Answers: 1. have   2. take   3. spend
4. waste   5. pass   6. saves

B Do the first one as an example, and allow students to work individually. Go through answers before moving on to consolidation, Exercise C.

Answers: 1. d   2. a   3. b   4. c   5. e

C You could put students into pairs and tell them to cover Exercise B. You might think that would be too challenging, and that they need the context to check the phrases. Make sure they write the phrases and not just the letters, as it will help them retain the language much better.

Answers:
1. a long time ago / ages ago
2. for a long time / for ages
3. at first / to begin with
4. immediately / straightaway
5. in the future / from now on

Grammar check

Read the first point with students. Ask them to translate the two meanings of 'time' into their own language. The words will probably be quite different. Read through the second point, and then look at the Watch out! box with them. Give them a minute to correct the errors.

Answers:
1. How many times have you met him?
   How long have you been here?

Pronunciation check

Tell students to read the pronunciation check box. Read the rubric with them, and then play the two examples on the recording. Play the three new examples, and allow a minute or two for students to practise saying the phrases to a partner.

Tapescript 🎧 81 (0 mins, 59 secs)

Pronunciation check

When one word ends in a sound that is similar to the sound at the beginning of the following word, the two sounds merge together. Listen to these examples from the unit.

1   waste time

2   spend time

Now listen to these new examples.

1 take care

2 big gun

3 time machine

Practise saying all the phrases.

Speaking 2

A The first task consolidates the point made in the grammar check. Give students a moment to read the questions before they answer with a partner. Encourage them to use full sentences so that they practise the time structures ('It takes me half an hour', rather than just 'half an hour'). Tell students to close the book, and then ask you the questions. Only answer if the question is properly formed.

B This task both consolidates and provides some typical speaking exam practice. Give students five minutes for this activity, and monitor to check that they are speaking fluently and accurately, as well as giving appropriate answers to the questions.

Speaking 3

The aim of this part is to emphasize the importance of listening to the examiner's questions, as well as answering appropriately.

A Read the rubric with students. Then give them a minute or two to read through the questions. Make sure they know they don't have to answer yet. Ask them which they think are difficult to answer and why.

Read the exam tip with students. Tell them to cover it, and then ask one student to tell you what the advice was.

B 🎧 Students will not understand everything the student on the recording says, but they should grasp enough to say whether the question is or isn't answered. Play the recording, pausing briefly after each speaker. Play the recording again if necessary. Go through the answers before students read the tapescript.

Tapescript 🎧 82 (1 min, 56 secs)

B **Listen to some students answering the questions in Exercise A. Mark each sentence (Y) if the student answers the question and (N) if the student doesn't.**

1
Examiner: Does modern technology really save us time, or is it just one more thing to worry about?

Student: Mm, I think both. Of course, washing machines and microwaves save people a huge amount of time. The trouble is, we then spend a lot of that time worrying about why our computer isn't working!

2
Examiner: Does modern technology mean that some people have *too much* free time?

Student: Of course, modern technology makes us too much free time. People can listen the music, watch some DVDs and play on computer games. Lot of free time activities is done with technology.

3
Examiner: Do people spend too long thinking about the future instead of enjoying now?

Student: The most important is think about your future. If you want have good job and have family, you need think about future and make plans about it.

4
Examiner: What is more important – time or money?

Student: I think time is more important, and too many people spend all time trying to make money, and then have no time for enjoy it. However, if you have a lot of time, it is difficult to enjoy it properly if you haven't money.

Answers: 1. Y 2. N 3. N 4. Y

C   🎧 Read the rubric with students. It is very important that they understand their priority is to answer the question, and say something valid, rather than worry about accuracy. Play the recording again as they read the tapescript.

Tapescript 🎧 **83** (0 mins, 15 secs)

C   **Listen again as you read the tapescript. Notice that answers do not have to be grammatically perfect to be good answers.**

[Play track 82 again]

D   Talking to different students will be more motivating than talking to the same person again. Encourage students to give their own answers, and not copy the answers they have heard.

For further speaking and vocabulary practice, tell students to complete the exercises on page 22 of the Workbook. Set as an extra activity or homework task.

Listening

Objectives

- To introduce the task of table completion.
- To emphasize the importance of prediction, and show students how to aid prediction by looking at a table.
- To revise and give further practice at listening for specific information, and spelling answers correctly.

Sometimes the Listening Modules practise a particular listening skill, like listening for gist or recognizing key vocabulary. As the course progresses, the focus will be more on particular task types, and helping students to approach that type of task. Here, the focus is on completing tables, which also revises listening for specific words and phrases.

Listening 1

A The aim of this speaking task is to provide some speaking practice, as well as to prepare and motivate students for the listening tasks that follow. Give students a couple of minutes to look at the pictures, and then ask the whole class the question. Once the topic of the talk has been established, students can describe each picture separately in pairs. Ask them to tell you something about each picture, and take the opportunity to elicit or pre-teach key words and phrases, like 'cave painting'.

Answers: The talk will be about recording events, and how the recording of history has changed.

Read the question-type tip with students. Point out that the task is really no different from sentence or note completion. Tell them that this task type usually occurs in the second or fourth parts of the listening exam.

B Tell students to look at the table, and then to cover the exam tip (this exam tip answers the questions in the task). Give them two minutes to discuss the first two questions. Then tell them to read the exam tip, and compare it with what they said. Now give them two more minutes to match parts of the table with the pictures in Exercise A.

Answers: The second and fourth squares of the table relate to two of the pictures.

c 🎧 The best way to approach this would be to listen to the whole recording once with pens down, and then listen again and complete the table. You should play the whole recording, as by now students should be coping, but pause if you feel it will make the task more manageable for your class.

Tapescript 🎧 84 (3 mins, 37 secs)

C **Listen to the first part of the talk and complete the table. Write <u>no more than two words or a number</u> for each answer.**

Voice: Good morning, again. I realize a few of you aren't here yet, but I'll make a start anyway. I'm going to talk this morning about an important aspect of history, and that is how history is recorded and how the way we record history has changed over the centuries. I'll talk about how the storytelling of primitive man has developed into the modern methods of communication that we have today. I've got some images that I'll show you as I talk, so just let me turn on the power point.

OK, now – man has been on Earth for something like two hundred thousand years, and we don't really know when man first used language to communicate. But we do know that as soon as man did have language, he used it to tell stories. Now, these stories were the first example of man recording his history. The stories were passed on from one generation to the next, and children would have known something about the people that came before them. One problem, of course, with a spoken history is that it's unreliable. The storyteller forgets facts and adds elements to the story that might not have been true.

The earliest attempts to record day-to-day life in anything other than spoken language were around 32 thousand years ago. That is when we believe the first cave paintings were made. Now, it might be that cave paintings were not an attempt to record history at all – the most common images in cave paintings are large wild animals, so perhaps man made them to bring him luck when he was hunting. They might have simply decorated his living space. Whatever they were for, they certainly are a record, and they tell us a great deal about how people so long ago lived their lives.

Many people believe that history really began when man learnt to write down information, and for that reason we say that what came before man could write is 'prehistoric'. However, you should remember that we have learnt a great deal from people in many parts of the world who could not write. The first people to record experience in written form were the Egyptians. Around 5,000 years ago – that's 3,000 BC – the Egyptians used hieroglyphics – a system of symbols and sounds – to record beliefs and events on the walls of their temples and on their monuments. Who knows if this was an attempt to leave something for future generations to understand?

The word 'history' comes from Greek, and it is the people of ancient Greece who, in around 500 BC, really began the long tradition of writing down everything that happened for future generations to read. In ancient Greece lived the first historians – the first people whose job was to record history.

D Give students time to compare before giving the answers. Ask them if they think the table format helped. Write the correct answers on the board as students give them to you.

Answers: 1. facts   2. paintings
3. (wild) animals   4. 3,000   5. of temples
6. 500   7. future   8. historians

Listening 2

The aim of this activity is to provide listening practice with a table completion. Note that the table task is a little longer than a similar task will be in the exam. This is in order to fully practise the techniques that have been the focus of the unit. The theme of recording history continues, and students should be left alone to complete the task.

A 🎧 Play the whole recording. Students might find it difficult to listen only once, but avoid playing it a second time. Students can discuss what difficulties they had, and then listen again later if necessary (see Exercises B and C).

Tapescript 🎧 85 (3 mins, 12 secs)

A Listen to the second part of the talk and answer the questions. For questions 1–12, complete the table. Write <u>no more than two words or a number</u> for each answer.

Voice: The next important development in how history is recorded came with print. In the eighth century, the Chinese invented paper and woodblock printing. Remember that up to this time very few people could read and write, and so only a very small number of people could understand written history. Suddenly, many books appeared, and many more people learnt to read.

In the fourteenth century, the first printing press was invented in Germany. This reduced how long it took to produce books. The new printing technique quickly spread to other parts of the world, more books appeared and even more people learnt to read. The first printed newspaper appeared in 1605 and the first daily newspaper in 1702. Now, people could read news stories soon after the event happened and every event was recorded and stored.

The problem with newspaper history is that newspaper reporters could tell the stories they wanted to tell and not necessarily the truth.

Photography was the next important development. We generally agree that

photography was born in 1839. Some of the earliest photographs that the public saw were images of the American Civil War. People were shocked by the photographs of dead soldiers, and for the first time saw the reality of war. By 1850, photographs appeared regularly in newspapers, and people now expected the truth. At the end of the nineteenth century came the first motion-picture camera. Soon, history was being recorded as moving images. In the 1930s, television brought moving images into people's homes. More and more people saw history as it happened, and more and more history was recorded.

Today, of course, we expect that every event in the world is recorded. Satellite TV and the Internet allow people to watch any event, anywhere in the world as it happens. It doesn't matter if the TV cameras are not there – people carry around mobile phones and can record any incident, and then share it online. Families have their own video cameras and record their own history. Children now grow up watching their parents and grandparents on film.

I'm sure you'll agree that the transition from storytelling to what we have today has been dramatic, and I hope that … *(fade out)*

B Give students sufficient time to check answers and think about why they may have answered incorrectly, before moving on to Exercise C.

Answers: 1. printing   2. to read
3. 14th / fourteenth   4. Books
5. (printed) newspaper   6. Photography
7. truth   8. moving   9. homes
10. Satellite   11. incident   12. their own

Note that students probably won't be penalized for not using capital letters at the beginning of a sentence in a note completion task.

C Students will by now be familiar with this type of reflective process, but note the questions here are more specific to table completion. Remind them that identifying what they are doing well and not doing so well is a very good way of focusing on what they can do better next time. Allow students time to reflect and complete the task. You might like to get some feedback from students to see what they have learnt from the practice.

Now would be a good time to reinforce the need for correct spelling of answers. Ask them if they are happy with the number of correct answers. Allow students to listen again and tell them to focus on why the correct answers are correct.

Key vocabulary in context

This activity focuses on some useful words from the listening task. Students can work individually. When they have finished, tell them to close their books, and then give them the definitions as they try to remember the words.

Answers: 1. a hundred   2. at the same time
3. done for a long time   4. study the past

Pronunciation check

Model 'century' a couple of times, and ask students to repeat. Play the recording, and then allow a minute or two for students to practise saying the phrases with a partner.

Tapescript 🎧 86 (0 mins, 38 secs)

Pronunciation check

Century is pronounced /'sentʃəri/. Listen to these phrases and then practise saying them.

1   eighteenth century

2   nineteenth century

3   twentieth century

For further listening practice, tell students to complete the exercise on page 22 of the Workbook. Set as an extra activity or homework task.

Reading

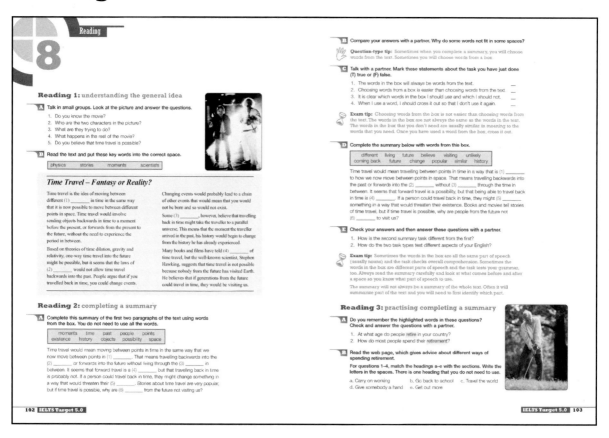

Objectives

- To introduce students to the task of completing a summary using words provided in a list.

- To help students understand the skills involved in completing a summary with words that are not from the text.

- To revise and further practise the skills required in the IELTS Reading Module.

Reading 1

The aim of the first two tasks is to provide an opportunity for some speaking practice, as well as to prepare students for the reading tasks that follow.

A The aim of this activity is to make the topic more appealing to students by focusing on a light-hearted story that they should be able to relate to. You might like to answer the first question together as a class, so that you have an idea how many students know the movie. Put students who have seen the film with those who haven't, so that they can answer the questions.

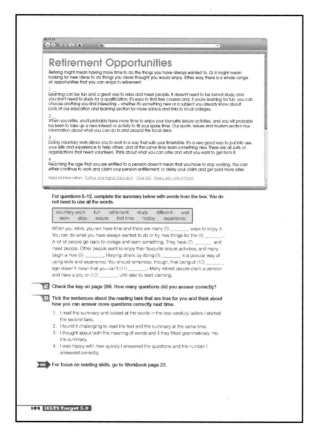

Give pairs or groups five minutes to answer the rest of the questions. Get answers from them, and find out who likes the movie and who doesn't. You can decide how long to spend discussing the final question, but make sure that any debate is beneficial. Note that getting a good answer to question 4 will make the concept in the text easier to manage.

Answers:
1. *Back to the Future*
2. Marty McFly and Doc Brown
3. travel back in time
4. They travel back in time, but then make things happen that will change the future from that point on (particularly the marriage of Marty's mother and father). They cannot travel back to the present because they realize that Marty would not have been born.
5. Students' own answers.

B This task aims to revise the importance of skimming (or at least reading fairly quickly for general meaning) before reading for detail. Note the words are all plural nouns, so only meaning is a factor. Students should work individually, and then compare with a partner. Set a time limit of about three minutes.

Answers: 1. moments   2. Physics
3. scientists   4. stories

Reading 2

A Read the rubric with students. They haven't seen this task type before, so make sure they understand what they have to do, and that the summary is of the first two paragraphs only. Ask them how many gaps they need to fill, and how many words are in the box. Leave the question-type tip until after they have attempted the task, as it introduces the task analysis in Exercise C. Tell students they can either read the summary and then look at the words in the box, or look at the words in the box first (there isn't really a right way of doing this task). Remind students that they will write their answers onto an answer sheet in the exam, rather than fill the gaps in the summary itself. End the task when about half the class have completed it, before moving on to Exercise B.

B Comparing answers is beneficial here because students can discuss why some answers don't fit. Some, for example, may have used 'time' to fill the first gap, which is wrong because we don't yet travel in time. Use this as an example of how you want them to compare answers, and then give them a few minutes to do so. Then provide the answers written on the board.

Answers: 1. space   2. past   3. time
4. possibility   5. existence   6. people

Now read through the question-type tip with students to set up Exercise C.

C Students are familiar with this type of task analysis now, and will know that the exam tip that follows usually answers the questions. Tell them to cover the exam tip, and give them three or four minutes to discuss the points. You can check their answers before reading the exam tip, if you like.

Allow them to read through the exam tip, and then tell them to cover it. Go back over the correct answers to the task. Emphasize that the distracters in the box are always chosen carefully to look like possible answers.

Answers: 1. F   2. F   3. F   4. T

D The summary that students now work on is more or less the same as in Exercise A, but with different words gapped. For that reason, you must tell them to cover the tasks they have already completed so that they cannot refer back to them. Work through the task as with the previous one, and stop when about half the class have completed it. Go through the answers before moving on to Exercise E.

Answers: 1. similar   2. future   3. living
4. unlikely   5. change   6. coming back

E As Exercise C.

Read this exam tip carefully with students. Ask them which of the two summaries was more challenging.

Reading 3

As students have not yet practised this type of gap-fill task, there is a little preparation. Once you have worked through this part, students should be left to cope with the exam practice tasks with minimal assistance.

A This is an opportunity to revise language learnt earlier in the course. Making sure that students understand the key highlighted words will make the text far more manageable. Give them three or four minutes to discuss the questions. Briefly get some feedback from the class, and then work through the exam practice.

B Read the introductory line with students, and set them a minute to read through the questions. Then set a time limit of about 15 minutes to complete the tasks.

C Give students sufficient time to check and think about why they may have answered incorrectly, before moving on to Exercise D.

Answers: 1. b   2. e   3. d   4. a
5. different   6. first time   7. fun
8. hobby   9. voluntary work   10. retirement
11. work   12. wait

D By now, students will be familiar with this type of reflective process, but note the questions are not the same as in previous units. Remind them that identifying what they are doing well and not doing so well is a very good way of focusing on what they can do better next time. Allow students time to reflect and complete the task, and then ask them if they are happy with the number of correct answers. You may like to ask one student what he or she will do differently next time.

The Workbook task for this unit provides practice looking at the parts of speech that are required to fill gaps in a summary. Now would be a good time to work through it or set it up as a homework task.

Writing

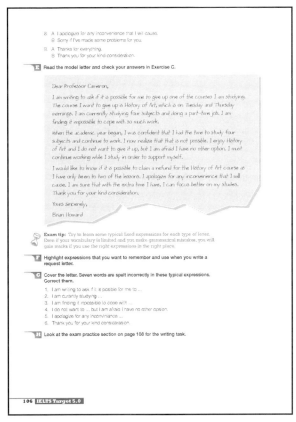

Objectives

- To practise writing a letter of request.
- To help students identify appropriate and inappropriate register.
- To present and practise some typical fixed expressions used in letter writing.

Writing 1

A The aim of this activity is to prepare students for the writing task, as well as provide some typical spoken exam practice. Give students five minutes to discuss the questions, and then work through them quickly with the whole class.

B The best way to conduct this would be to have an OHP transparency on the board, so that students can come and highlight the key points in the instructions. If that isn't possible, ask students what they consider to be the key points once they have had a minute or two to read through, and write them on the board.

C Students can discuss all the points with a partner, or you can answer questions 1–3 as a class and then look at 4 together in pairs for a little longer. Make sure students cover Exercise D before they start. To give feedback, find out how many students now feel that this task is relatively easy, establish that the letter should be formal, and get one of them to come up and write the opening line on the board. You don't need to provide a correct opening line, as students will see that in the model letter shortly.

D The aim of this activity is to present the typical formal expressions that make up a letter of this type. Although the formal language looks quite challenging, students should find it easy to identify which option is more appropriate. Give them the time they need to work individually, and then a couple of minutes to compare with a partner. The model letter provides answers, so there is no need for feedback.

E Make sure students know they are reading in order to check their answers to Exercise D.

Dear Professor Cameron,

I am writing to ask if it is possible for me to give up one of the courses I am studying. The course I want to give up is History of Art, which is on Tuesday and Thursday mornings. I am currently studying four subjects and doing a part-time job. I am finding it impossible to cope with so much work.

When the academic year began, I was confident that I had the time to study four subjects and continue to work. I now realize that that is not possible. I enjoy History of Art and I do not want to give it up, but I am afraid I have no other option. I must continue working while I study in order to support myself.

I would like to know if it is possible to claim a refund for the History of Art course as I have only been to two of the lessons. I apologize for any inconvenience that I will cause. I am sure that with the extra time I have, I can focus better on my studies. Thank you for your kind consideration.

Yours sincerely,
Brian Howard

The exam tip introduces the task that follows. Read it through with students, and then give them a few minutes to highlight what they want to. Monitor as they work, so that you know they are identifying the right kind of expressions.

F See above.

G Students should work individually, and then compare with a partner. They can look back at the model to check correct spelling.

H In this unit, the writing task can be found in the exam practice section, at the end of the Course Book unit. See instructions for that section on page 167 of this book.

Consolidation

Speaking

A The aim of this activity is to revise the various time expressions from the unit. Set a time limit of about ten minutes, as students may need to take some time to do this task. Monitor, and correct errors, so that the sentences students have are as accurate as possible by the time they compare with a partner.

Read the grammar check box with students.

B Refer students back to the relevant task. Make sure they know that they don't need to answer the questions again now.

C 🎧 Read the rubric with students, and play the whole recording. See if anyone can tell you one of the phrases used, or explain that one student repeated the question.

Tapescript 🎧 **87** (1 min, 23 secs)

C **Listen to some students answering the questions. How do they give themselves time to think?**

1

Examiner: Does modern technology really save us time, or is it just one more thing to worry about?

Student: Mm, that's a very good question. I think it's a bit of both. Of course, ... *(fade out)*

2

Examiner: Does modern technology mean that some people have *too much* free time?

Student: Too much free time? Of course, modern technology ... *(fade out)*

3

Examiner: Do people spend too long thinking about the future instead of enjoying now?

Student: Mm, I haven't really thought about it before. I guess the most important is ... *(fade out)*

4

Examiner: What is more important – time or money?

Student: Oh, I don't know if I can answer that in only a minute. It's a very big question. It depends ... *(fade out)*

D 🎧 Give students a moment to read the sentences, and then play the recording again, pausing after each speaker to allow time to write. You might need to play each extract a couple of times. Students can check in the tapescript, or you can write answers on the board. Point out the rising intonation when the student repeats the examiner's question.

Tapescript 🎧 **88** (0 mins, 12 secs)

D **Listen again and fill the gaps below.**

[Play track 87 again]

Answers:

1. a very good
2. Too much free time
3. thought about it
4. I can answer / a very big

Read the exam tip with students.

E Write a couple more examples of 'difficult-to-answer' questions on the board, and then tell students to work individually to write a couple more of their own. Give them five or six minutes to practise, and encourage them to think of some more questions spontaneously as they talk.

Vocabulary

A You can set this up as a competition if you like. Students can work in pairs to see which team can finish first. Tell them not to look back to the unit for answers. Write the answers on the board to give feedback.

Answers: 1. truth   2. inconvenience
3. exists   4. century   5. cope   6. unlikely
7. generation   8. tradition

Errors

A Students know that each unit ends with an error-correction task. Tell them there are no errors of spelling. They can either complete the task individually or in pairs. Write the correct sentences on the board for clarity.

Answers:

1. How long have you been in Europe?
2. How long will you stay in Paris?
3. How long have you known your best friend?
4. It's not good to waste time.
5. In the future, I hope to study in the USA.
6. At first, I didn't like Tony, but now I think he's really nice.
7. I spend a lot of my free time playing golf.
8. I spent two weeks in Greece last year.

Exam Practice

Exam Practice

8

Writing

A Look carefully at the instructions for this writing task. Highlight the key words and make sure you understand what you have to do.

You are currently studying on a full-time course at a university. Something has happened and you need to take two weeks off.

Write a letter to the principal of the university requesting the time off and explaining why you need it.

Write at least 150 words.

Exam tip: Sometimes you will need to invent some of the information that you write in your letter – what course you are studying, when you need to take time off and why you need to take time off, for example.

B Look at these pictures and answer the questions with a partner.
1. Why does the student want to take time off from his studies in each case?
2. Do you think they are all good reasons for taking time off from a course you are studying?

C Answer these questions with a partner. You will need to invent answers.
1. What course are you studying?
2. When do you need the time off?
3. What has happened? Why do you need the time off?
4. Are you going to apologize?
5. Are you going to request that your lecturers tell you in advance what they will do in the lectures that you miss?
6. Are you going to request that your lecturers give copies of any materials to one of your classmates?
7. How are you going to close your letter?

D Write the letter. For now, you should take 30–40 minutes to write your letter, but remember that in the exam that will mean less time for the more difficult second composition.

108 IELTS Target 5.0

IELTS Target 5.0 109

Writing

A Students should be more confident about writing letters by now, but will still need preparation. Read through the instructions, and ask how many students feel they can manage the task fairly easily this time.

Read the first line of the exam tip with students, and ask them what sort of information they will need to invent. Then read through the rest of the tip.

B The aim of this part is to give students ideas for the content of their letter, but also to provide some speaking practice. Tell students to look at the pictures and questions, and to plan what they want to say before speaking with a partner. Encourage them to tell you why they think the reasons are acceptable or unacceptable. Get some feedback from the class, before moving on to Exercise C.

C The aim of this activity is for students to use the questions to plan quite carefully what they want to say in their letter. Give them five or six minutes to answer the questions. You can discuss their answers with them, or monitor as they talk.

D Go over the point about timing the first and second writing task again with students.

Monitor as students work, but check specifically that they are organizing their letters, making relevant points and using appropriate register. There should be a little more accuracy now.

If you collect students' letters to mark, you should still be using the process to get an idea of what they are capable of, and to give constructive feedback, though you should correct mistakes that are not appropriate at this level.

Tell students to look at the model composition on page 269 of the Course Book. Make sure they understand that, as with all the model compositions, they are not expected to produce something of this standard.

The model letter is reproduced on the following page.

Dear Sir,

I am writing to request some time off from my studies from next week until the end of the month. I am studying American History, and I am enjoying the course very much. However, my father is ill in hospital and I want to spend some time with him. I also want to help my mother, who is finding it very difficult to cope alone.

I will ask my lecturer, Professor Watkins, to tell me in advance what the class will study while I am away, and I will ask one of my classmates to scan and e-mail the notes he takes during the lectures I miss. I will do everything possible to keep up with my studies.

I hope you understand the decision I have made. I would like to apologize and hope my request will not cause too much inconvenience. Thank you for your kind consideration.

Yours sincerely,

Martin Wood

Unit 8 Workbook answers

Speaking and Vocabulary

A 1. of   2. in   3. in   4. on   5. of   6. at
7. for   8. with

B Students' own answers.

Listening

A 1. B   2. F   3. A   4. D

Tapescript 🎧 **89** (1 min, 55 secs)

A **Listen and match each extract to one of the speakers A–F. There are two speakers that you do not hear. Write the letters into the spaces 1–4.**

Extract 1
Voice: I never have enough time. When I arrive at my office, there are four or five important e-mails that need to be answered, and usually a phone message or two as well. I have one or two meetings every day, and I have to travel to them. I really wish there were more hours in a day.

Extract 2
Voice: People think we have lots of free time and only have one or two lectures a week, but actually I'm always really busy. I am doing three courses, and I have a part-time job, too. I don't want my parents to have to support me.

Extract 3
Voice: There are parts of the day when I'm very, very busy, and other parts when I can relax for a while. I'm always in a hurry in the morning, getting breakfast ready, and then taking the children to school. In the afternoon, when I've tidied up and done the shopping, I take my time to read a magazine or watch some TV.

Extract 4
Voice: As everyone knows, the kitchen can be very hectic. Orders are coming in all the time, and the waiters and waitresses are hurrying in and out. I feel that I'm always short of time, but that is the challenge and I enjoy it.

Reading

A and B Looking back, the summary in the course might be too challenging, as the summary here is worded differently. Provide the answers if necessary.

Answers: 1. D   2. E   3. B   4. C   5. A
(Probable words – 1. putting   2. flexibly
3. enjoy   4. new   5. volunteers)

Writing

A I am writing for to ask if it is possible for me to give up one of the courses I am studying. The course I want to give up is the History of Art, which it is on Tuesday and Thursday mornings. I am currently studying four subjects and doing a part-time job. I am finding it too impossible to cope with so much work.

When the academic year was began, I was confident that I had the time to study four subjects and continue to work. I now realize that that is not possible. I enjoy History of Art and do not wish to give it up, but I am afraid I have no other option. I must to continue working while I study in order to support myself.

Money

Unit overview

The ninth unit is based around the theme of money. Students will talk about having and not having money, and about shopping. There is a focus on understanding unknown words and phrases in context, and on reference words in texts. Students will get further practice with various aspects of the IELTS exam.

Speaking and Vocabulary

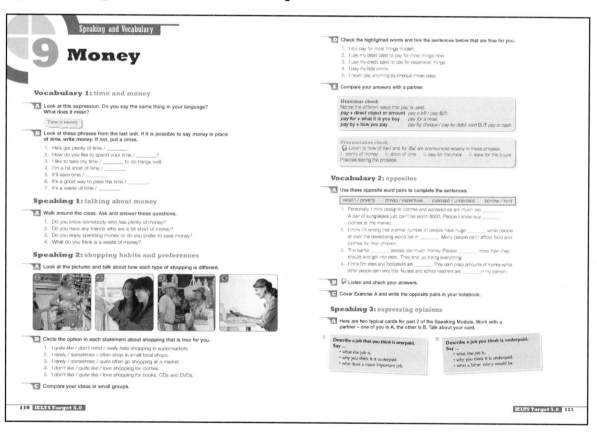

Objectives

- To give students further practice answering the type of questions they can expect in the second part of the speaking exam.

- To further practise expressing opinions and preferences.

- To present and practise vocabulary connected with money, and to learn how the same phrases are used when talking about time and money.

Vocabulary 1

The aim of this activity is to revise some of the expressions from the last unit, as well as show students how many of the same phrases can be used to talk about money.

A   Ask the question to the class. The response you get will depend largely on whether students are all from the same country or from various parts of the world. Try to agree that the expression is used a lot in business, and means that if you waste time you will not make any money.

B Students should work in pairs so that they can discuss each phrase as they work through the task. You could tell students that five of the phrases can be used with money. It would be a good idea to write the five correct phrases on the board for consolidation.

Answers: 3 and 6 are not possible and should be crossed.

Speaking 1

A Students can work with a partner, but it may be more productive to talk with a variety of people and listen to different views. Give them five or six minutes to ask each question to at least two classmates.

Speaking 2

A Students will not talk about pictures in the exam, but the pictures in this task can motivate students to start thinking about preferences when shopping. Give students five minutes to talk in pairs, and then discuss the topic together as a class. Teach the difference between 'go shopping' (generally for enjoyment), and 'do the shopping' (generally an obligation). Ask students which of the situations they can relate to, and whether they shop a lot online nowadays.

B This task revises frequency adverbs, as well as presenting some ways of expressing preference. Tell students to check with you any phrases they don't know as they work through the task individually. Make sure they understand that 'don't mind' is used to talk about something that is considered all right, but not something that is usually popular.

C Students work in small groups and use the sentences as prompts to develop discussion

about their shopping preferences. Monitor to check how well students are doing, rather than go through feedback that will ultimately mean saying the same things again.

D The theme of discussing habit and preference continues, but students also learn some key vocabulary. Read through the sentences with students, while they tick or don't tick them. Explain or give examples when they don't understand something.

E Give students five minutes to discuss their answers in pairs, or in the same small groups they were in for Exercise C.

Grammar check

Read the points with students, or give them time to read through by themselves.

Pronunciation check

Tell students to read the pronunciation check box. Then play the recording. Allow a minute or two for students to practise saying the phrases to a partner.

Tapescript 🎧 **90** (0 mins, 47 secs)

Pronunciation check

Listen to how *of* and *for* are pronounced weakly in these phrases.

1 plenty of money

2 short of time

3 pay for the meal

4 save for the future

Practise saying the phrases.

Vocabulary 2

A There is quite a lot of new vocabulary here, and some of it is fairly challenging. Note that there are new items in the sentences, as well as the word pairs in the box. Go through the word pairs with students first, eliciting and giving definitions or examples. Tell students to try to understand the items in the sentences from the context as they read. Go over the sentences to check the answers.

Answers:

1. expensive / cheap
2. wealth / poverty
3. lend / borrow
4. overpaid / underpaid

B 🎧 Give students a couple of minutes to do this, and tell them to look back at the Course Book to check.

Tapescript 🎧 91 (1 min, 12 secs)

B **Listen and check your answers.**

1

Personally, I think designer clothes and accessories are much too <u>expensive</u>. A pair of sunglasses just can't be worth $500. People I know buy <u>cheap</u> clothes at the market.

2

I think it's wrong that a small number of people have huge <u>wealth</u> while people all over the developing world live in <u>poverty</u>. Many people can't afford food and clothes for their children.

3

The banks <u>lend</u> people too much money. People <u>borrow</u> more than they should and get into debt. They end up losing everything.

4

I think film stars and footballers are <u>overpaid</u>. They earn crazy amounts of money while other people earn very little. Nurses and schoolteachers are <u>underpaid</u>, in my opinion.

For further speaking and vocabulary practice, tell students to complete the exercises on page 24 of the Workbook. Set as an extra activity or homework task.

Speaking 3

A By now, students know how to work through this type of task. Monitor to check that they are saying the right kind of thing, and generally improving with this type of task.

Listening

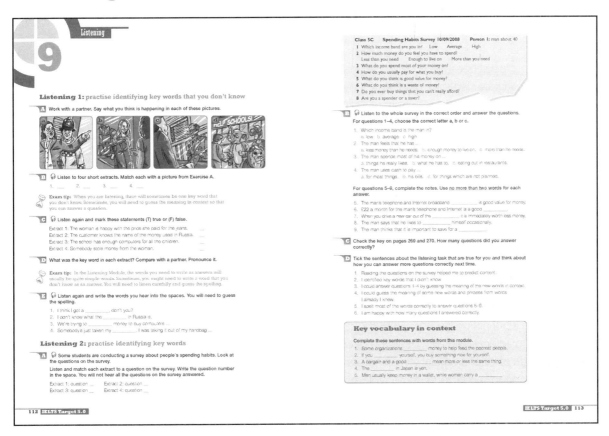

Objectives

- To help students deal with words and phrases they don't know.
- To help students guess the spelling of words they don't know, but need to use in answers.

Listening 1

A The aim of this speaking task is to prepare and motivate students for the listening tasks that follow, and repeat the importance of making predictions before listening. Give them a few minutes to talk in pairs, and then get a few ideas from the class. Don't give answers, as students will listen to check now.

B 🎧 Read through the instructions, and then play whole recording. Don't play the recording again, as it will be played more for the following tasks.

Tapescript 🎧 **92** (1 min, 55 secs)

B Listen to four short extracts. Match each with a picture from Exercise A.

Extract 1

Young adult 1: ... and look at these. Aren't they great?

Young adult 2: Oh, they're really lovely. They must have been really expensive.

Young adult 1: No, not at all. They were only £35 in Topshop – down from £70. I think I got a bargain, don't you?

Young adult 2: Definitely!

Extract 2

Man 1: Good afternoon.

Man 2: Oh, good afternoon. I'm going to Moscow tomorrow, and I want to change some money – say, about £200. To tell you the truth, I don't know what the currency in Russia is.

Man 1: In Russia, the currency is roubles, sir.

Man 2:	Roubles? OK, well, can I have £200 worth of roubles then, please?

Extract 3

Old man:	Hello, there. What are you collecting for?
Young man:	We're trying to raise money to buy computers for our school. St Mary's, do you know it?
Old man:	Yes, of course. Here you are.
Young man:	Thank you very much.
Old man:	I think it's great that you're trying to raise the money yourselves. Is it going well?
Young man:	Well, a lot of people are giving money, but we need to raise two thousand pounds.
Old man:	Well, good luck.

Extract 4

Woman:	Excuse me, officer.
Policeman:	Yes, madam, are you all right?
Woman:	No, not really. Somebody's just taken my purse. I was taking it out of my handbag to pay for something, and a young man just grabbed it and ran away. I don't know what …
Policeman:	Try to calm down, madam. Now, how long ago was this?
Woman:	Just a couple of minutes. I was … (fade out)

Answers: 1. B   2. C   3. D   4. A

Read the exam tip with students. Emphasize that by 'key' word we mean a word that the listener or reader must understand in order to comprehend a whole message or, in an exam sense, to answer a question.

C 🎧 Give students time to read the four sentences before playing the recording again. Tell them to concentrate on the true/false questions, but to think about the key word that provides the answer. Play each extract a couple of times if necessary. Go over the answers, but don't give them key words yet.

Tapescript 🎧 93 (0 mins, 14 secs)

C Listen again and mark these statements (T) true or (F) false.

[Play track 92 again]

Answers: 1. T   2. F   3. F   4. T

D Students should do this in pairs so that they don't tell everyone the answer if they already know the word. Give them a minute to compare, and try to spell the word they hear, but don't give any answers yet.

Tell students to read the exam tip, and then to cover it. Ask one student to tell you what the advice was.

E 🎧 Read the rubric with students, and then set them a minute or so to read the four sentences. Play the recording again, pausing after each speaker, so that they can attempt to write the key word. Write the answers on the board, or ask students to come up and do so.

Tapescript 🎧 94 (0 mins, 14 secs)

E Listen again and write the words you hear into the spaces. You will need to guess the spelling.

[Play track 92 again]

Answers: 1. bargain   2. currency   3. raise   4. purse

Listening 2

The aim of this activity is to provide listening practice, which will require students to decipher unknown key words and sometimes spell those words. The nature of the focus is quite challenging, so students are provided with a gist task to familiarize themselves with the recording, before attempting the exam practice.

A 🎧 Elicit or teach 'do a survey', and tell them that 'conduct' is a more formal way of saying 'do'. Read the introductory line with students, and check that they understand 'spending habits'.

Read the instructions for the first task with students, and make sure they know what to do. Give them a minute or so to look through the survey so that they know what they are listening for. Play the whole recording once only. Go over answers before moving on to the exam practice.

Tapescript 🎧 **95** (2 mins, 22 secs)

A Some students are conducting a survey about people's spending habits. Look at the questions on the survey. Listen and match each extract to a question on the survey. Write the question number in the space. You will not hear all the questions on the survey answered.

Extract 1

Male: I use my debit card for most things these days. I have two credit cards, but I don't like using them. I prefer to pay for things immediately, otherwise I feel I'm getting into debt. I pay my bills online or over the telephone. I usually have between ten and twenty pounds in cash with me to pay for emergencies – taxi fares and that kind of thing.

Extract 2

Male: Yes. I collect radios – old radios. I have nine now, and they're quite expensive. I paid £350 for a 1950s radio last month – I didn't have much money for the rest of the month after that! My wife thinks I'm crazy, but it's important to treat yourself occasionally – don't you think? My wife buys nice perfume and lots of clothes, and I have my radios.

Extract 3

Male: Personally, I don't understand why anyone buys a new car. They are so expensive, and as soon as you drive them out of the showroom, they're worth three thousand pounds less. Perhaps I'm just saying it because I can't afford a new car myself, but to me it seems so much more sensible to buy a good second-hand car for half the money.

Extract 4

Male: Well, most of it goes on monthly expenses. I've got a big mortgage on my house, and my children's school fees are very high. After I've paid for gas and electricity and water, and all the insurance on the house and my car, I don't have much left. I like taking my wife out to a nice restaurant once a month, but I don't very often buy clothes. Oh – and I collect radios – old radios.

Answers:

Extract 1: question 4   Extract 2: question 7
Extract 3: question 6   Extract 4: question 3

B 🎧 Now students should be ready to work through the rest of the practice. Give them a minute to look at the questions. Remind them that they will need to guess the spelling of some answers. Play the whole recording. Students might find it difficult to listen to the recording only once, but avoid playing it a second time. Students can discuss what difficulties they had, and then listen again later if necessary (see Exercises C and D).

Tapescript 🎧 **96** (4 mins, 33 secs)

B Listen to the whole survey in the correct order and answer the questions. For questions 1–4, choose the correct letter a, b or c.

Female student: Excuse me – good morning – we're students from St Anne's School, and we're doing a class survey. Have you got five minutes to answer a few questions?

Man: Um, I suppose so. What are the questions about?

Female student: About spending habits – people's attitudes to money and what they spend money on.

Man: Well, yes, OK. But only five minutes.

Female student: Thank you. OK, first of all – if you don't mind answering – what income band are you in?

Male student: You just need to say low, average or high.

Man: Oh, that's difficult to say – I don't know how much everyone else makes. I'm certainly not poor, but I'm not rich either – certainly not after I've paid all my bills.

Male student: Shall we say in the middle then?

Man: Yes, I think so.

Female student: And how much money do you feel you have to spend? You said that you have to pay a lot of bills.

Man: Yes, I feel that I don't have very much. I earn quite good money, but it doesn't feel like that most of the time. I guess everyone would like to have a bit more money, though.

Male student: OK, so what do you spend most of your money on?

Man: Well, most of it goes on monthly expenses. I've got a big mortgage on my house, and my children's school fees are very high. After I've paid for gas and electricity and water, and all the insurance on the house and my car, I don't have much left. I like taking my wife out to a nice restaurant once a month, but I don't very often buy clothes. Oh – and I collect radios – old radios – that's my hobby.

Female student: And how do you usually pay for the things you buy?

Man: I use my debit card for most things these days. I have two credit cards, but I don't like using them. I prefer to pay for things immediately, otherwise I feel I'm getting into debt. I pay my bills online or over the telephone. I usually have between ten and twenty pounds in cash with me to pay for emergencies – taxi fares and that kind of thing.

Male student: What do you think is good value for money?

Man: Mm, not very much to tell you the truth. Everything seems to cost more than it should these days. I think my telephone and Internet broadband package is good value for money, though. That's my telephone line, any number of national calls and unlimited Internet use for only £22 a month. I think at least one member of my family is online for an hour or more every day. I think £22 is a very good deal.

Female student: And what do you think is a waste of money?

Man: Personally, I don't understand why anyone buys a new car. They are so expensive, and as soon as you drive them out of the showroom, they're worth three thousand pounds less. Perhaps I'm just saying it because I can't afford a new car myself, but to me it seems so much more sensible to buy a good second-hand car for half the money.

Male student: Do you ever buy anything you can't afford?

Man: Yes. I collect radios – old radios. I have nine now, and they're quite expensive. I paid £350 for a 1950s radio last month – I didn't have much money for the rest of the month after that! My wife thinks I'm crazy, but it's important to treat yourself occasionally – don't you think? My wife buys nice perfume and lots of clothes, and I have my radios.

Female student: OK – so, finally – would you say that you're a spender or a saver?

Man: Well, as I said, I don't really have much to save, but I guess I'm a saver rather than a spender. It's good to enjoy money if you have it, but you must save for a rainy day. You never know what will happen in the future.

Female student/
Male student: Thank you very much for talking to us – have nice day, now.

For questions 5–9, complete the notes. Use no more than two words for each answer.

[Play track 96 again]

For further listening practice, tell students to complete the exercise on page 24 of the Workbook. Set as an extra activity or homework task.

C Give students sufficient time to check answers and think about why they may have answered incorrectly, before moving on to Exercise D. Some key words are given with the answers below. Students should check any words they feel they need to with you, as they look at the answers and tapescript.

Answers:
1. b
2. a
3. b (expenses, mortgage, fees)
4. c (emergencies)
5. package
6. deal (note that 'value' is uncountable, and so does not fit)
7. showroom
8. treat
9. rainy day

D Students will by now be familiar with this type of reflective process, but note the questions here are more specific to guessing the meaning of new words and phrases. Remind them that identifying what they are doing well and not doing so well is a very good way of focusing on what they can do better next time. Allow students time to reflect and complete the task. Ask students how many answers were wrong due to incorrect spelling. Play the recording again if necessary, and tell students to focus on why the correct answers are correct.

Key vocabulary in context

This task revises the vocabulary that was used to answer the question in the exam practice task. See if students can answer any of the questions without looking back, but then allow them to look back and check. Students can work individually. You can give answers orally, as students already have the words written down.

Answers: 1. raise   2. treat   3. deal
4. currency   5. purse

Reading

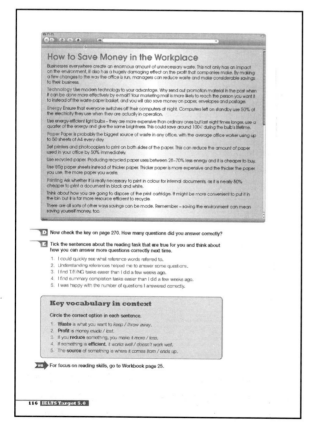

Objectives

- To show students the importance of understanding reference words in a text.

- To help students understand what is being referred to in a text more quickly.

- To revise and further practise the skills required in the IELTS Reading Module.

Reading 1

The best way to present this part of the lesson would be to use an OHP transparency.

A The aim of the first task is to provide an opportunity for some speaking practice, as well as prepare students for the reading tasks that follow. It also presents and revises some useful vocabulary. Read the questions with students, and check any new key words. Give them three or four minutes to answer. Get some ideas from the class, and provide answers if necessary.

Answers:

1/2. Students' own answers.

3. If you pay with a debit card, the money comes out of your account immediately. If you pay with a credit card, the money will come out on a fixed date at the end of each month.

4. Most people are now paid by direct transfer.

B This task revises different genres of text and a variety of register, as well as preparing students to practise the reference words. Go through the four options with students, and explain 'online advice service'. Tell them not to worry about the highlighted words for now, but to skim the text. Give students a time limit of about two minutes. Provide answers before moving on to Exercise C.

Answers: 1. C   2. D   3. A   4. B

C Write the first line of the first text on the board (not necessary if you are using an OHP transparency) whilst students are working on Exercise B, and circle 'one'. Ask students what 'one' refers back to, and then draw a circle around 'car'. Draw a line between the two circles, and explain that 'one' is a reference word because it refers to another word in the text. Ask for a couple more examples of reference words. Show students that this is an example of the task in the book, and make sure they know what to do. Give them about ten minutes for this activity. Students should work individually, and then compare ideas with a partner. If you are using the OHP transparency, feedback will be much easier. You can circle and join each reference word and the word or phrase it refers back to as you go through the answers. Otherwise, you can write the pronouns and answers next to each other on the board.

Answers:

Text A   one – car / him – my dad / that – ask my dad for money / it – the money

Text B   This – a basic bank account / his or her / he or she – the customer

Text C   there – to the USA / it – opening an account (without an address) / they – banks

Text D   this – my debit card was not returned from the machine / one – debit card

Read the exam tip with students.

D Students should work individually to complete this practice task. Those who finish early can compare answers. Write the answers on the board for clarity. Ask students which of the texts they found most interesting.

Answers:

(Correct options) A: these / their

B: They / it / one   C: there / they

D: them / then

Students can read through the 'Watch out!' box in their own time.

Reading 2

It is almost impossible to provide exam practice that practises reference words on their own, but the questions in this activity require students to understand the references in the text.

A Students can probably guess which is the correct summary without reading. Set it up as a gist task, and then tell students to skim the text to confirm their thoughts. Set a time limit of about three minutes.

Answers: The correct summary is 2.

B Students are not required to identify every reference word and say what it refers to. Set a strict time limit of three minutes for them to highlight words individually. Give them another three minutes to compare and discuss with a partner. Monitor, and check what each pair has achieved (formal feedback for this activity would be laborious and not especially useful).

C Students should now be ready to work through the practice tasks. They have practised these tasks before, so should only need minimal help. Give them a minute to read through the questions, and set a time limit of about 15 minutes.

D Give students sufficient time to check and think about why they may have answered incorrectly, before moving on to Exercise E. The answers, together with the parts of the text that provide answers, are reproduced here.

Answers:

1. T (it also has a hugely damaging effect on the profit that companies make)
2. NG
3. F
4. NG
5. T (it might be more convenient to put it in the bin ...)
6. profit
7. to reduce
8. left on / left on standby
9. light bulbs
10. both sides
11. in colour

E By now, students will be familiar with this type of reflective process, but note the questions are not the same as in previous units. Remind them that identifying what they are doing well and not doing so well is a very good way of focusing on what they can do better next time. Allow students time to reflect and complete the task, and then ask them if they are happy with the number of correct answers. You may like to ask one student what he or she will do differently next time.

Key vocabulary in context

The vocabulary in this activity is closely related to money, and some of the words are easily confused. Students should work individually. To check answers, tell students to cover the task, and then give the definitions as they tell you each correct word.

Answers: 1. throw away   2. made   3. less   4. works well   5. comes from

The Workbook task for this unit looks at how general nouns are used to refer back in a text. Work through the task in the lesson if you have time, or set it up now for homework.

Writing

Objectives

- To make students aware of various features that contribute to a well-written discursive composition.

- To present and practise fixed expressions which introduce opinion.

- To practise writing a discursive composition.

Writing 1

The best way to make feedback easier in this writing task will be to have the composition on an OHP transparency.

Start by telling students to look at the two pictures. Students have seen a few discursive compositions now, and will probably be able to guess what the topic of this one will be. Try to elicit key words like 'wealth' and 'poverty'. Teach 'be paid' by asking how much they think Ronaldo is paid every week.

A Give students a minute or two to read the task instructions, and check they understand everything. They might need to check 'feed'.

Emphasize that the question says 'Do you agree?', and that the statement starts 'It is not right that…' Make sure they understand that they can agree, disagree or present both sides of the argument. Get a general consensus about whether the task is fairly manageable or very challenging.

B Before you start this task, tell students to cover Exercise C (the teacher's notes). Make sure students understand that they are going to read a student's composition. Set a time limit of two minutes for them to read the composition on their own. Ask a couple of students if they think it is good, quite good or not so good. Don't give your own opinion yet. Tell students that later they will see what a teacher said about the composition, but now they are going to say more about what they think. Give them another five minutes to read more carefully, and make their notes individually. Finally, give them three minutes to compare their notes with a partner. Monitor to check what they are saying, but don't give any feedback.

C Read the rubric with students. Note that it might seem quite daunting for students to take the place of the teacher, but it is fairly easy to see which of the comments are totally unfair. Give them the time they need to read through the comments individually. Help with anything they don't understand as you go. Students who finish quickly can compare with others. Go through the answers before moving on to Exercise D. Write the numbers of the five true comments on the board, but don't show students any examples of each yet. You can point out, if you like, that it is unrealistic that the student would make no spelling or grammatical mistakes (the aim here is to focus on other aspects of good writing).

Answers: 1. N 2. Y 3. N 4. N 5. Y
6. Y 7. N 8. N 9. Y 10. Y

D Give students a few minutes to work on their own. They should have already identified some examples if they completed Exercise C properly. Give them another couple of minutes to compare. Write the examples on the board with the number of the comment if you are not using an OHP transparency.

Answers:
Comment 2: (This is clear from the whole composition.)
Comment 5: It's absolutely terrible that ...
Comment 6: (This is clear from looking at the start of each paragraph.)
Comment 9: They can't afford to feed their children ...
Comment 10: They can't afford ...

Writing 2

A Students should be quite eager to read the second composition now. Tell them not to worry about some phrases being underlined. Give them six or seven minutes to read and highlight. To give feedback, explain how each of the points in Exercise 1D above had been corrected by the second attempt.

B Tell students to look carefully at how each of the underlined words and expressions are used to introduce an opinion. You can clarify anything

that students are not sure about, but these items should all be fairly simple to understand. Read the rubric for the task with students, and make sure they know what to do (you could do the first one as an example). Students can work individually or in pairs. They should use dictionaries if they need to. Go over answers orally here.

Answers:
1. To my mind   2. Clearly   3. I think it is wrong
4. To my mind   5. In conclusion   6. I wonder if

Read the exam tip with students.

Writing task

The writing tasks are found either in the Workbook or in the exam practice section at the end of the unit. For this unit, the task is in the Workbook.

A Students will still need assistance with preparation before attempting to write a complete composition of this type. Tell them that the important thing is to attempt the composition, to make some valid points, and to organize the points as well as they can.

Give students a minute or so to read the task instructions, which for this task are very simple.

B This stage will be very important for students at this level. They can work in pairs as suggested, or in small groups. Give them at least ten minutes for this activity, and monitor, giving some of your own ideas (but not too many). Get some points up on the board, so that everyone has some points they can include.

Once students are ready to start writing, set a time limit of 40 minutes, and now try to ensure that students use the time they have. Tell them to use the composition in the Writing Module as a model. Monitor as students work, but check that they are organizing their ideas and making relevant points. There should be a little more focus on accuracy too now.

When students have completed the task, tell them to look at the model composition on page 270 of the Course Book. Put them into pairs to compare their composition against the model. The model is reproduced on the following page.

If you collect students' compositions to mark, it would be better to use the process to get an idea of what they are capable of, rather than correct too heavily. At this stage, you will be correcting most of what they write.

There are some people who are materialistic and want the good things in life. For them, having money is very important, and they think it makes them happy. There are other people who believe that the simple things in life matter more than money. For them, it is more important to have friends and family, and to be in good health.

I do not think it is really possible to say who is right and who is wrong, and I think it also depends on what people mean when they say 'happy'. Of course, if people are so poor that they have no home and nothing to eat, it is impossible to be happy, but there are plenty of people who do not have much money and really enjoy life.

There are also a lot of very rich people who are not happy at all. You always hear about rich movie stars who take drugs because money does not bring them everything they want. I think some rich people are happy because they have more than other people. They see money as proof that they are successful. Perhaps if everyone else was also rich, they would not be so happy.

Personally, I do not think that having more money than other people will make me happy. I want to be successful and I want to have nice things, but having a job I like and being with a man I love are the most important things. I have an uncle who is very rich, but does not have a wife and does not have any children. He does not seem happy to me.

Consolidation

Speaking

The aim of this activity is to show students how a follow-up comment (either an example or giving a reason) makes their language sound so much more natural and conversational.

A, B and C 🎧 Give students the time they need to work on the matching task. Play the whole recording to check answers. Play the recording again, pausing after each extract. Focus on stress and intonation, and drill parts of the extracts that you think students should practise. Students should work in pairs so that they can say each sentence to a partner. Tell them to practise each example a couple of times.

> **Tapescript** 🎧 **97** (1 min, 2 secs)
>
> **B** **Listen and check your answers.**
>
> **1**
>
> **Man:** I don't mind shopping in supermarkets. It's not much fun, but everyone has to do it.

2

Woman: I prefer shopping in small local shops. The shopkeepers are so much more friendly.

3

Man 2: I don't really like shopping for clothes. I always want a pair of shoes or a jacket that I can't afford.

4

Woman 2: I really enjoy shopping for DVDs. I usually find something I want to see.

5

Man 3: I don't enjoy shopping in markets. They're too busy and a lot of what they sell there isn't very good.

Answers: 1. b 2. e 3. a 4. c 5. d

D Give students a couple of minutes to plan what they want to say before they start talking. Tell them to talk with a partner, and after a few minutes get some opinions from the whole class.

Vocabulary

Students have previously seen that this can be an interesting and effective way of storing useful words and phrases. Ask whether any students have done something like this before, without being told to do so by the teacher.

A Set the first task for individual completion, and as students work, put the web on the board. Write the phrases in the box on the board web, as students tell you the correct groups.

Answers:
verb + money: borrow
pay + phrase: pay a bill
adjectives: cheap
nouns: debt
useful phrases: value for money

B Give students five minutes to add what they want to the web, or tell them to find two more examples for each column. Then get ideas from the class, and add them to the board web.

Errors

A Students know that each unit ends with an error-correction task. Tell them that there are no errors of spelling. They can either complete the task individually or in pairs. Write the correct sentences on the board for clarity.

Answers:
1. Who's going to pay the bill?
2. I spend a lot of money on clothes.
3. My brother lent me some money.
4. Can I borrow your dictionary a minute?
5. I'm interested in the USA, but I've never been there.
6. My parents have never travelled in their lives.
7. My sister wants a new bicycle, but my dad won't buy her one.
8. In my opinion, people should try to save money.

Exam Practice

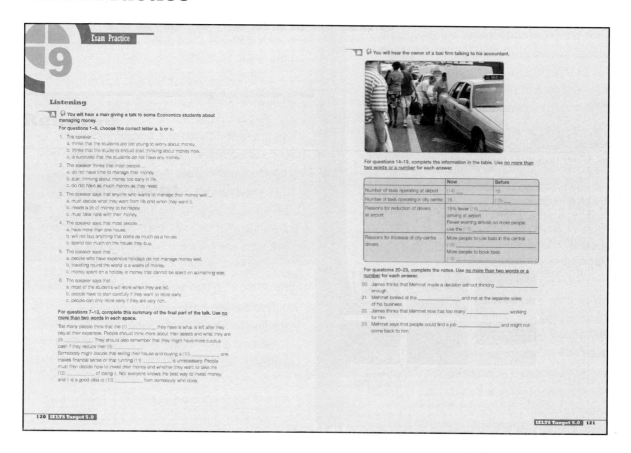

Exam Practice

9

Listening

A You will hear a man giving a talk to some Economics students about managing money.
For questions 1–6, choose the correct letter a, b or c.

1. The speaker...
   a. thinks that the students are too young to worry about money.
   b. thinks that the students should start thinking about money now.
   c. is surprised that the students do not have any money.

2. The speaker thinks that most people...
   a. do not have time to manage their money.
   b. start thinking about money too early in life.
   c. do not have as much money as they need.

3. The speaker says that anyone who wants to manage their money well...
   a. must decide what they want from life and when they want it.
   b. needs a lot of money to be happy.
   c. must take risks with their money.

4. The speaker says that most people...
   a. have more than one house.
   b. will not buy anything that costs as much as a house.
   c. spend too much on the house they buy.

5. The speaker says that...
   a. people who have expensive holidays do not manage money well.
   b. travelling round the world is a waste of money.
   c. money spent on a holiday is money that cannot be spent on something else.

6. The speaker says that...
   a. most of the students will retire when they are 50.
   b. people have to plan carefully if they want to retire early.
   c. people can only retire early if they are very rich.

For questions 7–13, complete this summary of the final part of the talk. Use no more than two words in each space.

Too many people think that the (7) _____ they have is what is left after they pay all their expenses. People should think more about their assets and what they are (8) _____. They should also remember that they might have more surplus cash if they reduce their (9) _____.
Somebody might decide that selling their house and buying a (10) _____ one makes financial sense or that running (11) _____ is unnecessary. People must then decide how to invest their money and whether they want to take the (12) _____ of losing it. Not everyone knows the best way to invest money, and it is a good idea to (13) _____ from somebody who does.

You will hear the owner of a taxi firm talking to his accountant.

For questions 14–19, complete the information in the table. Use no more than two words or a number for each answer.

	Now	Before
Number of taxis operating at airport	(14) __	10
Number of taxis operating in city centre	16	(15) __
Reasons for reduction of drivers at airport	15% fewer (16) _____ arriving at airport. Fewer evening arrivals so more people use the (17) _____	
Reasons for increase of city-centre drivers	More people to use taxis in the central (18) _____ More people to book taxis (19) _____	

For questions 20–23, complete the notes. Use no more than two words or a number for each answer.

20. James thinks that Mehmet made a decision without thinking _____ enough.
21. Mehmet looked at the _____ and not at the separate sides of his business.
22. James thinks that Mehmet now has too many _____ working for him.
23. Mehmet says that people could find a job _____ and might not come back to him.

120 IELTS Target 5.0

IELTS Target 5.0 121

Listening

Tell students that these recordings are what they can expect from various parts of the exam. The recording and degree of challenge in the task is close to what they will deal with in the exam. Students are not given preparation, and have to work on their own to get some experience of realistic exam practice.

A and B Read through both the task introductions with students. Make sure students understand 'managing money'. Allow students to read the question instructions themselves. Give them a minute for each, as there is quite a lot to read. Remind them, however, that they will only have 30 seconds in the exam.

You should play the whole recording once only. However, you could pause after the first part, and give your students a moment to write and check answers, depending on how well you feel they can manage the task. Write all the answers on the board.

Tapescript 98 (5 mins, 35 secs)

A You will hear a man giving a talk to some Economics students about managing money. For questions 1–6, choose the correct letter a, b or c.

Voice: Good morning, everyone. I think you all know me now. For anyone who doesn't, my name's Brian Sinclair, and I work for an independent financial advice service. Coming in and talking to students makes a nice change.

Now, you might think that because you're young, you don't really need to start worrying about money yet. You might feel that now is the time to enjoy life, and that you have plenty of time before you really need to start managing your money. Some of you probably think that you haven't got any money to manage anyway. I hope that by the end of my talk, you'll see that it's never too early to start planning ahead, and never too early to start making your money work for you.

Now, first of all, the key to good money management is time. The more time you are prepared to spend managing your finances, the better your money will work for you. So, the earlier you start managing your money, the more effective the process becomes. Too many people start that process too late in life. Rather than managing their money, they end up trying to manage on the money they have.

Basically, there are four questions that any money management programme should answer: What are your financial goals? When do you want to achieve them? What money is available to you now? And what risks are you happy to take in order to reach your goals?

Now, the first question is really the key question, and the first thing I want to talk about is houses. You might say that a house is a necessity rather than a financial choice – everyone needs a house – but buying one, or more than one, is the biggest financial transaction that most of you will make in your life. How much money you invest in a house or apartment, and how much that property costs each month, will affect all other aspects of your financial programme. You will also need to think about the kind of lifestyle you want to enjoy. If travelling round the world or taking holidays in exotic places is very important to you, you will have less money to save and less to invest. Now, I'm certainly not saying that good money managing means not having a holiday. I'm saying that managing your money well means that you have to consider each choice you make. It puts a cost on the choices you make, if you like.

Now, when you have set yourself financial goals, you have to think about timing. The most obvious consideration is retirement. When do you want to stop having to work? It may seem a long way off to most of you, but if you want to retire when you're fifty, you will need to start planning very soon. To achieve your goal in terms of timing, a lot will depend on how much surplus money you have. By surplus money, I mean money that you have left after you have paid all your expenses.

Now, it is important that you don't simply accept that what you have left after you pay all your expenses is the only money you have. Far too many see finance in this very simple way. You must think about your assets – what you have that is worth money, and whether your expenses can be reorganized so that you have more surplus cash. Let me give you some examples. One asset might be your house. You might decide to sell it, and buy another one in an area where property is cheaper – you might decide to rent one of the rooms to a student for a while. One expense might be keeping a car on the road – you might realize that it makes more financial sense to sell the car and use the train or take taxis.

Now, this is where investment and risk-taking come in. When you have decided how much surplus money you have, you should think about how you can best invest it. The more risk you are prepared to take, the more money you can make. Remember, though, you can also lose money – so, unless you know a lot about the area in which you invest money, it is best to get advice from people who know what they are doing.

Now, like all programmes, you need to revise your financial management programme from time to time. You might suddenly earn more money, or you may find a way of freeing money that was previously unavailable. Perhaps some of the goals that you set … *(fade out)*

For questions 7–13, complete this summary of the final part of the talk. Use <u>no more than two words</u> in each space.

[Play track 98 again]

Tapescript 🎧 99 (3 mins, 39 secs)

B You will hear the owner of a taxi firm talking to his accountant. For questions 14–19, complete the information in the table. Use no more than two words or a number for each answer.

Accountant:	Hello, Mehmet. How are you?
Businessman:	Oh, good morning, James. I'm not too bad. I'm glad you could come and see me.
Accountant:	Yes, when you spoke to me on the phone I got the impression that things are not going so well. Is there a problem?
Businessman:	Please sit down. Would you like a coffee?
Accountant:	No, I'm OK – I had a coffee on the train. So, Mehmet, tell me.
Businessman:	I'm very worried. I just don't understand what's been happening recently – business is down, and the money is just not coming in like it was.
Accountant:	Mm, well, have you made any changes to the way you operate the business – changes that could affect profit?
Businessman:	Well, yes. I've cut the number of drivers operating at the airport.
Accountant:	By how many?
Businessman:	Down from ten to eight.
Accountant:	Why?
Businessman:	Because I expected a fall in the number of people using the airport. The number of flights coming in has reduced by fifteen per cent. There are fewer evening arrivals – during the day, more people take a bus into the city centre – it saves them a lot of money, and it doesn't take that long. The drivers were waiting longer for customers.
Accountant:	OK. Have you made any other changes?
Businessman:	No. Well, I transferred the two airport drivers to the city centre.
Accountant:	Why did you do that?
Businessman:	Well, I didn't want to just dismiss them. It wouldn't be fair. Anyway, I predicted a rise in business in the central business district – everyone is talking about expansion there – more jobs and so on. I expected

	more people to use pre-booked taxis.
Accountant:	So, you've reduced the number of drivers operating at the airport, and increased the number of drivers operating in the city centre?
Businessman:	Yes, James. I've explained that.
Accountant:	So, how many drivers do you now have operating in the city centre?
Businessman:	Sixteen.
Accountant:	Did you look carefully at the profitability of airport taxis and city-centre taxis when you made your decision?
Businessman:	You mean, separately? No, not really. I just looked at the overall figures, and then made predictions.
Accountant:	Mm, it might have been better to lay off two or three of the airport drivers – at least for a month or two – and then re-employ them if business improved.
Businessman:	No, all the drivers have worked for the company for a long time – they have families to support. I couldn't do that. Anyway, who says they would be available when I wanted to re-employ them? They might find a job somewhere else. Good drivers are difficult to find.
Accountant:	Mehmet – I think you're trying to keep everyone happy. You must think more like a businessman. It seems clear to me that the problem here is that ... (fade out)

For questions 20–23, complete the notes. Use no more than two words or a number for each answer.

[Play track 99 again]

Answers: 1. b 2. a 3. a 4. b 5. c 6. b
7. only money 8. worth 9. expenses
10. cheaper 11. a car 12. risk 13. get advice 14. 8 / eight 15. 14 / fourteen
16. flights 17. bus 18. business district
19. in advance 20. carefully 21. overall figures
22. drivers 23. somewhere else

Once you have given students the answers, and if there is time, you might like to play the recording again as students read the tapescript. Pause to point out why some are incorrect if students are still unsure.

Unit 9 Workbook answers

Speaking and Vocabulary

A 1. on   2. of   3. from   4. to   5. for
6. in / by   7. in   8. for

B 1. c   2. b   3. e   4. a   5. d

Listening

A Extract 1: T – capital   Extract 2: F – overheads
Extract 3: T – stock   Extract 4: F – branch

Tapescript 🎧 **100** (2 mins, 1 sec)

A **Listen to some short extracts about starting up a business. For each extract, circle (T) true or (F) false after the statement and then write the key word that you hear in the space.**

Extract 1
Voice: Anyone starting up their own business will need some capital. Of course, you will have to borrow money from the bank – quite a lot of money, in fact – but you will need to have capital, too. The bank will not take you seriously if you do not have capital.

Extract 2
Voice: You must remember that you will have overheads. Apart from large expenses, like equipment, rent on a building and any salaries that you have to pay, you will also have regular overheads, like electricity, repairs and cleaning. A lot of people do not realize just how much money goes out.

Extract 3
Voice: If your business involves selling products, it is important that you order the right amount of stock. If you have too much stock, you might not sell it, and you will lose money. If you do not have enough stock, it might not be available when people want it, and they will go somewhere else to find it.

Extract 4
Voice: You should not think that as soon as business is good, it is time to open another branch somewhere else. Very often, what makes a business successful does not work everywhere. Too many businesses expand too quickly, and a second or third branch is much less successful than the first.

Reading

A 1. d   2. b   3. a   4. f   5. c   6. e

B reading task

C 1. 'this incident' refers to b
2. 'buildings like these' refers to a

Writing

A and B The writing task is dealt with in the main section of the Teacher's Book.

10 Feelings

Unit overview

The tenth unit is based around the theme of feelings and emotions. Students will talk about how they feel in various situations. There is further practice with topic sentences and linking words in texts, and students will work more on various aspects of the IELTS exam.

Speaking and Vocabulary

Objectives

- To give students further practice answering the type of questions they can expect in the first and second parts of the speaking exam.

- To help students talk about their feelings and emotions.

- To present and practise adjectives that describe how somebody feels.

- To clarify the difference between '~ed' and '~ing' endings on adjectives.

Speaking 1

A This activity aims to provide some speaking practice, as well as prepare students for the vocabulary task that follows. Students should practise using dictionaries if possible. Say that an emotional person normally shows his or her feelings, while an unemotional person usually hides them. Give students a few minutes to talk in pairs.

Vocabulary 1

A Give students time to look at the pictures and the words in the box, and think carefully. The aim here is for students to talk, and not to correctly match the words and pictures. Point out that when they listen in a moment, they will hear that more than one adjective can go with each picture. Don't go over any answers, as they are dealt with in Exercise B.

B 🎧 Play the whole recording whilst students check their ideas, and then once more, pausing after each exchange. Deal with any confusing words, and drill them to focus on correct pronunciation.

> **Tapescript 🎧 101** (2 mins, 13 secs)
>
> B **Listen to some students and check the pronunciation. Then practise saying the words.**
>
> **1**
> Student 1: They're very happy with their new baby.
> Student 2: Yes, and probably very proud, too.
>
> **2**
> Student 1: He looks very relaxed. He doesn't have to worry about anything.
>
> **3**
> Student 1: She's disappointed. She expected to get the job.
>
> **4**
> Student 1: The little boy's sad.
> Student 2: Yes, he looks very upset. His toy's broken.

> **5**
> Student 1: He looks bored.
> Student 2: Yes, it must be a very boring lesson.
>
> **6**
> Student 1: They're confused. They don't know which way to go.
>
> **7**
> Student 1: I think he's feeling quite nervous.
> Student 2: Yes, he's worried that he's going to fail his test.
>
> **8**
> Student 1: They're really excited about going on the ride.
> Student 2: They might be feeling a bit nervous, too.
>
> **9**
> Student 1: They're scared. They don't want to go up to the castle.
> Student 2: Yes, they're really frightened.
>
> **10**
> Student 1: She's surprised. She wasn't expecting a present.
>
> **11**
> Student 1: Oh dear, he's very annoyed. They've broken his window.
> Student 2: I think he's really angry.

C Encourage students to give reasons, and give them an example: 'I'm feeling a bit tired because I was working on my computer until late last night.'

> **Grammar check**
>
> Although there are various structures here, this is really as much about vocabulary as it is about grammar. The assumption is that students will have seen these ways to express feelings, and that this is revision. Read through each point with students, giving a few examples where necessary. Tell them that it is difficult to say why we can use 'get' with some adjectives, and not others (we can say 'get excited', but not 'get happy'). Tell them that we don't usually use 'make' with participle adjectives ('it frightens me', rather than 'it makes me frightened'). Students

will probably still be a little confused about when to use '~ed' or '~ing' adjectives. You could set Exercise B in the Workbook to check.

Pronunciation check

The aim of this activity is to raise awareness, and help students to recognize the sound if they hear it. It isn't really essential that they can produce these words exactly like a native speaker. Read the point with students, and then either replay the recording or model the words yourself. Give students a minute or two to practise saying the words, but don't expect perfect production.

Tapescript 🎧 102 (0 mins, 59 secs)

Pronunciation check

Words like *frightened* and *frightening* are difficult for students to say. Most native speakers produce a sound that you cannot find on the phonetic chart. The sound is made in the top of the nose.

Listen to these words that have the sound. Then practise saying them.

1 frightened   2 frightening

3 certainly   4 curtains

5 important

Speaking 2

A Make sure students know that they don't have to answer the questions yet. Give them a few minutes to read and think about their answers.

B 🎧 Play the whole recording with pens down, and then again, pausing after each extract as students make notes. You can either check what students grasped quickly, or play the recording once more as students read the tapescript.

Tapescript 🎧 103 (1 min, 41 secs)

B **Listen to some students answering the questions. Make notes.**

1
Examiner: What makes you happy?
Student: Being with my family at the weekend makes me happy – and sunny weather.

2
Examiner: When were you last excited about something?
Student: I went to see Germany play during the World Cup. I was very excited, and a bit nervous, too – I didn't think we would win that game.

3
Examiner: What makes you really angry?
Student: I get angry when people drop rubbish in the street or write things on the walls. I just don't understand why people want to make the place they live in look horrible.

4
Examiner: What do you worry about?
Student: I worry quite a lot about money. I always feel that I should have more.

5
Examiner: When did you last get nervous about something?
Student: I got very nervous when I took all my exams last year. It was OK, though – I passed them. I sometimes get nervous before I fly, too.

6
Examiner: What do you do to relax?
Student: I listen to music with my headphones on, or go for a swim.

C Talking to a variety of classmates should be more motivating than talking to one other person that they probably know well anyway. Monitor as students talk, and check that they are communicating appropriately.

Vocabulary 2

A There is a lot of new vocabulary in this activity. Encourage students to use dictionaries because it isn't possible to check each of the extreme adjectives without doing the task yourself. Tell them to work in pairs so that they can discuss meanings. Check answers by writing the word 'pairs' on the board. Model some typical pronunciations as you do so ('it was really good', 'it was absolutely fantastic!').

Answers: 1. c   2. e   3. f   4. d   5. a   6. b

Watch out!
Read through the errors in the box with students. It might be a good idea to tell them to correct the sentences this time.

Answers:
I'm absolutely furious.
I'm very happy.
I was amazed to see her again.

B 🎧 Play the whole recording with pens down.

Tapescript 🎧 **104** (1 min, 8 secs)

B Listen to some students using extreme adjectives to answer questions.

1
Examiner: So, what sort of thing makes you really angry?
Student: I get absolutely furious when people are cruel to animals. People think animals are less important than people.

2
Examiner: Parachute jumping sounds very exciting. How many jumps have you made?
Student: I've made five now. I made my first jump last year. I was absolutely terrified before I jumped, but then when I was in the air, it was absolutely fantastic.

3
Examiner: And so how did you feel when you got your exam results?

Student: Well, I was in Italy with some friends. My mother phoned to tell me I had passed them all. When I heard the news, I was absolutely delighted.

C 🎧 Note that this task not only practises the extreme adjectives, but also provides some exam-type listening practice. Play the recording again, pausing after each extract as students complete the notes. Write the answers on the board.

Tapescript 🎧 **105** (0 mins, 10 secs)

C Listen again and complete these sentences.

[Play track 104 again]

Answers:
1. cruel to animals
2. made my first jump / jumped / was in the air
3. I heard the news

Read the exam tip with students, and tell them to try to put the advice to use in the practice that follows.

D and E By now, students know how to work through this type of task. Make sure they spend time reading the cards and planning before they talk. Monitor to check that students are saying the right kind of thing, and generally improving with this type of task.

Listening

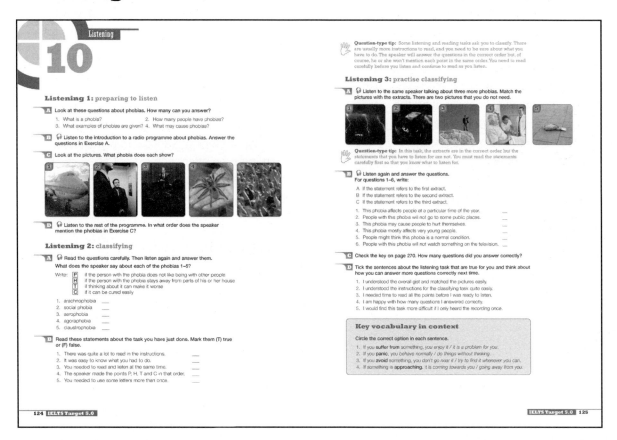

Objectives

- To introduce students to the exam task of classifying.
- To familiarize students with complicated task instructions, and to practise coping with them.

Listening 1

The aim of the first section is to prepare students for the challenging exam practice that comes later in the lesson.

Some key words and phrases are presented, and students become familiar with the recording through doing some gist listening tasks.

A Tell students that they are going to hear a recording about phobias, but don't explain the meaning of 'phobia' yet. They can talk in pairs to answer the questions, or discuss as a whole class. Make sure they understand that saying 'I don't know' is perfectly acceptable, and that they can't possibly answer question 3 before they listen.

B 🎧 Make sure students understand that this is only the introduction to the programme. Play the whole recording with pens down, as students check that each question is answered. Then play it again, pausing so that students can note the points down. Go over answers with them, writing any key words on the board.

Tapescript 🎧 **106** (1 min, 44 secs)

B Listen to the introduction to a radio programme about phobias. Answer the questions in Exercise A.

Voice: Good afternoon. On today's programme, we're going to hear about phobias, and learn what some of the most common phobias are. Now, a phobia is really a fear or an anxiety, but it's a very strong fear or anxiety. In fact, phobias are often called anxiety disorders – a disorder is something that is wrong. People don't understand why they have a phobia – they can't explain why they are so afraid of what it is they have a fear of. It is difficult to know exactly how many people are affected, but some doctors think around fifteen per cent of us have a phobia of one kind or another. Some phobias can make it very difficult for people to live a normal life – a fear of water or of open spaces, for example. Nobody knows exactly why people have phobias, but it is probably a mix of brain chemistry – something that is just there inside us – and past experience – fears caused by what has happened to us some time earlier in our life. Today, I have in the studio Doctor Alan Carling. He is an expert on phobias, and he is going to tell us about the five most common phobias. Later, he will talk about how people can overcome a phobia, or at least learn to live with one.

Answers:
1. a very strong fear or anxiety
2. about 15% of people
3. a fear of water and open spaces
4. brain chemistry or past experience

C Give students a moment to discuss the pictures in the same group or together as a class. It is not important to know the name of the phobia at this point.

D 🎧 Tell students that this is a gist listening task, and that they shouldn't worry about not understanding everything. Play the whole recording, and write the phobias in order on the board as students tell you them. It is probably best not to play the recording a second time now, or students will become too familiar with the content before the more exam-focused listening.

Tapescript 🎧 **107** (4 mins, 49 secs)

D **Listen to the rest of the programme. In what order does the speaker mention the phobias in Exercise C?**

Female voice: Doctor Carling, welcome to World Wise.

Dr Carling: Good afternoon. Now, Anne has described what a phobia is, so I won't go back over that. I'll go straight on to talk about the most common phobias, and how some phobias have similar qualities and cause similar difficulties to the people who suffer from them.

The most common phobia is arachnophobia. Now, that might not be surprising – most people don't like spiders – but a phobia about spiders is more than just a fear. People who suffer from arachnophobia may panic if they see a spider – however big or small it is. They don't want to go to places where there could be spiders, so they will feel uncomfortable if they go down to the cellar, up to the attic or find themselves in any room that hasn't been cleaned. They may not want to go out into their garden.

Female voice: Mm, I don't like spiders, but I don't think my fear is quite that bad.

Dr Carling: No, probably not. The second most common phobia is social phobia. Now, this is complex, and the person who suffers will be afraid of a range of situations. The real fear is of being with other people, especially large groups of people. People who have social phobia have very little confidence, and feel that other people are judging what they do and say all the time. They feel that what they say is stupid and that people are laughing at them. A person with social phobia could not speak in front of a group of other people, for example. Some sufferers do not like eating with other people – even members of their family. The phobia can make it very difficult for those who have it to live a normal life.

Female voice: That's very interesting. I have friends who are uncomfortable in large groups. They don't like parties, and so on.

Dr Carling: Yes, it's a common fear, but not necessarily a phobia. Now, another phobia that will probably not surprise people is aerophobia – the fear of flying. A lot of people don't really like flying, but a small number of people simply cannot fly. They know it is safer than driving a car, but they panic as soon as they are near a plane. It is usually a result of seeing a plane crash on TV or reading about one in the news. Aerophobia is unusual because it seems that the person who suffers from it can do something about it. It seems that if the person makes one successful flight, they may not be frightened again in the future, and will fly quite happily.

Female voice: That's amazing. I really didn't know that.

Dr Carling: Now, the fourth phobia is agoraphobia. This is similar in some ways to social phobia, and certainly means that the person who suffers doesn't like to be around a lot of other people. Agoraphobia is a fear of not being able to escape from a crowded place. The person who suffers will panic in a crowd, and will often feel physically sick. The condition is made worse because the person who suffers is then afraid of having a panic attack in front of so many other people. In some cases, those who suffer will not want to leave their house.

Female voice: That sounds terrible.

Dr Carling: Yes – a very serious condition. So, the fifth and final phobia I'm going to talk about is claustrophobia – a fear of being trapped in a very small space. People with claustrophobia will not want to be in a lift, or 'elevator', as the Americans say. They will often avoid travelling by train or bus, as they are afraid that an accident could mean being trapped somewhere. They do not like a room with all the doors closed. It seems that people who suffer from claustrophobia can become very anxious simply by imagining being in a small space, and not being able to escape.

Female voice: That sounds terrible. Even if they are not in a small space, they can experience fear and anxiety?

Dr Carling: Absolutely.

Female voice: OK, now, thank you for that summary. I think what we really want to know now is ... *(fade out)*

Answers:

The correct order is:

1. arachnophobia – fear of spiders
2. social phobia – fear of being with other people or being judged by other people
3. aerophobia – fear of flying
4. agoraphobia – fear of crowds of people
5. claustrophobia – fear of small confined spaces and of being trapped

Listening 2

Do not give students help with the instructions to this task because the aim is to show students how confusing the activity can seem.

A 🎧 Give students a couple of minutes to read and work out what they have to do. Remind them that they will have far less time in the exam. Note that two of the questions should be fairly easy, as students have already defined those phobias. Play the whole recording. You can give students a moment to compare answers or give direct feedback. Write the lines that provide answers on the board with the answers, and then play the recording again for students to check.

Tapescript 🎧 108 (0 mins, 17 secs)

A **Read the questions carefully. Then listen again and answer them. What does the speaker say about each of the phobias 1–5?**

[Play track 107 again]

Answers:

1. arachnophobia – H (... feel uncomfortable if they go down to the cellar, up to the attic or find themselves in any room ...)
2. social phobia – P (The real fear is of being with other people, especially large groups of people.)
3. aerophobia – C (It seems that if the person makes one successful flight, they may not be frightened again in the future ...)
4. agoraphobia – P (... the person who suffers doesn't like to be around a lot of other people.)
5. claustrophobia – T (... can become very anxious simply by imagining being in a small space ...)

B Students are now familiar with this type of reflective task analysis, and know that answers are usually given in the tip that follows. Make sure they cover the question-type tip first. Give them time to read and mark each statement individually, and then a couple of minutes for discussion. Then tell them to read the tip to check their answers. You can clarify if necessary.

Answers: 1. T   2. students decide   3. T
4. F   5. T

Listening 3

The aim now is to practise the task type, but this activity is slightly different from the one they have seen. The first task is to further practise gist listening, so that students feel more confident with the classifying task.

A 🎧 Read the rubric with students, and then give them a moment to look at the pictures and make predictions. Don't discuss the phobias with them at this point, as you will give away answers to the tasks. Play the whole recording whilst students match. Write answers on the board.

Tapescript 🎧 **109** (2 mins, 49 secs)

A **Listen to the same speaker talking about three more phobias. Match the pictures with the extracts. There are two pictures that you do not need.**

Extract 1
Voice: Acrophobia is a fear of heights. A lot of people confuse it with vertigo, which is a normal feeling that people get in a very high place. Acrophobia is a phobia and can be very dangerous. The person who suffers may panic and want to escape the situation – the quickest way to escape is to jump. People who suffer from acrophobia will avoid being at the top of tall buildings, and will not like going up long staircases. It may be a phobia that is a result of past experience. Children see things fall and break, and so become very frightened of the same thing happening to them.

Extract 2
Voice: Now, this phobia has a number of different names – brontophobia, astraphobia and keraunophobia. It is a phobia of storms – especially storms with thunder and lightning. It is especially common in children, but can continue into adult life. People who have a serious phobia worry when the spring turns to summer – they expect there to be more storms during that time. When a storm is approaching, they feel very uncomfortable and even physically sick. Many of those who suffer – especially children – hide when there is a storm, perhaps in a cupboard or under the bed. Adults with the condition may watch weather forecasts on television every thirty minutes to check that the weather is good.

Extract 3
Voice: Now most people are, to some degree, afraid of dying, but necrophobia is a fear of anything connected with death. It is more than a fear of dying. People who have necrophobia are terrified of seeing dead things. They will stay away from museums where there are mummies or skeletons, and avoid any images of dead people. They will panic if they see a dead animal in the street or in a forest, and will avoid watching a programme or movie that shows people dying or near to death. This phobia may be something that is natural in all of us to some degree, but is probably made worse by seeing a dead person or a favourite pet dying at some time in the past.

Answers:
Extract 1 – picture 3   Extract 2 – picture 1
Extract 3 – picture 5

B 🎧 Again, the instructions are complicated, and students will need a little more time to understand the activity than they will have in the exam. Often what you need to do becomes clear as you are listening, and it is important that students understand that once they have done this type of task a couple of times, they will know what to do. They may also notice that they have a one-in-three chance of guessing the answer, and feel that that makes the task easier. Read through the question-type tip with students, and then allow them the time they need to read. Play the recording when they are ready. Students might find it difficult to listen to the recording only once more, but avoid playing it a third time. Students can discuss what difficulties they had, and then listen again later if necessary (see Exercises C and D).

Tapescript 🎧 **110** (0 mins, 25 secs)

B   **Listen again and answer the questions.**

For questions 1–6, write:

A   If the statement refers to the first extract.

B   If the statement refers to the second extract.

C   If the statement refers to the third extract.

[Play track 109 again]

C Give students sufficient time to check answers and think about why they may have answered incorrectly, before moving on to Exercise D. Some key phrases are given with the answers below. Students should check any words they are unsure about with you, as they look at the answers and tapescript.

Answers:
1. B (... worry when the spring turns to summer ...)
2. A (... avoid being at the top of tall buildings ...)
3. A (... may panic and want to escape the situation – the quickest way to escape is to jump)
4. B (... especially common in children ...)
5. A (... people confuse it with vertigo, which is a normal feeling ...)
6. C (... will avoid watching a programme or movie ...)

D Students are now familiar with this type of reflective process, but note the questions here are very specific to the task type. Remind them that identifying what they are doing well and not doing so well is a very good way of focusing on what they can do better next time. Allow students time to reflect and complete the task. Play the recording again if necessary, and tell students to focus on why the correct answers are correct.

Key vocabulary in context

The task focuses on useful verbs from the lesson. Students can work individually or in pairs. You can give answers orally, or ask students to read the correct complete sentences.

Answers:
1. it is a problem for you
2. do things without thinking
3. don't go near it
4. coming towards you

Reading

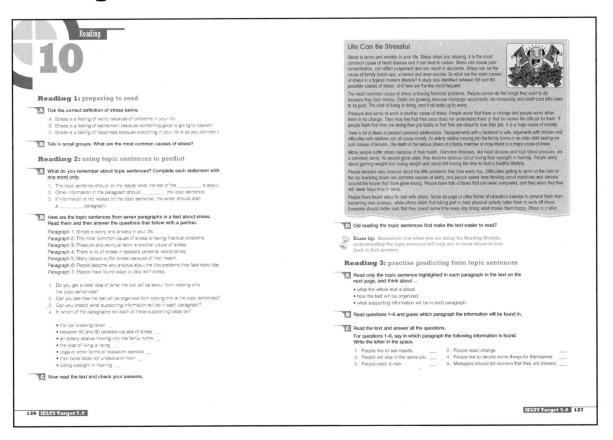

Objectives

- To further emphasize the need to focus on topic sentences.

- To practise using topic sentences to aid prediction.

- To revise and further practise the skills required in the IELTS Reading Module.

Students have already looked at the purpose and function of topic sentences. The aim in this unit is to show how students can get a good idea of what a text is about, by only reading the topic sentence of each paragraph. This section also aims to show how the topic sentence helps the reader make predictions as he or she reads.

Reading 1

The purpose of the first two tasks is to provide an opportunity for some speaking practice, as well as prepare students for the reading tasks that follow. Make sure students don't read the text for this unit before working on the preceding tasks.

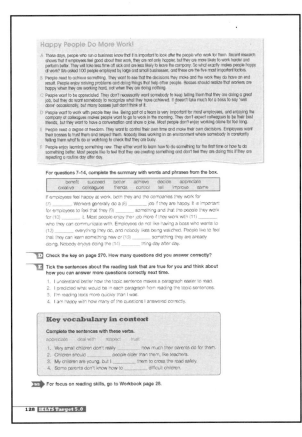

A Students will need to be clear about exactly what 'stress' is. Give them a minute to read the three definitions and make their choice. Tell them to cover the task, and then ask one student to define 'stress'.

Answers: The correct definition is A.

B Ask the class for one cause of stress, and write the answer on the board. Then set a time limit of three minutes, and allow them to talk in their groups. Write a few of their ideas on the board as feedback.

Reading 2

A This part of the lesson starts by revising what students already know. They should work individually, and then compare answers with a partner. Write the correct words on the board to check the spelling.

Answers: 1. paragraph   2. support   3. new

B Read the rubric with students, emphasizing that the seven sentences are the first sentences from the seven paragraphs that make up the following text. Give them adequate time to read the sentences properly. Then give them plenty of time to discuss the questions with a partner. End the task when about half the class have completed it. Note that the final question is the real task, and will take much longer to answer than the other questions. You might like to discuss questions 1–3 as a whole class, and then set 4 as pairwork. Go over students' answers to 4, but don't tell them the correct answers, as they will check in the text in a moment.

C There are no follow-up tasks with this text, so checking answers to Exercise B is the only task. The aim is to check that by looking at the topic sentences first, students felt they read more quickly and understood more. Tell students to correct any wrong guesses in Exercise B as they read.

D Get a general consensus from the class.

Read the exam tip with students.

Reading 3

This is a preparation phase for students to practise topic sentence reading before getting on to the more exam-related tasks. Read through the introductory line with students.

A Read through the three points with students, and check they know to read only the topic sentences. Set a time limit of two minutes, and then tell them to cover the text again. Go over the answers as a whole class, writing notes on the board.

Answers: The whole text is about what makes people happy at work.

It is organized typically – an introductory paragraph and then a list of examples. Each paragraph is a different example.

Supporting information will consist of examples, reasons and explanations. Sometimes the supporting sentences paraphrase the topic sentence.

B Students read the exam-type questions here, but don't attempt to answer them yet. Make sure they understand that they are still predicting from topic sentences. Students will need to look at the text again now, but only at the topic sentences. Tell them to write the letters of the paragraphs into the spaces provided, but lightly in pencil, so that answers can be changed when they read the text. Set a time limit of about three minutes. Ask students to tell you their answers, so you can check how well they have predicted, but don't give correct answers.

C Students should now be ready to work through the practice tasks. They have practised these tasks before, and should need minimal help. Give them a minute to read the questions, and set a time limit of about 15 minutes.

D Give students sufficient time to check, and think about why they may have answered incorrectly before moving on to Exercise E. The answers, together with the parts of the text that provide answers, are reproduced here.

Answers:
1. B (They want to see ... an end result.)
2. F (Most people ... don't feel they are doing this if they are repeating a routine day after day)

3. A (... are less likely to leave the company)

4. E (The whole paragraph explains the point.)

5. D (... they want to have a conversation and share a joke.)

6. C (The whole paragraph explains the point.)

7. benefit   8. better   9. achieve

10. appreciate   11. colleagues   12. control

13. improve   14. same

E   The number of questions in this reflective process will gradually decrease from now on. Students are aware of how it works and its benefits, and need a little less guidance. Remind them that identifying what they are doing well and not doing so well is a very good way of focusing on what they can do better next time. Allow students time to reflect and complete the task, and then ask them if they are happy with the number of correct answers. You may like to ask one student what he or she will do differently next time.

Key vocabulary in context

The task focuses on verbs that could be confused. Students can work individually or in pairs. You can give answers orally, or ask students to read out the complete sentences.

Answers: 1. appreciate   2. respect   3. trust   4. deal with

The Workbook task for this unit provides further practice of making predictions about a text using topic sentences. Work through this task if there is time in the lesson, as it will be more beneficial if conducted in pairs.

Writing

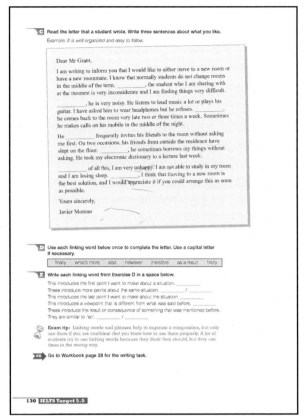

Objectives

- **To present and practise linking devices typically used in formal letters.**

- **To practise writing a formal letter that is typical of the IELTS writing exam.**

Writing 1

The aim of the first stage is to provide an opportunity for some speaking practice, to present more useful vocabulary students may need for talking about feelings and to prepare students for the writing tasks that follow.

A You can either encourage students to use dictionaries here, or go through the highlighted words with them.

Drill the words so that pronunciation is practised. Give students a few minutes to discuss the questions in pairs.

B Point out that different forms of the highlighted words are practised. Deal with meaning, as in

Exercise A. Model the adjectives within the phrases at the beginning of each sentence with exaggerated stress and intonation, so that students get a sense of how the words are really used ('It is <u>really</u> an<u>noy</u>ing when ...'). Give students about ten minutes to complete the sentences, and monitor to check accuracy.

C Tell students to say the sentences with real emphasis. Stop students if they sound flat, and drill the sentences they have written more naturally.

D This discussion is direct preparation for the writing task that follows. If most students have not been in a position like this, talk about it as a class so that those who have shared a room can talk.

Writing 2

The best way to clarify some parts of the feedback process here will be to have the composition on an OHP transparency.

A Give students a minute or two to read the task instructions, and then ask questions to check they understand ('Where are you living?', 'Do you have a room to yourself?', 'Is "inconsiderate" positive or negative?' and so on). Make sure everything is clear before moving on to Exercise B.

B Students are familiar with this type of writing preparation task. Give them a few minutes to talk through the points, and then get some feedback. Get a general consensus about whether the task is fairly manageable or very challenging, and establish that the letter should be formal.

C The aim of this activity is to revise what students focused on in the last unit. They have previously discussed what they like and don't like about a composition, and have read a teacher's comments about one. However, they haven't yet written their own comments, and this will be more challenging. Read through the example with them, and then give them ten minutes to read the letter, and write three sentences of their own. Tell them not to worry about the spaces for now. If students don't have as many ideas as they should, open it up as a class discussion, and get some comments up on the board.

D These linking words are very difficult to define, and students will learn them better by trying to use them in context, and by gradually becoming familiar with them. The meaning is checked in Exercise E anyway. Students can either work individually and then compare, or work in pairs straightaway. Tell them to use the words they know first so that the others are easier to guess at. End the task when about half the class has finished. Go through answers before going on to Exercise E. The best way to give clear feedback would be to have the composition on an OHP transparency.

Answers:
paragraph 1: however
paragraph 2: Firstly / What's more
paragraph 3: also / Finally
paragraph 4: As a result / Therefore

E The aim of this activity is to check that students have grasped the real meaning of the words, and to consolidate so that they can start to use the words themselves. Students can either work

individually and then compare, or work in pairs straightaway. Once again, an OHP transparency would be the best way to give clear feedback.

Firstly: This introduces the first point I want to make about a situation.
What's more / Also: These introduce more points about the same situation.
Finally: This introduces the last point I want to make about the situation.
However: This introduces a viewpoint that is different from what was said before. It is like 'but'.
As a result / Therefore: These introduce the result or consequence of something that was mentioned before. They are similar to 'so'.

Read the exam tip with students.

Writing task

The writing tasks are found either in the Workbook or in the exam practice section at the end of the unit. For this unit, the task is in the Workbook.

A Students should be more confident about writing letters by now, but will still need preparation. Read through the instructions, and ask how many students feel they can manage the task fairly easily this time.

B Put them straight into pairs to answer the questions. The aim of this activity is to provide them with a few points to make when they come to write the letter. You can go through answers with them, or monitor as they talk.

C Monitor as students work, but check specifically that they are organizing their letters, making relevant points and using appropriate register. There should be more accuracy now, especially with simple structures and fixed expressions.

When students have completed the task, tell them to look at the model composition on page 270 of the Course Book. Put them into pairs to compare their composition against the model. The model is reproduced on the next page.

If you collect students' letters to mark, use the process to get an idea of what they are capable of now, and to give constructive feedback. You should correct mistakes that you feel they shouldn't be making at this level.

Dear Mr Hardwick,

I am writing about some problems I have been having with students who are renting one of your houses. They are at 47, Colwell Gardens, which is the house next door to mine. I am at 45.

Your tenants are very inconsiderate, and seem to have no respect for neighbours living around them. Firstly, they play loud music all day and until late at night. What's more, there is frequently a lot of shouting and arguing. If they go out for the evening, they come home in the middle of the night and make a lot of noise.

I tried to speak to them about their behaviour, but they were very rude. When I complained about the noise, they seemed to find it funny, and nothing has changed. I am really very angry about the situation now.

Please could you speak to your tenants about their behaviour, and warn them that other people in the street have had enough. If nothing changes, I will report the problem to the local council and I do not want to have to do that.

Yours sincerely,

Greg Warren

Consolidation

Student: No, it's very boring most of the time.

3

Examiner: Are you nervous about the exams that you're taking next month?

Student: No, I'm not nervous. I like exams.

4

Examiner: What did you think of London? Did you get confused travelling around on the tube?

Student: No, it was easy.

B 🎧 Read the rubric with students, and then play the second recording. Try to elicit responses like 'more friendly', and establish that fuller answers sound so much more natural.

Speaking

The aim of this activity is to provide more focus on and practice with sounding natural and chatty, rather than sounding abrupt and uninterested.

A 🎧 Give students a moment to read through the exchanges, and then play the whole recording. Ask the class what they think. Try to elicit responses like 'rude', 'not friendly' and so on.

Tapescript 🎧 111 (1 min, 2 secs)

A **Look at these exchanges between an examiner and some students. Then listen. What do you think about the students' answers?**

1

Examiner: So, were you disappointed when you didn't get into university?

Student: No, I didn't care.

2

Examiner: So, working in advertising must be very exciting.

Tapescript 🎧 112 (1 min, 11 secs)

B **Listen to these students answering the same questions. How are their answers better?**

1

Examiner: So, were you disappointed when you didn't get into university?

Student: Actually, I didn't mind too much. I wasn't sure that I really wanted to go to university anyway.

2

Examiner: So, working in advertising must be very exciting.

Student: Mm, yes and no. It can be quite boring, actually. You do the same thing a lot of the time.

3

Examiner: Are you nervous about the exams that you're taking next month?

Student: I'm quite looking forward to them, actually. I quite like doing exams.

4

Examiner: What did you think of London? Did you get confused travelling around on the tube?

Student: It wasn't too bad, actually. I've been to a few big cities before.

Read the exam tip with students. Ask them if they can remember any words or expressions used to introduce disagreement.

C ⌁ Give students time to read the tapescript, and monitor as they highlight useful language. Point out how frequently 'actually' is used to introduce responses like these.

Tapescript ⌁ 113 (0 mins, 13 secs)

C **Look at the tapescript and listen again. Highlight expressions you want to use.**

[Play track 112 again]

D Students should practise the exchanges once as they read. Focus on stress and intonation patterns. Then tell one student to close the book and try to remember the responses whilst his or her partner reads the first line.

Vocabulary

A and B ⌁ Students have previously seen a few of these tasks to do with spelling correction and marking stress. They should work individually, then compare the spelling, and say the words aloud to a partner in order to mark the stress. You or they should write the answers on the board. Play the recording for students to check their pronunciation.

Tapescript ⌁ 114 (1 min, 8 secs)

B **Listen and mark the main stress on the words in Exercise A above. Then practise saying them.**

1	emotional	2	disappointed
3	annoying	4	frightened
5	furious	6	anxious
7	anxiety	8	pressure
9	sociable	10	appreciate

Answers: 1. e<u>mo</u>tional   2. disap<u>poin</u>ted
3. an<u>noy</u>ing   4. <u>frigh</u>tened   5. <u>fu</u>rious
6. <u>an</u>xious   7. an<u>xi</u>ety   8. <u>pre</u>ssure
9. <u>so</u>ciable   10. ap<u>pre</u>ciate

C By now, students know how to work through this type of task. It revises vocabulary learnt in the unit, emphasizes the need to learn the different forms of common words, and checks spelling. Students should complete the task individually. For feedback, either you or students should write the answers on the board.

Answers: 1. confusing   2. terrified
3. happiness   4. excitement   5. stressful
6. relaxation

Errors

A Students know that each unit ends with an error-correction task. Tell them that there are no errors of spelling. They can either complete the task individually or work in pairs. You will need to write the correct versions of each sentence on the board to clarify corrections.

Answers:
1. This film is really boring.
2. I'm feeling (absolutely) exhausted today.
3. She's very disappointed about it.
4. It really makes me angry when people say that.
5. Most people are afraid of spiders.
6. It's a difficult problem to deal with.

Exam Practice

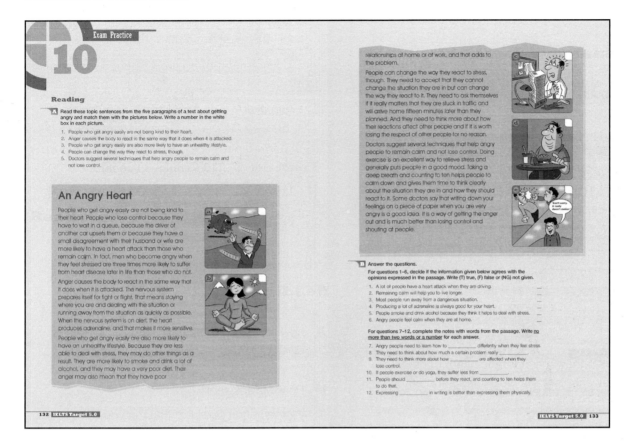

Exam Practice

10

Reading

Read these topic sentences from the five paragraphs of a text about getting angry and match them with the pictures below. Write a number in the white box in each picture.

1. People who get angry easily are not being kind to their heart.
2. Anger causes the body to react in the same way that it does when it is attacked.
3. People who get angry easily are also more likely to have an unhealthy lifestyle.
4. People can change the way they react to stress, though.
5. Doctors suggest several techniques that help angry people to remain calm and not lose control.

An Angry Heart

People who get angry easily are not being kind to their heart. People who lose control because they have to wait in a queue, because the driver of another car upsets them or because they have a small disagreement with their husband or wife are more likely to have a heart attack than those who remain calm. In fact, men who become angry when they feel stressed are three times more likely to suffer from heart disease later in life than those who do not.

Anger causes the body to react in the same way that it does when it is attacked. The nervous system prepares itself for fight or flight. That means staying where you are and dealing with the situation or running away from the situation as quickly as possible. When the nervous system is on alert, the heart produces adrenaline, and that makes it more sensitive.

People who get angry easily are also more likely to have an unhealthy lifestyle. Because they are less able to deal with stress, they may do other things as a result. They are more likely to smoke and drink a lot of alcohol, and they may have a very poor diet. Their anger may also mean that they have poor

relationships at home or at work, and that adds to the problem.

People can change the way they react to stress, though. They need to accept that they cannot change the situation they are in but can change the way they react to it. They need to ask themselves if it really matters that they are stuck in traffic and will arrive home fifteen minutes later than they planned. And they need to think more about how their reactions affect other people and if it is worth losing the respect of other people for no reason.

Doctors suggest several techniques that help angry people to remain calm and not lose control. Doing exercise is an excellent way to relieve stress and generally puts people in a good mood. Taking a deep breath and counting to ten helps people to calm down and gives them time to think clearly about the situation they are in and how they should react to it. Some doctors say that writing down your feelings on a piece of paper when you are very angry is a good idea. It is a way of getting the anger out and is much better than losing control and shouting at people.

Answer the questions.

For questions 1–6, decide if the information given below agrees with the opinions expressed in the passage. Write (T) true, (F) false or (NG) not given.

1. A lot of people have a heart attack when they are driving.
2. Remaining calm will help you to live longer.
3. Most people run away from a dangerous situation.
4. Producing a lot of adrenaline is always good for your heart.
5. People smoke and drink alcohol because they think it helps to deal with stress.
6. Angry people feel calm when they are at home.

For questions 7–12, complete the notes with words from the passage. Write no more than two words or a number for each answer.

7. Angry people need to learn how to _____ differently when they feel stress.
8. They need to think about how much a certain problem really _____.
9. They need to think more about how _____ are affected when they lose control.
10. If people exercise or do yoga, they suffer less from _____.
11. People should _____ before they react, and counting to ten helps them to do that.
12. Expressing _____ in writing is better than expressing them physically.

132 IELTS Target 5.0   IELTS Target 5.0 133

Reading

This preparation phase provides a little more specific practice with topic sentence reading, before students get on to the real exam tasks. It should also provoke interest in the text, and provide a little speaking practice.

A Look at the heading, but don't allow students to read the text yet. Read the rubric, and make sure students understand the topic. Point out that 'anger' is the noun giving rise to 'angry', before or whilst students read the topic sentences. Give them about five minutes for the matching task. Give the correct answers, as it will make the text more manageable. Write the letters and numbers on the board for clarity when checking answers.

Answers:
Topic sentence 1 – picture c
Topic sentence 2 – picture a
Topic sentence 3 – picture d
Topic sentence 4 – picture e
Topic sentence 5 – picture b

B Students should now be ready to work through the practice tasks. They have practised these tasks before, and should need minimal help. Give them a minute to read the questions, and set a time limit of about 20 minutes. Write the answers on the board so that they are clear. It would be a good idea to give students the lines that provide the answers to some of the questions.

Answers:
1. NG
2. T (much of the first paragraph provides the answer)
3. NG
4. F (the heart produces adrenaline, and that makes it more sensitive)
5. T (Because they are less able to deal with stress, they may do other things as a result)
6. F (Their anger may also mean that they have poor relationships at home)
7. react   8. matters   9. other people
10. stress   11. take a breath
12. your feelings

Unit 10 Workbook answers

Speaking and Vocabulary

A 1. about   2. of   3. of   4. about
   5. of / with   6. about   7. about   8. of

   Read through the grammar check with students.

B 1. bored   2. exciting   3. annoying
   4. surprised   5. amazing   6. relaxing

C Students' own answers.

D 1. c   2. d   3. e   4. a   5. b

Listening

A Speaker 1 – anger
   Speaker 2 – fear
   Speaker 3 – disappointment
   Speaker 4 – confusion

> **Tapescript** 🎧 **118** (1 min, 33 secs)
>
> **A** **Listen and match each speaker with a feeling below.**
>
> **1**
> I just can't believe you did that when I specifically told you not to. When I say 'DON'T DO something', LISTEN and DON'T do it. Now, you're not going to watch any TV for the rest of the day.
>
> **2**
> No, I'm really sorry. I've thought about it, and I just can't do it. I'm really proud that you asked me, but speaking in front of that many people terrifies me. I'm really sorry, but you'll just have to ask somebody else.
>
> **3**
> Oh, no. Josh has just phoned to say the party's been cancelled. Apparently, the neighbours said they didn't want him to have a party with so many people. I was really looking forward to it, too – now what am I going to do on a Saturday night?
>
> **4**
> Oh, I can't do this. I've been trying for hours, and it just doesn't make sense. Look, every time I do this, this happens. Do you know why?

B 1. Speaker 2   2. Speaker 4   3. Speaker 1
   4. Speaker 3

> **Tapescript** 🎧 **119** (0 mins, 11 secs)
>
> **B** **Listen again and answer these questions.**
>
> [Play track 118 again]

Reading

A how men and women express their emotions differently

B Possible answers:

   Women often complain that men do not express their feelings. (Men are cold. / Men are still little boys. / Men don't understand women.)

   Expressing feelings and having feelings is not the same thing. (Just because men don't talk about feelings doesn't mean they don't have feelings.)

   Men may feel that expressing their feelings is pointless. (It doesn't make the problem go away.)

   A lot of men prefer talking to other men. (Men understand each other. / Men understand the problems that men have.)

   The situation will probably never change. (This is all human nature. / Men and women must learn to accept their differences.)

Writing

The writing task is dealt with in the main section of the Teacher's Book.

Review 2

Review 2

Speaking and Vocabulary

A Answer these questions with a partner.

1. Do you feel that your speaking is generally improving?
2. Do you know what kind of questions the examiner will ask you in each part of the exam?
3. Do you feel more confident about answering those questions?

B The questions below practise the topics that you learnt in Units 6–10. Work in pairs. One of you is student A, the other is B. Ask and answer with your partner.

Student A
1. What do you like about the town or city you live in?
2. Do you prefer a city lifestyle or a more rural lifestyle?
3. How do you usually travel around your town or city?
4. Do you usually have enough time to do all the things you want to do each day?
5. Do you like shopping?
6. What makes you happy?

Student B
1. What is the most beautiful city you have visited?
2. Does your town or city have good facilities for entertainment and leisure activities?
3. How often do you fly? Do you enjoy flying?
4. How do you usually spend your free time?
5. When it comes to money, are you a saver or a spender?
6. What annoys you or makes you really angry?

C Write important words and phrases that you have learnt in Units 6–10 under each heading.

places	city and country life	travel and transport

feelings	**my words and phrases**	time expressions

money	say how often you do something

Listening and Reading

The thoughts below are from the 'exam tips' in the reading and listening sections of Units 6–10.

A Complete each sentence about listening, using one word only.

1. When I am listening for specific information, like writing names of places on a map, the speaker will often _____ information that I need to answer a question.
2. Sometimes I will have to complete a short _____ of what I heard on the tape. I need to spell words correctly and make sure they _____ grammatically. However, if I'm not sure how to fill a space, I should write what I think I hear.
3. Having a table will help me when I listen, because I can predict how the talk will be organized and _____ into parts. I will know that the speaker is going to move to a new topic within the talk.
4. I will sometimes need to understand the meaning of a key word I don't know from the context. I might have to _____ the spelling of a new word if it is part of an answer.
5. If a task asks me to classify, I will need to read the _____ carefully so that I know exactly what to do. I will need to look at points as I listen because they will not be in the same _____ as I hear them.

B Complete each sentence about reading using one word only.

1. In the IELTS Reading Module, passages which are advertisements, leaflets or information pages will be clearly divided into sections. Texts will be clearly divided into _____.
2. Reading the _____ sentence, which is usually the first sentence, of each paragraph will help me to read more quickly. I will often be able to predict quite a lot about a text just by reading the _____ sentence.
3. I will understand a text better if I can quickly see what is _____ and what is opinion.
4. When you complete a summary, you will either need to use words from the text or choose words from a _____. If the words come from a _____, they will not always be words from the text. I should always look at what comes before and after a space in a summary so I can check that answers _____ grammatically.
5. I will read more quickly and understand texts better if I see how one word or phrase _____ back or forwards to another. I need to understand how _____ words, like 'it', 'this', 'there' and 'one', are used.

C Answer the questions (Y) yes or (N) no.

1. Has your listening and reading improved since the last review section?
2. Do you feel more confident about doing well in the tasks?
3. Are you dealing better with words and phrases that you don't know?
4. Are you happy with the number of correct answers you are achieving in the tasks?

Exam tip: Don't worry if your scores for some tasks are the same as they were earlier in the course. The tapescripts are getting longer. Vocabulary and grammatical structures are more challenging!

Writing

You will hear an interview with an IELTS examiner. He talks about marking compositions.

A Look at the interviewer's first question and then listen to the first part of the interview. Mark these statements (T) true, (F) false or (NG) not given.

What is the difference between the Academic exam and the General Training exam in terms of the Writing Module?

1. The General Training writing exam is easier than the Academic writing exam.
2. In the General Training writing exam, students need to write about graphs and charts.
3. Not many students do well in the second part of the Academic writing exam.
4. For General Training students, writing a letter is usually the easier of two tasks.

B Look at the interviewer's second question and then listen to the second part of the interview. Put the points into the order in which you hear them.

What do you look for when you mark an IELTS composition?

___ A letter or composition should have paragraphs.
___ The student should use the appropriate register.
___ The student must use the right number of words.
___ Points or ideas need to be linked with both reference words or linking words.
___ The composition must be easy to read.
___ Each paragraph should start with a topic sentence.
_1_ The student must answer the question.
___ Points must be organized into a logical order.

C Look at the interviewer's third question and then listen to the third part of the interview. Complete the summary below. Use no more than two words for each answer.

What about vocabulary, spelling and accurate grammar?

If students are aiming for a lower score in the IELTS exam, they do not need to use very (1) _____ vocabulary. They should try to use the (2) _____ or phrase if they know it, but it is important to keep things simple. They should only use words and phrases that they know how to use (3) _____. For students aiming for a lower score, it is more important to use (4) _____ grammatical structures accurately than to try to use complicated structures that they do not really know how to use.

D Read the tapescript on pages 302 and 303.

E Give yourself a mark out of ten for how much your writing has improved.

```
0 ——————— 5 ——————— 10
My writing has not          My writing is much better
really improved at all.      than it was at the beginning
                             of the course.
```

What next?

You've now completed two-thirds of the course. You've heard most of the different types of talk or conversation that you will hear in the Listening Module, and you've read most of the different types of text that you will have to read in the Reading Module. You've practised almost all of the task types for each Module. You should feel more confident about taking the exam now, but don't worry if there are still parts that you find difficult. There is plenty of time to practise those parts and to deal with any problems you are having. Here are some things that you should do now. Decide which ones you'd like to do first. Number them.

☐ Continue to speak English every time you get the opportunity. Now you know what sort of things the examiner will ask you in the spoken exam, practise talking about those things. If you have friends or relatives who speak good English, try to have short conversations with them that practise what you have been learning and try to use new vocabulary that you have learnt.

☐ There are lots of websites that have short clips with people speaking English. Even if you don't understand everything people say, you will pick up some words and phrases and become more familiar with the pronunciation patterns of the language. Watch a movie in English from time to time if you can. Continue to borrow CDs to listen to if you need extra practice with the Listening Module of the exam.

☐ Continue to read as much as you can. You should be able to follow more challenging texts now, so look at English newspapers and magazines more frequently. There are thousands of websites in English, and you can always find something that you are especially interested in. Continue to think about the organization of a text and note down new vocabulary that you think will be useful to remember. Try to use the vocabulary when you speak or write.

☐ As your English improves, you may feel that you want to learn and remember more vocabulary than is realistic. Make sure you learn and revise vocabulary that is useful and that you can use to communicate. As well as single new words, you should learn words that you already know used in new ways. You should learn how words go together to form common phrases and expressions.

☐ If you are still having difficulty with basic writing skills, continue to practise writing sentences and short paragraphs. Practise your spelling and punctuation. If you feel that your writing has improved, practise writing more compositions. Continue to look at as many model answers to exam questions as you can. This will help you know what to write and how to write it in the exam.

Go on to the next section of the Course Book. Make sure you practise all aspects of your English, but focus on what you are having problems with. Don't worry if you don't make progress in all areas at the same time.

Overview

The review units are very much reviews rather than revision units. The aim is for students to consolidate what they have learnt about the IELTS exam, and how to go about getting the grade they require. There are tasks which are purely designed to encourage students to reflect and discuss, and there are tasks which consolidate and have correct answers. The instructions given to teachers for the review sections are brief, as the aims and procedure for each task are fairly self-explanatory.

Speaking and Vocabulary

A Give students three or four minutes to discuss the questions in pairs. Then get a general class consensus.

B The aim is to practise typical exam questions, and to see if students have gained in confidence from practising tasks of this type. Students should read the questions to their partner and not allow their partner to see the question. Encourage them to practise asking about anything they don't catch. Monitor carefully, and check students' performance. Don't go through each question as feedback, as it will be repetitive and not at all beneficial.

C Give students a moment to look at the web, and then read through the headings with them. You could start by telling them not to look back at the units in the Course Book, and see what they have retained. After five minutes, allow them to look back, adding words and phrases from the unit. Try to encourage them to do this in order to store new language rather than simply to fulfil a task.

Listening and Reading

A Students can either work individually and then compare with a partner, or work directly with a partner so that they can discuss the points as they read. Go over answers as a class, and write the missing words on the board for clarity.

Answers: 1. repeat   2. summary / fit
3. divided   4. guess
5. instructions / order

B As in Exercise A above.

Answers: 1. paragraphs   2. topic / topic
3. fact   4. box / box / fit
4. refers / reference

C Give students a few minutes to reflect and answer. Then get some feedback from the class.

Read through the exam tip with students. This is important, as students might think they are not progressing because their task scores are not improving.

Writing

A Make sure students know that the speaker that they will listen to is an examiner, and that he will talk about the Writing Module. Read through the interviewer's question with them, and give them time to look at the sentences that follow. Play the recording right through as students answer. Play the recording again if necessary. Go over answers orally.

Tapescript 115 (1 min, 31 secs)

A **Look at the interviewer's first question and then listen to the first part of the interview. Mark these statements (T) true, (F) false or (NG) not given.**

Examiner: Well, the first composition is completely different. I think it's fair to say that the General Training writing exam is easier. In the Academic exam, students need to look at a graph or chart and then explain what they see. They need to learn how to use a very specific type of academic language.

In the General Training exam, they write a letter. It is usually formal, but it can be informal. Of course, they must learn how to write various types of letter, but generally it is an easier task. The second composition is similar in both versions of the exam. It involves discussing a topic or agreeing or disagreeing with a statement. In the General exam, the topic may be a little more general – about a social issue, for example. In the Academic exam, the topic can be more academic – discussing technology or space travel, for example. Students taking the General Training Module often find the second composition much more difficult than the first.

Answers: 1. T   2. F   3. NG   4. T

B 🎧 Read through the interviewer's second question with students, and give them time to look at the points that follow. Play the recording right through, as students answer. Play the recording again if necessary. Using an OHP transparency would be the clearest way of giving feedback. Otherwise, you will need to write each point in order on the board, or simply tell students to check the order themselves in the tapescript.

Tapescript 🎧 **116** (2 mins, 48 secs)

B Look at the interviewer's second question and then listen to the second part of the interview. Put the points into the order in which you hear them.

Examiner: Well, there are quite a lot of different things to look for and, of course, it depends on the level of the student who's writing. I can quickly see if the composition is written by a student with a lower level of English, or if it's been written by a very advanced learner. I need to look for different things then, so I can decide what grade to give. However, there are certain aspects of a composition that are very important – in fact, essential – and that is the same for any student who takes the exam. Firstly, what the student writes must be relevant to the question – it doesn't matter how well written a composition is, if it doesn't answer the question, it won't pass. Then, there's the word count – the letter must be at least a hundred and fifty words, and the second composition two hundred and fifty. Sometimes a student writes very well but just doesn't say enough, and I'm afraid I can't pass the composition. All examiners say that a composition must be easy to read. That means they can understand what the student is trying to say. It doesn't have to be perfect English, but it must be easy to follow – sometimes that means that the student should keep it simple. A simple composition that is easy to follow is better than a very complex composition that is difficult to follow. Now, organization: all compositions should be organized – of course, that's what makes them easier to read. The student must make his or her points in a logical order, and they should introduce and conclude their ideas. Any type of composition should be divided into paragraphs, and each paragraph should have a purpose. Even lower-level students should understand that a topic sentence introduces a paragraph, and helps the reader to follow what the writer is saying. Students should be able to use reference words – at lower levels, these can be simple references, like 'this' and 'that', but at higher levels I expect to see more advanced reference and linking words. Finally, the student needs to use language that is appropriately formal or informal. If the composition is a letter to a college principal, it's not good to have lots of contractions and very informal vocabulary.

Answers:

5 A letter or composition should have paragraphs.

8 The student should use the appropriate register.

2 The student must use the right number of words.

7 Points or ideas need to be linked with both reference words or linking words.

3 The composition must be easy to read.

6 Each paragraph should start with a topic sentence.

1 The student must answer the question.

4 Points must be organized into a logical order.

C Read through the interviewer's third question with students, and give them time to look at the summary that follows. Play the recording right through, as students answer. Play the recording again if necessary. Write answers on the board for clarity.

Tapescript 117 (1 min, 33 secs)

C Look at the interviewer's third question and then listen to the third part of the interview. Complete the summary below. Use <u>no more than two words</u> for each answer.

Examiner: Well, these are all important, but not quite as important as what I mentioned before. In order to score a very high mark, students need to use an advanced range of vocabulary – which is all spelt correctly, of course. To score a lower grade, but to get the grade they want, students should keep it simple. Of course, if they know the right word or phrase, they should use it, but it is more important to make their point simply and clearly. Too many students try to use words and phrases that they have only heard once or twice and don't really understand properly. As for grammar, the same applies. Advanced students will show that they can use all sorts of grammatical structures and score a high mark, but it's just not necessary if you are aiming for a lower score. Lower-level learners should make sure they use basic structures accurately. Then, if they feel confident

with more challenging structures, they can try to use them. Students shouldn't try to say what they don't know how to say – they can usually make their point without having to use very complicated grammar.

Answers: 1. advanced   2. right word
3. properly   4. basic

D Students should read the tapescript, as this gives invaluable information about the writing exam.

E Tell students not to be too critical or modest with the score they give themselves. Once students have given themselves a grade, have a quick class discussion and get a general consensus as to whether writing skills are improving.

What next?

You might like to tell students to read this at home. You can check by asking questions, or by having a brief feedback session. If there is time to read it in class, it might be better to read through one section at a time and getting some feedback, rather than reading it right through in one go.

Now instruct students to complete mock test 2.

11 Health

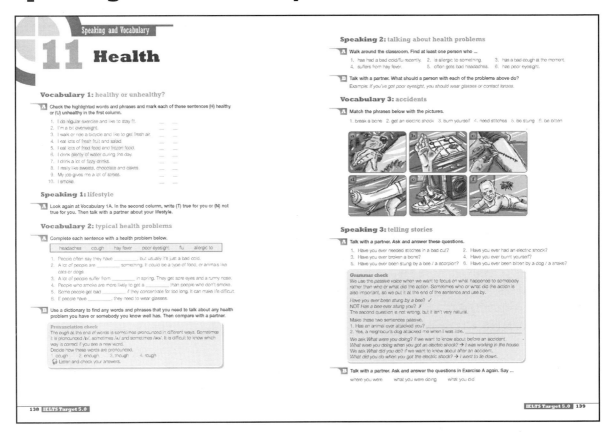

Unit overview

The eleventh unit is based around the theme of health. Students will talk about their lifestyles and what they do to stay healthy and keep fit. They will also talk about some typical problems with health and how they can be treated. Students will get further practice with various aspects of the IELTS exam.

Speaking and Vocabulary

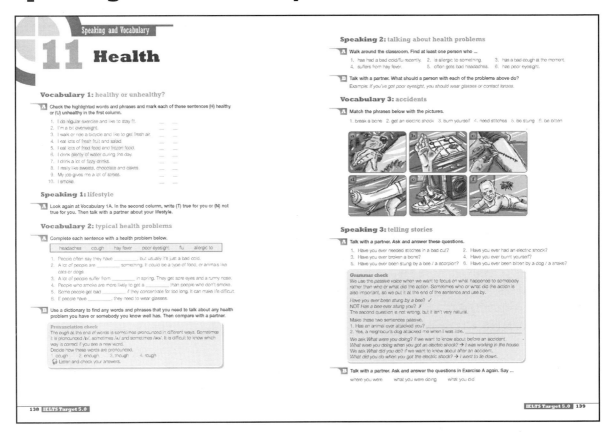

Objectives

- To give students further practice answering the type of questions they can expect in the first part of the speaking exam.

- To present and practise vocabulary related to health issues.

- To revise the use of active and passive forms, and the use of past simple and past continuous questions.

Vocabulary 1

The aim of this activity is to revise some vocabulary that students should already know, and to present some new ways of talking about healthy and unhealthy lifestyles.

A Students should use dictionaries as they go through and mark the sentences. Pre-teaching all the vocabulary will be time-consuming, and students should be more independent about words they need to check. You could ask the students questions to check some of what you think might be new to them ('Which word means "heavier than you should be"?', 'Give me an example of a fizzy drink', etc.).

Answers: 1. H   2. U   3. H   4. H   5. U
6. H   7. U   8. U   9. U   10. U

Speaking 1

A Tell students to complete the second column in Vocabulary 1A as preparation to talk in a moment. Then tell them they should use words and phrases from Exercise A to talk to a partner. Encourage them to use new language rather than language they know and is safe. After a minute or two, tell them to look back at the task if they want to use a particular new phrase.

Vocabulary 2

A The aim of this activity is to present and practise language relating to health problems that students are likely to need to talk about, rather than a long list of possible ailments. It will be difficult to pre-teach the words in the box without almost doing the whole task yourself. It would be better to encourage dictionary use. Students can complete the task individually or in pairs. Clarify anything that students don't understand as you feed back answers.

Answers: 1. flu   2. allergic to   3. hay fever
4. cough   5. headaches   6. poor eyesight

B You can either set a time limit, or tell students to find a certain number of words or phrases. They should talk to a partner about why they have chosen to learn certain words, but make sure they know they don't have to talk about anything too personal.

Pronunciation check

Read the explanation with students. Pronounce each letter of the first '~ough' – o-u-g-h – as no single pronunciation exists for this spelling. Then model each of the sounds written in phonetic script. Students should work in pairs to decide how the four words are pronounced, so that they can say them aloud to each other. Play the recording for them to check. Drill the words, and then give them a couple of minutes to practise saying them again correctly.

Tapescript 🎧 **120** (0 mins, 57 secs)

Pronunication check

The *ough* at the end of words is sometimes pronounced in different ways. Sometimes it is pronounced /ɒ/, sometimes /ʌ/ and sometimes /əʊ/. It is difficult to know which way is correct if you see a new word.

Decide how these words are pronounced.

1 cough   2 enough

3 though   4 rough

Listen and check your answers.

Speaking 2

A Make sure students understand that the aim is to find at least one person who answers each question 'yes'. You might like to give them a couple of minutes to form the correct questions that they need to ask, but they may be able to ask them more spontaneously. Tell them to sit back down when they have one 'yes' for each question.

B Look at the example, and give students a few minutes to find a way of dealing with each problem. Get some ideas from the class to finish the activity.

Vocabulary 3

A You could tell students to cover the words and phrases and talk about what the accident is in each picture, to see what they already know. Once students see the words and phrases, give them a minute or two to match, using dictionaries to check what they don't know. Feed back by pointing at each picture and asking students to use the phrases to give you answers.

Answers: a. b, be bitten   b. 3, burn yourself
c. 4, need stitches   d. 1, break a bone
e. 2, get an electric shock   f. 5, be stung

Speaking 3

A Allow students to answer the questions without going over the grammatical structures. Listen to see how much they need to focus on the grammar check in a moment. Give them a few minutes to talk in pairs, and then ask various students the questions yourself.

Grammar check

Read through the first two lines of the grammar check, and then ask students which two sentences in Exercise A above are passive. Then read through the example, and emphasize that learning the passive is as much about being natural about how a structure is formed as about being right or wrong.

Give students a minute or two to work through the two transformation sentences individually, and then get two students to come and write the correct passive forms on the board.

Answers:
1. Have you ever been attacked by an animal?
2. Yes, I was attacked by a neighbour's dog.

Read through the next part of the grammar check slowly, making sure students see the difference between the two questions. The speaking task that follows practises the two structures.

B Give students a couple of minutes to plan what they want to say this time, and make sure the focus is on accuracy. Monitor as students are talking, and make sure that they are using the target language properly.

For further speaking and vocabulary practice, tell students to complete the exercises on page 30 of the Workbook. Set as an extra activity or homework task.

Listening

Listening

Listening 1: flow charts

A Look at part of a flow chart below and then answer these questions with a partner.

1. What is a flow chart?
2. What does this flow chart show?
3. What do these words mean?
   symptoms   diagnosis   treatment

Cold and flu

Follow the chart so that you know how to treat the symptoms of a cold or the flu and whether or not you need to see a doctor. Other conditions can have the same symptoms as a cold or the flu.

SYMPTOMS	DIAGNOSIS	TREATMENT
↓ BEGIN HERE		
① Do you have a fever? → NO	You may have a cold.	Get plenty of rest and drink lots of water.
↓ YES		
② Do you have a sore throat and headache but not a runny nose? → YES	You may have strep throat – a bacterial infection.	Get plenty of rest and drink lots of water. See a doctor if the fever lasts more than 48 hours. He may give you antibiotics.
↓ NO		
③ Did your symptoms start suddenly? Do your muscles ache? Do you have a sore throat and a runny nose? → YES	You may have the flu.	Get plenty of rest and drink lots of water. Medicine that you can buy at a chemist will relieve some of the symptoms.
↓ NO		

Grammar check
First conditional type sentences can be used to talk about possibility and give advice.
If you have a sore throat and a runny nose, you may have the flu.
If you have the flu, you should get plenty of rest.

B Look at the next part of the flow chart. Listen and complete the notes using no more than two words for each answer.

④ Do you have a bad cough and is it difficult to (1) _____? → YES	You may have bronchitis.	Get plenty of rest and drink lots of water. If you (2) _____, stop completely for a while. Medicine that you can buy at a chemist will relieve the (3) _____. If symptoms get worse, contact (4) _____
↓ NO		
⑤ Do you have a runny nose and sore eyes? → YES	You may be (5) _____ something.	Try medicine that you can buy at a chemist or ask your doctor for advice.

140 **IELTS Target 5.0**

Question-type tip: A flow chart shows a series of events or actions and their possible results. In the Listening Module of the exam, you will sometimes need to complete notes on a flow chart. Having a chart like this helps you, because you can predict how the talk will be organized and divided into parts. You know when the speaker is going to go from one topic to another.

Listening 2: practice with flow charts

A Look at the first part of a flow chart that shows you what to do if you have a headache. Listen and complete the notes using no more than two words for each answer.

Headaches

There are different reasons why you may have a headache. You may also have other symptoms. Follow the chart so that you know what to do if you have a headache.

SYMPTOMS	DIAGNOSIS	TREATMENT
↓ BEGIN HERE		
① Do you have a fever or other symptoms of a cold? Have you been sick? → YES	You may have a bad cold or (1) _____	Get plenty of rest and drink lots of water. (2) _____ that you can buy at a chemist will relieve some of the symptoms.
↓ NO		
② Do you have a very bad headache and a stiff (3) _____? Does normal light hurt (4) _____? → YES	You may have meningitis – a serious condition that can affect your (5) _____	You MUST see your doctor or go to a (6) _____ immediately.
↓ NO		
③ Have you hit (7) _____ recently? → YES	You may have concussion – a serious condition caused by (8) _____ pushing against your brain.	You MUST get immediate treatment.

B Check the key on page 270. How many questions did you answer correctly?

C Tick the sentences about the listening task that are true for you and think about how you can answer more questions correctly next time.

1. Looking at the flow chart helped me make predictions about what I would hear.
2. I understood the speaker and knew which words to write in the spaces.
3. I spelt most of my answers correctly.
4. I am pleased with how many questions I answered correctly.

Key vocabulary in context

Match the words 1–4 with the words a–d to make common noun phrases from the text.

1. runny	a. muscles
2. sore	b. nose
3. aching	c. neck
4. stiff	d. throat / eyes

IELTS Target 5.0 141

Objectives

- To introduce students to the concept of a flow chart.
- To show students that completing a flow chart is similar to completing a table, and that having the flow chart can aid prediction.
- To practise completing a flow chart, and to provide further practice with correctly spelling answers.

Listening 1

A Write 'flow chart' on the board, and ask whether anyone knows what it means. Don't tell students yet. Tell them to look at the flow chart for a couple of minutes. Read the three questions with them, pronouncing the three words in red. Then give students three or four minutes to answer the questions in pairs. Tell them not to look up the words for these questions, but to use the context to work them out. Go over answers orally with students.

Answers:

1. Flow charts show how a process works. They often show how a situation could be addressed in different ways, and what each of the consequences would then be.
2. This flow chart shows how symptoms of a health problem could be diagnosed in different ways, and what the treatment would be for each diagnosis.
3. Symptoms – show that somebody is ill / they are what people can see, like evidence.
   Diagnosis – is what the expert says the illness is by looking at the symptoms.
   Treatment – is how the health problem can be made better.

Grammar check

Tell students to read through the grammar check box.

B 🎧 Tell students to look at the next part of the flow chart before they read the task instructions. Then read the instructions with them and see if they can predict any answers (questions 1, 2 and 4 are very predictable, and it would be good for their confidence if you guided them towards predicting a couple of these correctly).

The aim of this activity is to familiarize students with the task type, so you can play the recording two or three times if necessary. Play it once right through with pens down, and then again, pausing for a moment in appropriate places so that students have time to write answers. Write the answer on the board for clarity. Point out the collocation, 'relieve pain'.

Tapescript 🎧 **121** (1 min, 38 secs)

B Look at the next part of the flow chart. Listen and complete the notes using <u>no more than two words</u> for each answer.

Voice: If you are not showing those symptoms, you may have another problem. You should ask yourself – do I have a bad cough, and is it difficult to breathe? If it is difficult to breathe or you feel out of breath, you may have bronchitis. Bronchitis is really a bad cold with a cough, but it can last longer than a typical cold and be more difficult to treat. If you have bronchitis, you should get plenty of rest and drink lots of water. If you smoke, you will make things much worse by smoking while you are ill. You should try to stop completely while you have the symptoms. You can buy medicine at a chemist that will relieve the pain of the coughing, but you really should contact a doctor immediately if the symptoms don't clear up or get worse.

Now, if you don't have a bad cough, but you do have a runny nose and sore eyes, it could be an allergy. Perhaps you are allergic to something common, like cat hair, or perhaps it's something unusual that you don't know about yet. Explain the symptoms to somebody at a chemist, and they may be able to give you medicine that will help. It might be better to see your doctor and get some advice, though.

Answers: 1. breathe   2. smoke   3. pain
4. your doctor   5. allergic to

Read the question-type tip with students, and point out how a flow chart is similar to a table, in terms of the advice given.

Listening 2

The aim now is to practise with flow charts. Students have had plenty of gap-filling practice already, so should be left to work through this activity on their own.

A 🎧 Look at the heading of the flow chart with students, and ask them to make a few predictions, such as 'Why might somebody have a headache?' and 'What should somebody do if they have a bad headache?' Give students a minute or so to look at the chart and make further predictions, and then play the whole recording. Students might find it difficult to listen to the recording only once more, but avoid playing it a third time. Students can discuss what difficulties they had, and then listen again later if necessary (see Exercises B and C).

Tapescript 🎧 **122** (2 mins, 37 secs)

A Look at the first part of a flow chart that shows you what to do if you have a headache. Listen and complete the notes using <u>no more than two words</u> for each answer.

Voice: There are various different reasons why you may have a headache. Some of them are not serious and can be treated easily – perhaps by simply taking a painkilling tablet, like an aspirin. Some headaches, however, may be a symptom of something far more serious, and you should get immediate advice.

First of all, ask yourself if you think you have other symptoms that suggest you have a cold. Do you have a fever, a runny nose, a cough or a sore throat? Have you been sick at all? If you have, then you probably have a bad cold or the flu, and the headache is just one of the symptoms. Get plenty of rest and drink plenty of water. There are many types of

---

medicine that you can buy at a chemist, and these will relieve some of the symptoms. Remember, though, medicine will not actually cure the condition, and you might prefer to just drink hot water with some lemon and honey, and take a couple of aspirin.

Now, if you don't think you have a cold, you must ask yourself how bad the headache is. If the headache is really bad and you have a stiff neck, there may be a bigger problem. If you feel that normal light is hurting your eyes, it may also be cause for concern. Meningitis is a serious condition. It is caused by an infection of blood around your brain and spinal cord. The condition can seriously affect your brain if not treated immediately. You must see your doctor or go immediately to the nearest hospital.

If you do not show these symptoms, you may still have something that needs treatment quickly. You may have an injury of some kind, and you must try to remember if you have hit your head at all in the last few days. If you have, you may be suffering from concussion. Concussion occurs after an injury to the head, when blood pushes against the brain. It is very serious and you must make sure that you get treatment immediately.

Now, if you don't remember any recent injury, you must ask yourself if you feel ... *(fade out)*

B Give students sufficient time to check answers and think about why they may have answered incorrectly, before moving on to Exercise C. Students should check any words they feel they need to with you as they look at the answers and tapescript.

Answers: 1. (the) flu   2. Medicine   3. neck
4. your eyes   5. your brain   6. hospital
7. your head   8. blood

C The number of questions in this reflective process will gradually decrease from now on. Students are aware of how it works and its benefits, and need a little less guidance. Remind them that identifying what they are doing well

and not doing so well is a very good way of focusing on what they can do better next time. Allow students time to reflect and complete the task. Play the recording again if necessary, and tell students to focus on why the correct answers are correct.

Key vocabulary in context

Students can work individually or in pairs. Note that 'aching neck' is quite possible, but is not present in the recording. Go over the answers, and then tell students to close their books and see how many of the complete phrases they can remember.

Answers: 1. b   2. d   3. a   4. c

For further listening practice, tell students to complete the exercise on page 30 of the Workbook. Set as an extra activity or homework task.

Reading

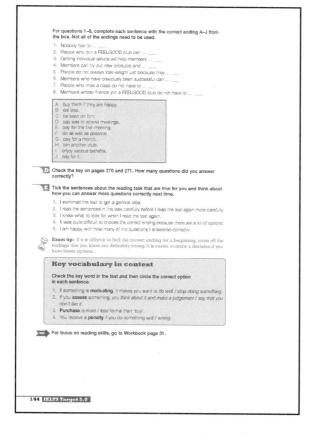

Objectives

- To introduce students to a sentence-completion task, and to focus on the skills required.

- To further practise skimming a text and reading a text for detail.

- To practise a task involving sentence completion.

This task occurs slightly less frequently in the exam than some other task types, but students will need to know how to approach it. The task involves scanning to identify the relevant part of the text and then reading very carefully to check the text says the same as the two parts of the sentence in the task.

Reading 1

The aim of this stage is to provide an opportunity for speaking practice, as well as to prepare students for the reading tasks that follow.

A Students will need to be clear about the exact meaning of 'lose weight'. Write it on the board, and then compare it with 'gain weight' and 'put on weight'. Tell them to think about how people lose weight in different ways. Give them five minutes to talk in pairs, and then open the questions up as a class discussion.

B This focuses on one of the topics in Exercise A, and serves as the basis for the tasks in Reading 2.

Reading 2

A Tell students that they are going to look at a task that they haven't seen yet. Tell them to read only sentence beginning 1, but all of the sentence endings A to G. Make sure they understand that C is the correct answer, and then give them a few minutes to discuss why. Talk about the reason together before students attempt the rest of the matching task. It is good if students say that some of the answers are illogical, but you must tell them that finding what is logical in the text is essential.

Now students should work individually to answer the remaining questions. When they have done so, tell them to compare with a partner and identify the parts of the text that provide the answers. Write the correct answers on the board.

Answers:
2. G (it's important to choose one that you are comfortable with so that you want to keep going.)
3. A (If you only go once a month, or stop going completely, you will waste a lot of money.)
4. E (There are usually some great offers available at fitness clubs, so you should shop around.)

B Students are familiar with this type of reflective analysis task, and know that the exam- or question-type tip that follows usually provides the answers. Tell them to cover the tips before they answer the question here. Give them three or four minutes to talk in pairs. Although the tips answer the questions, you should go over the answers with them now, clarifying anything if necessary.

Answers:
1. B (Some sentences are illogical, but students must check in the text.)
2. B
3. B (All endings begin with a modal verb, an auxiliary verb or a link verb (means).)

Read the tips with students, checking that they understand the points being made.

Reading 3

Students are practising a challenging task for the first time, so here is some preparation work to give them confidence and motivate them to read the text.

A Read the rubric with students, making sure that they take a quick look at the advertisement as you do so. Remind them that scanning means searching for specific information, and then tell them there is a time limit of two minutes for the scanning task. Read through the questions with students, and start the clock. Write the answers on the board and find out how many students answered all the questions correctly.

Answers:
1. FEELGOOD
2. a customer / somebody who goes to a FEELGOOD club
3. call the number at the bottom of the advertisement

B Read the instructions here with students, and make sure they understand why they are skimming. Make sure they stay within the time limit. Monitor to listen to what students have retained of the text. To finish the activity, ask a couple of students to tell you what they remember.

C The exam-type practice focuses only on the new task, and students should read the instructions themselves and work through the task. Set a time limit of about 15 minutes.

D Give students sufficient time to check and think about why they may have answered incorrectly, before moving on to Exercise E. The answers, together with the parts of the text that provide answers, are reproduced here.

Answers:

1. E (The first meeting is free for all!)
2. I (The whole ad provides this answer)
3. F (... individual advice that will ensure you achieve your goals ...)
4. A (... provide new products that you can try out and purchase if you are satisfied.)
5. B (... simply eating less doesn't necessarily equal weight loss.)
6. C (... people who we have already helped and show you videos that tell the story of their progress.)
7. J (There are no penalties for missed classes!)
8. G (... a whole month of free meetings if you introduce a friend to FEELGOOD!)

E Remind students that identifying what they are doing well and not doing so well is a very good way of focusing on what they can do better next time. Note that one question focuses specifically on this task type. Allow students time to reflect and complete the task, and then ask them if they are happy with the number of correct answers. You may like to ask one student what he or she will do differently next time.

Read the exam tip with students, and point out that this advice relates to a number of the tasks.

> **Key vocabulary in context**
>
> This task checks and consolidates various useful words from the text. Students can work individually or in pairs. You can give answers orally, or ask students to read the complete sentences.

Answers: 1. do well 2. think about it and make a judgement 3. more 4. wrong

The Workbook task for this unit provides further practice with this type of task. Now would be a good time to set it up as a homework task.

Writing

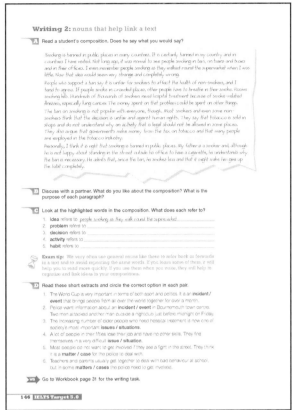

Objectives

- To present and practise nouns that link a formal text together.

- To practise writing a discursive composition that is typical of the IELTS writing exam.

Writing 1

The aim of the first stage is to provide an opportunity for some speaking practice, as well as prepare and motivate students for the writing tasks that follow. Start with a class discussion and try to pre-teach some language that occurs later in the lesson. Ask how many students smoke and how many are trying to 'give up'. Ask them why they want to give up, and teach 'tobacco' and 'lung cancer'. Teach 'non-smoker', and ask the non-smokers if they think smoking is a horrible 'habit'. Ask them if they think that 'passive smoking' is a serious problem, and if 'breathing in' a smoker's cigarette smoke is the same as smoking.

A Tell students to look at the pictures and make sure they understand that there are two pairs of pictures that show change. Point out the 'no smoking' sign in one of the pictures, and pre-teach 'ban' and 'banned'. Give students a moment to read the questions, and then five minutes to discuss them in pairs. You can either get some feedback or start the next task.

B Students are accustomed to seeing these writing instructions now, and should know that they need to check key words. Give them a minute or so to read, and make sure that 'banned' is absolutely clear now.

C Students are familiar with this type of writing preparation task. Give them five minutes to talk in pairs, and then open it up as a class discussion. See how many students would elect to express a strong opinion for this topic. Remind them they should still acknowledge the opposite point of view.

Writing 2

The best way to clarify some parts of the feedback process here will be to have the composition on an OHP transparency.

A Make sure students understand that they are looking to see if the writer made the same points that they would. There is no need to check whether or not this is the case.

B Students have assessed compositions a couple of times now, and should be more confident about expressing opinions. Give them some time to do this and monitor to check that they are saying the right kind of thing. The composition is obviously proficient and students should find all sorts of things they like about it. Put the paragraph order on the board like this to finish the activity.
1 – Introduce the topic and show that you understand the question.
2 – Say why some people are in favour of a ban.
3 – Say why some people are opposed to a ban.
4 – Conclude by expressing your own opinion.

C Students should work individually, and then compare with a partner. Placing the composition on an OHP transparency will make some parts of the feedback process clearer here. Make sure students know they are checking to see if the writer made the same points that they would. There is no need to check whether that is the case or not. Tell them not to worry about the highlighted words yet. Go through the answers in the same way as with the example.

Answers:

1. idea	refers to *people smoking as they walk round the supermarket*
2. problem	refers to *smokers need hospital treatment because of smoke-related illnesses*
3. decision	refers to *The ban on smoking*
4. activity	refers to *smoking*
5. habit	refers to *smoking*

Read the exam tip with students.

D The aim here is to present and practise some more typical reference nouns. Six are presented, but in three pairs of words that are often confused. This may appear challenging at this level, but note that in each sentence there are only two options and students should manage. They can work individually or in pairs. Feed back answers orally and explain the difference between words if the context doesn't make that clear. Note that these words are almost impossible to define accurately, and students will learn them by seeing them used again and again in context.

Answers:
1. event – something that is planned / arranged
2. incident – something that happens unplanned (often with unwanted effects – a mistake, a crime or an accident)
3. issues – what people are talking about / what worries people
4. situation – where people find themselves
5. matter – something that needs to be discussed and resolved
6. cases – particular examples of a situation or issue

Once students have completed the task, point out how frequent they are, especially in more formal texts. Tell students that they should notice them when they read and to start using them in their compositions when they understand them properly.

In this unit, the writing task can be found in the exam practice section at the end of the Course Book unit. See instructions for that section on page 228 of this book.

Consolidation

Speaking

The aim here is to encourage fluency and to show students how they can use typical introductory words and phrases to sound natural.

A Students know how these tasks work now. Make sure they just read the questions for now and don't start answering them. Get a general consensus about whether the topic is easy or challenging.

B 🎧 Tell students that they will hear a student performing the task, and give them a moment to look at the new question forms. Play the whole recording with pens down, and then again, pausing to allow time to write answers in note form. Go over the answers orally.

B Listen to a student talking and answer the questions.

Examiner: OK, so are you ready?

Student: Yes, I think. OK, I was on my bicycle. I was riding quite fast, but there was not much traffic. ... um ... um ... there were a lot of cars parked along the side of the road. One man – he opened the door of the car and, bang, I didn't have time to stop ... um ... I hit the door and came off the bicycle.

Examiner: And?

Student: Err ... oh, yes ... let me see the card again. What did I do? Um ... I was in the road ... and I could see a car was coming towards me. Um ... I jumped up and the first thing I wanted to know was 'is my bicycle OK?' ... I thought I was OK, but I was worried about my bicycle. Um, my bicycle was OK, and I took it to the side of the road. I realized that my chest hurt quite badly. I sat down, and the driver of the car called an ambulance. I discovered that one of my ribs was broken.

Answers:

1. in the street
2. riding his bicycle
3. there was an accident
4. he ran to check his bicycle

C Conduct this as a whole-class discussion. Don't be too critical, as students at this level will probably not be able to perform much better. Try to elicit the fact that the student wasn't very fluent, but he got his story across and he used a fairly good range of vocabulary. He paused a lot, and he needed to look at the card again. He could have used words and phrases to introduce key points and make his story more interesting.

D 🎧 Make sure students know that they are going to hear a different version. Read the rubric with them before they listen. Let them tell you what they think, and then establish that the negative points mentioned in Exercise C above have been resolved.

To exploit the language in the tapescript more robustly, write the following sentences with the gaps on the board – you might like to write it up while students are working through some of the earlier tasks. Alternatively, you could photocopy this for pairs of students.

1. _____, this was about a year ago.
2. _____, the driver of one car opened the door of his car.
3. _____, I remember that I was lying in the road.
4. _____ I realized that my chest hurt quite badly.
5. I _____ discovered that one of my ribs was broken.

Tell students that the focus is now on words that introduce points in spoken language. See if they can remember the word that fills the first gap, and then play the first part of the recording again to check. Play the rest of the recording, pausing briefly to allow students time to write the missing words. You can either write the words on the board, or refer students to the tapescript on page 304.

Tapescript 🎧 **124** (1 min, 25 secs)

D **Listen to the same student trying again. What does he do better the second time?**

Examiner: OK, so are you ready?

Student: Yes. Well, this was about a year ago. I was on my bicycle, and I was riding quite fast on a main road. It was a new bicycle, and I was really happy with it – maybe I was riding too fast. There wasn't much traffic, but there were a lot of cars parked along the side of the road. Suddenly, the driver of one car opened the door of his car. I'm sure he checked to see if any cars were coming, but he didn't see me on my bicycle. I tried to brake, but I didn't have time to stop and, bang, I hit the door and came off the bicycle. Then, I remember that I was lying in the road, and I could see a car was coming towards me. I jumped up and the first thing I wanted to know was 'is my bicycle OK?' I thought I was OK, but I was worried about my bicycle. My bicycle was OK, and I took it to the side of

the road – the pavement, I think. That is when I realized that my chest hurt quite badly. I sat down, and the driver of the car called an ambulance. I soon discovered that one of my ribs was broken.

Answers: 1. Well 2. Suddenly 3. Then 4. That is when 5. soon

Read the exam tip with students.

E The aim is for students to improve on what they might have said at the beginning of the lesson, and they will need a little time to prepare. Monitor as students practise, and allow them a second attempt with a new partner if necessary.

Vocabulary

A Students can work individually or in pairs. Write the correct preposition on the board for clarity.

Answers: 1. in 2. of 3. to 4. from

B Tell students that not all of the words are spelt incorrectly here. They should work individually, and then compare with a partner. You or they should write the answers on the board.

Answers: 1. chocolate 2. headache 3. gym 4. symptoms 5. assess 6. attitude

C By now, students know how to work through this type of task. It revises vocabulary learnt in the unit, emphasizes the need to learn the different forms of common words and checks spelling. Students should complete the task individually. For feedback, either you or students should write the answers on the board.

Answers: 1. weight 2. fitness 3. allergic 4. treatment 5. activity

Errors

A   Students know that each unit ends with an
    error-correction task. Tell them that there are no
    errors of spelling. They can either complete the
    task individually or work in pairs. You will need to
    write the correct versions of each sentence on
    the board to clarify corrections.

Answers:
1. I was cooking when I burnt my hand.
2. I was bitten by a friend's dog once.
3. I cut myself with a knife.
4. Have you ever been stung by a bee?
5. I discovered that my arm was broken.
6. I need to lose weight.

Exam Practice

11

Writing

A Look at the pictures and the first line of some writing task instructions below.

All over the world, life expectancy is increasing.

B Answer these questions with a partner.

1. What is good about more people living to an old age?
2. What are some of the problems of people living to an old age?
3. In your country, who usually cares for people when they are too old to look after themselves?

C Look carefully at the complete instructions for the writing task. Highlight the key words and make sure you understand what you have to do.

All over the world, life expectancy is increasing. Governments are finding it difficult to provide money for health care, and some people think that everyone should arrange private insurance to pay for health care.

Should health care be free for everyone, or should people pay for the care they need?

Give reasons for your answer and include any relevant examples from your experience.

Write about 250 words.

D Discuss these points with a partner.

1. Are you going to express a strong opinion or present a balanced argument?
2. Which of these points will you include in your composition?
 • Governments cannot afford to provide free health care for everyone.
 • Everyone should have free education and free health care.
 • Wealthy people should pay for health care.
 • Poorer people should have free health care.
 • How rich you are should not affect the quality of the health care you receive.
 • People who pay for health care should have the best doctors and hospitals.
 • Everyone should have free health care until they are 18.
 • People who smoke or drink a lot of alcohol should pay for their health care.
3. Are there any other important points you want to make?

Exam tip: When you do the second writing task, you may feel that it is difficult to find enough to say and that you can't write 250 words. The introduction is often the easier part to write, so make sure you write a solid introduction. The introduction to the composition in the Writing Module of this unit is 70 words.

E Look at this introduction to the composition that a student has written. Put the sentences into the most logical order. Do you like the introduction?

__ In the future, most people might live to be a hundred or more.
__ Of course, this is good if people can remain healthy, but most old people need more health care and governments are finding it difficult to provide the money that is needed.
__ People are living longer.
__ In some parts of the world, the number of young people is staying the same, while the number of old people is growing all the time.

F Write the composition. You can use the introduction above or you can write your own. Remember – you don't need to include all the points you discussed. Try to write around 250 words, but don't worry if your composition is a little shorter.

Writing

Students will still need assistance with preparation before attempting to write a complete composition of this type. Tell them that the important thing is to attempt the composition, to make some valid points and to organize the points as well as they can.

A The aim of this activity is to engage students in the topic and get them thinking about the problem they will write about. There is no actual task here. Tell students to look at the pictures and the first line of instructions and to think about the situation. Ask students where the old people live, and pre-teach 'nursing home' and 'health care'.

B This can be conducted as pairwork as suggested, or as a whole-class discussion. Note that question 3 will be more of a discussion point if students are from different countries. If students are all from the same country you may prefer to have an open discussion and introduce any key vocabulary as you go. Finish the activity by asking students if they have elderly relatives, and whether they live at home or in a nursing home.

C Students know how to read these task instructions now and should ask you about anything that is unclear. They have previously met the challenging words and phrases in these instructions, but will probably need to check 'life expectancy' and 'private insurance'.

D This stage will be very important for students. They can work in pairs as suggested, or in small groups. Give them about ten minutes and monitor to check that everyone feels they can contribute something when they start writing. Ask if there are any other points and write them on the board to finish the activity.

Read the exam tip with students. Then tell them to cover it and tell you what it said.

E The aim here is to show students how an introduction can be extended so that it does more than simply repeat the instructions. It will also provide students with an introduction that they can use if they want to, so that they feel confident about tackling the rest of the composition and have less to organize and produce. Students should work individually and then compare.

Write the correct order on the board as below.

Answers: 3, 4, 1, 2

Tell students that the introduction here is 74 words.

F   Once students are ready to start writing, set a time limit of 40 minutes and try to ensure that students use the time that they have. Monitor as students work, but check that they are organizing their ideas and making relevant points. At this point, there should be a little more focus on accuracy.

When students have completed the task, tell them to look at the model composition on page 271 of the Course Book. Put them into pairs to compare their composition against the model (the model here gives an example of how the student may not have very strong arguments, but can still answer the question. It is important to tell your students that they don't need to have 'expert' solutions to a problem like this). The model is reproduced below.

If you collect students' compositions to mark, use the process to get an idea of what they are capable of and give general feedback. Correcting everything they write will not be very motivating.

People are living longer. In some parts of the world, the number of young people is staying the same, while the number of old people is growing all the time. In the future, most people might live to be a hundred or more. Of course, this is good if people can remain healthy, but most old people need more health care, and governments are finding it difficult to provide the money that is needed.

It would be nice to say that everyone should have free health care, but I do not think that is realistic. Younger people would have to pay more and more tax, and there are other things the government needs to spend the money on. Perhaps private insurance is the answer.

The problem with people paying privately for health care is that not everyone can afford it. Richer people would have better health care in their old age than poor people, and that is not really fair. Of course, there are a lot of rich people now who have private health insurance, but poorer people can still get treatment in hospitals if they are ill. These poorer people might not get this treatment in the future if they cannot afford the insurance.

Unit 11 Workbook answers

Speaking and Vocabulary

A 1. g 2. e 3. d 4. b 5. a 6. h 7. c
8. f

Tapescript 🎧 **125** (1 min, 54 secs)

A **Listen and match each speaker with a health problem below.**

1

It's always the same at this time of year when the flowers come out. I get really sore eyes, and my nose never stops running. It's not fair because I can't go in the garden or walk through the park in the morning.

2

I was chopping onions in the kitchen when the knife slipped. It was really painful, and there was lots of blood. I ran my hand under cold water, but it didn't stop the bleeding. I had to put quite a big plaster on it.

3

Well, my wife told me that a lamp in the living room wasn't working and asked me to fix it. I should have unplugged the lamp before I touched it, of course, but I didn't. I suddenly felt a terrible pain and found myself lying on the floor. My arm felt strange for a few hours after that. I guess I was lucky really.

4

We were having our tea in the garden – a sort of picnic. Anyway, there were a lot of sweet things on the table – some jam and peanut butter. I reached out to take the jar of jam and I suddenly felt a sharp pain in my finger. I looked at my finger and it was all red. My mum ran it under cold water, but it was still hurting.

B and C speaking task

Listening

A Speaker 1 – b   Speaker 2 – d
Speaker 3 – c   Speaker 4 – a

Reading

A 1. D (they turn and twist a lot)
2. F (causes the bone in the leg to become weaker and means that a leg can break more easily)
3. E (they are avoided if sportsmen make sure they stay in shape and protect themselves)

Writing

Read through the exam tip with students.

A first paragraph – sentence 4
second paragraph – sentence 1
third paragraph – sentence 3
fourth paragraph – sentence 2

12 Nature

Unit overview

The twelfth unit is based around the theme of nature, and more specifically around the theme of weather and natural disasters. Students will talk about the climate and the weather in their country. There is a focus on the different styles of language that students can expect from the various types of recording and text genres that they tackle.

Speaking and Vocabulary

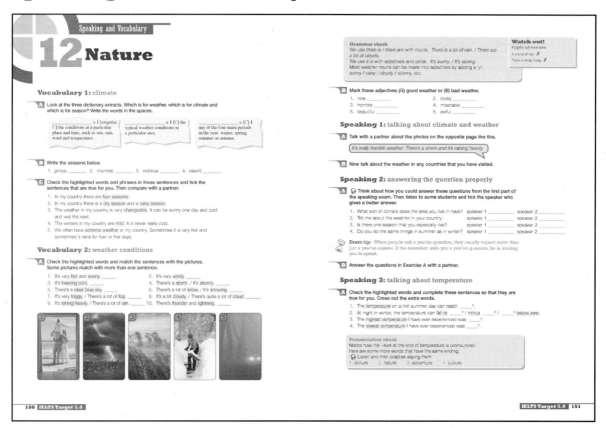

Objectives

- To give students further practice answering the type of questions they can expect in the first part of the speaking exam.

- To present and practise vocabulary related to weather and climate.

- To encourage students to give fuller, more communicative answers to the examiner's questions.

Vocabulary 1

A The aim of the first stage is to focus on the basic vocabulary that everyone needs for talking about climate, regardless of the specific weather conditions in their country.

Answers: a. climate   b. weather   3. season

B Give students a minute or so to work individually, and then write the correct spellings on the board.

   Answers: 1. spring   2. summer   3. autumn
   4. winter

C The highlighted words are defined in the sentences, but students should use a dictionary to check as they go.

   If your students come from different countries, they should compare with a partner. If they are all from the same country, you might prefer to just check that everyone agrees as a class. This will help you verify that they have understood the key words and phrases.

Vocabulary 2

The aim now is to focus on the most common types of specific weather conditions.

A If you tell students to cover the sentences and talk about the pictures, you will see what they already know. Once they start the matching task they should use dictionaries. It will be difficult to pre-teach all the vocabulary without doing the task yourself. Students should work in pairs so that they can talk and say the new words and phrases as they go. Monitor to check what students are saying, rather than repeat the activity as formal feedback.

   No answers are provided here as answers should be clear.

Grammar check

You will know whether your students confuse these two structures or not. Read through the grammar check box with them, and ask them if the distinction is clear. See if they can give you another example or two of adjectives that are formed by adding '~y' to the noun ('snowy', 'foggy', for example). You can tell students to correct the errors in the 'Watch out!' box now if you like.

   Answers: There is a lot of rain. / It is windy today.

B Allow students to mark the adjectives they know, and then use any they are not sure about in context with the appropriate intonation ('It's really miserable today'). This way, they should be able to hear if the adjective is positive or negative. Go over the answers orally, or mark them on the board to be clear if necessary.

   Answers: 1. nice: G   2. lovely: G
   3. horrible: B   4. miserable: B   5. beautiful: G
   6. awful: B

Speaking 1

A and B The aim now is for students to use all the vocabulary they have learnt and for you to be able to check what has been retained. Tell them to cover all of the vocabulary on the opposite page so they can see only the photos. After a couple of minutes, tell them they can quickly look to check a new word or phrase that they particularly want to use. Round up by asking a couple of students about a country they have visited.

Speaking 2

The aim of this speaking task is to encourage students to give fuller answers to questions, and to use a range of vocabulary that will make them generally more communicative.

A Give students time to look at the questions. Make sure they know that they don't have to answer them yet. Tell students that they will hear each question answered twice by two different speakers and that they need to decide who gives the better answer. Play the whole recording and then ask students to explain the answers they have given, as you also provide the correct answers. Ask students what the examiner expects when he asks the apparently yes/no questions 3 and 4.

   Play the recording again as students read the tapescript. Pause after each speaker so that they can absorb the answers given.

Tapescript 🎧 **126** (3 mins, 10 secs)

B Think about how you could answer these questions from the first part of the speaking exam. Then listen to some students and tick the speaker who gives a better answer.

Question 1 – Speaker 1

Examiner: What sort of climate does the area you live in have?

Student 1: Sometimes it's hot, and sometimes it's cold.

Question 1 – Speaker 2

Examiner: What sort of climate does the area you live in have?

Student 2: Well, it's quite an extreme climate. Summers are usually very hot and sunny, but winters are very cold. There's usually snow in January and February.

Question 2 – Speaker 1

Examiner: Tell me about the weather in your country.

Student 1: It's always very hot.

Question 2 – Speaker 2

Examiner: Tell me about the weather in your country.

Student 2: Well, it depends on the time of year. In summer, it's always very hot and dry. The temperature can reach forty-five degrees. It doesn't rain for months. In the winter, it is quite cold, especially at night. It rains a lot in spring.

Question 3 – Speaker 1

Examiner: Is there one season that you especially like?

Student 1: Yes, I like spring. I always feel happy because winter is over and it's like a new start. The weather is nice, but it's not too hot.

Question 3 – Speaker 2

Examiner: Is there one season that you especially like?

Student 2: Yes.

Examiner: Err ... which season do you like?

Student 2: I like summer.

Question 4 – Speaker 1

Examiner: Do you do the same things in summer as in winter?

Student 1: No.

Examiner: Oh, err ... so you different things in the winter?

Student 1: Yes, different things in the summer and the winter.

Question 4 – Speaker 2

Examiner: Do you do the same things in summer as in winter?

Student 2: Um, well, a lot of things are the same. I go to work the same, and spend free time with my family, but some things are different. During the summer, I take my little girl to the park a lot and have days out with her. In the winter, we stay at home more. During the winter, I go skiing at least once a month.

Answers:

1. Speaker 2 gives the better answer.
2. Speaker 2 gives the better answer.
3. Speaker 1 gives the better answer.
4. Speaker 2 gives the better answer.

Read the exam tip with students.

B Students should attempt to give fuller answers now and try to sound interested. Monitor, and tell students to try again if they sound flat or uncommunicative.

Speaking 3

Talking about the temperature is common, especially if students live in very hot or very cold countries.

A Draw a vertical line on the board and put '0°' at the bottom and '100°' at the top. Tell students that when we talk about temperature we use the word 'degrees'. Ask students what the temperature is today, and put that on the line in the appropriate place. Drill 'temperature', and write it in phonetic script on the board if possible. Now students should use dictionaries to check any words that are not clear as they complete the task. Use the board to clarify 'minus' and 'below zero'. Point out that 'reach' is for high temperatures, and 'fall to' is for low temperatures.

Pronunciation check

Read through the first line with students, and drill 'temperature' again. Play the recording for them to hear the four other examples, and then give them a couple of minutes to practise saying them to a partner.

Tapescript 🎧 **127** (0 mins, 42 secs)

Pronunication check

Notice how the *~ture* at the end of *temperature* is pronounced. Here are some more words that have the same ending.

Listen and then practise saying them.

1 picture

2 nature

3 adventure

4 culture

For further speaking and vocabulary practice, tell students to complete the exercises on page 33 of the Workbook. Set as an extra activity or homework task.

Listening

Objectives

- To familiarize students with the different register that they will hear in the various parts of the listening exam.
- To practise various listening exam task types with a focus on the register used.

Listening 1

The aim of the first stage is to compare the formal register of a weather forecast with the informal register of an everyday conversation.

A Give students a moment to look at the picture, and then a minute or so to talk with a partner. Don't pre-teach anything, as this would answer the questions for them. Check their answers orally and drill 'weather forecast'.

Answers:
1. She is a weather forecaster, and she is presenting a weather forecast.
2. They are symbols that show different weather conditions.

3. It will be quite cold and very wet. / It will rain a lot.

B 🎧 Play the whole recording so that students can confirm their predictions for 3 above.

Tapescript 🎧 128 (0 mins, 43 secs)

B **Listen to the weather forecast and check your predictions.**

Voice: Tomorrow will be another wet day across most of the country. The south-east can expect the worst of the weather, with heavy rain early in the day. Towns along the south-east coast may experience severe storms with thunder and lightning. Later in the day conditions should improve, but showers are still likely in most places during the afternoon. It will also be cold for the time of year, with the temperature remaining at around six degrees.

C 🎧 Give students a minute to read through the sentences. Tell them that you will play the recording through without pausing. Ask them to write some answers in when the recording has finished, if they don't have time when they are listening. They will need to get accustomed to writing answers more quickly. Students can compare answers with a partner for spelling, or you can give answers directly. Students should use an article with question 5.

Tapescript 🎧 **129** (0 mins, 14 secs)

C Listen again and complete the notes. Use <u>no more than two words</u> for each answer.

[Play track 128 again]

Answers: 1. expect   2. heavy rain
3. (severe) storms   4. improve
5. The temperature

Listening 2

Work through as in Listening 1 above.

A **Answers:**
1. colleagues / workmates
2. the (terrible) weather / the rain

B 🎧 Play the whole recording so that students can confirm their predictions for 2 above.

Tapescript 🎧 **130** (0 mins, 58 secs)

B **Listen to the conversation and check your predictions.**

Male 1: Oh, no – is it raining out there?
Male 2: Raining? It's absolutely pouring down. They said on the weather forecast that it would rain, but I didn't think it would be like this. How come you're not wet?
Male 1: Ah, well, I heard the forecast, too, so I took a taxi from the station.
Male 2: Mm, you're lucky. I'm absolutely soaked. It's really chilly out there, too. I hope I don't get pneumonia!
Male 1: Well, never mind. They say it's going to get better later on.
Male 2: Yes, but that doesn't help me. I'm going to be in these wet clothes all day!

C 🎧 As Listening 1C.

Tapescript 🎧 **131** (0 mins, 14 secs)

C Listen again and complete the lines. Use <u>no more than two words</u> for each answer.

[Play track 130 again]

Listening 3

A Give students a moment to talk, before reading the exam tip that answers the question together.

B Encourage students to find examples of formal language with corresponding informal language. You can show them 'heavy rain' and 'it's pouring down' as an example. Give them two or three minutes to work individually and then a couple more to compare with a partner. You can either write examples on the board or highlight an OHP transparency of the tapescript.

Answers:
Formal: can expect / heavy rain / experience (verb) / severe / conditions should improve / later in the day / are still likely / temperature remaining ...

Informal: it's absolutely pouring down / How come …? / absolutely soaked / really chilly / get better / later on

Listening 4

The aim of this activity is to expose students to exam practice in which various registers are used. For that reason, there are a number of short extracts with accompanying tasks, rather than the usual single longer recording. You can tell students that they will not have to deal with a number of short extracts like this in the exam.

A 🎧 The aim here is to practise gist listening and to familiarize students with the extracts, so they will feel more confident with the exam-type tasks. Give students a minute or so to read the instructions and the options and make sure they know what to do. Play the whole recording. Go over answers before moving on to Exercise B.

A Listen to the four extracts and match them with the descriptions below.

Extract 1

Voice: Hi, everyone – I'm a bit nervous about doing this, so ... err ... Anyway, as you all know, I come from Libya, and I'm going to talk about sandstorms. Sandstorms are very common in the Sahara desert, and so people in Libya, which is near the Sahara desert, know all about them. Now, we say 'sandstorm', but it's not really a storm – there's no rain or thunder and lightning. There are sandstorms when a strong wind picks up sand and carries it. As the wind blows, the sand in the wind causes more sand to move around, and that is also picked up. A very strong wind can pick up a huge amount of sand – look at my first image on the board, here. As you can see, a severe sandstorm looks like a huge wall or wave of sand. Can you imagine that coming towards you? Now, I will tell you what you should do if you know a sandstorm is coming, or even if you get caught in a sandstorm ...

Extract 2

Female 1: So, have you decided where you're going on holiday yet? You were talking about Spain.

Female 2: No, we've changed our minds. We're going to Egypt for two weeks.

Female 1: Wow, really? When are you going?

Female 2: The second week in August.

Female 1: Egypt in August – you're brave. It'll be absolutely boiling then, won't it?

Female 2: Yeah – that's what I want! We'll go and see the sights early in the morning when it's still quite cool, and then lie around by the swimming pool in the midday heat.

Female 1: Mm, I went to Morocco in the summer a few years ago. I couldn't sleep until about two in the morning. I always said that if I went anywhere like that again, I'd go in the spring or autumn.

Female 2: Well, I can't wait. You just see my tan when I get back!

Extract 3

Female: Good evening, Professor Drake, and welcome to the programme.

Prof: Good evening.

Female: Now, as we have heard, it appears that there are a greater number of hurricanes now, particularly in the Atlantic, and that hurricanes are becoming more violent and causing more damage. First of all, could you explain what causes a hurricane?

Prof: Yes, certainly. Hurricanes – or tropical cyclones, as they are also known – are really huge storms, or a number of storms that occur together within a small area. They are caused by low pressure and moist air rising from the Earth's surface – usually the surface of the sea. As the moist air rises it becomes warmer, and this is what forms the hurricane. If the hurricane is strong enough, it will develop an eye. The eye, which is circular, is at the centre of the hurricane and can be huge – three hundred kilometres in diameter, perhaps. The eye is usually calm – it is the area around the eye – the eyewall, where the storms occur. The eyewall surrounds the eye like the wall of a huge vertical passage, and is made up of the strong winds that cause the damage when the hurricane passes over land. Spreading out from the eyewall is the vast area of clouds and rain that we call the rain bands. These rain bands can spread for hundreds of kilometres.

Female: Thank you for that, professor. Now, why is it that the world is experiencing a greater ... *(fade out)*

Extract 4

Voice: Floods occur when the water level rises in an area where there was previously little or no water. Floods can be dramatic – they occur suddenly, and the water level rises quickly – or creeping – the water level rises over a longer period of time. They occur either because there is a larger amount of rainfall in an area than is usual, or because ice melts. Floods generally cause damage and negatively affect the economy of an area, but they can also be beneficial. The River Nile floods annually, and the water brings nutrients to the soil in surrounding fields. This, of course, means better crops. Most floods occur naturally, but they can be ... *(fade out)*

Answers: 1. extract 2   2. extract 4
3. extract 1   4. extract 3

B 🎧 Although students have practised all the task types and should be more independent now, the fact that there are four very different topics and four very different styles of language will make this challenging. Tell students that you will pause between each extract for about 20 seconds so that they can read the instructions and questions. Students might want to listen to the recording a third time, but avoid doing this, as they can discuss what difficulties they had and then listen again later if necessary (see Exercise D).

Tapescript 🎧 **133** (0 mins, 12 secs)

B **Listen again to each extract and complete the tasks below.**

[Play track 132 again]

C Give students sufficient time to check answers and think about why they may have answered incorrectly before moving on to Exercise D. Students should check any words they feel they need to with you as they look at the answers and tapescript.

Answers: 1. Sahara Desert / desert
2. strong wind   3. wave   4. c   5. b
6. a   7. eye   8. eye wall   9. rain bands
10. dramatic   11. ice   12. crops

D Students are aware of how this reflective process works now and its benefits, and need less guidance. Remind them that identifying what they are doing well and not doing so well is a very good way of focusing on what they can do better next time. Allow students time to reflect and complete the task. Play the recording again if necessary, and tell students to focus on why the correct answers are correct.

> **Key vocabulary in context**
>
> Give students a few minutes to work individually, and then a couple more to compare with a partner. Monitor, and check that students are spending the time productively.

Answers: 1. F   2. F   3. F   4. I   5. I   6. I

The Workbook task develops the theme of formal and informal ways of saying the same thing, and now would be a good time to work through it.

Reading

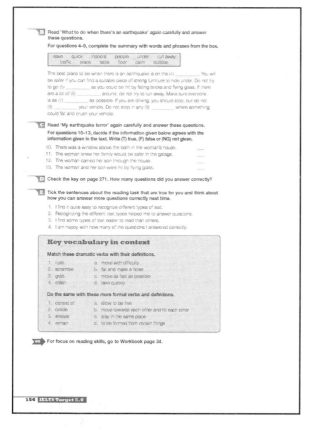

Objectives

- To remind students that there are various different genres of text, and practise identifying their typical features.

- To practise identifying genres of text from reading them quickly.

- To practise reading tasks with a focus on text genre.

Reading 1

A The aim of this task is to introduce the theme of the reading lesson, as well as pre-teach the key word 'earthquake'. Once students have spoken for a minute or so in pairs, open the task up as a class discussion and pre-teach words and phrases that occur later in the lesson, like 'collapse' and 'rubble'.

B Conduct this as a continuation of the whole-class discussion. Students will probably not know why an earthquake occurs, but if one student does, see how well he or she can explain it.

C Give students a moment to look at the three images. You can ask them how they differ and what more they can tell you about earthquakes. Tell them to work for a minute on their own to match the headings with the images. As you check answers, ask them why they have made their decision. Provide the answer before moving on.

Answers: 1. picture 1   2. picture 3
3. picture 2

D Students should use dictionaries for this. Teaching all the words and phrases yourself will be difficult without doing the task for them. If students need to share dictionaries, they should still work individually before comparing, as they need to think rather than converse straightaway. Before they begin, point out that the words and phrases from the first story will be more connected with advice, those from the second story more dramatic and those from the third more technical. Monitor and deal with anything individual students are not sure about.

Once students have checked the words and phrases individually, they should compare. Write on the board 'I think 'tectonic plates' goes with heading 3 and image b because it's a technical phrase'. Tell students to discuss the other items in the box in a similar way. Give them five minutes for this, and monitor to check what they are saying. Tell them that you are not going to go over the answers, as it will help them too much with the matching tasks that follow.

Answers:
Heading 1, picture a – stay calm / take cover / avoid being injured
Heading 2, picture c – grab / scramble / rush
Heading 3, picture b – fault lines / release energy / tectonic plates

Reading 2

Students know what the extracts are about, so it is important that they appreciate that they are skimming to recognize the style of writing and therefore the genre of each extract. The key words and phrases that they learnt in Exercise D above will help. Set a time limit of about two minutes, though students may need less. Go over answers before working through Exercise B.

A Give students a minute or two to think individually, and then another two or three to discuss meanings with a partner.

Answers:
extract 1 goes with picture c and heading 2
extract 2 goes with picture b and heading 3
extract 3 goes with picture a and heading 1

B Set a time limit of only a minute this time and then ask students whether they are confident with their matches. If not, give them a further minute. Go over the answers.

Answers:
extract 1 in B continues extract 3 in A
extract 2 in B continues extract 1 in A
extract 3 in B continues extract 2 in A

Students may feel a little frustrated that they haven't had a chance to read all the extracts properly yet. Tell them they have read well enough to complete the tasks and that they will be able to read more carefully to answer exam-type questions later.

C Give students about five minutes to answer the questions in pairs. They will need to look back at the extracts to answer some questions. Tell them to use the heading when giving you answers during feedback.

Answers:
1. The science of earthquakes
2. My earthquake terror
3. What to do when there's an earthquake
4. My earthquake terror
5. The science of earthquakes
6. What to do when there's an earthquake

Read through the extracts slowly with students, checking that they follow one sentence at a time.

Read the exam tip with students and point out that this advice relates to a number of the tasks.

Reading 3

A, B and C The practice stage is divided into three parts because each part relates to one of the texts about earthquakes from the previous stage. However, students have practised all the task types and have already skimmed the text, so they should be able to work straight through independently now. Make sure students realize that they will have to read both parts of each text in order to answer the questions. Set a time limit of 20 minutes to complete questions 1–13.

D Give students sufficient time to check and think about why they may have answered incorrectly, before moving on to Exercise E. The answers, together with the parts of the text that provide them, are reproduced here.

Answers for questions 1–3 here are in alphabetical order, but any order is fine as long as the three correct letters are given.

Answers:
1. C   2. D   3. F   4. floor   5. outside
6. people   7. calm   8. leave   9. place
10. T (my little boy was in the bath. I knew that
    he was in a place that was very unsafe –
    under a window with a huge piece of glass
    right above his head)
11. T (there were no safe places inside the
    house and we had to try to get out to the
    garage)
12. T (I grabbed Daniel in my arms)   13. NG

E Remind students that identifying what they are doing well and not doing so well is a very good way of focusing on what they can do better next time. Note that the questions focus specifically on reading different types of text. Allow students time to reflect and to complete the task, and then ask them if they are happy with the number of correct answers. You may like to ask one student what he or she will do differently next time.

> **Key vocabulary in context**
>
> This task checks and consolidates various verbs from the texts. Students can work individually or in pairs. When they have completed the task, tell them to cover up the verbs as you read the definitions and they provide the answers.

Answers:
1. c   2. a   3. d   4. b
1. d   2. b   3. a   4. c

The Workbook task for this unit focuses on recognizing different genres of text and the register used. Now would be a good time to either work through it or set it up as a homework task.

Writing

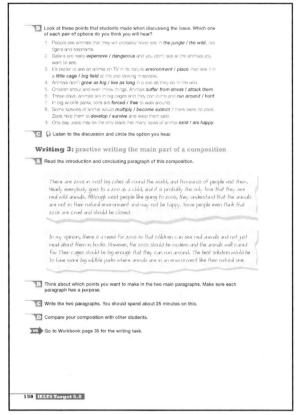

Objectives

- **To give students further guidance with deciding what to say in a discursive composition.**

- **To help students plan and organize the main body of a discursive composition.**

- **To practise writing a discursive composition that is typical of the IELTS writing exam.**

As previously stated, students often find the most difficult aspect of the second writing task is thinking of what they can say (what they know about the topic and what points they can make). Students have already spent time looking at how they can brainstorm ideas and thinking about what they might say in their own language first. This lesson develops that, and goes on to practise writing the main body of a composition in the lesson.

Writing 1

The aim of the first stage is to provide an opportunity for some speaking practice and to prepare and motivate students for the writing tasks that follow.

A Give students a moment to look at the pictures, and check and drill 'environment' in the third question. Then set three or four minutes to answer the questions. As you go over their answers, try to develop a class discussion, and pre-teach some language that occurs later in the lesson ('zoo', 'cages', 'natural environment', etc.). Try not to develop the discussion so far that you answer the questions in Exercise B (see below).

B If your students are from different countries, this should be conducted as pairwork. If they are all from the same town or city, you might prefer to talk through the points as an extension of the feedback from Exercise A.

C Students are accustomed to seeing these writing instructions now, and should know that they need to check key words. Give them a minute or so to read, and make sure that 'cruel' and 'wild animals' are clear.

Writing 2

A Students have previously seen points organized into columns like this, and it will be beneficial for them to use the technique again here. Try to organize your groups so that there is at least one stronger speaker who you think will have ideas and guide the group through the discussion. Set a time limit of about six minutes and then get some ideas back. There is no need to write the points up on the board as students will see a number of possible points in the task that follows.

B The aim of this activity is to provide students with more ideas and some more key vocabulary that they will be able to use in the main body of the composition that they will write later. It should also help them think more about what is relevant and logical. They should also be comparing their own ideas with the ideas here. Make sure students know that they will listen to a discussion to check their answers. They can continue to work in the same group that they are working in, or work individually and then compare with a partner. Go through their answers to check that they have understood the logic of some answers, but don't correct them before they listen.

C 🎧 It might be best to play the whole recording with pens down, and then play it again as students circle the correct option. If necessary, you can pause at appropriate points for students to absorb ideas. Students should read the tapescript on page 306 to check answers. Go over any key language that students feel is important.

Tapescript 🎧 **134** (3 mins, 19 secs)

C Listen to the discussion and circle the option you hear.

Teacher: So, personally, I have quite strong views about this issue, but I want to hear what you have to say. I don't need to practise my English. I'll tell you what I think at the end. Now, I'm not going to ask individual people what they think, but I'd like to hear from everyone, if possible – OK? So ...

Student 1: Well, I have mixed feelings. I think zoos are quite cruel, but I enjoy going to them. I like to see animals that I know I will probably never see in the wild – like tigers and elephants.

Student 2: But if you really want to see them, you can go on a safari or a jungle trek.

Student 3: No, that's not true for everyone – safaris are really expensive and you don't see all the animals you want to see anyway.

Student 2: I think in this day and age, people can see wild animals on TV all the time. There are really realistic DVDs and Internet pages.

Student 1: But that's not the same as seeing the real animal.

Student 2: I think it's better to see an animal on TV in its natural environment – hunting or playing with its babies – than see it in a little cage at the zoo looking miserable. Big animals that hunt, like lions, tigers and bears, always look very unhappy in a zoo. I heard that they don't live as long in a zoo as they do in the wild.

Student 4: Yes, in my country, zoos are not very well-kept. The children shout at the animals and sometimes even throw things at them. The animals suffer from stress.

Student 1: Well, somebody should stop them doing that. In most countries, zoos are better these days. Animals are in big cages and they can climb and run around.

Student 2: Um, I'm not so sure. When did you last see a lion chasing a zebra in a zoo?

Student 1: Well, there are some big wildlife parks in most countries. Lions might not hunt zebras, but they are free to walk around. People drive their car through the park and take photos.

Student 2: Yes, maybe they are better than small zoos, but they can't keep every type of animal. People go to a zoo to see as many animals as possible.

Student 3: Yes, and these days there are lots of interactive activities, too – like in a museum.

Student 1: People say that zoos are cruel, but I think some species of animal would become extinct if there were not

---

zoos. Zoos help them to survive and keep them safe.

Student 3: Yes, that's true – animals like pandas in China find it very difficult in the wild because their homes are destroyed. They are safer in zoos, and people can help them to produce more pandas. I know it's not perfect to have animals in zoos, but one day it may be the only place that many types of animal exist.

Student 4: I really hope not. People should be doing more to protect the environments of animals in the wild.

Teacher: Um, that's true, but I think it's a whole new question. So – do you want to hear what I think?

Answers: 1. the wild   2. expensive
3. environment / little cage   4. live as long
5. suffer from stress   6. run around
7. free   8. become extinct / survive   9. exist

Writing 3

A You might like to get students attempting to write an introductory paragraph that they can compare to the one here in the model. However, there is quite a lot of writing in this lesson so it might be best to concentrate on writing the main body of the composition.

Give students the time they need to read and understand the two paragraphs, and establish that it looks like a balanced composition. Go over any points students are unclear about. Point out that the two paragraphs together are nearly 150 words and that they need to write just over 100 words more.

B Tell students to keep looking at the tapescript of the class discussion and to use the points that were made. If they are confident enough they can make their own points. It would be a good idea to agree that the second paragraph should focus on why some people don't like zoos these days, and then the third on how zoos are changing and why they still serve an important purpose. This order is more logical in terms of the final paragraph following on from the third.

C You can decide whether you want students to write collaboratively and share ideas, or to write individually. Some students find it very difficult to write with a partner and feel that writing is an individual skill. Keep within the time limit, and monitor to check that students are making progress. You can make suggestions and correct obvious errors now, so that compositions are as successful as possible when it is time to compare them.

D When students have completed the task, allow them some time to exchange and compare with a partner. Then tell students to look at the model composition on page 271 of the Course Book. The two main paragraphs are reproduced here. Put them into pairs to compare their composition against the model.

In a lot of zoos, animals are in small cages and they are miserable. Big animals cannot run around or hunt as they do in the wild. In some zoos the animals are not treated well, and children shout and throw things at them. Some people think that because nowadays we can see wild animals on TV whenever we like, it is no longer necessary to keep them caged up in zoos.

However, I think the conditions in most zoos are improving. There are more wildlife parks where big animals can run around. Near my city, there is a big park where you can drive your car and take photos of animals. Some people argue that we need zoos because some rare animals would die out and become extinct if they were left in the wild. Zoos help animals like pandas to multiply and survive.

Writing task

The writing tasks are found either in the Workbook or in the exam practice section at the end of the unit. For this unit, the task is in the Workbook.

A Students will still need assistance with preparation before attempting to write a complete composition of this type. Tell them that the important thing is to attempt the composition, to make some valid points and to organize the points as well as they can.

Students know how to read these task instructions now, and should ask you about anything that's unclear. The instructions are short and fairly simple and so should be quite clear. Note that this time it will not be so easy to write a balanced composition as it is not really a case of discussing two points of view. It will be more a case of discussing why a situation might exist, giving some examples and expressing an opinion about it (see model).

B This stage will be very important for students. They can work in pairs as suggested, or in small groups. Give them about ten minutes for this, and monitor to check that everyone feels they have something to say when it is time to write. Ask if there are any other points and get some up on the board to finish the activity.

C Once students are ready to start writing, set a time limit of 40 minutes, and now try to ensure that students use the time they have. Monitor as students work, but check that they are organizing their ideas and making relevant points. There should be a little more focus on accuracy too now.

When students have completed the task, tell them to look at the model composition on page 271 of the Course Book. Put them into pairs to compare their composition against the model (note that the model here is fairly simplistic, and expresses ideas that a student would feel able to produce. You might like to indicate that another point that could be made is how much some people pamper their pets). The model is reproduced below.

If you collect students' compositions to mark, use the process to get an idea of what they are capable of and give general feedback. Correcting everything they write will not be very motivating.

In most countries pets are important, but I think that they are more important to people in some countries than in others. Pets are important to people at different times in their life, too. I think pets are more important to children and to old people than to people who are busy and out of the house a lot. I suppose it is true that pets are even more important to some people than other people are.

If people are very old and they spend a lot of time alone, a dog or a cat can be very important.

A dog can be an old person's best friend, and taking the dog for a walk can be an opportunity to get out of the house and take a walk. A cat can provide a lot of comfort if somebody is unable to get out of the house so easily.

Some children do not have brothers and sisters. Others are shy and not good at making friends. For them, a pet can be a best friend. I can imagine that if something happens to a child's pet dog, it seems worse than something happening to another person. When I was little I had a rabbit, and I came home from school every day to see him. However, I cannot say that he was more important than my sister or my friends.

Personally, I find it difficult to understand how a pet can be more important than other people. In my country, old people live close to other people in their family and they see people every day. When I stayed in Scotland I saw that old people seem to spend more time alone, and I can imagine why their pet becomes so important. I think it depends on the country how important pets are to people.

Consolidation

Speaking

The aim here is to provide more practice answering the more challenging questions that students will be asked in the third part of the speaking exam.

A and B Students know how these tasks work now. Make sure they just read the questions for now and don't start answering them. Read through the questions with them and deal with any words and phrases that are unclear.

Get a general consensus from the class about how challenging each question is.

C 🎧 Tell students that they will hear students answering each question, and make sure they know what to do. Play the whole recording as they do the matching. Note that the questions here are similar, and students may need to listen again to distinguish one answer from another. Play the recording a final time, pausing to check the answers. Students can listen again as they read the tapescript if they want to. Write the answers on the board if necessary.

Tapescript 🎧 **135** (1 min, 39 secs)

C Listen to some students and match the answers they give to the questions in Exercise B.

Speaker 1: Yes, I think so. We are cutting down forests to build towns and cities, and using the wood from the forests for industry. We are polluting the air and the seas and rivers.

Speaker 2: Yes, I think everyone can see that it is. The ice is melting in the Arctic and Antarctic, and some countries are getting hotter. There are natural disasters, like hurricanes, in more places now.

Speaker 3: Yes, especially big animals like pandas and rhinos that people love. They must have special places where humans are not allowed to build and animals are safe from hunters.

Speaker 4: Mm, I'm not sure. It seems to rain much more than it did when I was little, but maybe I just remember the sunny days.

Speaker 5: Yes, if any more ice melts, some parts of the world will be under water. Some islands will disappear. I heard that some diseases from Africa and Asia will be common in Europe if it gets any warmer.

Answers:

Speaker 1: question 4   Speaker 2: question 3
Speaker 3: question 5   Speaker 4: question 2
Speaker 5: question 1

Read the exam tip with students.

D The aim is for students to improve on what they might have said at the beginning of the lesson, and they will need a little time to prepare. Encourage them to express their own ideas and not repeat those in the examples. Monitor as students practise and allow them a second attempt with a new partner if necessary.

Vocabulary

A and B You could conduct these two tasks as a competition between individuals or pairs of students. Set a time limit of ten minutes and see how many questions they can answer correctly. You may prefer to ask students to complete them individually so that you can check better what each student has retained. Either you or students can write answers on the board during feedback.

Answers:

A 1. winter   2. mild   3. thunder
    4. lightning   5. foggy   6. extinct

B 1. flood   2. hurricane / earthquake
    3. below zero   4. freezing / boiling
    5. natural environment

C Tell students that all of the words are spelt incorrectly here. They should work individually and then compare with a partner. You or they should write the answers on the board.

Answers: 1. weather   2. autumn
3. temperature   4. occur   5. damage
6. previously   7. release   8. remain
9. survive

Errors

A Students know that each unit ends with an error-correction task. Tell them that there are no errors of spelling. They can either complete the task individually or work in pairs. You will need to write the correct versions of each sentence on the board to clarify corrections.

Answers:
1. There was a big storm last night.
2. Do you think the weather will be good tomorrow?
3. It's raining very heavily outside.
4. At night, the temperature can fall below ten degrees.
5. It's very hot. / It's absolutely boiling today.
6. Floods usually cause a lot of damage.

Exam Practice

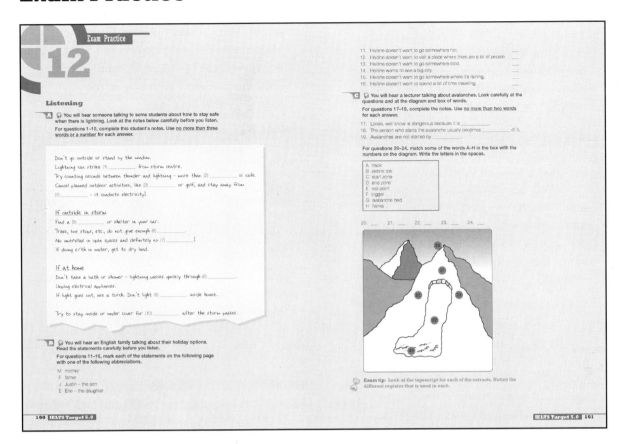

Listening

A, B and C 🎧 Tell students that the recordings here are what they can expect from various parts of the exam. The recording and degree of challenge in the task are close to what they will deal with in the exam. Students are not given preparation, and are left to work on their own to get some experience of realistic exam practice.

Read both the task introductions with students. Quickly check that students remember 'lightning' and 'avalanches' in the third part. Allow students to read the question instructions themselves. Give them a minute for each, as there is quite a lot to read through. Remember that they will only have 30 seconds in the exam.

You should play the whole recording once, though if you really feel your students are not ready for that, pause after each part and give them a moment to write and check answers. Write all the answers on the board.

Tapescript 🎧 136 (3 mins, 32 secs)

A You will hear someone talking to some students about how to stay safe when there is lightning. Look at the notes below carefully before you listen. For questions 1–10, complete this student's notes. Use <u>no more than three words or a number</u> for each answer.

Voice: Now, a big storm can be quite exciting, and you may want to go outside or stand by a window to get a better view, especially if it's not something you have seen much of before. However, it's not really a good idea. Thunder and lightning can be very frightening, and lightning can be very dangerous, too. You will all know that recently there have been a lot of storms, and that's why I want to warn you of the dangers.

Now, first of all, if you can hear thunder that means the storm is close, and it's close enough for you to be struck by lightning. Lightning can strike as far as fifteen kilometres away from the centre of the storm. Have you tried counting how many seconds there are between the thunder you hear and the flash of lightning that you see? The less you can count, the closer the centre of the storm. If there's less than thirty seconds between the thunder and the lightning, there is a danger.

If they say on a weather forecast that there will be a thunderstorm you should cancel any outdoor activities that you have planned, especially if they are in areas where it will be difficult to get to safe cover. Don't go camping and don't play golf. Avoid any activities near still water, like fishing – water conducts electricity.

If you are outside when a thunderstorm starts, take cover inside a building as quickly as possible. If there are no buildings and you have a car, shelter in that. Make sure all the windows are closed. Sheltering under a tree or in a bus stop is not really safe – you do not have as much protection as you should. If you are in an open space, don't put up an umbrella and, whatever you do, don't use a mobile phone. The metal directs electricity into the body and can make any injury much worse. Anyone who is swimming or rowing a boat must get to dry land as quickly as possible.

Inside your home there are dangers, too. Don't take a bath or a shower when there is a thunderstorm – if lightning strikes a house, it can send surges of electricity through metal pipes. If a storm appears to be serious, unplug electrical appliances, like TVs and music systems. If the light goes out during a storm, try to use a torch – lighting matches or holding cigarette lighters inside the house is very dangerous.

Finally, don't go out or leave your shelter too soon after the storm has passed. Many lightning strikes occur after the storm has passed. Stay indoors for at least half an hour. Now, I hope I haven't frightened you too much, and I hope you enjoy the rest of ... *(fade out)*

Tapescript 🎧 **137** (2 mins, 51 secs)

B You will hear an English family talking about their holiday options. Read the statements carefully before you listen. For questions 11–16, mark each of the statements below with one of the following abbreviations.

Mother: OK, since we're all together for a change, let's talk about holidays. It's the summer holiday soon, and Dad and I have been discussing some places that everyone might like. Now, I don't want arguments, so let's hear what everyone has to say. Justin, have you thought about a summer holiday yet?

Justin: Can we go skiing again?

Ellie: I don't want to go skiing – not in the summer. It was freezing last time we went skiing – I had the flu for most of the holiday.

Mother: OK, Ellie – let's calm down. We can all make suggestions. We don't have to decide on anything today.

Father: Mum and I were talking about Turkey. Lots of people go to Turkey in the summer. It's very popular at the moment. There's lots to see and some lovely beaches to relax on, too.

Justin: Yeah, but it'll be absolutely boiling – probably about fifty degrees.

Father: I think you're exaggerating a bit, Justin.

Justin: Maybe. But anyway, you know I get bored just lying on the beach all day.

Mother: Yes, but like Dad said, there's lots to see as well. We can go for day trips to sights and museums.

Ellie: Boring!

Father: I was thinking we could spend some time by the beach, and then go up to Istanbul for a few nights.

Mother: Mm, I don't know about that. I don't really want to go anywhere that's too crowded. I want to get away from stress – not go looking for it.

Father: Well, OK – perhaps just a day trip, then. I'd like to see it. They say it's one of the most exciting cities in the world.

Justin: A day trip from the coast to Istanbul – no way. We'd be on the bus for five hours there and five hours back. That's not my idea of fun.

Mother: OK, it's just one of the options. I said we don't have to decide anything today. I wouldn't mind staying in this country. We could drive to Cornwall or the Lake District. We could go up to Scotland – we've never been there.

Ellie: Mm ... except ... it'll be wet every day – probably pouring down most days. That's the trouble with holidays in Britain.

Father: Look ... we're not getting very far here, are we? Everyone is saying where they don't want to go and nobody is being very positive.

Justin: I said I want to go skiing.

Tapescript 🎧 138 (2 mins, 43 secs)

C You will hear a lecturer talking about avalanches. Look carefully at the questions and at the diagram and box of words. For questions 17–19, complete the notes. Use <u>no more than two words</u> for each answer.

Voice: Most of you have probably never experienced an avalanche – they only occur in mountainous areas and not very often – but you've probably seen one on TV.

The most dangerous type of avalanche occurs when snow is loose and wet. Wet snow is very heavy – it moves slowly, but it causes a huge amount of damage. Most avalanches are started by the victim – that means the person who starts the avalanche is usually killed or injured in it. Not many avalanches destroy towns or villages, like you see in movies. People think that the wind can cause an avalanche, but that's not true. The wind can make snow loose and dangerous, but it doesn't actually make the avalanche start.

Now, look at this diagram on the board. Right at the top here, you see the trigger. That means the cause – what makes the avalanche start. It's usually a person walking on loose, unstable snow. Below that is the start zone – the area where the avalanche builds up, and the snow starts moving. As the snow starts to move with more force, it creates a track. This is the

path down which the snow slides. As the snow moves, it creates its own track. As more snow becomes loose, it follows the track down the mountain. On each side of the track are the flanks. The snow here is pulled into the track by moving snow. Finally, down here at the bottom, is the debris toe. This is where the avalanche ends. It will either be on the mountain, where there is not a steep enough slope for the snow to continue moving downwards, or it will be at the bottom of the mountain. Obviously, if it's the bottom of the mountain, a huge amount of damage could be caused. As I said before, however, this is not common, and ... *(fade out)*

For questions 20–24, match some of the words A–H in the box with the numbers on the diagram. Write the letters in the spaces.

[Play track 138 again]

Answers:
1. 15 / fifteen km / kilometres
2. 30 / thirty seconds   3. camping   4. water
5. building   6. protection   7. mobile phones
8. metal pipes   9. matches
10. half an hour
    (Note that for 10, 30 / thirty minutes is not what was said on the recording.)
11. J (it'll be absolutely boiling – probably about fifty degrees)
12. M (I don't really want to go anywhere that's too crowded)
13. E (It was freezing last time we went skiing)
14. F (and then go up to Istanbul / it's one of the most exciting cities in the world)
15. E (it'll be wet every day – probably pouring down most days)
16. J (We'd be on the bus for five hours there and five hours back. That's not my idea of fun.)
17. heavy   18. the victim   19. (the) wind
20. F   21. C   22. A   23. H   24. B

Once you have given students the answers, play the recording again as students read the tapescript. Pause to point out why some answers are incorrect if students are still not sure about the reason, and tell them to check the register, as suggested in the exam tip.

Unit 12 Workbook answers

Speaking and Vocabulary

A 1. d   2. c   3. a   4. e   5. b

B Students' own answers.

C 1. flood   2. earthquake   3. avalanche
4. hurricane   5. sandstorm

D Students' own answers.

Listening

A Answers:
1. F: improve – INF: get better
2. F: occur / large amount – INF: happens
3. INF: chilly
4. F: extreme heat – INF: boiling
5. F: negative effect
6. F: previously
7. F: summer – INF: can't wait

Tapescript 🎧 **139** (1 min, 39 secs)

A Listen and complete these pairs of sentences. Use two words in the longer spaces.

1

Weather forecaster: Conditions should improve later in the day.

Young man: They say things will get better later on.

2

Lecturer: Floods occur when there is a large amount of rainfall.

Student: So, what happens when there's lots of rain? Does it flood?

3

Weather forecaster: Most parts of the country can expect a cold night.

Woman: They say it's going to be a bit chilly tonight.

4

Lecturer: The extreme heat lasts from early morning until late afternoon.

Student: It's boiling hot all day.

5

Newsreader: Generally, a flood has a very negative effect on the economy.

Young man: Floods are not usually very good for the economy.

6

TV presenter: In many parts of the world there is water where previously there was ice.

Girl: There's water now, but there was ice there before.

7

TV presenter: Around this time, families begin to look forward to their summer holiday.

Young woman: I can't wait to go away this year.

Reading

1. a   2. c   3. b   4. e   5. d

Writing

The writing task is dealt with in the main section of the Teacher's Book.

Unit overview

The thirteenth unit is based around the theme of buildings, engineering and architecture. Students will talk about their homes and their neighbourhoods. There is a focus on spelling answers correctly and students will deal with a longer text in the Reading Module.

Speaking and Vocabulary

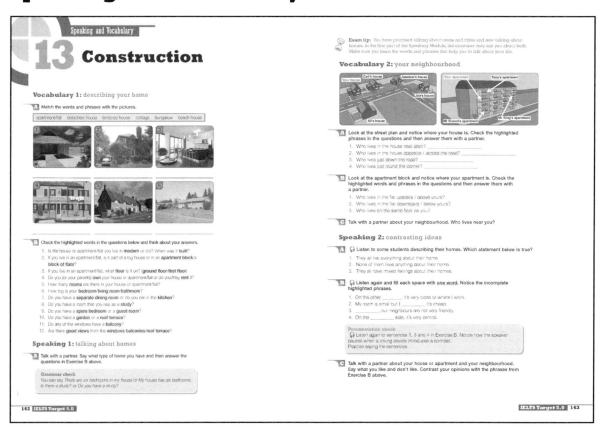

Objectives

- To give students further practice answering the questions they can expect in the first part of the speaking exam.

- To give students further practice talking about where they live.

- To present and practise vocabulary related to houses, homes and neighbourhoods.

- To present and practise ways of introducing contrast in spoken language.

Vocabulary 1

The aim of the first stage is to focus on the basic vocabulary that somebody needs to describe the building he or she lives in.

A It is probably best here to use the pictures to teach vocabulary for the different types of home. Dictionaries may not clarify meanings as well as the pictures do, and definitions might be quite complicated. Tell students something about each type of home – for example, a bungalow always has just one floor.

Answers: 1. beach house
2. detached house   3. apartment/flat
4. terraced house   5. cottage   6. bungalow

B Make sure students understand that this is a vocabulary task and that they don't need to answer the questions yet. They should use a dictionary to check the highlighted words, and think about how they will answer the questions in a moment. Give students about ten minutes for this, and monitor to help if necessary. Drill 'separate' with only two syllables, and check students can pronounce it properly.

Speaking 1

A Give students as long as they need for this. Perhaps you could end the discussion when about half the pairs have finished. To finish the activity, ask a couple of students to tell you about their partner's home, so that you check they have been listening.

Grammar check

You will know whether your students are aware that these two structures can be used to express a similar idea.

Read through the grammar check box with them. You might like to give them the following sentence to transform:

There are eighty rooms in the hotel.

Answers: The hotel has eighty rooms.

Read the exam tip with students. Remind students about the importance of taking control over exactly what vocabulary they learn.

Vocabulary 2

Before starting this section, check that students know 'neighbour', and teach 'neighbourhood'. Draw a very simple house on the board, and then another next door. Elicit 'neighbour', which students should know. Make sure they pronounce it correctly, and write it phonetically on the board if possible. Then draw a few more houses around and teach 'neighbourhood'. You might like to ask if your students generally like their neighbours and why.

A Read through the rubric with students. Don't pre-teach the highlighted words before they attempt the task, as this would more or less do the exercise for them. Let them work out anything they don't know by looking at the street plan and talking to a partner. Check answers by asking the questions to the class. Drill the highlighted phrases at this point. Point out that 'opposite' doesn't need a preposition 'of' or 'to', which is a typical mistake.

Answers: 1. Carl   2. Ali   3. Jasmine
4. Lisa

B Conduct as Exercise A above.

Answers: 1. Tony   2. Mr Brown   3. Mr King

C The aim now is for students to practise talking about their own lives with the new vocabulary. Write on the board, 'My best friend lives …' , 'My sister and her husband live …' and 'One of my cousins lives …' as prompts, and see if anyone can complete one with something that is true. Once students know what they are doing, give them some time to talk about their neighbourhoods. Get some feedback by asking a couple of students what their partner told them.

Speaking 2

A 🎧 The aim of this task is to prepare students to focus on the ways of introducing contrast in Exercise B. Give them time to read the options, and then play the whole recording. Play the recording again if students are really not sure. Provide the answer before moving on to Exercise B.

Tapescript 🎧 **140** (1 min, 20 secs)

A **Listen to some students describing their homes. Which statement below is true?**

Speaker 1: Mm, my apartment is very small, but very expensive. On the other hand, it's very close to where I work, so I save money on bus fares.

Speaker 2: I rent a house with some friends. It's not in very good condition, and my room is small, but I guess it's cheap, and it's better than being at home with my parents.

Speaker 3: I moved to a new house with my husband last year. It's very comfortable, and in a part of the city that we like. However, our neighbours are not very friendly, and they make a lot of noise.

Speaker 4: My apartment is right next to a busy main road – it's really noisy, and the windows are always black! On the plus side, it's very central, and I can walk everywhere.

Answers: The correct option is sentence 3.

B 🎧 Give students a moment to read the sentences, and then play the recording again, pausing after each to allow them time to write. Write the correct answers on the board.

Tapescript 🎧 **141** (0 mins, 15 secs)

B **Listen again and fill each space with <u>one word</u>. Notice the incomplete highlighted phrases.**

[Play track 140 again]

Answers: 1. hand   2. guess   3. However   4. plus

Pronunciation check

Read through the advice with students, and then play the recording so that they can listen especially for the pausing. Then give them time to practise saying each sentence. Monitor to check the pausing is natural.

Tapescript 🎧 **142** (1 min, 8 secs)

Pronunciation check

Listen again to sentences 1, 3 and 4 in Exercise B. Notice how the speaker pauses when a linking device introduces a contrast.

Practise saying the sentences.

C Students will probably need a little planning time if they are going to practise the spoken language feature properly. Give them a moment to plan, and then allow time for them to talk in pairs. Get a few ideas from various students to finish the lesson.

For further speaking and vocabulary practice, tell students to complete the exercises on page 36 of the Workbook. Set as an extra activity or homework task.

Listening

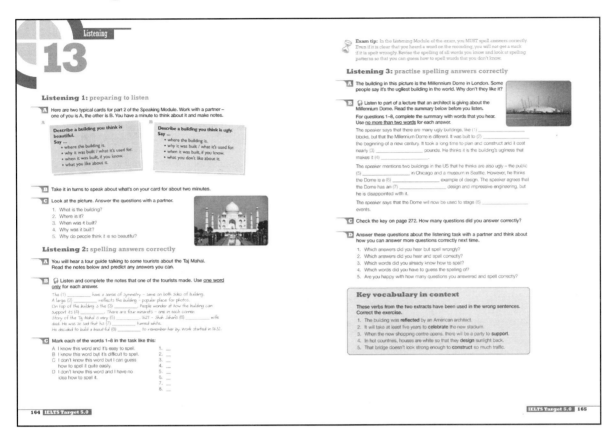

Objectives

- To familiarize students with the different register that will be used in the various parts of the listening exam.

- To practise various listening exam task types with a focus on the register used.

Listening 1

The first stage is very much preparation for the listening focus later in the lesson.

A and B Although this provides practice for a speaking exam task, the aim is to activate the listening topic of beautiful and ugly buildings. Work through the task as you have done with previous tasks of this type. When students have finished, get some feedback and see if any useful vocabulary has arisen.

C Students probably know something about the Taj Mahal, but the fact that they probably won't be able to answer all the questions doesn't

matter. Give them a minute or two to talk in pairs, and then open it up as a class discussion. Don't provide the answers yourself yet, as students will hear the answers in a moment.

Listening 2

The main focus of the module is on spelling answers correctly, but there is also a lot of useful prediction practice.

A Tell students to read the notes carefully, but not to write anything into the spaces yet. Look at the first gap as an example with them. Guide them towards making sensible predictions ('What can be on both sides of a building?' and so on). If students ask you to explain 'symmetry', they are thinking along the right lines, and you should explain it to them. Then give students five minutes to make predictions in pairs. Monitor to check suggestions are logical, and to help with any difficult key words, but don't actually correct their answers yet.

B 🎧 The real focus here is on spelling, so students will need time to hear the answers properly. Remind students that they will sometimes need to fill a gap with a word they don't know, and that they will have to guess the spelling. Play the whole recording once with pens down, and then again, pausing after each gap. Go straight on to Exercise C. Don't allow students to compare and don't provide answers yet.

Tapescript 🎧 **143** (2 mins, 44 secs)

B **Listen and complete the notes that one of the tourists made. Use <u>one word only</u> for each answer.**

Voice: OK, is everybody still with me? Good. Now, before we walk up to the building, I would like to tell you a few things. You will enjoy looking around the building more if you have some background.

As I'm sure you know, many people think the Taj Mahal is the most beautiful building in the world, and I hope you now understand why. Look at the gardens and how they have been designed. They are the same on both sides of the building, so there is a sense of symmetry. The fountains and pools create a sense of calm. You will see as we approach the building that it is reflected in a large pool. This is where most tourists stop to take their first photos, and I'm sure you will, too.

We will see the building up close, of course, but from here what you notice is the dome on top of the building and the four towers, or 'minarets' as they are properly called, in each corner.

Most people are surprised by the size of the dome, and wonder at how its weight is supported. When you are closer, you will see how the light at this time of the day makes the dome appear a blue-white.

Now, I expect most of you will know something about the story behind the Taj Mahal, but I will quickly summarize for those who do not. It is a truly romantic story – perhaps the most romantic story ever told. Shah Jahan

was one of the most important men in India. He had built wonderful constructions all over the north of India. Suddenly, in 1629, his favourite wife died, and the Shah was terribly sad. They say his beard turned white in one night. He wanted to create something to remember her by, and he decided to build the most beautiful monument he could imagine. The work started in 1632. It was finished thirty years later. 20,000 men worked on the construction.

Unfortunately, Shah Jahan did not have very long to enjoy his project. His son …
(fade out)

C Students are familiar with this type of reflective task analysis. Read the rubric and the four options with them. Make sure they understand that they are marking each of the eight gaps in the notes with one of the four options. Allow students a few minutes to do this.

Answers: 1. gardens   2. pool   3. dome
4. weight   5. romantic   6. favourite
7. beard   8. monument

Read this important exam tip carefully with students. Then cover it up, and ask one student to tell you what the advice was.

Listening 3

The aim now is to expose students to exam practice in which spelling will play an important part. Tell them that the recording is shorter than the one they will hear in any part of the exam, but that the level of challenge is what they can expect from the actual exam.

A Read the rubric with students and revise the meaning of 'dome'. Ask them if they know where the building is and why it was built. Discuss why people might think it is ugly. Ask students whether they think it's ugly.

B 🎧 Remind students that the summary is shorter than the recording, and that they will hear a lot that is not part of the summary. Emphasize, though, that they will hear the words that actually fill the gaps. Give students a minute to read through the summary. Don't help with anything at the moment. Tell them to make predictions, and then play the whole recording. Students might find it challenging to listen to the recording only once, but avoid playing it again, as they can discuss what difficulties they had and then listen again later if necessary (see Exercises C and D).

Tapescript 🎧 **144** (3 mins, 3 secs)

B Listen to part of a lecture that an architect is giving about the Millennium Dome. Read the summary below before you listen. For questions 1–8, complete the summary with words that you hear. Use <u>no more than two words</u> for each answer.

Voice: Now, you might ask why the Millennium Dome is so unpopular – why people are so upset by it. After all, there are ugly buildings all over the world. Blocks of flats and office blocks in every city in the world are truly unpleasant to look at. I'm sure you have plenty of ugly buildings in your city.

However, the important difference is that the Millennium Dome was not constructed quickly and cheaply like some 1950s block of flats. It was built to celebrate a special occasion. It took years of planning and years of construction – and it cost an enormous amount of money – not far off a billion pounds.

The Millennium Dome is supposed to be beautiful. It is, however, quite horrible. It was built to bring one of the world's great cities into the twenty-first century. Now, less than ten years later, nobody wants to look at it. I am afraid that it will always be famous for its ugliness.

In the United States, we have our ugly buildings, too. The Chicago Public Library is a good example and the Experience Project Museum in Seattle is awful. But there is something about the Millennium Dome that makes it worse – in my opinion, at least.

I admit that the design of the building is ambitious and, of course, is a great achievement of engineering. However, I'm afraid that for me that is not enough. To my mind, the Millennium Dome was, and is, a huge disappointment.

So, what will become of the building now? I understand that it has been bought by a company that hope to turn it into a venue for entertainment events, like shows and concerts. I suppose that considering how much it cost, it is good that it will be used for something. Personally, however, I would prefer to see it pulled down.

C Give students sufficient time to check answers and think about why they may have answered incorrectly, before moving on to Exercise D. Students should check any words they feel they need to with you as they look at the answers and tapescript.

Answers: 1. office   2. celebrate   3. a billion
4. famous   5. library   6. worse   7. ambitious
8. entertainment

D Students are now aware of how this reflective process works and its benefits. Note that here, the focus is mainly on the correct spelling of answers. Allow students time to reflect and complete the task. Play the recording if necessary, and tell students to focus on why the correct answers are correct.

Key vocabulary in context

Make sure students understand what to do in this activity. Give them a few minutes to work individually, and then a couple more to compare with a partner. Students should read the complete correct sentences to you as feedback.

Answers: 1. designed   2. construct
3. celebrate   4. reflect   5. support

For further listening practice, tell students to complete the exercise on page 36 of the Workbook. Set as an extra activity or homework task.

Reading

Objectives

- To prepare students to read longer texts.

- To revise various reading skills and apply them to reading longer texts in particular.

- To practise various task types based on reading a longer text.

Reading 1

The aim of the first activity is to introduce the theme of the main text in the practice stage. Some vocabulary is pre-taught so that students are better able to manage the length of the passage.

A Tell students to look at the image but not to say anything about it yet. Then give them a moment to read through the questions before talking to a partner. Work through students' ideas, but avoid too much lengthy or irrelevant discussion (especially with question 6). Provide quick, concise, correct answers, and take the opportunity to check any key words and phrases.

Answers:

1. a dam
2. to stop water flowing down a river / to create a lake or reservoir
3. in Egypt
4. in 1970
5. because the desert needed water / irrigation
6. It has improved many aspects of their lives.

B You might like to conduct this as a whole-class activity, as students have practised a lot of pairwork with dictionaries. Elicit or explain the meaning of each word, and then ask students how they think it will relate to the topic. Note that most of the words have occurred previously in the course.

Tell students that they will read the text once they have talked about reading longer texts.

Reading 2

A Read the rubric with students and establish that the text is longer than those they have read so far.

Give students the time they need to read and mark the points, and then get a general class consensus. There is no need to suggest correct answers to students as the points are covered in the lesson.

Read the exam tip with students. Then tell them to cover it, and ask them what points were made.

B Students will probably feel daunted by some of the longer texts they will see in authentic IELTS exam practice, especially the single passage in the third part. They have previously seen most of these points made in exam tips, but now they should apply the advice especially to reading longer texts. Students can work individually and compare answers with a partner, or work in pairs directly. Write answers on the board during feedback to check spelling.

Answers: 1. heading or title   2. topic
3. instructions   4. word   5. answer / context

Read the exam tip with students.

Reading 3

The aim now is to give students practice dealing with a longer text. The preparation stage earlier should give them more confidence when reading the text.

A Although you have gone over answers to the questions in the first stage of the lesson, students will probably need reminding due to the tasks in between. Give them a moment to look back and refocus on the topic. Set a time limit of two minutes to skim and check their earlier discussion.

B Students should now be able to work independently, but may need a little guidance with the first task. Although they have seen a number of matching tasks they have not actually matched headings with paragraphs yet. Give them some time to read the question-type tip in the middle of the task and check that they know what to do. Point out that although there are not Roman numerals in this task, such numerals may be used instead of letters in tasks similar to this. Students have used them previously. Remind students that the letters chosen in the third task can be given in any order. Set a time limit of 20 minutes.

C Give students sufficient time to check and think about why they may have answered incorrectly, before moving on to Exercise D. The answers, together with the parts of the text that provide answers, are reproduced here.

Answers:

1. d (Around 95% of the population of Egypt lives within ...)
2. g (There is a long history of ...)
3. i (The whole paragraph provides the answer.)
4. j (The statistics in the paragraph provide the answer.)
5. e (... has brought many benefits.)
6. a (... there have been problems, too.)
7. c (... how similar problems can be overcome in other countries ...)
8. 500km / kilometres   9. 35km / kilometres
10. 90 metres   11. 1,000 metres
12. 111 metres

Answers for questions 13–17 here are in alphabetical order, but any order is fine as long as the three correct letters are given.

13. A   14. B   15. C   16. E   17. G

D Remind students that identifying what they are doing well and not doing so well is a very good way of focusing on what they can do better next time. Note that the questions relate specifically to the practice focus. Allow students time to reflect and complete the task, and then ask them if they are happy with the number of correct answers. You may like to ask one student what he or she will do differently next time.

In this unit, the focus of the Workbook reading task ties in with the key vocabulary in context. Students are given advice about the amount of new vocabulary they may have to deal with in a longer text, and about how to decide what is important and less important in terms of answering questions. Now would be a good time to either work through it or set it up as a homework task.

Writing

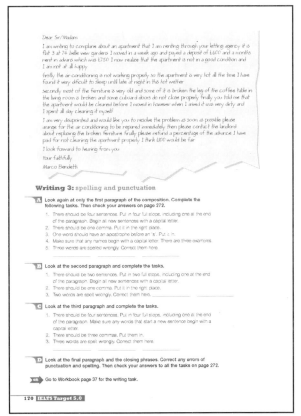

Objectives

- To show students the importance of spelling and punctuation in their compositions.

- To identify and correct errors of spelling and punctuation.

- To practise writing a letter that is typical of the IELTS writing exam.

Writing 1

The aim of the first stage is to engage students with the topic of the writing task and to pre-teach some key vocabulary.

A If your students are from different countries this exercise should be conducted as pairwork. If they are all from the same locality, you might prefer to talk through the points.

B Students should use dictionaries for this, and compare ideas with a partner as they work. When about half the class has finished, go over the words, drilling for correct pronunciation.

C Look at the example with students, and get one or two more from the class. Then give groups three minutes to brainstorm some more problems. Get some ideas from the students, and write any useful key words on the board.

D Tell students that the first time they listen, they should check which of their own ideas they hear mentioned. Check these with them and then play the recording again as students read the tapescript. Clarify the meaning of any vocabulary that is new to them.

Tapescript 145 (1 min, 24 secs)

D Listen to some students talking about problems they had when they rented an apartment. Did you mention any of the same things?

Speaker 1: I moved in and the apartment was really dirty. The agency hadn't arranged for anyone to clean it properly.

Speaker 2: The landlord kept coming round to the house without telling us first.

Speaker 3: The shower didn't work, so I had to have a bath all the time. It took a long time for the water to get hot.

Speaker 4: The heating didn't work, and it took the landlord a month to repair it.

Speaker 5: The furniture was old, and some of it was broken. There were only two cooking pans and we didn't have enough plates or glasses.

Writing 2

A Students are accustomed to seeing these writing instructions now, and should know that they need to check key words. Give them a minute or so to read and make sure that the words learnt in Exercise C above are clear, and check the meaning of 'in advance'.

B Students are familiar with this type of writing preparation task. Give them five minutes to talk in pairs, and then open it up as a class discussion.

C Tell students that they should simply read the letter to check the content and for now, not to worry about anything they think is an error. When they have read it, ask whether the letter is generally what they were expecting.

D Students should read again carefully and choose the option individually. Provide the correct answer before moving on.

Answers: The correct option is sentence 3.

Writing 3

A, B, C and D The clearest way to feed back this task is to have the composition on an OHP transparency. If that is not possible, you will probably have to tell students to check each paragraph of the model themselves.

It would be best to work through each task separately and check answers before moving on to the next. Students will gradually have a better idea of what to look for and feel more confident. Students should work individually on each task and then check with a partner. Go over answers on the OHP transparency, or refer students to the appropriate paragraph of the model. Note that Exercise D is more challenging, as students are left to work on their own more. They should work in pairs to discuss errors before getting some feedback. The correct version of the letter is on page 272 of the Course Book, and is reproduced below.

Dear Sir/Madam

I am writing to complain about an apartment that I am renting through your letting agency. It is Flat 3 at 74 Belle View Gardens. I moved in a week ago and paid a deposit of £600 and a month's rent in advance, which was £750. I now realize that the apartment is not in a good condition and I am not at all happy.

Firstly, the air conditioning is not working properly so the apartment is very hot all the time. I have found it very difficult to sleep until late at night in this hot weather.

Secondly, most of the furniture is very old and some of it is broken. The leg of the coffee table in the living room is broken and some cupboard doors do not close properly. Finally, you told me that the apartment would be cleaned before I moved in. However, when I arrived it was very dirty and I spent all day cleaning it myself.

I am very disappointed and would like you to resolve the problem as soon as possible. Please arrange for the air conditioning to be repaired immediately, then please contact the landlord about replacing the broken furniture. Finally, please refund a percentage of the advance I have paid for not cleaning the apartment properly. I think £100 would be fair.

I look forward to hearing from you.

Yours faithfully,
Marco Bendetti

Writing task

The writing tasks are found either in the Workbook or in the exam practice section at the end of the unit. For this unit, the task is in the Workbook.

A Students should be more confident about writing letters by now, but will still need preparation. Read the instructions and ask how many students feel they can manage the task fairly easily this time.

B Put them straight into pairs to answer the questions. The aim here is to provide them with a few points they can make when they come to write the letter. You can go through answers with them or monitor as they talk.

C Monitor as students work, but check specifically that they are organizing their letters, making relevant points and using appropriate register. There should be a particular focus on spelling and punctuation for this task.

When students have completed the task, put them into pairs to compare their compositions.

If you collect students' letters to mark, use the process to get an idea of what they are capable of and to give constructive feedback. There should be a particular focus on spelling and punctuation.

The model letter in the Course Book provides a good example of what a letter of this type should look like.

Consolidation

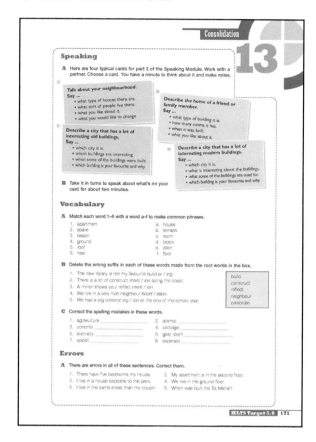

Speaking

The aim here is to provide more practice answering the more challenging questions that students will be asked in the third part of the speaking exam.

A and B Students now know how these tasks work. Make sure they follow the usual procedure, and monitor to check their performance as they talk. Once each student has had a turn, he or she should each choose one of the remaining cards and repeat the process.

Vocabulary

A Students can work individually or in pairs. Get them to say the complete phrases to check answers.

Answers: 1. d   2. c   3. a   4. f   5. b
6. e

B Students know how to work through this type of task, but here they simply have to choose an option. Students should complete the task individually. Write the answers on the board for clarity.

Answers: 1. building   2. construction
3. reflection   4. neighbourhood
5. celebration

C Tell students all of the words are spelt incorrectly here. They should work individually and then compare with a partner. You or they should write the answers on the board.

Answers: 1. agriculture   2. attempt
3. concrete   4. cottage   5. electricity
6. guest room   7. opposite   8. separate

Errors

A Students know that each unit ends with an error-correction task. Tell them that there are no errors of spelling. They can either complete the task individually or work in pairs. Write the correct sentences on the board for clarity.

Answers:
1. There are five bedrooms in my house.
2. My apartment is on the second floor.
3. I live in a house opposite the park.
4. We live on the ground floor.
5. I live in the same street as my cousin.
6. When was the Taj Mahal built?

Exam Practice

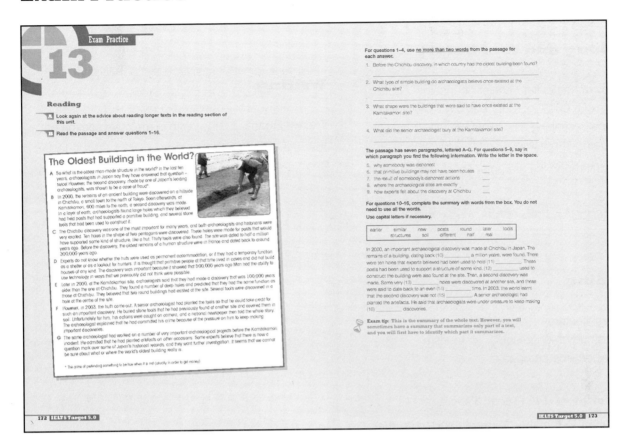

Reading

Although the text is longer, students should work completely alone now. They have practised all the task types and know how to approach the text. Some of the questions are a little easier than they will probably have to deal with in the exam.

A Give the students a few minutes to look at the advice again.

B Set a time limit of 20 minutes, which will include reading questions. Point out that 'fraud' is explained at the bottom of the text, and remind them there is occasionally a short glossary with a text. Write answers on the board for clarity.

Answers: 1. France   2. a hut   3. round
4. (stone) tools   5. F   6. D   7. G   8. B
9. C   10. half   11. posts   12. Tools
13. similar   14. earlier   15. real   16. new

Unit 13 Workbook answers

Speaking and Vocabulary

A types of home: flat / chalet / bungalow / cottage
parts of a building: roof / balcony / wall / floor
words describing a building: beautiful / ugly /
modern / impressive

Read through the grammar check with students.

B 1. d   2. a   3. e   4. c   5. f   6. b

Writing

The writing task is dealt with in the main section of
the Teacher's Book.

Listening

A 1. architecture   2. accidents
3. historic / monuments   4. tourism
5. millionaires / property

> **Tapescript** 🎧 **146** (1 min, 3 secs)
>
> **A** **Listen to the short extracts and write the
> missing words with the correct spelling.**
>
> **1** The Chinese city of Shanghai is now famous
> for its unusual architecture.
>
> **2** The construction industry can be dangerous,
> and there are occasionally serious accidents.
> Workers must follow safety procedures.
>
> **3** Rome is famous throughout the world for its
> many historic buildings and monuments.
>
> **4** Thousands of hotels have been built along
> the Spanish coast as a result of increased
> tourism.
>
> **5** In the last twenty years, many people have
> become millionaires through buying property
> at the right time.

Reading

Read the exam tip with students.

A 1. N   2. I   3. I   4. N   5. I   6. N   7. I
8. I   9. N   10. N   11. I   12. N

14 Technology

Unit overview

The fourteenth unit is based around the theme of technology. Students will talk about the appliances and gadgets they have in their homes, and how technology is changing their lives. There is a focus on taking control of your learning, such as by timing yourself when you read and making sure you have enough to say when you write.

Speaking and Vocabulary

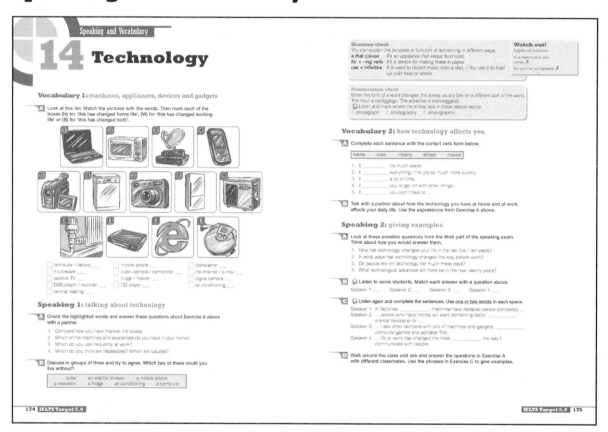

Objectives

- To give students further practice answering the questions they can expect in the first and third parts of the speaking exam.

- To give students practice talking about the machines and appliances they have in their homes.

- To present and practise vocabulary related to technology.

- To present and practise different ways of talking about a machine's function.

- To present and practise ways of giving examples in spoken language.

- To present and practise ways of introducing contrast in spoken language.

Vocabulary 1

It is important to note that the general terms in the heading – 'appliances', 'devices', 'gadgets' – are actually more challenging than some of the words in the task that follows. These words are used in the heading because they capture the topic of the module, and they occur frequently within the unit as a whole. There is no specific task with these words, so it would be a very good idea to pre-teach them before starting Exercise A.

Start the lesson by writing the four words on the board and then elicit examples of each. As you go, ask students if any words they suggest could go under more than one heading. You could start by writing 'car' under 'machine', and then 'fridge' under 'appliance'. Establish that a fridge is indeed also a machine, but that a car is not an appliance – appliances are generally found in the home and plug into the electricity supply. Point out that 'household appliance' and 'kitchen appliance' are typical phrases. For 'device', establish that a mobile phone and a tin opener are each a device – something clever that does a particular job. Some devices are machines and some are appliances. Finally, establish that 'gadget' is a more informal word, and implies that something is modern and very clever – 'modern cars are full of gadgets'.

Students might ask where 'tool' fits in here, and you might want to make sure that it's included in the lesson for distinction purposes. Tools are generally used to do a particular manual job – a 'screwdriver' is a tool and also a simple device; an 'electric drill' is a tool, a device and also a machine. If students are interested and can cope with more new vocabulary, teach them 'gizmo' – a very modern word that means a small, very clever new gadget.

A Conduct the matching task as individual dictionary work or as a whole-class activity. The latter approach will give you the opportunity to drill and get pronunciation right. Students should then work individually to mark each item appropriately. There is no need to give feedback, as students will compare ideas in the speaking task that follows.

No answers are necessary here.

Speaking 1

A It might be best to check the two highlighted words in question 4 as a class, before students talk in pairs. Check the meanings, and drill for accurate pronunciation. Point out that 'necessities' is related to the more basic word 'necessary'. Give students five minutes to talk in pairs, and then get some class feedback on the last question. Avoid a lengthy debate, which could waste valuable learning time.

B There will be more debate if students talk in groups. Set a time limit of five minutes and make sure students know they are supposed to try to agree. Get some feedback but avoid repeating the whole task.

Grammar check

Make sure students understand that the structures mean more or less the same thing. As you read through the information, ask them if they know what each item is (a fridge, a hole punch, a CD burner and a microwave). You could ask them to use each structure to explain the function of an appliance or device that you have in the classroom. At this point, you might like to ask students to correct the sentences in the 'Watch out!' box.

Answers:
1. It's a machine that dries clothes.
2. You use it to cut vegetables.

Pronunciation check

Read the advice with students, modelling the example words clearly. Drill the words until pronunciation is accurate. Give students a minute to say the three new words in pairs and attempt to mark the stress, and then play the recording. Write the words with stress marked on the board, and then give them time to practise saying each again more accurately.

Vocabulary 2

The aim here is to present students with a range of ways that they can talk about more or less the same thing. It is really an exercise in developing the accurate use of some very common fixed expressions.

A The verbs themselves may not be new to students, but they will probably not be confident using the whole of the fixed expressions accurately. Students should work individually, and then compare with a partner. When they have finished the task, tell them to cover it up, and then see if they can remember the whole expressions as you write them on the board.

Answers: 1. makes   2. does   3. saves
4. allows   5. means

B The aim here is for students to use the expressions in Exercise A accurately, so they should plan for a moment before talking. Monitor, and check they are using the target language properly.

Speaking 2

A Make sure students know that they are only thinking about how to answer each question, and that they don't start answering them straightaway. When they have looked at them,

ask if they think the questions are easy or difficult to answer. Students have seen questions like these a lot now, so you might like to see if anyone can answer some before listening to the examples.

B 🎧 As well as providing an example of typical spoken language, this stage also practises listening skills. Make sure students understand what to do, and play the whole recording. You can pause briefly between each speaker if necessary, but don't check answers. Provide the answers at the end before moving on to Exercise C.

c 🎧 Ask students if they liked the answers the students on the recording gave. Tell them that each student gave an example to explain his or her point. Give students some time to read the extract sentences, and then play the recording again with pens down. Play the recording once more, pausing to allow students to write the missing word. Either write answers on the board or refer students to the tapescript.

Tapescript 🎧 **149** (0 mins, 14 secs)

c **Listen again and complete the sentences. Use <u>one or two words</u> in each space.**

[Play track 148 again]

Answers: 1. for example   2. like   3. such as
4. especially

D In order to use each of the target items, students will need to plan for a minute or so before they start talking. Talking to a variety of classmates will be motivating, so tell students to ask each question to two or three people. Monitor, and check performance, rather than looking at it all again as formal feedback.

For further speaking and vocabulary practice, tell students to complete the exercises on page 39 of the Workbook. Set as an extra activity or homework task.

Listening

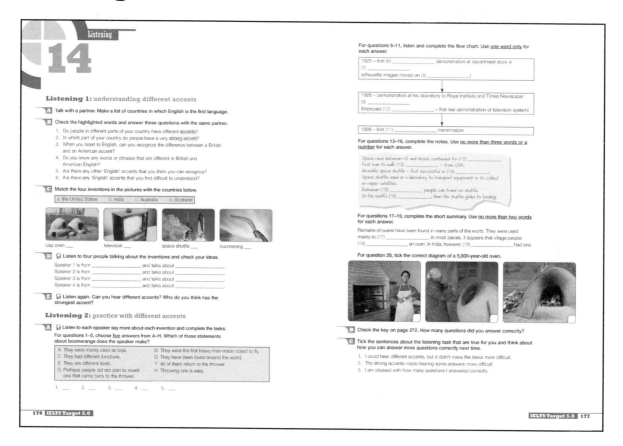

Objectives

- **To familiarize students with various accents that they might hear in the listening exam.**
- **To practise various exam listening tasks.**

In the exam, students may not have to listen to speakers with accents that are too strong for them to understand. The aim of the module is to make students aware of the varieties of English they might hear at any time, and to provide a motivating context for some listening exam practice.

Listening 1

A You can conduct this as pairwork or open it up as a class discussion. Write the names of some countries on the board, so that students can refer to them during the rest of the lesson.

Answers: Britain / Ireland / The United States / Canada / Australia / New Zealand / India

B Check the two highlighted items first, and drill 'accent' for accurate pronunciation. If your students are all from the same country you might like to answer questions 1 and 2 together as a class, as an extension of Exercise A. Give students about five minutes to talk, and then get some feedback. Introduce some of the ideas below during feedback.

Example answers:

4. lorry / truck   main road / highway
   trousers / pants   sweets / candy, etc.

6. Irish and Scottish accents can be very strong, even for native speakers. Mention that people in some cities (Liverpool) have very strong accents.

C Conduct this as a quiz. Put students into pairs and set a time limit of a minute. Check their ideas, but don't give the answers yet. You can say how many pairs matched everything correctly.

Answers: a. space shuttle   b. clay oven
c. boomerang   d. television

D 🎧 Students will probably not recognize the accents, but should listen for clues. Give them a moment to check what they have to fill in and then play the recording. Pause after each speaker, but don't check answers. Play the recording once more if students feel they need to listen again. Provide the answers before moving on to Exercise E.

Tapescript 🎧 **150** (2 mins, 55 secs)

D **Listen to four people talking about the inventions and check your ideas.**

Speaker 1: Most people probably don't realize what a clever thing a boomerang is. People think they're toys or used for sport. In fact, they were the very first objects made by human beings that were heavier than air and could fly. They were used for weapons and for hunting. The oldest Aboriginal boomerangs date back to 10,000 years ago. At that time, they would have been very advanced in terms of technology.

Speaker 2: Of course, it's not really clear who exactly invented the television – a number of different scientists and inventors were working on similar projects at the same time. But a man from my country, John Logie Baird, is the man who created the first working television system. He first demonstrated his invention to the public in 1925.

Speaker 3: Everyone knows that we have achieved a huge amount in terms of space exploration. The space race between ourselves and Russia went on for nearly twenty years, but we were the first to land a man on the Moon. At that time, the space race was very close, and the Russians very nearly got to the Moon before us. For me, the most exciting invention, and the invention that really showed we were ahead in the space race, was the reusable space shuttle. It was first successful in 1981 and has since been used on many missions.

Speaker 4: Although the remains of very early ovens have been found in many parts of the world, it was here that they were first used frequently in people's homes.

In ancient Greece and in other parts of Europe and Turkey, it seems that people used ovens to bake bread. But it seems there was only one large oven that everyone shared. Here, the remains of villages from 5,000 years ago show that each mud-brick house was constructed with an oven, and that baking bread and perhaps cooking meat was common.

Answers:
Speaker 1 is from Australia and talks about boomerangs.

Speaker 2 is from Scotland and talks about television.

Speaker 3 is from the United States and talks about the space shuttle.

Speaker 4 is from India and talks about clay ovens.

E 🎧 Once students have listened a couple of times, tell them to focus only on the accents. Play the recording again, and see if they agree about who had the most detectable accent.

Tapescript 🎧 **151** (0 mins, 14 secs)

E **Listen again. Can you hear different accents? Who do you think has the strongest accent?**

[Play track 150 again]

Listening 2

In the actual exam, students will not have to deal with this number of speakers and tasks, so you might like to pause between speakers. However, it will be difficult for students to check answers to one task without seeing the answers for the following task. You will need to work right through before students answer. The fact that they have prepared for the topic should give them confidence and make the tasks more manageable. Students have previously practised all the task types.

A 🎧 As there are so many tasks, give students a couple of minutes to read through the instructions and questions. They might find it challenging to listen to the recording only once, but avoid playing it again as they can discuss what difficulties they had, and listen again later if necessary (see Exercises B and C).

Tapescript 🎧 152 (6 mins, 14 secs)

A **Listen to each speaker say more about each invention and complete the tasks. For questions 1–5, choose <u>five</u> answers from A–H. Which of these statements about boomerangs does the speaker make?**

Speaker 1: Most people probably don't realize what a clever thing a boomerang is. People think they're just toys or something used for sport. In fact, they were the very first objects made by human beings that were heavier than air and could fly. They were used for weapons and for hunting. The oldest Aboriginal boomerangs date back to 10,000 years ago. At that time, they would have been very advanced in terms of technology. The remains of boomerangs have been found in North Africa, India and parts of America, but it's the Aboriginal boomerang that everyone knows about. When it's thrown correctly it follows a curved path and comes back to where it was thrown from. Some boomerangs are only about ten centimetres long, but the biggest can be over two metres. Not all boomerangs are designed to come back to the thrower. Hunting boomerangs, some of which are still used by Aborigines in Australia, are designed as flat throwing sticks and are used for hunting. These boomerangs that followed a straight path and flew very fast were actually more difficult to make, and it could

be that the famous returning boomerang was actually invented by accident as attempts were made to develop a faster hunting weapon. Nowadays, boomerangs are made mainly for tourists. It can be quite difficult to learn to throw one so that it comes back to you, and you may need a few lessons before you can do it properly.

For questions 6–11, listen and complete the flow chart. Use <u>one word only</u> for each answer.

Speaker 2: Of course, it's not really clear who exactly invented the television – a number of different scientists and inventors were working on similar projects at the same time. But a man from my country, John Logie Baird, is the man who created the first working television system. He first demonstrated his invention to the public in 1925. At one of London's most famous department stores, Logie Baird demonstrated how silhouette images could be seen to move on a screen. In 1926, he demonstrated his invention again – this time at his laboratory, to the Royal Institute and to reporters from the *Times* newspaper. The quality of the projected image had improved greatly and the event is considered to be the first real demonstration of a television system. In 1928, Logie Baird developed his invention and demonstrated the first transmission in colour.

For questions 12–16, complete the notes. Use <u>no more than three words or a number</u> for each answer.

Speaker 3: Everyone knows that we have achieved a huge amount in terms of space exploration. The space race between ourselves and Russia went on for nearly twenty years, but we were the first to land a man on the Moon. At that time, the space race was very close, and the Russians very nearly got to the Moon before us. For me, the most exciting invention, and the invention that really showed we were ahead in the space race, was the reusable space shuttle. It was first successful in 1981 and has since been used on many missions. The reusable shuttle can carry astronauts on space missions and can serve as a laboratory in which to conduct experiments. It can be used to transport equipment to space stations, or to collect or repair satellites. The shuttle carries between five and seven crew members. When a mission is complete, the shuttle fires thrusters, which propel it back into the earth's atmosphere. It then glides down to make its landing.

For questions 17–19, complete the short summary. Use <u>no more than two words</u> for each answer.

Speaker 4:   Although the remains of very early ovens have been found in many parts of the world, it was here that they were first used frequently in people's homes. In ancient Greece and in other parts of Europe and Turkey, people used ovens to bake bread. But it seems there was only one large oven that everyone shared. Here, the remains of villages from 5,000 years ago show that each mud-brick house was constructed with an oven, and that baking bread and perhaps cooking meat was very common. The ovens were made of clay and shaped like a beehive. Inside they had shelves, so that a number of loaves could be cooked together, and an opening at the bottom from which ash could be removed.

B Give students sufficient time to check answers and think about why they may have answered incorrectly, before moving on to Exercise C. Students should check the new words they need to with you as they look at the answers and tapescript.

Answers:
1. B   2. C   3. D   4. E   5. G

Note that the answers above are in alphabetical order, but they can be in any order as long as the five correct letters are given.

6. public   7. London   8. (a) screen
9. reporters   10. projected image   11. colour
12. nearly 20 / twenty years   13. on the Moon
14. 1981   15. 5 and 7 / five and seven
16. atmosphere   17. bake bread   18. shared
19. each house   20. 3 is the correct diagram

C Students are aware of how this reflective process works now and its benefits. Note that here, the focus is on the accents of the speakers. Allow students time to reflect and complete the task. They may want to talk about other factors that made tasks more challenging. Play the recording again if necessary, and tell students to focus on why the correct answers are correct.

For further listening practice, tell students to complete the exercises on pages 39 and 40 of the Workbook. Set as an extra activity or homework task.

Reading

Objectives

- To emphasize the need for students to time themselves when they read under exam conditions.

- To clarify which parts of the reading exam will involve reading longer and more challenging texts.

- To practise reading more quickly and to improve reading speed.

Reading 1

The aim of the first stage is to revise what students know about the IELTS Reading Module, to clarify exactly what the module consists of and to start students thinking about timing themselves more deliberately.

A   Students can either answer the questions in pairs or as a whole class. The exam tip is very thorough in this module, and answers the two questions, but you can give the answers if you wish.

Answers:
1. three
2. two (occasionally three) texts in the first two parts, one text in the third part

B Students should know what type of text to expect in each part of the Reading Module, and it isn't important whether students remember the labels for the various parts. Give them a minute or so to match and then check answers.

Answers:
Part 1 – social survival
public information leaflet / product information / advertisements

Part 2 – training survival
page of information related to work

Part 3 – general reading
article from newspaper, journal or magazine

C Students are familiar with this type of task in which the answers are given in the exam tip that follows. Tell them to cover up the exam tip, and give them a few minutes to discuss the points. There is no need to check their answers or provide answers yourself. Go straight on to the exam tip.

Read the exam tip slowly, checking that students have absorbed each piece of information. You could ask them the questions in Exercise C again now, if you think it would be beneficial.

Reading 2

The aim here is to guide students through the first part of the following reading practice, in terms of timing themselves and improving their reading speed. Make sure they cover the text itself while they are working through this stage.

A There is no task here (this is preparation for Exercise B that follows). You might like to read through the points with students, so you can check they have absorbed them.

B Make sure students understand that they are only planning how they are going to approach the first text, and that they are dividing ten minutes up into smaller sections of time. Students should work individually and then

compare with a partner. Within reason, give them as long as they need for this. There are not definite correct answers here, but you should provide a rough guide as feedback.

Answers: 1. one minute   2. two minutes
3. two minutes   4. one minute
5. three minutes   6. one minute

Reading 3

The aim of this activity is to give students practice with timing and reading quickly. Treat Exercises A and B as totally separate tasks this time.

A Students have the advantage of knowing what the text is about and what type of questions they have to answer. Read the rubric and set a very strict 10-minute time limit. Monitor to see whether students are following the advice about the timing of each stage. You can allow students to check answers now if they want to, but they must cover up the answers to Exercise B at the same time. Otherwise, work through Exercise B before checking answers to both tasks. The answers for Exercise A are provided below.

B Read the rubric carefully with students, and make sure they plan to apply the same timing breakdown to the various stages. Monitor as they work and apply the time limit as with Exercise A.

C Give students sufficient time to check and think about why they may have answered incorrectly, before moving on to Exercise D. The answers, together with the parts of the text that provide answers, are reproduced here.

Answers:
A 1. B   2. D   3. A   4. C   5. the cable / (the) supply cable / electricity supply cable
6. detergents   7. (a) qualified engineer
8. (your) local council

B 1. T (e-mail is now the most common form of communication)
2. NG
3. NG   4. F (most of fourth paragraph)
5. T (all of sixth paragraph)
6. F (all of seventh paragraph)
7. NG

D The questions relate specifically to the practice focus. Allow students time to reflect and complete the task, and then ask them if they are happy with the number of correct answers. You may like to ask one student what he or she will do differently next time.

> ### Key vocabulary in context
>
> Students may have noticed the prepositions as they read, but will probably need to refer back to the texts. To save time, you could tell them that the first two come from the first text and the others from the second text. Students should work individually or in pairs. Go over answers orally.

Answers: 1. in 2. of 3. with
4. in / with 5. to 6. in

The Workbook task for this unit provides further practice with timing and reading speed. Now would be a good time to set it up as a homework task.

Writing

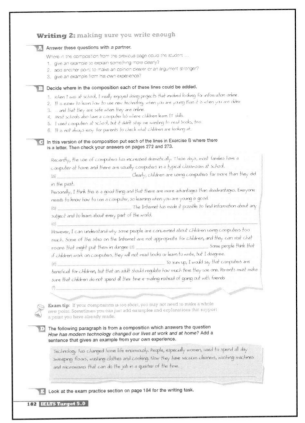

Objectives

- To focus once more on the problem of not having enough to say in a discursive composition.

- To give specific guidance on where content can be added to a composition, to ensure the word count is met.

- To practise writing a typical discursive composition.

Writing 1

A The aim of this activity is to revise what students know about the two parts of the Writing Module, as well as check how they now feel about each. Give them a couple of minutes to talk and then get a general class consensus.

Answers: 1. 150 words   2. 250 words

B Students are accustomed to seeing these writing instructions now, and should know that they need to check key words. Give them a minute or so to read, and then go over any difficulties. They will probably want to check 'harm' and be clear about what 'harming their development' means. Get a general consensus about whether this is a fairly easy or difficult topic to write about.

C and D Read through the instructions with students and look at the two examples. Establish that they are examples of both sides of the argument. Set a time limit of five minutes, and tell students to note down any points they think they would include in a composition. At the end of five minutes, students should answer the questions in Exercise D. Ask for a few possible arguments from the class to finish the activity.

E Tell students that there is something obviously wrong with the composition. Give them a moment to skim it and then establish that it is too short (that it doesn't meet the word count). Tell them that they will be able to read the composition more carefully in a moment.

Writing 2

The best way to give and get feedback for this task will be to have the composition on an OHP transparency.

Tell students that you are going to look at some ways of adding to the composition to make it long enough. Make sure students do not see the second version of the composition before working on this section.

A Read the three questions with students so that they know what they are looking for when they read again. They should work individually and then take some time to compare with a partner. You can check their ideas, and if you are using the OHP transparency, put the numbers in the places they suggest. There is no need to give correct answers, as they are dealt with in the task that follows.

B Students now see some lines that could be added and decide where they go. Note that the task that follows is more or less the same task, but with more guidance. Monitor, and check how well students are doing with this activity (if it is too difficult, move on to Exercise C). Set a time limit of about three minutes for this, and then to go on to Exercise C without worrying about checking answers. If you are using the OHP, check their ideas as in Exercise A.

C This is the same version of the composition but with spaces marked for the six additional lines. Stronger students will use this to confirm what they suggested in Exercise B, while weaker students will probably start all over again. How long they need for this will depend on what they have already achieved.

Refer students to the model on pages 272 and 273 of the Course Book to check their answers. It is provided below also. Point out that the composition now meets the required word count.

Recently, the use of computers has increased dramatically. These days, most families have a computer at home and there are usually computers in a typical classroom at school. Most schools also have a computer lab where children learn IT skills.

Clearly, children are using computers far more than they did in the past.

Personally, I think this is a good thing and that there are more advantages than disadvantages. Everyone needs to know how to use a computer, so learning when you are young is good. It is easier to learn how to use new technology when you are young than it is when you are older. The Internet has made it possible to find information about any subject and to learn about every part of the world. When I was at school, I really enjoyed doing projects that involved looking for information online.

However, I can understand why some people are concerned about children using computers too much. Some of the sites on the Internet are not appropriate for children, and they can visit chat rooms that might put them in danger. It is not always easy for parents to check what children are looking at. Some people think that if children work on computers, they will not read books or learn to write, but I disagree. I used computers at school, but it didn't stop me wanting to read books, too.

To sum up, I would say that computers are beneficial for children, but that an adult should regulate how much time they use one. Parents must make sure that children do not spend all their time e-mailing instead of going out with friends and that they are safe when they are online.

Read the exam tip with students. Then tell them to cover it, and ask a student what it said.

D This task focuses specifically on giving an example from personal experience. Read the rubric and make sure students understand what the topic of the composition is. Set a time limit of five minutes and tell students to work individually. Ask for ideas, and write the two you like best on the board to finish the activity.

E In this unit, the writing task can be found in the exam practice section at the end of the Course Book unit. See instructions for that section on page 284 of this book.

Consolidation

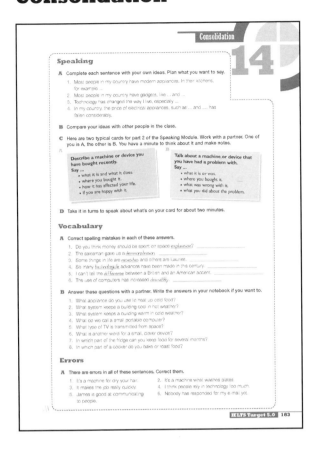

Speaking

A and B Students should look back to the first module of the unit to find the vocabulary they need. Help them with any challenging vocabulary in the sentences as they read and plan. Set a time limit for the planning stage and then allow them the time they need to talk.

C and D Students know how these tasks work now. Make sure they follow the usual procedure, and monitor to check their performance as they talk. If you feel students could do better, get them to go through the tasks again with a different partner.

Vocabulary

A Students have seen this error-correction task before. They should complete the task individually. See if they can correct the spelling without looking back at the unit. Then give them a minute to check their answers. Write the answers on the board for clarity.

Answers: 1. exploration   2. demonstration
3. necessities   4. technological   5. difference
6. dramatically

B This task checks their retention of vocabulary and their spelling. You could conduct it as a quiz, with pairs playing against each other. Set a time limit and award points for correct answers and correct spelling. You or they should write the answers on the board for clarity.

Answers: 1. microwave   2. air conditioning
3. central heating   4. laptop   5. satellite
6. gadget   7. freezer   8. oven

Errors

A Students know that each unit ends with an error-correction task. Tell them that there are no errors of spelling. If students are having difficulty identifying the errors, tell them that 4–6 are all errors with dependent prepositions. They can either complete the task individually, or work in pairs. Write the correct sentences on the board for clarity.

Answers:
1. It's a machine for drying your hair.
2. It's a machine that washes plates.
3. It does the job really quickly.
4. I think people rely on technology too much.
5. James is good at communicating with people.
6. Nobody has responded to my e-mail yet.

Exam Practice

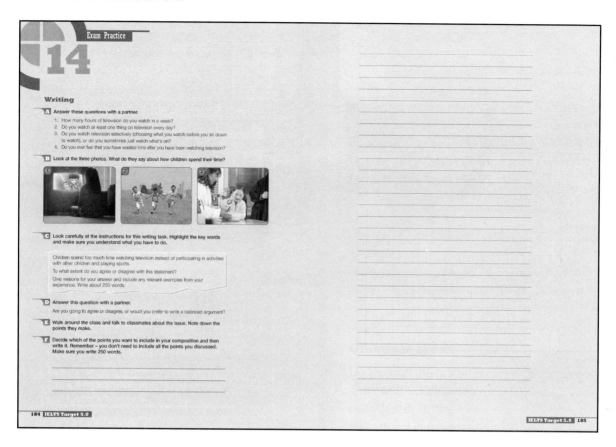

Writing

Students should now be more independent when it comes to writing a composition of this type, but will benefit from some guided preparation.

A Tell students to read through the questions and plan what they want to say. Tell them to add up and calculate how many hours of television they watch in a typical week. Give them four or five minutes to answer the questions, and then get some feedback. However, avoid going through all the questions again and repeating what they have already done.

B The aim of discussing the pictures is to prepare students for the content of the writing task (to start them thinking about whether children should be watching television or doing other things). They should focus on the first picture and compare it with the other two, as they have already been talking about television. When students have spoken in pairs, choose a few to tell you what they think.

C Students know how to read these task instructions now, and to ask you about anything that's unclear. Here, instructions are fairly simple and so should be quite clear.

D This can be conducted as pairwork as suggested, or as a whole-class discussion. The discussion earlier in the lesson should have given students ideas.

E This makes a change from the typical pairwork preparation. Students should have an opinion about this topic and will enjoy discussing it before they write. Make sure students use the discussion stage to note down any points they could use as arguments in the writing stage.

F Once students are ready to start writing, set a time limit of 40 minutes and try to ensure that students use the time they have. Monitor as students work, but check that they are organizing their ideas and making relevant points.

Once students have finished writing their compositions, tell them to look at the model composition on page 273 of the Course Book. The model is reproduced below. If you collect students' compositions to mark, use the process to get an idea of what they are capable of and give general feedback. Correcting everything they write will not be very motivating.

Nowadays, almost every family in the world has a television, and in the developed world there might be a television in every room in the house. Many children have their own television in their bedroom. All this probably means that children are watching a lot of television. The question is, though, are they watching more television than is good for them, and are they watching television when they should be doing other things?

There are some people who think that children spend all day, every day sitting in front of the television. They think that children never leave the house, never meet their friends and never play any sports. What's more, these people probably think that children only watch cartoons and action movies. In my experience, this is just not true. Most parents limit how much television their children watch and encourage them to watch programmes that are educational. There are a lot of programmes now that encourage children to go out and do things, or make things at home. I know that my nephew started playing tennis because he loved watching tennis on television so much.

I think it is important to say that children can learn a lot from watching television. There are all sorts of documentaries about different parts of the world and the history of the world. When I was young I couldn't watch the programmes that children can watch now.

To sum up, I would say that I disagree with the statement. There are some children who watch too much television, but most children watch the same amount as children did twenty years ago.

Unit 14 Workbook answers

Speaking and Vocabulary

A   Students have worked with dictionary entries before. Give them time to plan before each speaking activity. Monitor to check fluency rather than accuracy.

B   Students' own answers.

Listening

A   Speaker 1: Ahmed   Speaker 2: Simon
    Speaker 3: Sally   Speaker 4: Julie

Tapescript 🎧 **153** (2 mins, 59 secs)

A   **Listen and match each speaker with a picture.**

1

We bought one of these last year because we wanted to have some film of the children as they grow up – you know, playing in the garden or on holiday at the beach. We've got hundreds of photos, but this means you can see all the family talking and laughing. We transfer the films to DVD, and then we can watch them on TV or on the computer. I think the children will love to see them when they are grown up – perhaps they will show the films to their own children. I hope they can still play DVDs in thirty years!

2

I think nearly everyone has one these days. I can't imagine living without one now. I can call the office from my car, or as I'm walking down the street to work. When I'm away on business, I can keep in touch with people at work, and with my wife. My daughter has one, too, and I feel much better knowing that she can call us anytime if she is in danger or needs our help. Sometimes my wife calls me from the supermarket to tell me what we are having for dinner! Of course, the bills can be high, especially if I make calls when I'm abroad, but it's definitely worth it for the convenience.

3

I think they have both advantages and disadvantages. Of course, they're very convenient if you want to warm up something that you cooked the day before, or if you're very busy and you just want a quick ready-made meal. I must admit, I often use mine just to heat up my coffee when I'm too busy to drink it! However, if you use them all the time, it's not healthy. Young people eat far too much junk food when they are out, and so when they are at home they should eat a proper meal that their mother has cooked for them. Personally, I think a lot of technology makes life easier, but not necessarily better.

4

Having one of these is just brilliant. I can download music from my computer, and get my friends to copy songs for me. I don't have to waste money buying CDs which only have one good song on. I can listen to my favourite tracks on the bus to school, when I'm with Mum and Dad on a long boring car journey, or even if I'm just walking in the street. Music should be throwaway – if I get bored of a song, I can just delete it and record something new. I don't have enough room in my bedroom for hundreds of records and CDs – they're so old-fashioned.

B   1. Sally   2. Simon   3. Ahmed   4. Julie
    5. Simon   6. Julie   7. Ahmed   8. Sally

Tapescript 🎧 **154** (0 mins, 18 secs)

B   **Read these questions carefully so that you know what to listen for. Then listen again and write a name from the pictures in Exercise A into each space.**

[Play track 153 again]

Reading

A   1. In the kitchen: Third paragraph
    2. The system could even be connected to other buildings: Fourth paragraph
    3. In the homes of the future: First paragraph

4. When you are out of the house: Second
   paragraph

Writing

A 1. Generally speaking / However   2. so
3. Although   4. Because

B Either set some time aside in class for students
to compare their paragraphs, or collect the work
in and give a quick impression mark. Focus on
the use of linking devices especially.

15 Society

Unit overview

The final unit is based around the theme of issues in society. Students will talk about social problems and crime. In the skills modules the focus is on transferring answers, checking answers and making sure answers are spelt correctly.

Speaking and Vocabulary

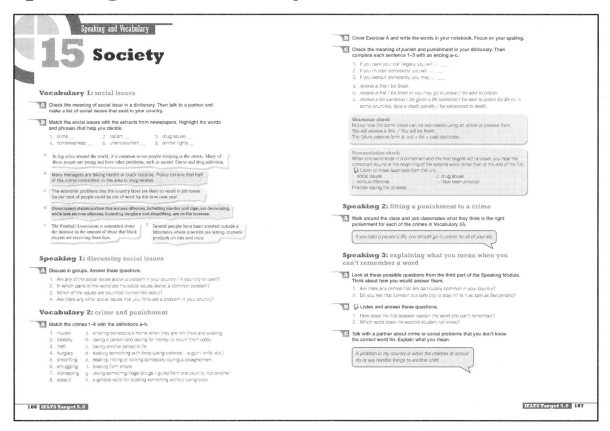

Objectives

- To give students further practice answering the questions they can expect in the third part of the speaking exam.

- To give students practice talking about social issues.

- To present and practise vocabulary related to social issues, and especially to crime.

- To practise explaining what you mean when you don't know the exact key word that you need.

Vocabulary 1

The first stage is a little more challenging in this final unit. Students need to read and understand vocabulary in context, and they have less in the way of visual support.

A They are accustomed to learning vocabulary through dictionary entries now. Tell students to cover up Exercise B first, and then give them a moment to read the entry. Elicit an example of a social issue and point out that it doesn't matter if they don't know the exact word for an issue (you could write 'not having a job' on the board, and explain that this is a way of saying what you mean if you don't know the word 'unemployment'). Give them three minutes to brainstorm in pairs. If you think students will be short of ideas, conduct this as a whole-class discussion. Rather than ask for ideas as feedback, it would be quicker for them to look at the list in Exercise B now.

B Tell students to look at the list of issues, but don't explain each issue yet (the reading task that follows deals with that). Ask them if they mentioned those on the list or if they mentioned any others. Tell students to work individually to do the matching, and to highlight key words and phrases as they work. Tell them to highlight the words and phrases that help them to match, and not to highlight everything they don't know. Students should check the matching task and compare what they highlighted. Go over the answers and write what you consider to be useful key vocabulary on the board. The first Workbook task for this unit focuses on language from these extracts, and now would be a good time look at and work through it together.

Answers: 1. d 2. e 3. b 4. a 5. c
6. f

Speaking 1

A If your students are all from the same country, you might like to answer the first question together as a class, and then deal with 2–4 as pairwork. Even if you feel your students won't have much to say about issues of this type, avoid conducting the whole task as a class discussion, as students should practise answering questions that they are not altogether confident about. Point out that for question 4, students should focus on anything that is currently an issue – something that has been in the news, for example. Have a time limit in mind and open the discussion up at some point. Try to elicit answers to the last question to finish the activity.

Vocabulary 2

A You could start by brainstorming crimes for a minute before looking at the task, or by covering up the definitions a–h and seeing how many of

the crimes students already know the terms for. However, avoid doing the matching task for them totally. Students can work individually and then compare answers or work directly with a partner. Write the number and letter matches on the board for clarity.

Answers: 1. c 2. d 3. h 4. a 5. f
6. g 7. b 8. e

B Make sure students cover up Exercise A and then say the eight words in a random order clearly, but naturally (don't read them through from 1–8). Pause briefly between each word to allow time for students to write. Students shouldn't need you to repeat words, but you can do so if they ask you to. When you have finished, students can check answers against Exercise A.

C Pronounce the two key words for students and then give them a moment to use their dictionaries. Clarify if necessary. Then ask students to tell you some different punishments, and try to elicit basic words like 'prison', 'fine' and perhaps 'death', to make the matching task more manageable. Then give students a minute or two to work individually to match. Students will probably complete the task quite easily, but will need clarification with exactly what some words and phrases mean as you give feedback.

Answers: 1. a 2. c 3. b

Grammar check

Read through the information and point out that the two structures in the example mean the same thing. Ask students for more examples of the same idea, expressed in two ways (go to prison / be sent to prison, receive a life sentence / be given ...). Go over the structure of the future passive, and substitute the various participles (be sent / be given, etc.) to make it clear.

Pronunciation check

It will be better to write the phrases on the board first this time and ask students to try saying them. Then play the recording, and show students how the final sound of the first word is transferred. Model each phrase as it is on the recording. Then give them time to practise saying each phrase again more accurately.

Speaking 2

A Students have walked around talking to different classmates a number of times. Doing so now should be more motivating than talking to one partner who they have probably spoken to most. Look at the example with them and ask who agrees or disagrees. Then tell them to get the views on each crime from three or four people. To finish the activity, see what the general consensus of opinion is for each crime.

Speaking 3

A Make sure students know that they are only thinking about how they would answer each question and that they don't start answering them straightaway. When they have looked at them, ask if they think the questions are easy or difficult to answer. For the second question they can substitute a city they have visited and compare it with their hometown.

B 🎧 Tell students that the focus is on continuing to speak, and explaining what you mean when you don't know the exact word for what you want to say. Read through the two questions with them and make sure they know what they are listening for. Play the whole recording with pens down, and then again, pausing between the two as students write their answers. Play it again if necessary. Write the answers on the

board and check that students understand that the first speaker didn't know the word 'kidnap'. Point out that in the first exchange the examiner provides the key word. In the second, he/she does not.

Tapescript 🎧 **156** (1 min, 14 secs)

B **Listen and answer these questions.**

1

Examiner: Are there any crimes that are particularly common in your country?

Student: Mm, I think we have the same as other countries. But one crime that is a big problem is, erm ... you know, when somebody takes a child and asks for money ...

Examiner: You mean kidnapping?

Student: Yes, kidnapping. It is a big problem in my part of the world.

2

Examiner: Do you feel that London is a safe city to stay in? Is it as safe as Switzerland?

Student: No, not really. I think people are a little more aggressive. Sometimes, I think there will be a fight. The first flat I stayed in was on the ground floor, and there was a ... erm ... when someone comes in the flat and he steals things, erm ... anyway, that happened in my first flat. I wanted to move to another one after that.

Examiner: Oh, I'm sorry to hear about that.

Answers:
1. takes a child and asks for money
2. burglary

C In order to practise this particular skill, students will need to plan for a minute or so before they start talking.

Look at the example with them, and make sure they understand that they don't need to know the key word that they are paraphrasing. Monitor while students practise, to check they know what to do. If all your students are from the same country you could put some social issues, written in their language, on the board.

Listening

Objectives

- To practise transferring answers to the answer sheet at the end of the listening exam.

- To practise a variety of listening tasks.

Listening 1

A The aim of this first stage is to prepare students for the topic of the recordings that they will focus on in the lesson. Tell students to look at the picture, and write 'homeless' and 'homelessness' on the board. Ask students if they can relate to the image (are there homeless people in their cities?). Students can talk in pairs as suggested, or in small groups. Tell them to make notes so that they can tick points as they listen in a moment. Give them five minutes to talk and then get some feedback. Write any key points on the board, as it will provide focus for the listening task that follows.

B 🎧 Students now hear the whole recording in order to check their ideas in Exercise A. Tell

them that they will listen to the recording two or three times more and that for now, they are listening for gist and will not understand everything. Tell them to tick the points they discussed if these are mentioned by the speaker. To finish this stage, ask a couple of students to tell the class one point they remember.

Tapescript 🎧 **157** (5 mins, 19 secs)

B **Listen to somebody giving a talk about homelessness and check your ideas.**

Part 1

Voice: Good evening. I'm so pleased that so many people have attended my talk. I know many of you are concerned about the number of homeless people that there are in the town centre. I know a lot of you will feel that the situation is becoming worse, and that nobody is doing anything about it. However, I think that coming along this evening shows that you want to know more about homelessness and understand the issue, and not simply see it as a problem that affects you as individuals.

Now, I'll start by explaining what 'homeless' means – and it means a little more than simply sleeping out in the street. The people you see in parks and gardens, or bus stops and shop doorways, are a small percentage of the people that we class as homeless. People are homeless if they are sleeping on the floor or on the sofa at a friend's house. They are homeless if they are sleeping in a hostel or shelter for homeless people. They are homeless if they are sleeping in a car or any other vehicle. We also class people as homeless if they are separated from family or other people that they would normally live with. People are homeless if they live in conditions that are so bad that their health is affected, and they are homeless if they are in danger of violence or physical abuse. That means, as I said before, that homelessness is a much bigger issue than a few people sleeping in bus stops or shop doorways. This is just what you see.

Part 2

So, why do people become homeless? People do not choose to be homeless. They are not sleeping rough because they have chosen to leave a safe home or families who love them. They are homeless because there is no other option. People become homeless because they are poor – because they cannot afford to pay rent, or sometimes because they cannot afford to pay the mortgage on a house or apartment that they have bought. People become homeless because they lose their job or have never had a job. There are related problems that often result in a person becoming homeless. Many homeless people have a drug addiction – they are either homeless because they spend their money on drugs, or they have become addicted to drugs because they are homeless. A high percentage of homeless people have mental health problems and find it difficult to make the decisions about their lives that most people can make. A number of homeless people are ex-prisoners – when they are released from prison, it is very difficult to

find a job and a place to live. Many people become homeless because the owner of their home – a landlord or landlady – evicts them. If people have lived in the same place for a long time and then suddenly lose it, they can find it impossible to afford the increased rent for a new home. Many people have to move out of the place they live because it is dangerous – a young person may have a violent father, or a wife a violent husband. These people are too afraid to stay in their home, and they risk making themselves homeless. Finally, in many parts of the country, there is just not enough housing – certainly not enough housing that poor people can afford. The increase in the value of property has made life difficult for many people – not just homeless people. I'm sure many of you will understand that.

So, how do we deal with a problem as big as this? It isn't easy. In this country, people with very poorly paid jobs or no jobs at all receive some kind of financial support. In some cases, all or part of their rent is paid by the government. This helps to stop people becoming homeless, but if you are already homeless, it doesn't help. Most towns, like this one, have shelters for people who are temporarily homeless, but they cannot stay at them permanently. They have to move on after a certain period of time. Some towns have food kitchens where homeless people can get a meal two or three times a week. The problem is that shelters and food kitchens don't really deal with the cause of the problem – they deal only with the effect. People can stay in a shelter for a while, but it will not help them to find a home of their own – and that is what they need, of course. Now, I'm going to go on in a moment to talk about some of the suggestions that have been made in terms of dealing with homelessness – ideas for dealing with the problem in a more permanent way. I'll also talk about some of the programmes that are in place and are, in some cases, very successful in other parts the world. Before that, does anyone have any questions about what I have said so far?

Listening 2

A Tell students that they will hear the recording again later, but for now you are going to focus on an important aspect of the exam. Read the section heading with students. They are familiar with this type of reflective analysis now, and will know how to discuss the questions. Give them five minutes to do so in pairs and then check their answers.

Answers:
1. multiple-choice / matching, etc.
2. completing sentences and notes / short answers / summary completion, etc.
3. on the question paper
4. on the answer sheet
5. ten minutes
6. spell words wrongly / miss words out / use too many words / run out of time if you write too slowly, etc.

B 🎧 The aim of this stage is to make students aware of the types of mistakes they can make when transferring answers, rather than to give actual listening practice. Don't worry then if students need to listen a couple of times in order to hear and write answers. Tell them that they are going to hear part of the recording they heard earlier, and give them a minute or two to read through the questions. Play the whole recording, and then again, pausing so that students have time to write answers. Don't go over the answers until students have looked at the answers given by the fictitious student in Exercise C (the answers are provided then).

> **Tapescript** 🎧 **158** (0 mins, 25 secs)
>
> **B** Listen to the first part of the talk about homelessness again and answer these questions. For questions 1 and 2, choose the correct answer a, b or c.
>
> [Play part 1 of track 157 again]
>
> For questions 3–7, complete the notes. Use <u>no more than three words</u> for each answer.
>
> [Play part 1 of track 157 again]

C The aim is for students to recognize the mistakes and understand why the student's answers will be marked as wrong. Tell students that not all answers are wrong, and that they must decide which are wrong and why. They should also compare their own answers with these ones. Give them five minutes to talk and then work through the answers, giving the correct answers as you do so. Write them on the board. Ask your students how they compared with the student who did the task.

Answers:
1. c is correct   2. b is correct
(point out that multiple-choice answers are easier to transfer)
3. The student has used too many words.
4. The student has misheard or spelt the first word incorrectly.
5, 6 and 7: The student has spelt the answers incorrectly.

Actual answers: 3. floor or sofa
4. hostel or shelter   5. vehicle   6. health
7. violence

Read the exam tip with students slowly and carefully. Then tell them to cover it and ask them to look at the points made.

Listening 3

The aim of this activity is to give students practice transferring answers onto the answer sheet. Tell them that they will practise this again when they come to the exam practice later in the unit.

A 🎧 The fact that students have prepared for the topic and already listened to the recording should give them confidence and make the tasks more manageable. However, because the focus here is on transferring answers, it would be best if students had a significant number of answers to transfer. If they need to listen again twice now, let them do so. Give them a minute to read through the instructions and questions first.

A Listen to the rest of the talk about homelessness again. Answer the questions. For questions 1–8, complete the summary below with words from the text. Use <u>no more than two words</u> for each answer.

[Play part 2 of track 157 again]

For questions 9 and 10, choose <u>two</u> answers from A–D.

[Play part 2 of track 157 again]

B Now give students exactly a minute to transfer answers. They can compare before looking at the answers, if you like. Monitor, and check whether students are finding it difficult and try to spot any spelling errors.

C Give students sufficient time to check answers and think about why they may have answered incorrectly before moving on to Exercise D. Students should check with you any words they feel they need to as they look at the answers and tapescript.

Answers: 1. option   2. afford   3. a job
4. drugs   5. mental health   6. prison
7. violent   8. property

Answers 9–10 are given in alphabetical order, but the order is not important.

9. A   10. C

D Students are now aware of how this reflective process works, and of its benefits. Note that here the focus is on transferring answers. Allow students time to reflect and complete the task. Play the recording again if necessary, and tell students to focus on why the correct answers are correct.

Reading

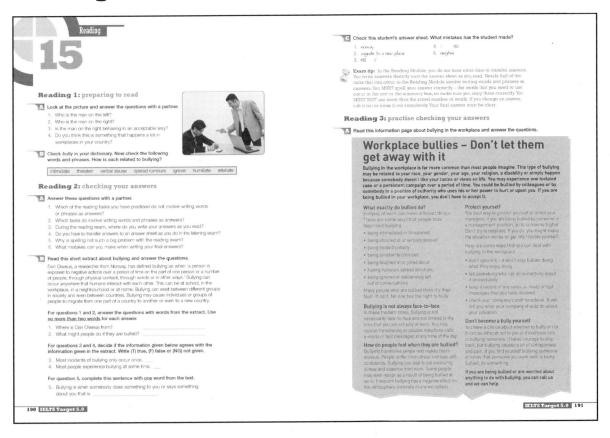

Objectives

- To practise writing answers directly onto the answer sheet.

- To emphasize the need to check answers carefully at the end of each part.

- To practise various typical reading tasks.

Reading 1

The aim of this first stage is to prepare students for the topic of the text that they will focus on in the lesson.

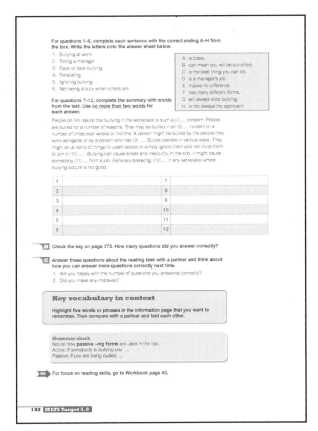

A Tell students to look at the picture and ask them to tell you what they think is happening. You don't need to respond to suggestions yet, as students will answer questions in pairs in a moment. Give students two or three minutes to answer the questions in pairs and then go over answers as a class. Take the opportunity to check useful words connected with work, like 'employee' and 'manager', and try to elicit 'bully' and perhaps 'victim' from the context. If you want to, you could use the opportunity to touch on a continuous passive, by writing 'he is being bullied' on the board.

Answers:
1. an employee
2. the other man's manager/boss
3. probably not / he is a bully
4. students' own answers

B If students haven't yet learnt 'bully', give them a moment to look it up and clarify the meaning for them. Tell students that these words occur in the text they will later read. Tell them to use dictionaries to check the words – bilingual dictionaries will be best here – and then to think about how each is related to bullying. They should work individually and then talk to a partner about what they have learnt. Get some feedback and clarify anything that students are not sure about. Point out that you can 'threaten somebody' or 'threaten to do something'. Distinguish between 'physical' and 'verbal' abuse.

Reading 2

A Tell students that they will read more about bullying later, but for now you are going to focus on an important aspect of the exam. They have just done something very similar in the Listening Module. Give them five minutes to complete the activity in pairs, and then check their answers.

Answers:
1. multiple choice / matching / T/F/NG, etc.
2. completing sentences and notes / short answers / summary completion, etc.
3. straight onto the answer sheet
4. no
5. because the words and phrases are from the text / you can copy them
6. copy them wrongly / use too many words / not make your answer clear

B The aim of this stage is to make students aware of the types of mistakes they can make when transferring answers, rather than actual reading practice. Don't worry then if students need a little longer than usual to understand and write answers. Tell them to follow the usual procedure of skimming, looking at the questions, and then

reading again more carefully. Don't go over the answers until students have looked at the ones given by the fictitious student in Exercise C (the answers are provided then).

C The aims here are for students to recognize the mistakes as well as understand why the student's answers will be marked as wrong. Tell students that here all the answers are wrong (or could be marked as wrong), and that they must decide why. They should also compare their own answers with those here. Give students five minutes to talk and then go over the answers, giving the correct answers as you do so. Write the correct answers on the board. To finish the activity, ask your students how they compared with the student who did the task.

Answers:
1. No capital is used.
2. There are too many words.
3. The first answer is not crossed out properly.
4. The first answer is not rubbed out properly.
5. The word has been copied wrongly and so misspelled.

Actual answers: 1. Norway   2. migrate
3. F   4. NG   5. negative

Read the exam tip with students slowly and carefully. Then tell them to cover it up, and ask them to go through the points made.

Reading 3

The aim now is to give students practice writing answers onto the answer sheet. The answer sheet is provided at the end of the text.

A As this text is new to students, tell them to look at it and establish that it is an information page, probably from a website. Remind them this is a typical text from the second part of the Reading Module.

Tell students that the focus is on writing answers onto the answer sheet, but that they should also apply the timing of each reading stage they practised in the last unit. Set a time limit of 15 minutes. Monitor to check that students are following the advice about timing and are confidently using the answer sheet.

B Give students sufficient time to check and think about why they may have answered incorrectly, before moving on to Exercise C. The answers are reproduced here.

Answers: 1. F   2. C   3. H   4. B
5. E   6. A   7. common   8. isolated
9. authority / power   10. conversations
11. to resign   12. the atmosphere

C The questions relate specifically to the practice focus. Allow students time to reflect and complete the task, and then ask them if they are happy with the number of correct answers. You may like to ask one student what he or she will do differently next time.

Key vocabulary in context

Remind students that taking control of the vocabulary they record and revise is important. Give them a few minutes to highlight, and then a couple more to compare and test each other.

Grammar check

Read through the information and examples with students. Then write 'if someone is ignoring you ...' on the board, and tell students to make it passive.

Answer: If you are being ignored.

The Workbook task for this unit provides further practice with writing answers. Now would be a good time to set it up as a homework task.

Writing

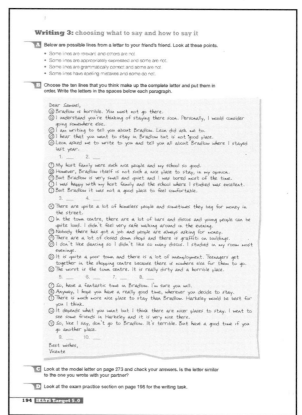

Objectives

- To practise writing an informal letter that gives advice.
- To focus on a variety of aspects of a composition, including relevance of content, register and errors.
- In this lesson, students will attempt to write a complete letter and then compare it with a model.

Writing 1

The aims of the first stage are to provide some speaking practice that is typical of the third part of the Speaking Module, as well as engage students with the topic of the writing task.

A You can conduct this as a whole-class activity. Deal with meaning and pronunciation as students match. Point out not only that begging, vandalism and graffiti are all examples of antisocial behaviour, but also that what people consider to be antisocial is not always the same. You can ask students if the boys in the picture are being antisocial. Point out other related words here, like 'vandal' and 'beggar', and that 'to spray' is a verb usually used in connection with graffiti.

Answers: 1. begging   2. graffiti
3. vandalism   4. antisocial behaviour

B Students can talk with a partner or in small groups. Give them five minutes and then ask for feedback from the class.

C Students are now accustomed to seeing these writing instructions, and should know that they need to check key words. Give them a minute or so to read, and then go over any difficulties. Get a general consensus about whether this is a fairly easy or difficult letter to write.

D Give students about five minutes to get ideas together, and then get some ideas back from the class. Write key points on the board so that students can refer to them during the lesson.

Answers:
1. something between formal and informal
2. Students will probably mention the points in Writing 1A.

Answers: 1. e   2. b   3. i
4. g (Note that h is not relevant)
5. p   6. n   7. k
8. l (Note that as the writer is listing problems, there is not one correct order here, especially with n and k)
9. u   10. s

Writing 2

A and B   Students have had plenty of practice with opening and closing letters, and should be able to tackle this now. Writing as a team should motivate students and will lessen the amount of writing that takes place when time might be short. Set a time limit of six or seven minutes, but give them an extra minute if necessary. Give them time to compare, and then ask pairs if they feel that their joint effort is what they expect to see in the model. Monitor to check work as you go (students will check against the model later).

C   Some students do not enjoy writing with a partner, but encourage them to do so here. You might like to put stronger and weaker students together, but if you do make sure one student doesn't do all the work. Set a time limit, as above, and monitor in the same way. Tell students that they will see the model later, but that they will do some more language focus first.

Writing 3

A   Read the rubric with students. 'Below' means in Exercise B, and the lines are lines a–v. Read through the points slowly with students, checking they understand as you do so.

B   Read the instructions with students. Make sure they can see that each paragraph is dealt with separately, so the task is less daunting than it may look at first. Make sure students understand that they must order, as well as select, the correct lines. Students should work individually, and then take some time to compare answers and explain their choices with a partner. Go over the answers one paragraph at a time, writing the numbers and letters on the board. This will be more methodical than simply referring students to the model. Ask students to explain why they have not chosen some of the lines.

C   Refer students to the model letter on page 273 of the Course Book, and give them time to read the whole thing. The letter is also reproduced here.

Dear Samuel,

Leon asked me to write to you and tell you all about Bradlow, where I stayed last year. I understand you're thinking of staying there soon. Personally, I would consider going somewhere else. I was happy with my host family, and the school where I studied was excellent. However, Bradlow itself is not such a nice place to stay, in my opinion.

It is quite a poor town and there is a lot of unemployment. Teenagers get together in the shopping centre because there is nowhere else for them to go. There are a lot of closed-down shops and graffiti on buildings. There are quite a lot of homeless people, and sometimes they beg for money in the street. In the town centre, there are a lot of bars and discos and young people can be quite loud. I didn't feel very safe walking around in the evening.

It depends what you want, but I think there are nicer places to stay. I went to see some friends in Harkeley and it is very nice there. Anyway, I hope you have a really good time, wherever you decide to stay.

Best wishes, Vicente

Tell the students to compare their letter with the model. Discuss any differences.

D   In this unit, the writing task can be found in the exam practice section at the end of the Course Book unit. See instructions for that section on page 303. Note though that because students practised writing the letter before seeing the model, the writing task practises something quite different, and is related to the reading passage in the same module.

Consolidation

Speaking

A The aim of this activity is to give students further practice at paraphrasing when they don't know a key word. They should use bilingual dictionaries, otherwise they will simply read the definition given. Tell them that once they know what the word means they should find a way of explaining it. Their partner should tell them if the meaning is clear from what they have said.

B and C Students know how these tasks work. Make sure they follow the usual procedure, and monitor to check their performance as they talk. If you feel students could do better, get them to go through the tasks again with a different partner.

Vocabulary

A Students will probably enjoy this more if they work in pairs. You could conduct it as a quiz to see which pair finds all the words first. The best way to go over answers will be to use an OHP transparency. Students can come and circle the words on the board.

Answers:

K	V	R	O	B	B	E	R	D	K
U	A	M	K	G	U	T	N	I	I
T	N	U	I	T	H	E	F	T	L
S	D	D	D	I	I	R	N	I	L
N	A	A	N	T	I	R	E	P	E
R	L	L	A	F	I	N	E	R	G
Y	I	B	P	R	U	M	M	I	A
E	S	M	U	G	G	L	E	S	L
O	M	U	R	D	E	R	I	O	N
P	U	N	I	S	H	A	C	N	R

B Students should complete the task individually. Write the answers on the board for clarity.

Answers: 1. racism   2. unemployment
3. burglary   4. assault   5. release
6. temporary   7. permanent   8. threaten

Errors

A Students know that each unit ends with an error-correction task. Tell them that there are no errors of spelling. They can either complete the task individually or work in pairs. Write each sentence on the board for clarity.

Answers:

1. If you murder, you will be given a life sentence.
2. If you rob a bank, you will be sent to prison.
3. Homeless people may be separated from their family.
4. If you are being bullied, you must tell somebody.
5. He is staying with friends temporarily.
6. I am writing to tell you about Bradlow.

Exam Practice

15

Listening

A 🎧 You will hear two people telephoning their local council to complain. Answer the questions.

For questions 1–5, choose the correct answer a, b or c.

1. The woman ...
   a. has called the council before. b. is calling for the first time. c. called the council yesterday.
2. The woman ...
   a. lives in the city centre. b. does not like football. c. is surprised by something.
3. The woman didn't call the police because ...
   a. she didn't want to call early in the morning. b. it was too late for them to do anything.
   c. she was too angry to stay calm.
4. The council telephonist says that ...
   a. everyone wants more cameras. b. it is right that homeowners must clean up graffiti.
   c. the council is very busy.
5. The council telephonist ...
   a. promises that telephone boxes will be cleaned soon.
   b. admits that the council must repair some public property.
   c. thinks that parents should stop their children spraying graffiti.

For questions 6–10, choose five answers from A–I. Which of the following is the man unhappy about?

A Rubbish is not collected regularly.	B Friday is not a good day for a rubbish collection.
C Birds make a problem worse.	D He was not told about a change.
E He has to clean the street himself.	F He has a difficult job.
G People put rubbish out on the wrong day.	H He does not like his neighbours.
I Rubbish collectors could do a better job.	

6. ___ 7. ___ 8. ___ 9. ___ 10. ___

B Transfer your answers to the answer sheet below. You have two and a half minutes.

1		6	
2		7	
3		8	
4		9	
5		10	

Reading

A Read the passage and answer questions 1–10.

A. The answer to this question depends on what, in your opinion, is the purpose of sending people to prison. Most people consider the impact that imprisonment has on criminals and how it affects their behaviour in the future. Some people will have different views about why we have prisons; politicians, policemen and the victims of crime, for example. Putting people behind bars appears to work for a number of reasons.

B. Most people regard a prison sentence as a fair punishment for certain serious offences or a number of less serious offences. The criminal does something wrong and society pays him back. He gets what he deserves. There are other forms of punishment, such as fines or community service, but imprisonment is what people expect when the crime cannot be ignored.

C. Violent criminals and those who offend again and again need to be locked up so that people are not in danger. A recent survey of offenders sent to prison showed that the typical offender admitted to committing 150 offences in the year before he was caught. On average, therefore, for each 1,000 criminals sent to prison for a year, there would be 150,000 fewer offences.

D. Many people believe that the fear of going to prison deters people from committing crime. People who might do wrong think again if they know that the punishment will mean being locked up. Some statistics suggest that in countries where punishment for certain crimes is very severe, the rate for that crime has fallen. Other people argue that people commit crime because they are desperate and that desperate people have no fear of punishment, whether it is prison or something else.

E. Prison is supposed to rehabilitate criminals. In prison, an offender has time to reflect on the crime he has committed and on the pain he has caused to his victim. Prisons have programmes for educating inmates and for teaching them new skills that they can use when they are released. Some people might argue, however, that in prison, offenders simply meet and mix with other criminals and come out knowing more about crime.

F. Finally, prison is an important institution. Every democratic country has prisons, and people believe that there are wrongdoers who should be inside them. If prisons did not exist or if softer punishments were given to serious criminals, people would not trust the justice system. It is possible that, in that situation, more people would take the law into their own hands and deal with criminals themselves.

For questions 1–6, match the section headings i–x with the sections in the text. You do not need to use all the headings. Write the numeral for each answer.

i.	Prison life is too easy	ii.	What sort of person goes to prison?
iii.	Public confidence	iv.	Fines might be the solution
v.	Changing for better or worse	vi.	Afraid of losing freedom
vii.	Does prison work?	viii.	An eye for an eye
ix.	Most criminals are not caught	x.	Protecting the public

1. Section A ___
2. Section B ___
3. Section C ___
4. Section D ___
5. Section E ___
6. Section F ___

For questions 7–10, answer each of these questions with words from the text. Use no more than two words for each answer.

7. Apart from imprisonment and fines, what form of punishment does the text mention?
8. How many crimes does the typical offender commit before he is caught?
9. Which word is the opposite of 'soft' when describing a punishment?
10. What are some inmates supposed to learn while they are in prison?

1		6	
2		7	
3		8	
4		9	
5		10	

Writing

A Look carefully at the instructions for this writing task. Highlight the key words and make sure you understand what you have to do.

> Prison is the only suitable way of dealing with the majority of offenders.
> To what extent do you agree or disagree with this statement?
> Give reasons for your answer and include any relevant examples from your experience.
> Write at least 250 words.

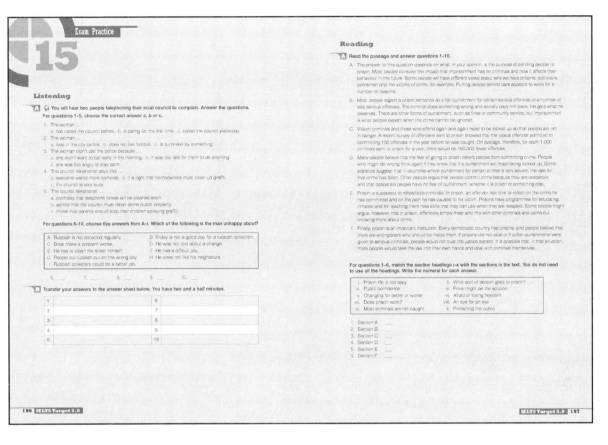

B Look back at the passage above. Highlight points that you could use in your composition.

C Walk around the class and talk to classmates about the issue. Note down the points they make.

D Decide which of the points you want to include in your composition and then write it.

In this final unit, the exam practice focuses on listening, reading and writing, and practises writing answers onto answer sheets. You can work through each part separately or set the whole thing up as a sort of mini-mock exam. It would probably be a good idea, however, to prepare a little for the writing task so that students feel confident that they have something to say.

Listening (A and B) and Reading (A)

For the listening and reading parts, you can either read the rubric with students, or leave them on their own completely. Write the answers on the board. For the listening practice, refer them to the tapescript to check why their answers are correct or incorrect.

Tapescript 🎧 **160** (5 mins, 2 secs)

A You will hear two people telephoning their local council to complain. Answer the questions. For questions 1–5, choose the correct answer a, b or c.

Telephonist: Good morning, you're through to Hereford Council. How can I help you?

Woman: Oh, good morning. I'm telephoning about graffiti. Not for the first time, I might add.

Telephonist: Oh, yes? Where is this graffiti? Which part of the city do you live in?

Woman: I'm in the Port Hall area. It's a quiet residential area – as you probably know. These days, I expect to see graffiti all over the city centre, but not round here. I looked out my window this morning and some ... well, someone has sprayed names and football teams all over the wall opposite. There's more on the house on the corner of the street. Can't somebody stop it happening?

Telephonist: I'm sorry. I know graffiti is a problem. Did you phone the police about it?

Woman: What's the point? I didn't actually see anyone spraying. What can the police do the next morning? There should be cameras in the streets. Then you'd know who did it. Oh, it makes me so angry.

Telephonist: Um, I'm not sure about having cameras in residential areas. A lot of people already think there are too many cameras in the street as it is.

Woman: Well, do you think you could tell me who's going to clean it off? You can't expect the people who own the houses to keep cleaning it off every time it happens.

Telephonist: Well, I'm afraid it is the responsibility of the owner to clean up graffiti. I know it's not really fair, but we just don't have people to come out and clean up all over the city. Walls usually need to be repainted.

Woman: And what about graffiti on telephone boxes and lamp posts – whose job is it to clean that off?

Telephonist: Well, that is the council's responsibility, but we can't promise that it will be done straightaway.

Woman: No, I didn't think you could. You know who I blame? The parents ... If only they ... *(fade out)*

For questions 6–10, choose <u>five</u> answers from A–H. Which of the following is the man unhappy about?

Telephonist: Good morning, you're through to Hereford Council. How can I help you?

Man: Oh, hello there. I'm phoning about the rubbish collections. Why the rubbish hasn't been collected again this week, to be more specific.

Telephonist: Oh, I see. Which part of the city do you live in?

Man: I live in Chester Road. That's in the West Cliff area.

Telephonist: And which day is your rubbish normally collected?

Man: Well, who knows? I thought it was supposed to be Friday, but it seems to be a different day every week at the moment. Some weeks there isn't even a collection. I'm really fed up with it.

Telephonist: Mm, the collection in West Cliff is supposed to be Tuesday, but the council has had a few problems recently. A new company has taken over the collection. It's taking a while to get the operation running smoothly. They had an issue with their drivers last month – I think that meant that collections were affected.

Man: Well, it's not good enough. If the rubbish isn't collected the streets look terrible. Seagulls fly down and peck at the bags for food. They pull the rubbish all over the street. For the last three or four weeks, I've had to go outside and sweep up the rubbish and put it in a new bag. I'm too busy to keep doing that every week.

Telephonist: Yes, I understand.

Man: You know, things are bad enough even when the collection is regular. Some neighbours put their rubbish outside the house whenever they like, anyway. They are supposed to put it out on the Tuesday morning – they know that, but they don't care. By the time the lorry comes round, the rubbish is all over the street.

Telephonist: Well, people know they shouldn't put their bags outside until Tuesday morning. If you know who's doing it, you can tell us what number they live at and we'll call them.

Man: Mm, I don't see why the men who do the collection can't pick up some of the rubbish that's in the street. They just throw the bags in the lorry and leave the loose rubbish where it is in the street.

Telephonist: I'm afraid it's not their job to clean the streets. They are paid to collect the bags from outside the houses – no more than that. The street cleaner comes to West Cliff on a Wednesday.

Man: Ah, yes – well, that's another thing ... *(fade out)*

Answers:
Listening   1. a   2. c   3. b   4. c   5. b
6. A   7. C   8. E   9. G   10. I
(Note that answers 6–10 can be given in any order)

Answers:
Reading   1. Section A: vii
2. Section B: viii   3. Section C: x
4. Section D: vi   5. Section E: v
6. Section F: iii   7. community service
8. 150   9. severe   10. new skills

Writing

A, B, C and D   If you feel that students have been given enough guidance with this type of composition now, and that this should be treated simply as exam practice, set a time limit of 40 minutes and let them use the picture and ideas from the text they have just read to tackle the task.

If you feel that students will still benefit, do some preparation work through the stages A, B, C and D, and then set the task. Students have worked through this series of tasks a number of times now. Monitor as students work, and check that they are organizing their ideas and making relevant points.

When students have completed the task, tell them to look at the model composition on pages 273 and 274 of the Course Book. The model is reproduced below. Collect students' compositions and give them feedback on all aspects.

There are a number of reasons why people think that offenders should be sent to prison. Firstly, they think that other people are safer if criminals are locked up and unable to commit more crime. Secondly, people think that somebody who does something wrong should be punished, and prison is the obvious solution. Finally, people think that the fear of going to prison stops people committing crime.

However, I think it too simplistic to say that prison is the only way of dealing with offenders, and it is certainly not the best way to deal with all offenders. There are all sorts of reasons why people commit crime, and some crimes are not very serious. There are other punishments.

Of course, if somebody commits a terrible crime they should be punished, and if there is no death penalty then prison is the only option. If a criminal is likely to hurt or even kill, he or she should be locked up so people feel safe. Society has always had prisons, so people would be very concerned if they did not exist.

On the other hand, I think there are arguments against sending people to prison. If the crime is not serious, it is better to fine the criminal or make him or her do community service. It costs a lot to keep somebody in prison so the other options make more sense financially. Also, when criminals go to prison they often learn more about crime, and when they come out they go straight back to a criminal lifestyle. There should be a way of helping offenders to learn and to not want to commit more crime.

Personally, I think prison should be for serious offenders who are a danger to society and not for everyone who commits a crime. If we lock up everyone who does wrong, prisons will be full in no time.

Unit 15 Workbook answers

Speaking and Vocabulary

A 1. e   2. d   3. h   4. a   5. c   6. g   7. f
8. b

B 1. murderer   2. robber   3. thief   4. burglar
5. smuggler   6. shoplifter   7. kidnapper

C Students' own answers.

Listening

A Students should use bilingual dictionaries for this.

Answers: Speaker 1: b   Speaker 2: c
Speaker 3: d   Speaker 4: a

Tapescript 🎧 **161** (1 min, 57 secs)

A **Look up the words below in a dictionary. Then listen to students answering questions during the spoken exam. Match each word with one of the speakers.**

1

Examiner: So, has a crime like that happened recently?

Student: Yes, there was that little girl in Portugal. She was ... erm ... she was erm ... well, she was taken from the room of the hotel when her parents were having dinner. It was really terrible.

2

Examiner: So, have you ever been the victim of a crime like that?

Student: Yes, when I was in Russia I bought something, but I didn't have change. I had to give the man in the market a big note – I can't remember how much it was worth. He gave me the change and I counted it. I thought it was OK, but later I realized the notes he had given me were ... erm ... I

don't know the word ... you know, when the money isn't real money.

3

Examiner: What do you think people should do in a situation like that?

Student: I think people should refuse to buy the product. They should ... uh ... I can't remember the word ... but ... yeah ... they should say that they will not buy that product because it's been made by children, or by people who are paid nearly nothing.

4

Examiner: What kind of antisocial behaviour annoys you?

Student: Mm, I'm not sure if it's antisocial behaviour or a crime, but ... erm ... you know, when the person drives his car much too fast. It makes me really angry if it's where there's a lot of people – near a school or something.

Reading

A 1. mistakes   2. his daughter   3. nine months
4. qualifications   5. interview   6. boring

Writing

A and B Personally / However / in my opinion / Anyway

Review 3

Review 3

Speaking and Vocabulary

A Mark each of the following topics like this:

> (↔) I can talk about this topic easily and have plenty to say.
> (+) I can talk about this topic quite well and have some things to say.
> (-) I don't enjoy talking about this topic and don't know what to say.

1. keeping fit and doing exercise
2. your diet
3. the natural beauty of your country
4. the climate and weather in your country
5. your home
6. your neighbourhood
7. buildings in your country
8. technology
9. social issues
10. crime

B Discuss your answers with a partner.

C Work in pairs. Take it in turns to ask and answer questions about the topics in Exercise A.

D Write important words and phrases that you have learnt in Units 11–15 under each heading.

staying healthy

accidents and injuries

climate and weather

homes, houses and neighbourhoods

technology

(my words and phrases)

crime

social issues

Listening and Reading

A Work in pairs. Take it in turns to ask and answer the following questions about listening. The student asking the questions can look back at the unit and check the exam or question-type tips.

1. What type of information will you hear in the different parts of the listening exam?
2. Why is it sometimes easier to complete a flow chart or a table?
3. Will the speakers on the tape use formal or informal language?
4. Why might one speaker be more difficult to understand than another?
5. What do you need to do at the end of the listening exam?
6. How long do you have to transfer answers to the answer sheet?
7. What mistakes can you make when you are transferring answers?

B Work with the same partner. Ask and answer these questions about reading.

1. What do you remember about matching beginnings and endings of sentences? How can you make it easier to choose from a number of options?
2. How many different types of text can you remember? How can you know quickly what type of text you are reading?
3. Which passage is the longest passage? What type of text will it be?
4. What can you do to cope with a longer text more successfully?
5. Why is it important to time yourself when you read a text?
6. What is usually a waste of time when you are reading?
7. Why is it easier to write answers onto the question sheet during the reading exam than it is during the listening exam?

C Mark each of these statements (T) true or (F) false.

1. My listening has improved since I started the course.
2. I know what to listen for in order to answer questions.
3. I am happy writing answers as I continue to listen.
4. I am good at identifying key words even if I don't know them.
5. I feel confident about transferring answers in ten minutes.
6. My reading speed has improved since I began the course.
7. I feel confident reading any type of text now.
8. I understand the main idea of almost any text I read now.
9. I know what to look for in order to answer exam questions.
10. I don't worry about words and phrases I don't know anymore.

D Look at these comments that students have made about taking exams. Tick the ones that you most agree with.

'I get very nervous in exams. I can't concentrate on the tasks.' ___

'Some people are good at doing exams and some people are not.' ___

'If other students in the exam are writing a lot and seem to be doing well, it makes me anxious. I think I am not as good as they are.' ___

'My mind goes blank as soon as I sit down in an exam hall.' ___

'I worry too much about getting the answers right and not enough about whether I understand.' ___

'I can't sleep the night before an exam, so I'm always really tired during the exam.' ___

'Revising for exams is really boring.' ___

'Revising just before an exam is a waste of time. You either know it or you don't.' ___

Writing

A Look at the instructions for a writing task below. Highlight the key words and check that you understand what you have to do.

> Write to a friend telling him/her that you are taking the IELTS exam. Say why you are taking the exam and how you feel about it. Tell your friend that he/she should do the exam and why.
> Write at least 150 words. You should spend about 20 minutes on this task.

B Look at this student's attempt to write the composition. Talk to a partner about what you like and don't like about the composition.

> Hi Henri, I'm Sorry that I didn't can come at your brothers weding last week. I am very bisy, recently, I'm taking an examination in english. It called IELTS. I need it for go university next year. I just finish a course that help me prepare for this examination. It difficult but I enjoy it too much. My speaking english is much better than before but I don't can write so good like can you see. Ha ha! The examination it is next friday and I am too nervos about it. There is a speaking part a lisening part a reading part and a writing part. The reading and writing parts is which I am nervos about. I think you should to take this IELTS examination too. Your good in english and so you can get high score I think it is good have this examination for find a work, ok goodby now William.

C Work in pairs. One of you is A, the other is B.

Student A: Highlight errors in the letter related to organization and grammar.
Student B: Highlight errors in the letter related to spelling and punctuation.

D Compare your ideas with a partner.

E Look at the version of the letter on page 274. The errors are highlighted. Then read the model letter below it.

F Write a similar letter to a friend of yours. Make sure you cover all the points in the instructions.

What next?

Congratulations! You've finished the course. You've heard the different types of talks or conversations that you will hear in the Listening Module and you've read the different types of text that you will have to read in the Reading Module. You've practised every task type for each module. Hopefully, you feel much more confident about taking the exam now. Here are some tips to prepare you for the exam.

✓ Revision doesn't have to be boring. It is boring if you do it for too long or try to do it all at once. It will make you feel anxious if you try to revise too much. Remember that revision means looking back at what you have learnt – not trying to learn things that you haven't learnt yet.

✓ Practise the Speaking Module with other students who are taking the exam. Revise the typical vocabulary that you need to talk about the most common topics of conversation. Make sure you know the words and phrases you need to talk about your own life.

✓ Revise for the Listening Module by borrowing tapes that practise IELTS listening tasks. Remember, though, that the important thing is to improve your all-round listening skills, so continue to follow the advice from the previous review sections.

✓ Revise for the Reading Module by doing reading sections from past IELTS papers and by doing the IELTS mock exams in this book. Look back at the Reading Modules from earlier units in this book. Look at how the texts have become more challenging and how your reading skills have improved.

✓ Revise when you would otherwise be wasting time. Revise at the bus stop or on the bus. Don't wait until the night before the exam to do all your revision. Remember that the important thing is to improve your all-round reading skills, so continue to follow the advice from the previous review sections.

✓ Practise writing compositions and ask your teacher or someone who reads English very well to check them. Continue to look at as many model answers to exam questions as you can.

✓ Try to get a good night's sleep the night before the exam. You don't want to feel tired. Make sure you arrive at the exam centre some time before the exam starts. You want to feel relaxed and confident – not in a terrible rush.

✓ Try not to be nervous. Remember that the important thing is to understand what you hear and what you read. If you can, you will answer questions correctly. Don't worry about how other people are doing – you are not in competition with them.

Overview

The review units are very much reviews rather than revision units. The aim is for students to consolidate what they have learnt about the IELTS exam, and how to go about getting the grade they require. There are tasks which are purely designed to encourage students to reflect and discuss, and there are tasks which consolidate and have correct answers. The instructions given to teachers for the review sections are brief, as the aims and procedure for each task are fairly self-explanatory.

Speaking and Vocabulary

A and B Give students time to read through the topics and think. Tell them to take into consideration whether they have something interesting to say, and whether they have the range of vocabulary they need. Allow them time to talk in pairs and then get a general class consensus.

C Give students a little time to plan some questions, or remember some of the questions they asked previously when working through the relevant unit. Students can ask one partner their questions, or walk around and ask various classmates.

D Give students a moment to look at the web and then read through the headings with them. You could start by telling them not to look back at the units in the Course Book, and see what they have retained. After five minutes, allow them to look back, adding words and phrases from the unit. Try to encourage them to do this in order to store new language, rather than simply to fulfil a task.

Listening and Reading

A Students may or may not need to look back in order to answer the questions. Make sure they know what to do, and give them about five minutes to work through the questions. Then check the answers as a class.

Answers:
1. part 1: a social situation (two speakers)
   part 2: a non-academic topic (one speaker)
   part 3: an education-related topic (two or more speakers)
   part 4: general academic topic (one speaker)

2. You see how the talk is organized, and know when the speaker will move on to a new point.
3. both
4. he/she may have an accent
5. transfer your answers to the answer sheet
6. 10 minutes
7. spell words wrongly / use too many words

B Conduct as Exercise A.

Answers:
1. It is not a grammatical exercise / decide which endings are impossible, so that you have fewer options to choose from.
2. students' own ideas / look at the layout and visual information, read the heading, notice the register
3. the last one / an article
4. apply the reading skills you have learnt – read selectively / don't worry about every word and phrase
5. so that you don't spend too long reading what is not important / so that you have time for each stage of the reading process
6. reading the whole text carefully before looking at the tasks / trying to understand very word
7. because you can copy words and phrases from the text

C and D Give students the time they need to mark each point, and then either get them to compare with a partner as suggested, or open it up as a whole-class discussion. Round up by asking whether students feel more confident generally about the Listening and Reading Modules.

Writing

A Students know how to read through instructions and check anything they need to. Ask if they think it is an easy or challenging writing task.

B Give students a few minutes to read the composition and then to talk about it. They should point out that it is not organized into paragraphs and that there are a lot of grammatical and spelling mistakes.

C Once students are in pairs they can decide which of them will work on which point. The aim is to make the task a motivating joint effort, and to give them something concrete to compare. It is probably best to set a time limit, but be flexible if most students have not completed their part of the task within that time.

D Give students the time they need now to compare and point out anything they think their partner didn't notice.

E Refer students to the model letters on page 274 to compare. Both are reproduced below.

Hi Henri I'm Sorry that I didn't can come at your brothers weding last week I am very bisy resently. I'm taking an examination in english It called IELTS. I need it for go university next year. I just finish a course that help me prepare for this examination It dificult but I enjoy it too much. My speaking english is much better than before but I don't can write so good like can you see. Ha ha! The examination it is next friday and I am too nervos about it. There is a speaking part a lisening part a reading part and a writing part. The reading and writing parts is which I am nervos about. I think you should to take this IELTS examination too. Your good in english and so you can get high score I think it is good have this examination for find a work. ok goodby now William.

Hi Henri,

I'm sorry that I couldn't come to your brother's wedding last week. I have been very busy recently. I'm taking an examination in English called IELTS. I need it to go to university next year. I have just finished a course that has helped me

prepare for this examination. It is difficult but I enjoyed it very much.

My spoken English is much better than before but I can't write very well, as can you see – ha ha! The examination is next Friday and I am very nervous about it. There is a speaking part, a listening part, a reading part and a writing part. The reading and writing parts are what I am nervous about.

I think you should to take this IELTS examination, too. You're good at English and so you can get a high score. I think it is good to do this examination to find work.

OK, I must get on now. Hope to see you soon.

Best wishes,
William

F Set the writing task for individual completion with a 20-minute time limit. Collect and mark the students' work if possible.

What next?

Give students time to read through the comments, and to ask you about anything that is not clear. Students can talk together as a class about how they feel about exams. Elicit some more exam advice from the students and get it up on the board.

You might then like to tell students to read the advice at home. If there is time to read it in class, it might be better to read through one section at a time and get some feedback, rather than reading it right through in one go.

Now instruct students to complete mock test 3.

IELTS
Academic
section

Introduction

How the Academic course works

IELTS Target 5.0 Academic is for students who have studied IELTS Target 5.0 General Training but want to sit the Academic exam. Scoring 5.0 in the General Training exam is more realistic than doing so in the Academic exam, but some students need the Academic exam for entrance to university or to apply for certain jobs. If students need to sit the Academic exam, but are concerned that their general level of English isn't high enough, this supplement will prepare them to deal with academic content of the reading passages and the more challenging writing tasks.

Since both the Listening and Speaking Modules of the Academic exam are the same as those in the General Training exam, this supplement practises only reading and writing. The course consists of five units and develops in terms of challenge, so that by the time students sit the exam, they will feel much more prepared and confident.

Since students will have no experience of the writing tasks that they have to tackle in the first part of the IELTS Writing Module, the Writing Modules in this book take a simple step-by-step approach, and gradually introduce them to possible task types.

As in the General Training course, the Reading Module is roughly divided into two parts. The first part aims to engage students in a topic, pre-teach key vocabulary and then focus on a key skill or particular IELTS exam technique. The second part aims to practise the skill or technique, and then encourages students to reflect and develop. The module ends with a focus on key vocabulary in context. The aim here is to focus on the semi-formal vocabulary that students are likely to meet in the texts which make up the IELTS exam.

The Writing Module focuses mainly on the first writing tasks, as students practised writing tasks that are very similar to those in the second part of the Academic Writing Module in the General Training course. Each unit focuses on how information can be presented in different types of figures, and on writing technique required for the exam. There is a focus on guided writing, and there are model compositions for all writing tasks. The final unit demonstrates how the discursive composition in the Academic exam is more challenging than that in the General Training exam.

Consolidation and exam practice at the end of each unit focuses on various elements of the two modules.

As in the General Training course, there are exam tips and question-type tips. They are there to help students know how to approach the various tasks that make up the exam, and to provide advice on how to achieve the highest score possible.

In the Workbook, there are tasks for each of the two modules in the Course Book units. Students can study these in class or as homework tasks. Reference is made to these Workbook tasks in the Course Book Reading Modules, as the tasks specifically focus on the content of the Reading Module.

As you work through the course, students will learn more about the exam and what they have to do in each module. By the end of the course, students will know everything about every part of the exam and what is expected of them.

An introduction to students

The aim of this introduction is to quickly familiarize students with the differences between the General Training exam, for which they have already prepared, and the Academic exam, for which this course prepares them.

Reading

A Students may not know the answer to this, but they will probably have prepared themselves for this course, having completed the General Training course. Give them a few minutes to compare ideas – one or two if they have very little to say. There's no need to supply the answers now, as students will discuss specific points in the task that follows.

B Students are familiar with these analytical tasks, for which the answers are given in the exam tip that follows. Make sure they cover the exam tip before answering the questions. They should work individually, and then compare, or work with a partner for the whole task. There is no need to provide answers, as the exam tip does that. A key is provided after the exam tip instructions (see below).

Read the exam tip with students slowly and carefully. Then tell them to cover it and go back through questions 1–7 in Exercise B, as they provide the correct answers.

Answers: 1. F 2. T 3. F 4. T 5. T 6. F 7. T

C Make sure students understand that two of the extracts are from texts that are typical of the type of texts they will read on this course and in the exam, and that three are not. Give them time to read the extracts, and then compare their thoughts with a partner. Go over the answers, pointing out the sources of each extract.

Answers: The two academic style extracts are 3 and 5.

The other extracts are written in a style that is more direct or more informal than is typical of academic style texts.

Writing

A and **B** Deal with as Reading A above.

B Answers: 1. is the same number of 2. the same amount of
3. the same number of 4. a formal report based on data that you are given
5. a discursive composition 6. more difficult than

C Go through the figures with students, pronouncing each carefully. You should write 'graph' phonetically on the board, if possible. Students should work individually and then compare with a partner, or work directly with a partner. To check answers, tell them to cover the words and tell you what each visual image is from memory.

Answers: 1. pie chart 2. bar chart 3. table 4. line graph 5. flow chart

Read the exam tip with students.

1 Work

Reading

Reading

1 Work

Reading 1: reading skills

A Answer this question with a partner.

1. Which of the reading skills that you learnt when you studied for the General Training exam will be most useful when you read texts for the Academic exam?

B Look at the list of advice below and then do these two tasks.

1. In the first column, tick the advice that you think is most helpful for reading longer, more challenging texts.
2. In the second column, give yourself a mark from 1–5.
   1 = I am not so good at this and still need practice
   5 = I am very good at doing this now

a. Use the instructions and any visual information to help you predict what the text is about.
b. Skim the text quickly to get a general idea of what it is about.
c. Notice how topic sentences tell you what a paragraph is going to be about.
d. Read through the questions and decide which parts of the text you need to read again more carefully.
e. As you read again, don't worry about the meaning of every word and phrase. Guess the meaning of new words and phrases in context.
f. Try to understand what is fact and what is opinion.
g. Learn to recognize language that is paraphrased in the questions.

C Compare your list with a partner.

Reading 2: preparing to read

A Look at the pictures and discuss these questions with a partner.

1. What are the advantages and disadvantages of working from home?
2. What sort of jobs can people easily do from home?

B Check these words and phrases if you need to. Then talk to a partner. Why will each of them be mentioned in the text?

| technology | a nine-to-five job | flexibility | having commitments |
| bosses | wasting time | working efficiently | feeling isolated |

> I think technology will be mentioned because new technology, like the Internet, allows people to work from home more easily.

C Skim the text quickly and check your ideas.

Reading 3: practise applying your reading skills to an academic text

A Read this text about working from home and answer the questions that follow.

The Changing Workplace

A Nearly 3.5 million people now work from home in the United Kingdom. That is around 12% or one-in-eight of the working population, and is an increase of 600,000 since the mid-nineties. Advances in technology, the growth of home computer and laptop ownership, and the development of the Internet are key drivers of this trend. It is becoming increasingly appealing for people to do their job from the comfort of their living room, a study, or even a local coffee shop.

B There is a growing number of people for whom the traditional nine-to-five job simply no longer works. They may have family commitments and other reasons why they need to be at home during the day. Many simply prefer working from home because of the flexibility it offers. Many women find themselves in this situation, because they find it difficult to go back to an ordinary job once they have children.

C There are several obvious advantages of working at home. First of all, people can arrange their working day in the way that best suits them. If they have other commitments, or things that they need to be doing, they can arrange their schedule so that work can fit around them. If people do not get work done during the day, they can catch up in the evening or at the weekend. Many people with creative jobs, like writing, designing and illustrating, find that a short break to pick up children from school or meet friends for lunch re-energizes them, so they function more productively and for longer periods of time when they are working.

D People often find that they can get their work done more quickly and efficiently at home, as opposed to working from an office. To start with, working in an office means having to commute to and from work five days a week. In most cases, that is a lot of valuable time wasted. In the office, people usually spend a significant portion of their day doing things other than their work. Much time is spent assisting other people, dealing with unexpected problems or simply socializing with colleagues. Getting work done more quickly means that people achieve more in a day, or have the time to do things that they previously could not do. There is the added bonus that home workers do not have to spend the day with people they do not get on with, particularly a difficult boss or line manager.

E However, there are disadvantages of working from home, too. People can feel isolated and miss the company of colleagues. Some companies that have encouraged more of their staff to work from home, have found that these employees complain about a lack of creative interaction. Home workers may also find that the companies that employ them are less sympathetic if they say they are sick, and that benefits, such as pension schemes and health care packages, are no longer on offer. Once businesses accept that people can get work done from home, they might use the opportunity to employ people in countries where salaries are lower and they do not have to pay them as much.

F At present, it seems that most companies still have reservations about allowing their employees to work from home whenever they like, but many are experimenting with a range of options. Workers might work from home one day a week, or work from home on a particular one-off project. Bosses are beginning to realize that this is the way forward. If companies do not offer workers the option of staying at home occasionally, more people may well look to work freelance or become self-employed. It is estimated that 10 million people could be working away from a traditional office environment by 2010.

For questions 1–6, match the headings in the box below with the paragraphs A–F. Write the numeral as your answer. There are more headings than you need.

i. Higher incomes for home workers
ii. Arranging your own schedule
iii. Inefficient use of time
iv. Too much time to relax
v. Working in an office is natural
vi. Not yet ready for total change
vii. New working trends
viii. Working from home is not all good
ix. Companies welcome home workers
x. Nine-to-five no longer works

1. paragraph A ___
2. paragraph B ___
3. paragraph C ___
4. paragraph D ___
5. paragraph E ___
6. paragraph F ___

For questions 7–11, decide if the information given below agrees with the information given in the text. Write (T) true, (F) false or (NG) not given.

7. People usually choose to work from home so that they can look after children at the same time.
8. Many people who work from home work irregular hours.
9. Not having to travel to work is a big advantage for most home workers.
10. People get more work done when they work in a traditional office environment.
11. Bosses do not have a good relationship with workers who choose to work from home.

For questions 12–14, complete these sentences about the disadvantages of working from home with words from the text. Use no more than two words for each answer.

12. Sometimes people need to share ideas with ___
13. Some companies might not ___ the same package of benefits to home workers.
14. Some companies might employ people to work from home in countries where they can pay ___

B Check the key on page 274. How many questions did you answer correctly?

C Tick the sentences about the reading task that are true for you and think about how you can answer more questions correctly next time.

1. I didn't find the text much more difficult than those in the General Training course.
2. Making predictions about the content helped me to read more confidently.
3. I applied the reading skills I have learnt, and followed the stages of the reading process.
4. I timed each stage, and had time to complete the tasks.
5. I checked all my answers carefully.
6. I'm pleased with how many questions I answered correctly.

Key vocabulary in context

Look at these sentences and then look again at the key word in the texts. Highlight the correct option.

1. Commitments are things you want to do / have to do.
2. If something has flexibility, it is always the same / can change easily.
3. If people function productively, they achieve a lot / don't do very much.
4. If people work efficiently, they do a job properly / don't do a job very well.
5. A bonus is something people want / don't want.
6. If people feel isolated, they have a lot of contact with other people / spend too much time alone.
7. If people are sympathetic they listen to you and respond to your problem / can help you recover if you are sick.
8. If you have reservations about something, you know it is the right thing to do / are not completely sure about it.

▶ For focus on reading skills, go to Workbook page 46.

Objectives

- **To remind students of the skills necessary for more effective reading and improved reading speed.**
- **To practise reading a typical text from the IELTS Academic Reading Module.**

Reading 1

A The aim is for students to look at the length of the text and the number of paragraphs. They should read the title, but no more than that. Remind them that towards the end of the General Training course, they were sometimes reading longer texts to practise the third part of the Reading Module. Give them time to discuss the question, but don't worry if they lack ideas. Ask for some feedback if students appear to have something to say. The task that follows develops the discussion and gives students guidance.

B Read through the two questions with students. Tell them to check with you for any new language in the list of points. Students should be familiar with this type of self-evaluation task, but make sure they know how to complete each column. The aim is for students to discuss the reading skills they have learnt and express their concerns, rather than complete the columns perfectly accurately. Make sure they spend more time comparing (see Exercise C) than worrying about the task individually.

C See above. Give students time to compare ideas before getting some feedback from individuals. All of the skills will help students cope with the Academic exam, but let them decide which they feel will be most helpful.

Reading 2

The aim of this stage is to prepare students for the reading exam and provide some speaking practice. Students discussed this topic in the General Training Module so should have something to say, and be able to predict something about the content of the text.

A Give students a minute to look at the pictures. Then read through the questions with them, clarifying the meaning and pronunciation of 'advantages' and 'disadvantages'. Tell them to plan at least one thing they want to say about each picture, and then give two minutes to think. Take the opportunity to revise 'commuting'. Tell them to try to remember some of the points made when they listened to a discussion on working from home, at the beginning of the General Training course. Either get a few ideas from the class or move straight on to Exercise B.

B Students should use dictionaries if possible. As they check the words, students can use the definitions to explain how and why each will be used in the text. Make sure they look at the example to help them know what sort of thing they should be saying. Students will check their ideas when they skim read in a moment.

C The aim now is to give students an opportunity to skim the text rather than pick out each of the words and phrases from Exercise B. Set a time limit of two minutes, and make sure students know that the aim is to get the general message of the text.

Reading 3

A Although students have dealt with some reading texts like this on the General Training course, the majority of the texts they have seen have been shorter and less academic and challenging in style. The preparation should have made the text more manageable, and they should be left to complete the tasks on their own. Look at the tasks together, and remind students that they have seen all the task types, though they have not had so much practise matching headings to paragraphs. Point out that this task is probably more common in the Academic exam than it is in the General Training exam. For this first attempt at a more academic text, you might like to give students the time they need rather than impose a rigid time limit. Perhaps you could end when about half the class have completed the task.

B Give students sufficient time to check and think about why they may have answered incorrectly, before moving on to Exercise C. The answers are given here as well as in the Course Book. Note that the reading task in the Workbook develops the matching task, and encourages students to analyze why certain answers are correct or incorrect. For that reason only answers are given now.

Answers: 1. A – vii   2. B – x   3. C – ii
4. D – iii   5. E – viii   6. F – vi   7. NG
8. T (… they can arrange their schedule so that work can fit around them. If people do not get work done during the day, they can catch up in the evening or at the weekend.)
9. T (… working in an office means having to commute to and from work five days a week.)
10. F (People often find that they can get their work done more quickly and efficiently at home, as opposed to working from an office – the rest of the paragraph provides more evidence)
11. NG   12. colleagues   13. offer
14. lower salaries

The following alternative answers to questions 1–6 might help you prepare students for the Workbook task.

i	Higher incomes for home workers	X
ii	Arranging your own schedule	C
iii	Inefficient use of time	D
iv	Too much time to relax	X
v	Working in an office is natural	X
vi	Not yet ready for total change	F
vii	New working trends	A
viii	Working from home is not all good	E
ix	Companies welcome home workers	X
x	Nine-to-five no longer works	B

C Students will be familiar with this type of reflective process having worked through these tasks on the General Training course. Remind them that identifying what they are doing well and not doing so well is a very good way of focusing on what they can do better next time. Allow students time to reflect and complete the task, and then ask them if they are happy with the number of correct answers. You may like to ask one student what he or she will do differently next time.

Key vocabulary in context

This task revises some of the words and phrases from the preparation stage of the lesson, as well as some additional vocabulary from the text. Encourage students to look back at the text, and check how each item is used in context rather than relying on memory. Students should read the correct sentences to practise saying the key items. Go over anything that needs clarifying and give examples, such as 'a lot of people get a bonus at Christmas'.

Answers:
1. have to do   2. can change easily
3. achieve a lot   4. do a job properly
5. want   6. spend too much time alone
7. listen to you and respond to your problem
8. are not completely sure about it

Now would be a good time to do the Workbook task, which matches headings to paragraphs, or to set it up as homework. You might like to use the second set of answers provided on this page, and tell students to write the correct answers onto the Workbook task to facilitate the analytical task.

Writing

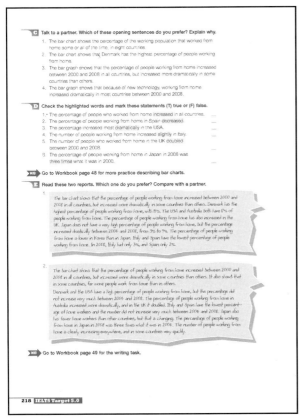

Objectives

- To familiarize students with bar charts and the type of information they show.

- To introduce students to some typical language used to describe bar charts and other visual diagrams.

- To revise and practise the comparatives and superlatives as used typically to describe charts.

- To practise writing a report based on information presented in a bar chart.

Writing 1

Students have to absorb a huge amount of information in order to fulfil the first writing task. This includes various types of visual data, and the different structures and fixed expressions they need to learn. The aim of the first Writing Module is to keep things simple. Students concentrate only on bar charts and affirmative comparatives for now. Some language of trends is introduced, and students will be able to apply what they learn when they describe pie charts and line graphs later in the course.

A The first bar chart that students see is simpler than the one they will see in the exam. Note that there is no need for a key here, as only one source of data is presented. Give students a minute to do the matching, and then go over answers, focusing on the pronunciation of 'horizontal' and 'vertical'. You could tell students that the plural of 'axis' is 'axes'.

B Tell students to cover Exercise C for now. Give them a minute or two to look at the information individually before they answer the questions in pairs. Go over answers clearly, and refer to countries written on the board to check their previous predictions. Point out that it is possible to say either 'the percentage of people who work from home' or 'the percentage of people working from home'. Students will see both structures in the models.

Answers:
1. the percentage of people who work from / working from home in eight countries
2. the eight countries
3. percentages from 0% to 50%
4. refer back to the board for their predictions

Once students understand the information presented, you might like them to tell you more about it as a diagnostic task before Exercise C. Students might not be accurate with the language they use, but it will help you to see what sort of things they notice, and are able to express.

C Once students have uncovered the task, encourage them to compare what is here with what they mentioned a moment ago. Give them two or three minutes to complete the task individually, and then compare. Students should read the sentences as feedback. Check their pronunciation of key words and expressions. Point out that while 'a bigger' or 'a smaller' percentage are not wrong, 'higher' and 'lower' are more accurate, and should be used.

Answers: 1. More 2. higher 3. Fewer
4. lower 5. highest 6. lowest

Grammar check

Go through the grammar check and Watch out! box with students. You can tell them that many people now use 'less' with countable nouns in spoken English, but that it is inaccurate, and that they should practise using 'fewer'.

D Don't go through the highlighted words with students as you will begin to do the task for them. Tell them to work with a partner, and discuss what they think the highlighted words mean as they complete the task. When you go over answers, check the meanings are clear, and use the target words to explain why answers are false.

Answers:
1. T   2. F (a far higher percentage ...)
3. T   4. F (slightly fewer ...)

Grammar check

Go through the grammar box one point at a time, and make sure that the rules are clear. If students ask whether 'many more' is possible, you can tell them that it is possible, but not very common. Note that 'many fewer' is not possible. 'A lot more' is common in spoken language, but not for this type of writing task.

E Students can either work individually or in pairs. Monitor to check, and correct student's work as they write, rather than correcting once they have finished the task.

Writing 2

Read the exam tip with students, and then go straight on to Exercise A.

A Let students read the rubric, and then discuss the questions in pairs. They should be able to work out what the key is by process of elimination. Go over answers to clarify before looking at the writing task.

Answers:
The key is to show that two years are represented by different coloured columns.

This chart shows what the previous chart showed, and how the percentage of people working from home changed over a four-year period.

B Students are familiar with writing task instructions, but not instructions for this first task in the Academic exam. Give them some time to absorb what the task demands. They are also familiar with the type of task analysis that follows, and know that the exam tip normally answers the questions for them. Tell them to cover the exam tip as they work through this task. Help students with anything they don't understand as they read the list of points. You might need to explain 'randomly' and 'stands out'. Students should spend about as long comparing with a partner as they do marking the points individually. There is no need to give formal feedback, as the exam tip covers the points, but you might like to get a few ideas from the class. You could check each point as you read through the exam tip. Students are not aiming to explain why certain information is true, even if the writer thinks that he or she can suggest a good reason.

Answers: 1. T   2. F   3. T   4. F   5. T
6. F   7. F   8. T   9. T   10. T

C Remind students that the first thing they should do is demonstrate that they understand the bar chart. Give them time to read through each of the opening line options, and then discuss which they prefer with a partner. Encourage them to say what is wrong with the other options.

Answers:
3 is the correct option
1 simply repeats the instructions
2 describes one fact from the information – not what the bar chart is designed to show
4 tries to explain – give a reason for what the bar graph shows

D The aim here is to introduce students to some typical language that they will need in order to compare information in charts and graphs. Take note that this language is even more likely when describing line graphs, and will be revised and added to when looking at those. Avoid studying too many other fixed expressions that students might want to use, as they will become confused by too many options. The Workbook exercise expands the options, and should be tackled having completed this task.

Don't go through the highlighted words before students attempt the exercise, as you will begin doing it for them. Tell them to work with a partner, and discuss what they think the highlighted words mean as they complete the task. Give them enough time to look back at the bar chart as they mark each sentence. As you check answers, clarify each key word, and use the board to illustrate when appropriate.

Answers: 1. T   2. F   3. F   4. T   5. T
6. T

Now would be a good time to look at the Workbook exercise before students see the language used in a composition. If there is not time now, set the task for homework while the language is fresh in students' minds. Take note that the Workbook exercise also introduces language that students will not yet need. You may feel that they have seen as much as they can manage.

E On the General Training course, students compared compositions, and talked about strengths and weaknesses. Give them time to read and assess the two pieces of work. Monitor as students talk in pairs or small groups, and ask questions that guide them towards seeing the shortcomings of the first composition. Finish by getting ideas back.

Answers:
The first composition is not divided into paragraphs, and so is not easy to follow.

The second composition has a fuller description of generally what the chart shows.

The first composition states facts and statistics without comparing data enough.

The first composition is rather repetitive in style.

The second composition has a concluding sentence.

All in all, the second composition is better planned, better organized and easier to follow.

Writing task

A Tell the students that in order to understand the instructions for the first writing task, they must look at the visual information as well. This might clarify something they wouldn't understand simply by reading it in the instructions. Tell them that they can check anything they need to when they have looked at the bar chart.

B This can be conducted as pairwork as suggested, or as a whole-class discussion. Students should tell you the answers to the questions.

Answers:
1. how people used different methods of transport to get to work in 1960 and 2000
2. the various methods of transport both in 1960 and 2000 (the years are represented by different coloured columns)
3. the percentage of people who used each method

C Remind students of what 'stand out' means. Tell them they cannot hope to describe everything that the chart shows, and then give them three minutes to make a list of information that stands out.

D Students should compare with a purpose. If they think other students have noticed more relevant information, they should think about changing the points they plan to make. Get some feedback, and write relevant points on the board (use the model below for ideas). At their first attempt, students will need as much guiding with this task as possible.

E The aim is to write one part of the report and feel confident about it, before moving on to the more challenging body of the report. Set a time limit of two minutes for the opening line, and then allow students to compare. Refer them to the opening sentence in the model on page 274 of the Course Book, which is displayed separately from the whole composition there. The model opening line has been kept simple so that students will feel more confident about what they have written.

F Remind students that they are advised to spend about 20 minutes on this first writing task so that they have 40 minutes for the more challenging discursive composition. However, students may feel that if they find this first task easier, they should spend a little longer on it, and gain as many marks as possible. Certainly for now, they should spend at least 30 minutes doing the task. Monitor as students work, but check more that they are organizing their reports, making relevant points, and using appropriate register. When they have finished, allow them time to exchange

and compare reports. Then refer students to the model on page 274 of the Course Book, which is also reproduced below.

If you collect students' reports to mark, you should get an idea of what they are capable of and give constructive feedback, rather than correct every mistake.

The bar chart shows that the way people travelled to work changed very much between 1960 and 2000. The percentage of people who used their car to get to work increased dramatically from only 22% in 1960 to 55% in 2000. At the same time, the percentage of people using public transport decreased. Nearly four times the number of people used the bus to get to work in 1960 than in 2000. The number of people who get to work by train fell by 50% too.

A small percentage of people use a motorbike to get to work, but the percentage of people who used a motorbike decreased by more than 50% between 1960 and 2000. Using a bicycle to get to work became slightly more popular.

The percentage of people who walked to work also fell dramatically. In 1960, 18% of the working population walked to work, but in 2000 half that number walked to work.

Consolidation

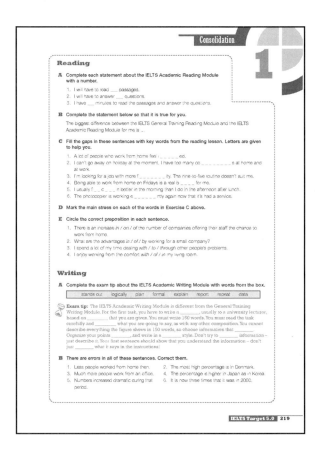

Reading

A This task quickly checks and revises what students know about the Academic exam. Give them a couple of minutes to complete the task individually, and then check answers.

Answers: 1. 3   2. 40   3. 60

B Read the rubric with students, give them a minute to think about what they want to say, and another two minutes to write it. Students can either compare what they have written with other students, or you can get a selection of ideas from the whole class.

C Students have seen tasks like this on the General Training course. They can work individually, but it might be more enjoyable to work in pairs. You could conduct it as a competition between pairs, and see who can get the most correct answers within a time limit. Either you or they should write correct answers on the board as feedback. Leave the words on the board for the task that follows.

Answers: 1. isolated   2. commitments
3. flexibility   4. bonus   5. function
6. efficiently

D Students have seen tasks like this on the General Training course, and know how to mark stress. Use the words on the board to go over answers.

Answers: 1. isolated   2. commitments
3. flexibility   4. bonus   5. function
6. efficiently

E Students can work individually or in pairs. Some of these might be challenging, and rather than simply guess, you might like to suggest that students look back, and try to find the answers in the unit. Give answers orally, but very clearly.

Answers: 1. in   2. of   3. with   4. of

Writing

A Tell students to read the extract through to the end before filling any gaps. They should complete the task individually. Ask a student to read the extract aloud as feedback, making sure pronunciation is clear so that the answers are not confused.

Answers: report / data / plan / stands out / logically / formal / explain / repeat

B Students know from having completed the General Training course that each unit ends with a correcting errors task. Students can work individually or in pairs. Write the correct answer on the board for clarity.

Answers:
1. Fewer people worked from home then.
2. The highest percentage is in Denmark.
3. Far more people work from an office.
4. The percentage is higher in Japan than in Korea.
5. Numbers increased dramatically during that period.
6. It is now three times what it was in 2000.

Exam Practice

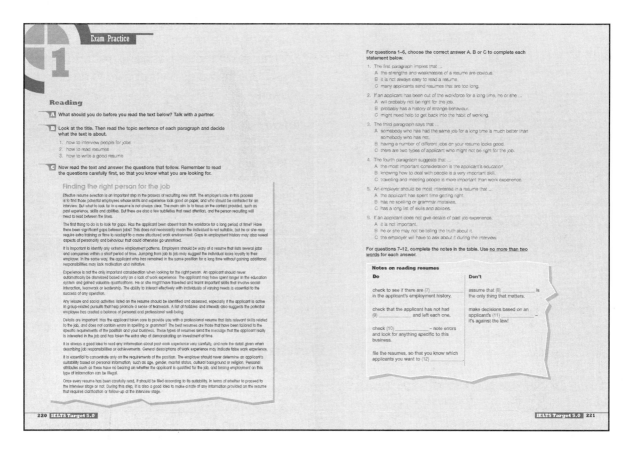

Reading

The aim of the exam practice sections is to provide practice that is close to what students will see in the exam. The length of the text is close to what students can expect, and although language is slightly simplified, it is close to the authentic level that students will have to deal with. For this first unit students are given some preparation, and there is a focus on the skills that students studied in the Reading Module.

A The aim is to show students that they have quite a lot to look at before they start reading the text itself. Read the question with students, and then give them a moment to think before they talk with a partner. Get some ideas back before moving on.

Answers:
They should read the title.
They should look at the visual image.
They should make predictions about the content of the text.
They could quickly look at the types of task they have to complete, but they might prefer to do this after they have skimmed the text for gist.

B The aim now is to encourage students to read topic sentences, and to reinforce the benefits of doing so. They will have already looked at the title. Read the three options with students, and give them about 30 seconds to read only the topic sentences. Ask two or three students what the text is about.

Answers: The text is about 2 (how to read resumes)

C Once students have read for gist, they should know to look at the questions so that they have a purpose when they read more carefully. Later in the course, they will not be given so much advice in the rubric of the exam practice sections. Point out that students have seen the exercise before, and then set a time limit of about 20 minutes to complete the exercises.

Answers: 1. B   2. C   3. C   4. B   5. A
6. B   7. gaps   8. experience
9. several jobs   10. details
11. personal information   12. interview

Unit 1 Workbook answers

Reading

(The key to this reading task is also provided at the back of the Workbook.)

A 1. i – Paragraph D mentions that people who work from home can earn money by working harder, but the text does not say that people who work from home earn more money than those who go to work.

iv – The text does not say anywhere that people who work from home can relax – the text says that they have time to do other things, but it implies that they work very hard.

v – The text does not say that either working in an office or from home is more natural.

ix – Paragraph B says why women especially might choose to work from home, but it does not say they are 'forced' to make this choice. The whole text is about people *wanting* to work from home.

2. The key parts that provide matches to headings are underlined. Supporting information that also helps you match is highlighted in light grey.

Answers: 1. vii   2. x   3. ii   4. iii   5. viii
6. vi

The Changing Workplace

A Nearly 3.5 million people now work from home in the United Kingdom. That is around 12% or one-in-eight of the population, and is an increase of 600,000 since the mid-nineties. Advances in technology, the growth of home computer and laptop ownership, and the development of the Internet are key drivers of this trend. It is becoming increasingly appealing for people to do their job from the comfort of their living room, a study, or even a local coffee shop.

B There is a growing number of people for whom the traditional nine-to-five job simply no longer works. They may have family commitments and other reasons why they need to be at home during the day. Many simply prefer working from home because of the flexibility it offers. Many women find themselves in this situation because they find it difficult to go back to an ordinary job once they have children.

C There are several obvious advantages of working at home. First of all, people can arrange their working day in the way that best suits them. If they have other commitments, or things that they need to be doing, they can arrange their schedule so that work can fit around them. If people do not get work done during the day, they can catch up in the evening or at the weekend. Many people with creative jobs, like writing, designing and illustrating, find that a short break to pick up children from school or meet friends for lunch re-energizes them, so they function more productively and for longer periods of time when they are working.

D People often find that they can get their work done more quickly and efficiently at home, as opposed to working from an office. To start with, working in an office means having to commute to and from work five days a week. In most cases, that is a lot of valuable time wasted. In the office, people usually spend a significant portion of their day doing things other than their work. Much time is spent assisting other people, dealing with unexpected problems or simply socializing with colleagues. Getting work done more quickly means that people achieve more in a day, or have the time to do things that they previously could not do. There is the added bonus that home workers do not have to spend the day with people they do not get on with, particularly a difficult boss or line manager.

E However, there are disadvantages to working from home, too. People can feel isolated and miss the company of colleagues. Some companies that have encouraged more of their staff to work from home have found that these employees complain about a lack of creative interaction. Home workers may also find that the companies that employ them are less sympathetic if they say they are sick, and that benefits, such as pension schemes and health care packages, are no longer on offer.

Once businesses accept that people can get work done from home, they might use the opportunity to employ people in countries where salaries are lower and they do not have to pay them as much.

(The topic sentence is the main key sentence here, but the whole paragraph summarizes the correct heading.)

F At present, it seems that <u>most companies still have reservations about allowing their employees to work from home whenever they like</u>, but many are experimenting with a range of options. Workers might work from home one day a week, or work from home on a particular one-off project. Bosses are beginning to realize that this is the way forward. If companies do not offer workers the option of staying at home occasionally, more people may well look to work freelance or become self-employed. It is estimated that 10 million people could be working away from a traditional office environment by 2010.

The writing task is dealt with in the main section of the Teacher's Book.

B Checking task

Writing

A
1. increased	d. rose
2. decreased	c. fell
3. changed a lot	a. fluctuated
4. did not change	e. stayed the same
5. was at its highest	b. reached a peak

B
a) did not change / stayed the same
b) increased / rose
c) was at its highest / reached a peak
d) decreased / fell
e) changed a lot / fluctuated

C
a) increased slightly
b) increased dramatically
c) increased steadily
d) increased gradually

D

present simple	past simple	present perfect
rise / rises	rose	have / has risen
fall / falls	fell	have / has fallen

Technology

Reading

Reading

2 Technology

Reading 1: preparing to read and reading for gist

A Discuss with a partner. Do you like shopping? How do you do your shopping?

B Look at the pictures and answer these questions with a partner.

1. What different types of shopping establishment can you see in the pictures?
2. Can you put the pictures into chronological order (from earliest to latest)?

1. __ 2. __ 3. __ 4. __ 5. __

C Skim read the text below. How quickly can you check the order of the pictures?

The Way We Shop

A The way we shop has changed drastically over time, and so have the buildings in which we do our shopping. In the Middle Ages, people shopped in markets. Market stalls were set up together in one place, and were often covered to protect shoppers from the sun or rain.

B The first shops sold one product and were typically adjoined to the producer's workshop. Bakers sold bread, tailors sold clothes and cobblers sold shoes. In the United States, retailers placed boardwalks outside their establishments so that shoppers did not have to walk in the mud.

C In the 19th century, the first arcades were constructed in Europe. These were narrow, covered streets with a number of shops, each selling a different product. In larger cities, the first department stores were opened in multi-storey buildings. The concept of a fixed price was introduced, and haggling became less common. People began to enjoy browsing, and consumerism as we know it was born.

D In the 1920s, the first supermarkets heralded the arrival of self-service and a revolution in the way people shopped. Around the same time, shopping malls combined elements of the arcade and the department store. Several retail establishments were linked by arcades within one huge building, and the retailers paid rent to the mall owner. Today, we see the fundamental elements of these concepts in the drive-in hypermarkets and retail parks of the 21st century.

Reading 2: reading for detail and dealing with unknown vocabulary

A Look at these questions. Without reading the text again, try to say in which paragraph you will find each answer. Write the paragraph letter in the space.

1. Where were the first shopping arcades built?
2. Where did people shop in the Middle Ages?
3. What type of shop introduced the concept of self-service?
4. What did early retailers in the United States put outside their shops?

B Read the text more carefully and check your answers in Exercise A. Then write the answers to the questions in the spaces below. Use no more than two words for each answer.

1. _____ 2. _____ 3. _____ 4. _____

Exam tip: Remember that skimming the text gives you a general idea of what the text is about. That will help you know where to look for answers to questions when you read more carefully for detail.

C Work with a partner. Find one example of each of the following.

1. a word in the text I don't know, and I didn't need to know

2. a word in the text I don't know, but I could guess the meaning of easily

3. a word I needed to know because it stopped me understanding an important point

4. a word I don't know that I had to use as an answer to a question

Exam tip: You don't need to worry about the meaning of every word in a text. Remember:
• You won't need to understand many of the words.
• You can use the context to guess the meaning of most words you do need to understand.
• You can use a word you don't understand as an answer to a question, if you understand the words around it.

D Guess the meaning of these words in the text from the context. Compare with a partner.

| stalls | adjoined | cobblers | boardwalks | multi-storey | haggling | browsing | combined |

Reading 3: practise reading for detail and dealing with unknown vocabulary

A Talk with a partner. What do the pictures tell you about how shopping has changed?

B Read the text and answer the questions that follow.

A Shopping Revolution

A There is something of a revolution occurring in the retail industry. Consumers are quickly becoming more adept when it comes to using technology, and they are increasingly choosing to go online to do their shopping. Internet sales are soaring, and traditional retail outlets are transferring to the web, just like all the specialist e-retailers.

B Recent research shows that online shoppers will spend nearly £50 billion this year. That is something like ten times the amount that will be spent in London's West End shops. More than 800 million parcels will be sent out to the UK's 25 million online shoppers. Online consumers will spend an average of £1,500 each. Some online retailers are reporting rises of over 100% in their sales from last year. One company boasts that over 2 million potential shoppers visited its website in one month recently.

C It is only fourteen years ago that the first Internet shopping transaction was conducted in the US. Eight years later, in the middle of the dotcom gold rush, UK online sales had reached the £800 million mark. Since then, despite reservations about the continuing popularity of the Internet, and concerns about the safety of using credit cards online, sales have grown by a staggering 5,000%.

D Shopping has been transformed in the same way it was when the first supermarkets opened, and over-the-counter interaction was replaced by self-service 100 years ago. Traditional retail establishments only have shelf space for the products that sell best. Online, the choice is unlimited, and consumers can find exactly what they are looking for, rather than what a particular shop is offering.

E When it comes to shopping online, there are no borders, and a huge global marketplace is taking shape. Last year, more than a billion people, nearly 20% of the world population, used the Internet. Online business is worth a staggering £260 billion. Every country in the world will need to develop an e-commerce sector in order to compete in a changing economy.

F There are several factors which have influenced the popularity of online shopping. The biggest factor is probably convenience. In the modern world, most people do not have the time to go out shopping like they once did. Now they can order online and have products delivered to their home or place of work. Recent research shows that 95% of 16-year-olds have purchased something online. Their concept of shopping is shaped by their experience and not what other people have done for the last hundred and fifty years. Broadband has had a huge effect. Products can be displayed in a far more appealing way than previously, and online shopping will become more and more of a virtual visit to a shopping mall.

G Most of the major retailers now see the Internet as an opportunity, rather than as competition. The biggest supermarkets and department stores have all announced a huge growth in online sales over the last year. An ever-growing percentage of consumers prefer to shop online, and even those who still enjoy a traditional visit to the High Street retailers go online first to check out product choice and prices. The popularity of eBay* shows how keen consumers are to find the right product at the right price, and that they are prepared to invest time in getting what they want.

H Despite the online shopping explosion, there are still many who believe traditional retail establishments are here to stay. Around half of all retail businesses in the UK do not have online stores, but do have sites on which they display and promote their products. For convenience, people like to buy books and small objects online, but appear to still enjoy shopping traditionally for personal items, like furniture and clothing. The most successful retailers will probably be those who combine the various methods that consumers can use to make their purchases.

* eBay is an American company that manages an online shopping auction (customers buy and sell products online).

The passage has eight paragraphs, labelled A–H. For questions 1–6, say which paragraph contains the following information. Write the appropriate letter in the space below.

1. that this is not the first revolution in the way people shop
2. the type of products people like to buy in different ways
3. that more people know how to use a computer
4. that young people know a lot about online shopping
5. that people do not like to pay too much for a product
6. the first time a product was bought online

For questions 7–10, label the blue segments in the charts below. Choose your answers from the options in the box.

7.

8.

9.

10.

A amount spent online this year, compared with six years ago
B retailers that have and do not have an online store
C 16-year-olds who have and have not bought something online
D number of people who do and do not shop online
E amount spent in the UK online, compared with amount spent in London's West End
F worldwide Internet users and non-users

For questions 11–14, complete this summary of why online shopping is so popular with words from the text. Use no more than three words for each answer.

Online shopping is very popular. The (11) _____ it offers is what most people find so appealing. Instead of going out to the shops, people can go online and wait for their order to be (12) _____ to their door. Teenagers grow up shopping online, and their (13) _____ is very different from that of their parents and grandparents. (14) _____ is making the online shopping experience even more enjoyable.

C Check the key on pages 274 and 275. How many questions did you answer correctly?

D Tick the sentences about the reading task that are true for you and think about how you can answer more questions correctly next time.

1. I found it quite easy to get the general idea of the text.
2. I found it quite easy to find details and answer questions.
3. There was a lot of vocabulary I didn't know.
4. I didn't worry about not knowing some vocabulary. I could answer questions without it.
5. I'm pleased with the number of questions I answered correctly.

E Look at these words from the text. Answer the questions with a partner.

| adept | soaring | staggering | unlimited |
| | convenience | purchase | concept | |

1. Which words did you know?
2. Which words could you guess from context?
3. Which words didn't matter at all?
4. Do any words relate to specific questions? Did you need to know them to answer questions?

▶ For focus on reading skills and key vocabulary in context, go to Workbook page 50.

Objectives

- To revise and practise the concepts of reading for gist and reading for detail.
- To revise and practise dealing with unknown vocabulary in context.
- To practise reading a typical text from the IELTS Academic Reading Module.

Reading 1

The aim here is to reinforce the importance of gist reading, as well as remind students that it is not necessary to understand every word and phrase in the text. The aim is also to contrast reading for gist with reading more carefully for detail, which students will practise later on.

A This can be conducted as pairwork as suggested, or as a whole-class discussion. You might like to teach 'retail outlet', and then brainstorm various examples. Take the opportunity to elicit or pre-teach more key vocabulary, like 'market', 'shopping mall', 'go online', 'pay by debit' or 'credit card' and so on.

B Read the rubric with students, making sure they understand 'establishment'. This is pre-taught in the rubric, as it is a key word in the text that follows. Make sure students also understand 'chronological order', so that they know what they need to do. Tell students that they don't need to know the words for all the different types of shopping establishments in the pictures, and don't tell them yourself, as it will spoil the first reading task that follows. Tell them to complete the exercise in pencil, or very lightly, so that they can change any answers when they read the text. You can check their answers, but don't give feedback yet.

C Make sure students understand the aim is to read for gist, and to read quickly. Students should work individually, and put up their hands when they have completed the exercise. Go over answers when about half the class have finished. Write the correct sequence on the board.

Answers: 1. C   2. E   3. B   4. D
5. A (you could say that D and A were at the same time)

Reading 2

The aim now is to reinforce the concept that successful gist reading will facilitate reading for detail. Students will be shown that while it is not always necessary to understand every word in a text, in order to answer some questions they will need to work out the meaning of some challenging vocabulary from the context.

A Students should realize that they are trying to remember where they should look for the answers to each question, and not try to answer the questions just yet. Tell them to complete the task without looking back – the pictures and the sequencing task should help them to remember in which paragraph information was given. If students start with the obvious questions, they should be able to work things out by process of elimination. Go over the answers now.

Answers: 1. C   2. A   3. D   4. B

B Students should work individually, and then compare with a partner. End the task when about half the class has completed it. Write the answers on the board.

Answers: 1. (in) Europe   2. (in) markets
3. (the) supermarket   4. boardwalks

Read the exam tip with students.

C Read the rubric and the statements with students. Use 'heralded' as an example of 1 (the other words tell them enough). If necessary, give 'boardwalk' as an example of 4 (they needed it for an answer and needed to guess its rough meaning, but they didn't need to understand its meaning exactly), and perhaps also of 2 (placed outside the shop / not have to walk in the mud). Tell students that they can use the same words as examples of more than one answer. Monitor as students work, and check that they are giving examples that you agree with. It is more important that students discuss their own ideas here than get a correct example for each question.

Answers: (further possible examples, it is important that there are not correct answers here)

1. drastically / mud / narrow / fundamental / retail parks
2. drastically / adjoined / tailors / cobblers / boardwalks
3. multi-storey fixed price / haggling / browsing / consumerism
4. boardwalks

Read the exam tip slowly with students, pausing after each point. Emphasize that students could use 'boardwalk' as an answer to a short answer question, without necessarily understanding it.

D Students can either think for a minute or two individually and then compare, or talk directly in pairs. The aim is for students to discuss whether or not they can guess the meanings, and how accurate they are, rather than give perfect definitions. You might like to do the first one with them as an example, 'stalls are like little shops in a market'. If students all speak the same language, you might like to allow them to translate to show that they can work out meaning. Monitor and give students prompts, or ask concept questions to guide them, such as 'what do you think a boardwalk was made of?' For feedback, allow students to explain the words, rather than you providing definitions for them.

Reading 3

A Students are hopefully becoming more familiar with these longer texts, and the sorts of skills they need to apply in order to cope. Having been introduced to the topic, students should find the text more manageable than they might under exam conditions, and this first preparation phase should further help students to make predictions.

Give students time to look at the pictures and plan what they want to say before they start talking. You can pre-teach some key vocabulary, such as 'online shopping', 'e-commerce' and 'deliver' if you want to, but avoid teaching too much, as the focus here is dealing with unknown vocabulary in context.

B Students should now be left on their own to complete the tasks. Take a look at the exercises with students, particularly the matching task questions 7–10, which they have not practised

as much as some of the other task types. Point out that this exercise is probably more common in the Academic exam than it is in the General Training. You can either give students the time they need, or set a time limit if you feel students are accustomed to that. Perhaps you could end the task when about half the class have completed it.

C Give students sufficient time to check and think about why they may have answered incorrectly, before moving on to Exercise D. The answers are reproduced here together with the lines that provide the answers.

Answers:
1. D (Shopping has been transformed in the same way it was when …)
2. H (people like to buy books and small objects online, but appear to still enjoy shopping traditionally for personal items …)
3. A (Consumers are quickly becoming more adept when it comes to using technology)
4. F (… 95% of 15-year-olds have purchased something online.)
5. G (… how keen consumers are to find the right product at the right price …)
6. C (It is only fourteen years ago that the first Internet shopping transaction was conducted in the US.)
7. C   8. F   9. B   10. E   11. convenience
12. delivered   13. concept of shopping
14. Broadband

D Students will be familiar with this type of reflective process by now. Remind them that identifying what they are doing well and not doing so well is a very good way of focusing on what they can do better next time. The focus here is on dealing with unknown vocabulary, and this time there is a follow-up task to develop that (see following page). Allow students time to reflect and complete the exercise, and then ask them if they are happy with the number of correct answers. You may like to ask one student what he or she will do differently next time.

E This task follows up the reflective process, and gives further practise with working out meaning from context. Once more, make sure students understand that the aim is to answer the questions, and not to give perfect definitions for the new words. You could get some feedback, and write the words against the numbers 1–4 on the board, based on what students tell you. Avoid trying to suggest there are correct answers.

The Workbook task focuses on dealing with unknown vocabulary, as well as key vocabulary in context, and deciding whether certain words are important for answering questions. Now would be a good time to work through it, or set it up as a homework task.

Writing

Objectives

- To familiarize students with pie charts and the type of information they show.

- To introduce students to some typical language used to describe pie charts and other visual diagrams.

- To present and practise the negative comparatives most typically used to describe charts.

- To practise writing a report based on information presented in pie charts.

Writing 1

Just as in the first module, the aim is to keep things simple to begin with and then gradually introduce more challenge. In this module, students concentrate only on pie charts. They will be able to apply what they learn when it comes to describing other sources of visual data.

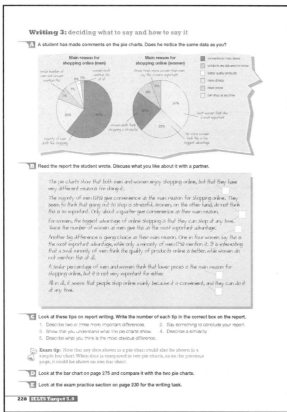

A The theme of the Reading Module continues, so students should be focused on the topic by now. Check whether students remember 'pie chart', and see if they can tell you how pie charts differ from bar charts in terms of the type of information they show (how 100% is broken down into shares/segments – it is not necessarily the relationship between one thing and another).

Tell students to look specifically at the blue segments in the pie charts. Make sure students understand that they are guessing here, and are not expected to know the correct answers. However, students should find it fairly easy to guess the correct answers. Give them time to look at the charts, and to read the opening lines. You can point out that the opening lines here are very simple, and designed for the purpose of the matching task. Allow students to compare answers, or get a general class consensus. Then provide the answers.

Answers: a. 2 b. 1 c. 3

You could ask students what a pie chart showing Internet users in their own country would look like, particularly if they are all from the same country.

B Read the rubric with students, and tell them there are two sentences for each chart. Tell them to look carefully at phrases such as 'half', 'three out of four' and 'three quarters' as they work through the task. When you get feedback, drill the key words and phrases to practise the pronunciation. Once you have provided answers, tell students to cover the task, and only look at the pie charts again. See if they can remember the descriptions of each.

Answers: 1. chart 3 2. chart 2 3. chart 1
4. chart 3 5. chart 1 6. chart 2

C Point out that 'approx' means 'approximately', and that percentages and fractions might not be exact. Students should work individually. Either you or they should write answers on the board for clarity during feedback.

Answers:
1. a quarter / one out of four
2. 33% / one out of three
3. 66% / two thirds

D The key structures are not highlighted in the task because the grammar check focuses on them. Tell students to notice the structures as they are working through the task. Give them the time they need to complete the task individually, and then compare. Write answers on the board for clarity.

Answers: 1. T 2. F 3. T 4. T 5. T
6. F

Grammar check

Go through the grammar check with students one point at a time. Make sure students see the examples, as well as the explanations. Point out that negative comparatives are used to compare one thing that is smaller or less than another, and that a sentence like 'an elephant isn't as small as a mouse' sounds ridiculous. When you come to 'not nearly as', give a couple of examples to exemplify its use, and use the comparison with 'much ... than' to clarify – 'Russia is much bigger than Spain' or 'Spain isn't nearly as big as Russia', for example. If you want to, you can tell students that many people now use 'amount' with countable nouns in spoken English, but that it is inaccurate, and that they should practise with 'number'.

You could ask students to correct the errors in the Watch out! box now.

Answers:
1. not as <u>many</u> Internet users
2. in France <u>as</u> in the United States

E Again the pie chart is very simple, but it is divided into more segments. Ask students if what the pie chart shows agrees or seems to disagree with what the longer text in the Reading Module suggests. Ask them if they are surprised that the biggest segment represents people who don't shop online.

Go through the words in the box, and check the meaning and pronunciation. Students should work individually to complete the task, and then compare. They should read the complete sentences as feedback to practise the pronunciation.

Answers: 1. Most 2. majority 3. Not many
4. minority

Grammar check

Go through the grammar box with students. Point out that 'small' is very often used with 'minority'. If students ask which adjective is used with 'majority', tell them that 'vast' is the most usual.

Writing 2

Read the exam tip with students. They should know this having seen the task based on bar charts previously.

A The aim is not only to prepare students for the writing task, but also to provide some speaking practice. Read through the two questions with students, and make sure they understand that the second question says 'for the same reasons', and not 'for the same things'. You might like to give an example. They can talk in pairs as suggested, or in small groups. Give them three or four minutes for the task, and then get some feedback.

B Tell students to look at the two pie charts, and remind them what the exam tip said about comparing information. Ask them if the task will want them to describe both charts in great detail, or compare the most interesting data in the two charts.

Give students a moment to read the instructions, and ask them if they think they understand exactly what the charts show. Point out that the segments show the percentage of people who gave a particular reason as their main reason, not their only reason. Ask students how the data shown compares with what they discussed in Exercise A, and whether they are surprised by anything.

Give students the time they need to answer the questions. The first question has been answered, but students can clarify if they need to. Monitor as students talk, and check that they are improving in terms of selecting data to include in a report. There is no need to ask for feedback or to provide an answer to the questions, as students will be given further guidance in the task that follows.

Writing 3

A The aim here is to give students guidance with the type of data they should be focusing on, how they look at charts and how they might go about noting or highlighting that data. Make sure students know that they are comparing the data they identified as relevant with what this student has. Get a general class consensus as feedback.

B Students are familiar with assessing compositions, having done so several times during the General Training course. Tell them not to worry about the boxes for now. Give them time to read the composition, and to think about what they want to say before they start talking. They can make notes or highlight as they read. Once students are in pairs, you might like to limit each pair to making three or four points, in order to give the task more clarity. Get some feedback from the class, and make notes on the board.

Answers: (possible points to make)

The report is well planned (the student has identified the right number of points, and they are all relevant).

The report is well organized and easy to follow (the points are made in a logical order, and relate to other points within the same paragraph).

The report is well expressed (grammatically, and in terms of vocabulary).

Points are made and data compared using a variety of structures (the language is not repetitive).

C The aim here is to guide students in terms of organization of points made. In this case, two paragraphs focus on differences, and one on similarities. Make sure students understand that there are alternatives. Students should work individually to complete the task, and then compare with a partner. The ideal way to give feedback would be to reproduce the report on an OHP transparency, so that you or students can write the numbers into the boxes. If that is not possible, give the numbers in the correct order going down through the report.

Answers: 3 / 1 / 5 / 4 / 2

Read the exam tip with students, and ask if they can imagine what the bar chart would look like. Then refer them to the appropriate page at the back of the book (see Exercise D).

D See exam tip above.

E In this unit, the writing task can be found in the exam practice section at the end of the Course Book unit. See instructions for that section on page 332.

Consolidation

Reading

A The aim of this task is to give students an opportunity to express how they feel about their reading skills, as well as talk specifically about the level of challenge that the Academic exam presents. Set a time limit of about five minutes, and monitor as students talk. To round up, ask each question, and see if any students want to share their feelings with the class.

B Students should work individually, and then compare with a partner. You or they should write the correct spellings on the board.

Answers: 1. retail   2. revolution   3. concept
4. purchase   5. combined

C This type of task tests both students' retention of vocabulary and their spelling. They know how the tasks work now. They should work individually, and then compare with a partner. Write the answers on the board for clarity.

Answers: 1. convenience   2. establishments
3. consumers   4. transactions   5. unlimited
6. popularity

Writing

A These words are all from the Writing Module, and are words that students will use in report writing. Make sure they understand that some words are spelt correctly. Students should work individually, and then compare with a partner. You or they should write the correct spellings on the board.

Answers: 1. (correct)   2. majority
3. minority   4. amount   5. half   6. (correct)
7. (correct)

B, C, D and E   Students can work on these tasks one at a time, getting feedback after each, or work through all the tasks, getting feedback at the end. Students can work individually, and then check any answers they are not sure of with a partner. You or they should write the correct spellings on the board.

Answers:

B 1. U   2. C   3. C   4. U

C 1. 75%   2. 66%   3. 80%   4. 90%

D 1. ½   2. ⅓   3. ¼

E 1. two out of three   2. three out of four
3. four out of five   4. nine out of ten

F Students know that each unit ends with a task like this. They can work individually or in pairs. Write the correct sentences on the board for clarity.

1. Not as many people use cash these days.
2. There are not as many smokers as there used to be.
3. The majority of people drive nowadays.
4. A small minority of the population shop only online.
5. A large number of people shop online.

Exam Practice

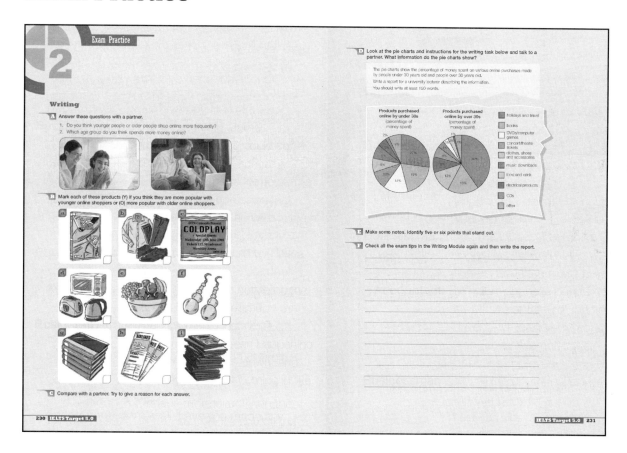

Writing

Although students have practised writing a report in the first unit, they will still need plenty of preparation and guidance.

A The aim here is not only to get students thinking about the topic of the report they will have to write, but also to provide them with some motivating speaking practice. Students can talk in pairs as suggested, or in small groups. Tell them to look at the pictures, and encourage them to support their answers with evidence or at least concrete reasons. Remind them that this is the type of topic the examiner might discuss in the final part of the speaking exam. Get some ideas from the class to finish off. You don't need to provide answers.

B and C Students should work individually to mark each product, and then spend some time discussing their decisions. Again, they should try to support their answers with evidence, and give concrete reasons for their thinking.

D Remind students that in order to understand the instructions for the first writing task, they must look at the visual information provided. The visual information might clarify something they wouldn't understand simply by reading it in the instructions. Give students time to look at the charts and read the instructions. Then tell them to cover the page or close the book so that they are not simply reading from the task to answer the question. Ask one student to explain to you what the charts represent in his or her own words.

Students often make inaccurate conclusions from looking at charts like this, and you might like to point out that the pie chart shows percentages of all money spent and not the number of any product purchased. Holidays can be very expensive, so it doesn't mean that holidays are the most frequently purchased online product. People over 30 might buy more books than people under 30, but the percentage of the total money they spend on books is lower, which is largely because they spend so much on holidays and travel.

E Remind students what 'stand out' means. Also remind them that they cannot hope to describe everything that the charts show in 150 words. Give them three minutes to make a list of stand-out information.

F Remind students they are advised to spend about 20 minutes on this first writing task so that they have 40 minutes for the more challenging discursive composition. However, students may feel that if they find this first task easier, they should spend a little longer on it, and gain as many marks as possible. Certainly for now, they should spend at least 30 minutes doing the task. Monitor as students work, but check more that they are organizing their reports, making relevant points and using appropriate register. When they have finished, allow them time to exchange and compare reports. Then refer students to the model on page 275 of the Course Book, which is also reproduced below.

If you collect students' reports to mark, you should get an idea of what they are capable of, and give constructive feedback rather than correct every single mistake.

The pie charts show that there are some differences between the products that under 30s and over 30s spend money on when they shop online. However, there are similarities between their shopping habits too.

Both groups spend the highest percentage on holidays and travel, though over 30s spend more than under 30s. Almost a third of the money that under 30s spend is on holidays and travel and an even higher percentage (40%) of the money that over 30s spend. Books are also a popular purchase for both age groups. Almost a fifth of the money spent online is on books.

A noticeable difference is with DVDs and computer games. Younger people spend five times as much as people over 30. Under 30s pay to download music far more than the over 30s while the over 30s spend twice as much on CDs. It is interesting that over 30s shop online for food and drink while under 30s seem not to.

All in all, whether people are under or over 30, they are buying quite a range of online products.

Unit 2 Workbook answers

Reading

A 1. T   2. B   3. T

B 1. No, the second sentence provides the answer
also.
2. Yes
3. Probably, though the second sentence
rephrases the point.

Key vocabulary in context

The aim here is to select the most useful words
from the lesson in terms of their frequency and
application to typical IELTS tasks. Make sure
students know where they are selecting the
words from. They can work individually, and then
compare or work in pairs. Students should read
the complete sentences as feedback to practise
pronunciation.

Answers: 1. convenience   2. combined
3. transaction   4. concept   5. purchase
6. unlimited

Writing

A 1. (example)
2. ... as much choice in most shopping malls as
there is online.
3. ... isn't as enjoyable as going out to the
shops.
4. ... as many people use cash these days.

B but / on the other hand / while / while / but /
All in all

Reading 1: preparing to read

A Check the highlighted words in these questions if you need to. Then answer them with a partner.

1. Do you think that the percentage of people in the world who smoke is increasing or decreasing?
2. Do you think that the consumption of cigarettes in your country is increasing or decreasing?
3. Where in the world do you think smoking is declining?
4. Are there any parts of the world where smoking is on the increase?
5. Do you think a smoking ban in public places makes people give up smoking?
6. Do you think a ban on the advertising of tobacco has an effect on the number of smokers?

B Look at the bar chart. What does it tell you? Compare with a partner.

Smoking is increasing in the developing world

C Write four sentences using data from the bar chart. Then look at the sentences on page 275.

Reading 2: recognizing paraphrased language

A Skim the first two paragraphs from an article about tobacco below. Does the text support the data in the bar chart?

World tobacco demand is expected to increase until the year 2010 due to population and income growth, but at lower rates than in the past, according to a new study just published. The report maintains that while in developed countries tobacco smoking will continue to decline, in developing countries consumption will increase.

World tobacco production is projected to reach over seven million tonnes of tobacco leaf in the year 2010, up from just under six million tonnes in 1998. This is lower than the record tobacco production of 7.5 million tonnes in 1992.

B Decide if these statements are (T) true, (F) false or (NG) not given.

1. Tobacco use will increase because there will be more people with more money.
2. People in developing countries will smoke far more than those in developed countries.
3. Fewer people will want tobacco over the next six years.

C Complete these sentences. Use no more than two words for each answer.

1. Over a million tonnes more _____ will be produced in 2010 than in 1998.
2. 1992 was a _____ year for tobacco production.

Exam tip: Remember that in some scanning exercises you need to look quickly for parts of the text that mean the same as the words and phrases in the question. You will not find the exact words and phrases from the question in the text.

D Talk to a partner. How is the language in each question different from the language in the text that provides the answer?

Reading 3: dealing with statistics

A Skim only paragraph 3 from the same text on the next page, and highlight all the statistics.

B Answer these questions (T) true, (F) false or (NG) not given. Then compare with a partner.

1. The number of smokers will probably increase by 0.2 billion by 2010.
2. If the number of smokers rises to 1.3 billion, it will be an increase of 1.6% since 1998.
3. Each adult will use on average 10% less tobacco in 2010 than now.
4. Anti-smoking and anti-tobacco policy is reducing the number of smokers.

Exam tip: You are more likely to read a text that has a lot of facts and statistics in the Academic exam than in the General Training exam. Sometimes you will need to answer questions about charts and graphs, as you did in Unit 2.

C Read only paragraph 6 and complete the table below with the correct figures. You will need to calculate number 7.

	developed countries		developing countries	
	1998	2010	1998	2010
tobacco demand	(1) ____ m tonnes	(2) ____ m tonnes	(3) ____ m tonnes	(4) ____ m tonnes
share of tobacco consumption	(5) ____ %	(6) ____ %	(7) ____ %	(8) ____ %

Question-type tip: Sometimes you will need to complete statistics in a table. You will use figures provided in the text and not have to make calculations, as you did for this Course Book task.

Reading 4: practice with paraphrased language and statistics

A Read the complete text and answer the questions 1–15.

World Tobacco Use on the Increase

1 World tobacco demand is expected to increase until the year 2010 due to population and income growth, but at lower rates than in the past, according to a new study just published. The report maintains that while in developed countries tobacco smoking will continue to decline, in developing countries consumption will rise.

2 World tobacco production is projected to reach over seven million tonnes of tobacco leaf in the year 2010, up from just under six million tonnes in 1998. This is lower than the record tobacco production of 7.5 million tonnes in 1992.

3 The number of smokers is expected to grow from 1.1 billion in 1998, to around 1.3 billion in 2010. This is an increase of about 1.5% annually. Despite the overall increase of tobacco use, consumption per adult is expected to decline by around 10% by 2010, and individual consumption will probably be around 1.4 kg per year from around 1.6 kg in 2000. If an aggressive anti-smoking and anti-tobacco policy were adopted, tobacco consumption per person could even drop by 20%. Consumption per person is noticeably declining in developed countries, and is now slightly declining in developing countries, including China.

4 Cigarette smoking is the most prevalent type of tobacco consumption; manufactured and hand-rolled cigarettes account for about 85% of all tobacco consumed worldwide. With around 320 million smokers, China is the world's major cigarette consumer.

5 Around 100 countries produce tobacco. The major producers are China, India, Brazil, the US, Turkey, Zimbabwe and Malawi, which together produce over 80% of the world's tobacco. China alone accounts for over 35% of world production.

Tobacco Consumption

6 The overall pattern of tobacco consumption is influenced by two contrasting trends. Tobacco demand in developed countries is declining slowly, and will reach about 2.05 million tonnes in 2010. This is 10% lower than the 2.23 million tonnes consumed in 1998. However, more tobacco will be smoked in developing countries, where tobacco consumption is expected to grow to 5.09 million tonnes by 2010 from 4.2 million in 1998. This shows an average annual growth rate of 1.7%. It is projected that by 2010, only 29% of world tobacco consumption will be in developed countries, down from 34% in 1998. In developing countries, the share will be 71%.

7 The decline in tobacco use in developed countries can be attributed to a slower population and income growth. In addition, in developed countries, an increasing awareness of the damaging health effects of smoking, together with the anti-smoking measures of governments, including intensified anti-smoking campaigns, the banning of advertising and increased taxation, have had a strong negative effect on the consumption of tobacco products.

8 A major part of the projected increase in demand is expected to be in the Far East, particularly in China. The share of China in total world tobacco demand is likely to remain around 37% in 2010. In India, the second most important tobacco consumer, the smoking of conventional cigarettes accounts for only 25%. Most people consume tobacco in the form of non-cigarette items, such as hand-rolled bidis* or chewing tobacco. Total demand for tobacco in India is likely to continue to increase, but more slowly than in the previous decades. In Africa, total tobacco demand increased in the 1990s, with record growth of 3.5% per year. Growth for the period to 2010 is expected to continue at a similar rate.

9 The report concludes that it is the higher demand for tobacco in the developing countries that drives the world tobacco economy, and that public policy to reduce tobacco usage should focus on demand rather than supply. Reducing demand in the developing countries will not be easy, given projected population and income growth, but by adopting a combination of tax and direct restriction policies, it is achievable. Reducing demand will in turn imply a decline in global tobacco production.

* Bidi: a tobacco item often flavoured, wrapped in a leaf and tied with a thread.

For questions 1–5, complete these notes with words from the text. Use no more than three words or a number for each answer.

Most common type of tobacco consumption (about 85%) – (1) _____
More tobacco smoked in (2) _____ than anywhere else –
(3) _____ people smoke.
80% of all tobacco is produced in seven (4) _____
(5) _____ of all tobacco is produced in China.

For questions 6–8, choose three of the reasons why there is a decline in tobacco use in developed countries. The order is not important.

A The population is decreasing.
B Most people do not suddenly have much more money.
C People understand that smoking is not good for them.
D People are not allowed to smoke in some of those countries.
E People no longer believe what advertisements tell them.
F Cigarettes are more expensive because of higher taxes.

6. ____ 7. ____ 8. ____

For questions 9–11, decide if the information given below agrees with the information given in the passage. Write (T) true, (F) false or (NG) not given.

9. Over a third of all tobacco use is in China.
10. Most people in India cannot afford to buy conventional cigarettes.
11. The number of smokers in Africa is expected to drop.

For question 12, mark the graph that shows projected tobacco use in India.

A   B   C   D

For questions 13–15, complete the summary below with words from the text. Use one word for each answer.

The tobacco industry relies on the fact that demand for their product is (13) _____ in developing countries. It will not be easy to make people smoke less in those parts of the world because there are more and more people with a better (14) _____. However, as awareness decreases, so too will the (15) _____ of tobacco.

B Check the key on page 275. How many questions did you answer correctly?

C Tick the sentences about the reading task that are true for you and think about how you can answer more questions correctly next time.

1. I found it quite easy to find the relevant information and answer questions.
2. I recognized when language was paraphrased.
3. I found it quite easy to work with statistics.
4. I'm pleased with how many questions I answered correctly.

For focus on reading skills and key vocabulary in context, go to Workbook page 52.

Objectives

- To revise and practise recognizing paraphrased language.
- To practise understanding statistics and answering questions about statistics.
- To practise reading a typical text from the IELTS Academic exam Reading Module.

Reading 1

The aim of this first section is to re-engage students in the topic of the lesson, and to pre-teach some key vocabulary connected with the topic. Start by looking at the picture, and ask students what they remember from the lesson in the General Training course about smoking.

A Students can use dictionaries to look up the highlighted words as they answer, but it would be better to go through the questions with them, making sure that the meaning of the highlighted words is clear, and helping them with deeper comprehension. Ask them which verb 'consumption' is from, and drill it for accurate pronunciation. Point out that 'decline' is similar to 'decrease', but is often used to mean 'become less popular', and is not so commonly used to describe graphs and charts. Point out that 'be on the increase' is a very common phrase used, instead of simply 'increase' in texts of the type they will read. Point out that 'ban' is both a verb and a noun, and that the past participle 'banned' is very common in passive structures. Remind students that 'give up' is a phrasal verb, and is very frequently used to talk about habits, especially smoking. Point out that 'tobacco' is uncountable, and that 'cigarettes' and 'cigars' are countable. Mention that doubling the 'b' instead of the 'c' is an easy mistake even for native speakers.

Give students four or five minutes to discuss the questions, and then get some feedback from the class. Avoid going through each question again in detail, as it will simply repeat what students have just done.

B The aim here is to further engage students in the topic, and to make predictions about the text. It is also a good opportunity to practise talking and writing about data in a bar chart. Give students a moment to look at the chart, and then clarify the meaning of 'developed' and 'developing'. Give examples of each. Read the vertical axis with them, and make sure they understand that the figures represent the number of cigarettes smoked on average by each individual member of the population. Make sure students understand that this doesn't mean that everyone smokes, but that some people obviously smoke far more. Give students another minute or so to talk about what the graph shows. Ask one student to explain as feedback.

Answers:
It shows that smoking declined in the developed world between 1972 and 1992, and is therefore probably still declining. At the same time, smoking increased in the developing world, and is probably still increasing.

C Encourage students to work in pairs to plan and write sentences about the chart. Tell them not to try to write a report at this point. Set a time limit of five or six minutes, and then tell students to compare with the sentences at the back of the Course Book, on page 275. Monitor as students work, so that you can check the accuracy of what they have written both in terms of fact and the language used. The model sentences are reproduced below.

Between 1970 and 1980, smoking in both the developed and developing world increased noticeably.

Between 1980 and 1990, smoking declined dramatically in the developed world.

At the same time, tobacco consumption continued to rise in the developing world.

Between 1980 and 1990, world tobacco consumption stayed at the same level, which means that all of the increase was in the developing world.

Reading 2

Start by asking students to explain what 'paraphrase' means, and establish why it is important to recognize paraphrased language. You don't need to provide a detailed answer, as the exam tip revises this. You could provide a simple example on the board, such as 'tobacco consumption' / 'amount of tobacco smoked'.

A Ask students to read the extract and see if it agrees with the chart. Establish that the extract does indeed support what the chart shows.

B Give students the time they need to answer the questions. Students should work individually, and then compare answers with a partner. Don't provide answers until students have worked through Exercise C.

C Work through in the same way as with Exercise B above, but make sure students know that this time they are filling in missing words.

Students should work in pairs to compare their answers to Exercise B, and decide together which language in the extract is paraphrased. Now provide answers to both tasks.

Answers: Exercise B: 1. T   2. NG   3. F
Exercise C: 1. tobacco leaf   2. record

Read the exam tip slowly with students.

D Give students an example of the type of thing you want them to look for (a formal verb 'demand' is paraphrased in the questions as 'want', an everyday verb). Monitor to check that students are noticing the right language. Give some feedback, but be careful not to over-complicate explanations, so that students understand less by doing the task.

Answers:
1. 'population and income growth' is formal, 'more people with more money' is far less so.
2. More formal structures, 'smoking will continue to decline' and 'consumption will increase' are paraphrased with 'far more people' in order to suggest that information is given when it is not.
3. 'Demand' is paraphrased as 'want' / 'until the year 2010' as 'over the next six years'.
4. The order of the information changes, 'up from six to seven million' is paraphrased as 'a million more'. Students need to make a very simple calculation.

5. The order of information given changes, and 'record' is used with a different noun phrase.

Reading 3

Begin by revising the different ways in which statistics can be presented, such as percentages, fractions, figures in a table, and so on.

A The best way to set up and give feedback on this task would be to use an OHP transparency. Allow students to read the title of the text, but not to start reading the text itself. Tell them to look at the third paragraph, and highlight in the extract on the transparency '1.1 billion in 1998'. If you cannot use a transparency, write this phrase on the board. Give students a few minutes to highlight the relevant parts of the paragraph. As feedback, you or the students can highlight all the statistics on the board. Writing each statistic on the board will be time-consuming and probably unnecessary, so it would be better to monitor to check progress.

Answers:
The number of smokers is expected to grow from 1.1 billion in 1998, to around 1.3 billion in 2010. This is an increase of about 1.5% annually. Despite the overall increase of tobacco use, consumption per adult is expected to decline by around 10% by 2010, and individual consumption will probably be around 1.4 kg per year (from around 1.6 kg in 2000). If an aggressive anti-smoking and anti-tobacco policy were applied, tobacco consumption per person could even drop by 20%. Consumption per person is noticeably declining in developed countries and is now slightly declining in developing countries, including China.

B This task not only practises understanding statistics, but also gives further practice with paraphrased language. Give students the time they need to answer the questions individually, and then compare with a partner. Provide the answers, clarifying anything students are not sure about.

Answers:
1. T (grow from 1.1 billion in 1998, to around 1.3 billion in 2010)
2. F (it is an annual increase, not a total increase)
3. T (consumption per adult is expected to decline by around 10% by 2010)

4. NG (the paragraph says that anti-smoking could work – not that it is working)

Read the exam tip with students, and then look at the table below with them. Ask them if they think the task looks easy or quite difficult.

C Now make sure students look only at paragraph 6. Tell them to quickly read it through once, and then to go back and read more carefully as they fill in the table. As students work, copy the table onto the board, so that you can provide clear feedback. Alternatively, make an OHP transparency of the table. Allow them a moment to compare answers before providing the key. Elicit answers from the class as you complete the table for them.

Answers:
1. 2.23m tonnes   2. 2.05m tonnes
3. 4.2m tonnes   4. 5.09m tonnes
5. 34%   6. 29%   7. 66%   8. 71%

Read the question-type tip with students. Tell them that it was necessary for them to make the calculation here; otherwise they would have been able to work out the answers mathematically.

Reading 4

A Students are hopefully becoming more familiar with these longer texts and the skills they need to apply in order to cope. Students should now be focused on the topic, and they have read two of the paragraphs already. They should find the text more manageable than they would under strict exam conditions.

Students should now be left on their own to complete the tasks. Take a quick look at the tasks, and remind them that they have practised all of them before. Remind them to skim the whole text, and then to read the parts that provide answers for each task in turn. You can give students the time they need to complete the tasks if you think they will be challenged, or you can set a time limit of about 20 minutes. Students should be applying the timing breakdown that they learnt on the General Training course.

B Give students sufficient time to check and think about why they may have answered incorrectly, before moving on to Exercise C. The answers are reproduced here, together with the lines that provide the answers.

Answers:
1. cigarette smoking / cigarettes   2. China
3. 320 million   4. countries
5. 35% / 35 per cent

(Answers here are given in alphabetical order, but any order is fine)

6. B (... can be attributed to a slower ... income growth)
7. C (... an increasing awareness of the damaging health effects)
8. F (... and increased taxation)
9. T (The share of China in total world tobacco demand is likely to remain around 37%)
10. NG (the text doesn't say why they smoke alternatives to conventional cigarettes)
11. F (In Africa ... demand increased in the 1990s with record growth of 3.5%. Growth for the period to 2010 is expected to continue at a similar rate.
12. C (demand for tobacco in India is likely to continue to increase, but more slowly than in the previous decades)
13. higher   14. income   15. production

C Students will be familiar with this type of reflective process by now. Remind them that identifying what they are doing well and not doing so well is a very good way of focusing on what they can do better next time. Note that the focus here is what was specifically practised in the unit. Allow students time to reflect and complete the task, and then ask them if they are happy with the number of correct answers. You may like to ask one student what he or she will do differently next time.

The Workbook tasks and key vocabulary in context focus on both paraphrased language and dealing with statistics. The text here is further exploited. Now would be a good time to work through them, or to set them up for homework.

Writing

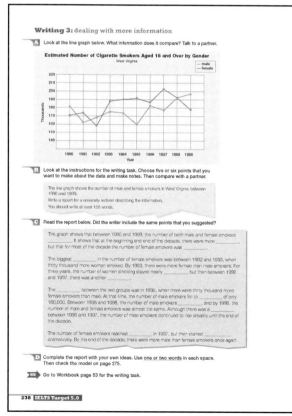

Objectives

- To familiarize students with line graphs and the type of information line graphs show.

- To revise language specifically used to describe line graphs, and to introduce some new ways of describing trends.

- To present and practise the use of verb + adverb and also adjective + noun combinations to describe graphs.

- To practise writing a report based on information presented in a line graph chart.

In this Writing Module, the topic of smoking continues throughout. In the Course Book module, students will see three line graphs, all of which show smoking habits in West Virginia. As in previous Writing Modules, the approach is to guide students through tasks, increasing the challenge gradually.

Writing 1

The aim of the first section is to revise the language of trends that students were introduced to in the first unit, as well as present further examples of descriptive language, so that they can draw from a greater range.

A   The aim here is to re-engage students in the topic that they worked on in the Reading Module, and to get them thinking again about how smoking might be changing. Read the rubric and questions with students, and tell them to think and plan for a couple of minutes before they start talking to a partner. Make sure students understand that the aim is not to give accurate answers, and that it doesn't matter if they don't know answers. Give them three or four minutes to talk, and then get some feedback from the class. If students are all from the same country as you, you might like to say whether you agree or disagree with them.

B   By now, students will be accustomed to talking about what charts and graphs show. Give them time to talk in pairs, and then check answers together as a class. As you check their answer to question 1, point out that line graphs usually show 'trends', such as how something changed or is changing over a period of time.

Now that students have seen bar graphs, pie charts and line graphs, it would be a good time to distinguish between them. Bar charts usually show one thing compared to another thing, but can also show trends; pie charts usually show shares or percentages of a whole; line graphs show trends. In Unit 2, students saw how what was shown in a pie chart could also be shown in a bar chart, so they know that information can be displayed in different ways.

Answers:
1. How the number of smokers in West Virginia increased and decreased (fluctuated) at various times between 1990 and 1999.
2. years
3. the number of smokers

C   This is very much revision, and students should complete the task easily. The aim is to check that they have retained the basic verbs they will need to write reports. Give them a minute or two to work individually, and then check answers. Ask individuals to read the correct sentences as feedback, so that you can check pronunciation of key words.

Answers: 1. decreased   2. rose
3. stayed almost the same

D and E   The aim now is to revise the adverbs that students met in Unit 1, and to introduce some new verbs that can be used in the same way. Exercise D focuses on the difference between those verbs, while Exercise E focuses on the similarity between some of them. You can set the tasks one at a time, checking the answers for each individually, or tell students to work through both tasks and then check. Again, for feedback, get students to read the correct sentences to you, and make sure that correct answers are clear. You might need to repeat answers or write them on the board. Note that in Exercise C, 1993 to 1994 is described as 'stayed almost the same', while in Exercise D the same period is described as 'rose very slightly'. Note also that in Exercise E, the suggestion is that 'steadily' and 'gradually' mean more or less the same thing, whereas in Unit 1, they learnt that they were different. Explain that 'gradually' means 'slowly' and 'by a little bit at a time', while 'steadily' means 'constantly' and 'without a stop'. 'Steadily' is more positive than 'gradually'. Emphasize though, that when describing simple trends, they can mean something very similar.

Answers:
Exercise D: 1. steadily   2. very slightly
3. noticeably

Exercise E: 1. 'slightly' is wrong
2. 'dramatically' is wrong

F   The aim now is to introduce the option of using nouns with adjectives, rather than verbs with adverbs. You don't need to explain this yet, as the grammar check focuses on it. For now, students should be able to understand the nouns and adjectives from the verbs and adverbs they already know. Give them a minute or two to work individually, and then check answers. Ask individuals to read the correct sentences as feedback, so that you can check pronunciation of key words.

Answers: 1. 1990   2. 1993   3. 1994
4. 1994

Writing 2

The aim of the second section is to develop the descriptive language that students will need. A couple more useful phrases are revised or introduced, and there is a focus on linking points rather than describing everything in crude one-phrase sentences.

A Conduct this as a whole-class discussion. Give students a minute or two to look at the new graph, and then establish that the graph shows smoking trends in the same part of the world at the same time, but now only amongst young smokers. The data is different from that on the first graph because it fluctuates far more noticeably. There are especially sharp increases and falls between 1994 and 95 and 1995 and 97. Although students don't have to explain why things happen in their report, for interest you might like to ask whether anyone can suggest why smoking declined, and then increased again so dramatically.

B Refer students first to the phrase 'reached a peak' in description 3, and see if they remember it from the first unit. Then refer them to 'fell to a low' in description 2, and see if they can tell you on the graph where that occurs. Give students two or three minutes to work individually to complete the task. As you check answers, make sure students appreciate that each of the descriptions contains more than one piece of information. Show how the linking words 'and', 'but' and 'until' are used.

Answers: 1. 1994   2. 1995
3. 1995, 1997   4. 1997

Read the exam tip with students. Make sure that you give your own advice that relates to your students' level and the amount of expression they are capable of.

C The aim now is to assess what students have retained, and the language they will be able to use when it comes to writing reports. Some students will more or less repeat what has already been presented while stronger students will attempt to link ideas together, and express their descriptions in new ways. Give students as long as you feel is beneficial for this exercise. Students can simply talk about the graphs or write some sentences together. Monitor, and give assistance where necessary.

Writing 3

A By now, students will understand that the exam writing task will ask them to compare two sources of information, rather than describe one, as they have done so far in this module. Give them time to look at the graph, and study it. Students can either talk in pairs as suggested, or tell you directly what the graph shows. Establish that the graph once again shows smoking trends in West Virginia, but that this time compares trends in smoking for males and females over the same ten-year period.

B Students are now familiar with the task instructions for this type of report writing. Set a time limit of five minutes for them to work individually to make notes about what they want to include. Remind them to focus on data that stands out. Give them another three or four minutes to compare ideas. Monitor, and check that students have identified relevant data, rather than go through it all as rather laborious oral feedback. Students will compare what they identified with what is included in the model report in a moment.

C Tell students to read through the report, aiming to compare the content with their own thoughts. Tell them not to worry about the spaces for now.

D Students can either work individually and then compare ideas, or work in pairs. Students will probably prefer to interact, and compare their ideas as they work. Give students the time they need to complete the task, and perhaps end when half the class has finished. Monitor, and check their suggestions as they work so that they can correct any errors they make. Students can check their spelling by looking back at the previous descriptions. There is no need to give feedback, as students will check the model report at the back of the book. When students check the model, they will probably want to ask you whether some of their alternative ideas are also acceptable. The model is reproduced below.

Note that there is a Workbook task that exploits this model further, focusing on linking devices.

The graph shows that between 1990 and 1999, the number of both male and female smokers fluctuated. It shows that at the beginning and end of the decade, there were more male smokers, but for most of the decade the number of female smokers was higher.

The biggest increase in the number of female smokers was between 1992 and 1993, when thirty thousand more women smoked. By 1993, there were more female than male smokers. For three years, the number of women smoking stayed nearly the same, but then between 1996 and 1997, there was another sharp rise.

The biggest difference between the two groups was in 1995, when there were thirty thousand more female smokers than male. At that time the number of male smokers fell to a low of only 160,000. Between 1995 and 1996, the number of male smokers rose dramatically, and by 1996, the number of male and female smokers was almost the same. Although there was a slight drop between 1996 and 1997, the number of male smokers continued to rise steadily until the end of the decade.

The number of female smokers reached a peak in 1997, but then started to fall dramatically. By the end of the decade, there were more male than female smokers once again.

Writing task

Although students have practised writing a report in the two previous units, they will still need plenty of preparation and guidance.

A Give the students the time they need to look at the graph, the instructions and the questions.

Then give them three or four minutes to answer the questions with a partner. Go over the answers carefully, making sure they understand exactly what the graph shows.

Answers:
1. from 1948 to 2005 – 57 years / not all years are shown on the graph – up to 1968, periods of five years are shown – from 1968 to 2000, selected periods are shown
2. that is when records of smoking trends began

B and C Conduct this step as you have done previously. Students should work individually, and then compare ideas. They should compare with a purpose. If they think other students have noticed more relevant information, they should think about changing the points they plan to make. Remind them they cannot hope to describe everything that the charts show in 150 words. Monitor to check that students are planning to include the relevant content. It would be a good idea to guide weaker students and make suggestions about what data to include. Look at the model report below yourself first, so that you can suggest including some of the points if necessary.

D Remind students they are advised to spend about 20 minutes on this first writing task, so that they have 40 minutes for the more challenging discursive composition. However, students may feel that if they find this first task easier, they should spend a little longer on it, and gain as many marks as possible. Certainly for now, they should spend at least 30 minutes doing the task. Monitor as students work, but check above all that they are organizing their reports, making relevant points, and using the appropriate language they have learnt. When they have finished, allow time to exchange and compare reports.

If you collect students' reports to mark, you should get an idea of what they are capable of, and give constructive feedback rather than correct every mistake.

The line graph shows that the percentage of the population that smoke decreased dramatically between 1948, when records began, and 2005. The percentage of male smokers decreased more rapidly than the number of female smokers.

In 1948, around 65% of men smoked compared

with around 41% of women. By 2005, the number of male and female smokers was almost the same.

Between 1955 and 1957, there was a rise in the number of both male and female smokers, though the rise in the number of female smokers was sharper. Over the next few years, the numbers of both male and female smokers fluctuated.

Between about 1961 and 1963, there was a noticeable fall in the number of men smoking, and the difference between the number of men and women smoking became smaller.

Between 1970 and 2000, the number of both male and female smokers fell steadily. By around 1990, less than 30% of both men and women were smoking. Despite a couple of slight rises in the percentage of male smokers, the numbers of both men and women smoking continued to fall until 2005.

Consolidation

Answers: 1. consumption   2. growth
3. production   4. awareness   5. global

Reading

A The aim here is to give students the opportunity to express how they feel about their reading skills, and to talk specifically about the level of challenge that the Academic exam presents. Set a time limit of three minutes, and monitor as students talk. To round up, ask each question, and see if any students want to share their feelings with the class.

B Students should work individually, and then compare with a partner. They should read the complete correct sentences, in order to practise appropriate pronunciation.

Answers: 1. stop (correct)   2. less (correct)
3. is increasing (correct)   4. cannot (correct)
5. want (correct)

C Students have seen this type of task previously with spelling mistakes. They should work individually, and then compare with a partner. Write the correct spellings on the board for clarity.

Answers: 1. consumption   2. growth
3. production   4. awareness   5. global

Writing

A and B   These tasks practise the alternative ways of expressing trends, as was the focus of the Writing Module. As suggested earlier, it may be better to work through the two tasks during the writing skills lesson. Students should work individually, and then compare with a partner. Write the answers on the board for clarity.

Answers:

A   1. (example)   2. decreased slightly
3. rose dramatically   4. fell noticeably
5. dropped steadily

B   1. (example)   2. a steady increase
3. a sharp rise   4. a dramatic fall
5. a slight drop

C   Make sure that students know what articles are, and write the options 'a', 'an' and 'the' on the board. Students should work individually, and then compare with a partner. As students are working, copy the incorrect sentences onto the board so that either you or they can add and delete articles for feedback.

Answers:
1. In 1994, there was a drop in the number of the smokers.
2. The number of the female smokers reached a peak in the 1997.
3. As the population in many developing countries grows and as a people have more money, the consumption of the tobacco will increase.

Exam Practice

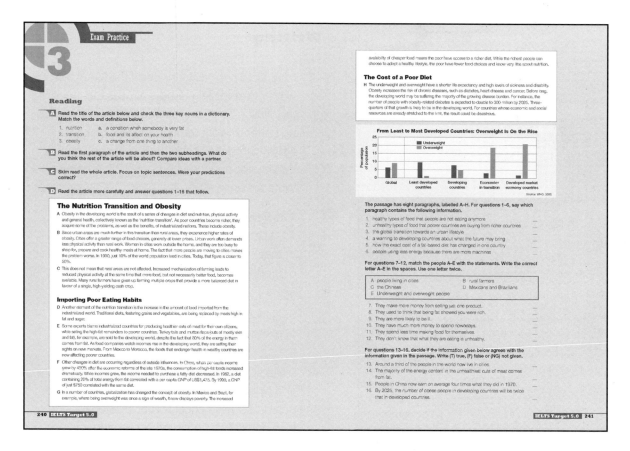

Reading

The aim of the exam practice section is to provide practice that is close to what students will see in the exam. The length of the text is about what students can expect, and although language is slightly simplified, it is close to the authentic level that students will have to deal with. Once again, students are given some preparation to boost their confidence, and make reading more enjoyable. There is a focus on the skills that students studied in the Reading Module, and a graph accompanying the text.

A It is important that students understand the words in the title, so that they have a basic comprehension of what the text is about. Students will understand 'nutrition transition' only by understanding the two words separately first. Pronounce the three key words for students, and then give them two or three minutes to use dictionaries to check meanings. If there is an insufficient number of dictionaries, students can share and work in pairs. As you go over answers with them, clarify meaning a little more, for example 'if somebody is obese, they are unhealthily overweight' and so on. Once

students understand the key words, you can ask them what the article will be about.

Answers: 1. b   2. c   3. a

B Give students time to read the first paragraph and the subheadings. Remind students of what 'developing' means. Point out that your 'diet' is what you eat, while 'nutrition' is the goodness in what you eat. Remind students that 'import' means bring something into a country, and tell them that 'poor' here means not good, rather than not having money. Once you are confident that students understand the first paragraph, you can give them two or three minutes to predict the content of the rest of the article. Get some ideas from the class, and write any key words and phrases on the board. If students have difficulty, you can ask direct questions, like 'What do you think people are eating that they didn't eat before?' or 'What do you think people have stopped eating?'

C Set a time limit of two minutes for students to skim the text. Emphasize that they must focus on the topic sentences. Make sure they

understand that for now they are reading to
check their predictions.

D Now students have to read for gist, they will
know that they should look at the questions so
that they have a purpose when they read more
carefully. Later in the course, they will not be
given so much advice in the rubric of the exam
practice sections. Point out that students have
seen all the task types before, and then set a
time limit of about 20 minutes.

Answers:
1. D   2. E   3. B   4. H   5. F   6. C
7. B (... in favour of a single, high-yielding cash
   crop)
8. D (... where being overweight was once a sign
   of wealth, it now displays poverty)
9. E (... high levels of sickness / obesity
   increases the risk of chronic diseases)
10. C (In China, when per capita income grew
    by 400% ...)
11. A (... they are too busy to shop for, prepare
    and cook healthy meals at home)
12. D (and know very little about nutrition)
13. F (half live in cities, 50%)
14. T
15. T
16. NG

Unit 3 Workbook answers

Reading

A   1. d   2. e   3. f   4. a   5. c   6. b

B   1. 7.5 million   2. 10% / 20%   3. 320   4. 71
   5. 25

Key vocabulary in context

The aim here is to check what students have noticed, both in the text they have read in this unit, and previously when working with this type of description. Note that the expressions are all expressions students might like to use in their writing. Encourage them to look for answers in the text if they find it difficult to remember them. They can work individually and then compare, or work with a partner. Students should read the complete expressions as feedback, but write answers on the board for clarity.

Answers: 1. of   2. to   3. from / to   4. by
   5. for   6. by   7. for   8. of

Writing

A   1. but   2. when   3. By   4. but   5. then
   6. when   7. At that time   8. and
   9. Although   10. until   11. but   12. by

The writing task is dealt with in the main section of the Teacher's Book.

4 Society

Reading

Reading

4 Society

Reading 1: preparing to read

A Look at this first line from a text you are going to read. Check the highlighted words in a dictionary and then answer the questions that follow with a partner.

> Disposing of all the waste we produce is a global problem.

1. What different types of waste do we produce?
2. Why is disposing of waste such a big problem?

B Look at this sentence from the same text. Check the highlighted words and then answer the questions that follow with a partner.

> One way waste is classified is by consistency; whether it is solid or liquid waste.

1. One example of solid waste is empty bottles. Can you think of a few more examples?
2. One example of liquid waste is bath or shower water. Can you think of any other examples?

C Use a dictionary. Match the words and phrases below with the pictures.

1. landfill ___ 2. incineration ___ 3. composting ___
4. waste injection well ___ 5. recycling ___

D Talk to a partner. Do you know any advantages or problems with any of the methods in Exercise C?

> landfill is cheap

> incineration can cause pollution

E Circle the correct option in each sentence.

1. If you **monitor** something, you watch it and check it / say it doesn't work well.
2. If you **dump** something, you want to keep it / throw it away.
3. If water is **contaminated**, it's good to drink / dangerous.
4. If something is **hazardous**, it could hurt you or kill you / is very good for you.
5. If something **leaks**, it breaks into pieces / allows water to escape.
6. If something is **harmful**, it is good / not good for you.
7. **Pollutants** are harmful to / good for the air that we breathe.
8. If something **decomposes**, it breaks down / comes together.

Reading 2: understanding references and linking

A Complete each of the sentences about waste with the reference words in the box.

1. The United States produces around 208 million tonnes of solid waste every year, and _____ is on the increase.
2. In many countries, people no longer throw away bottles and jars. _____ take _____ to bottle banks, where _____ can be recycled.
3. A long time ago, people simply took their rubbish out into the country and dumped _____.
4. When rubbish was first disposed of in an organized way, _____ was dumped into large open holes. Since _____, complex systems of rubbish disposal have been developed all over the world.

> it (x 2)
> this
> then
> there
> they (x 2)
> them

B Complete each of these sentences about waste with the linking words in the box.

1. Most rubbish is taken to landfill sites, but it can _____ be incinerated.
2. Most people are not happy about living close to landfill sites _____ they are afraid that drinking water may become contaminated.
3. In most big cities, there are recycling systems in place. In smaller towns, _____, recycling is not such usual practice.
4. _____ the constant monitoring of waste injection wells, dangerous pollutants can sometimes escape.
5. Composting is popular with many people because it is a natural process. _____ it can be cheaper than producing chemical fertilizers.

> however
> in addition
> despite
> also
> because

Reading 3: practice understanding references and linking

A Read the text and answer the questions 1–15 that follow.

Where Does All the Rubbish Go?

A Disposing of all the waste we produce is a global problem. Every area of our lives involves throwing something away, whether it is household rubbish, plastic, paper, metal, commercial waste or anything else we simply do not want or need. The United States alone produces 208 million tons of solid waste every year, and this is on the increase. Each person produces more than four pounds of waste a day. We have developed various different ways of disposing of waste, but certainly not yet a way that is absolutely safe.

B We have not always monitored the way we dispose of waste as we do today. In 18th century Europe, people with carts were paid to carry rubbish out of town and dump it. The first municipal cleaning system originated in the United States in the middle of the eighteenth century. This made the dumping of rubbish in open pits usual practice. However, since then, our waste has become more complicated, and cannot simply be placed in a hole in the ground. We have many different types of waste, and it must be disposed of properly to prevent contaminating the environment.

C There are different types of waste, and it is classified according to its physical, chemical and biological characteristics. One way it is classified is by consistency; whether it is solid or liquid waste. To classify as a solid waste, the material must contain less than 70% water. This type of waste includes materials such as household rubbish, industrial waste, mining waste and some oilfield waste. Liquid wastes must be less than 1% solid and is often from wastewater. Wastewater often contains high levels of dissolved salts and metals. Sludge is the final consistency classification, being somewhere between a liquid and a solid. Sludge contains between 3 and 25% solids, and the rest of it is made up of water-dissolved materials.

D Waste can also be classified into three categories; non-hazardous, hazardous and special waste. Non-hazardous waste does not pose any immediate danger to health or the environment. This category includes household rubbish. Hazardous waste can either be flammable or leachable. This means that it can either easily catch fire, or it can leak toxic chemicals. Examples of special waste would be radioactive and medical waste, and there are very clear rules about how this can be disposed of.

E There are a number of ways that we dispose of rubbish and waste. Landfill is the most common, and can account for more than 90% of a country's waste. It is the most cost-effective way of disposing of rubbish, as collection and transport represents 75% of the total cost involved. A landfill site is carefully constructed site located away from heavily populated areas, and in areas where there is no flooding. Rubbish is buried in thin layers and then covered with clay, sand and fresh soil. When the landfill is full, it is covered with a layer of plastic and then more soil. Grass and other vegetation is planted, so that the site is hidden completely. Despite all this effort to minimize danger, however, it is known that landfill can contaminate drinking water. A 10-acre landfill site will leak between 0.2 and 10 gallons of liquid every day through the plastic liner.

F Waste can also be burnt in incinerators. This method is more expensive, but safer than landfill. Modern incinerators can destroy more than 90% of organic waste material. In addition, incineration recovers energy in the waste, which can be used to generate electricity. Older incinerators, however, do not separate the material that is burnt, and there are concerns that harmful pollutants are released into the air. People who live near incinerators usually object to them because of the health risk.

G Some hazardous waste can be pumped into deep wells inside the earth. This is called waste injection. The wells are constantly monitored to check that pollutants cannot escape and contaminate drinking water. Many people are strongly opposed to this method because it has caused explosions and even earthquakes in the past.

H Organic material that contains little or no heavy metals can be detoxified biologically. This is done by composting and land farming. Waste materials are spread over a large area of land so that they decompose more quickly. Hazardous waste must be detoxified because it can leak into the groundwater, causing water contamination.

I Presently, the aim of governments all over the world is to reduce the amount of waste that we need to dispose of. Firstly, to reduce the amount of waste that is created in the first place, and then to reuse and recycle waste rather than discard it. Many strategies are in place or are being considered. They might cost us more now, but will almost certainly bring benefits to future generations.

For questions 1–6, match the headings below with some of the paragraphs A–I. Write the letter of the paragraph as your answer.

1. It used to be easy ___
2. Up in flames ___
3. Don't throw it away ___
4. How dangerous is it? ___
5. We all produce rubbish ___
6. Most rubbish goes under the ground ___

For questions 7–10, choose the correct answer a, b or c to complete each statement below.

7. The methods used to dispose of waste in the eighteenth century ...
   a. were very complicated.
   b. meant that town centres were very dirty.
   c. would not be appropriate today.

8. Sludge is ...
   a. mostly solid.
   b. mostly liquid.
   c. is about the same amount of solid and liquid.

9. All special waste ...
   a. can easily catch fire.
   b. must be disposed of carefully.
   c. cannot be destroyed.

10. Landfill is popular because ...
   a. it is not expensive to move rubbish from one place to another.
   b. it helps to prevent flooding.
   c. once rubbish is under the ground, it is not at all dangerous.

For questions 11–15, mark each of the statements below with one of the following abbreviations. Use some abbreviations more than once.

I   incineration
WI waste injection
C   composting

11. Experts check the process very carefully. ___
12. Disposing of waste in this way can produce power. ___
13. This process is natural, but not totally without risk. ___
14. Only newer equipment is really efficient. ___
15. This process has been linked to natural disasters. ___

B Check the key on page 276. How many questions did you answer correctly?

C Tick the sentences about the reading task that are true for you and think about how you can answer more questions correctly next time.

1. I could quickly see what reference words referred to.
2. Understanding references helped me to answer some questions.
3. I understood how linking words and phrases were used.
4. I didn't need to understand every word of the text to answer the questions.
5. I'm pleased with how quickly I did the tasks and how many questions I answered correctly.

Exam tip: Technical words in a text are often explained. Notice how sludge, flammable and leachable are explained in the text that you have just read. Recognizing that a word or phrase you don't know has been explained will help you to read more quickly and understand more of a text.

Key vocabulary in context

There are a lot of synonyms (words that have a very similar meaning) in the text. Delete the one word in each list that is different from the others.

1. waste / rubbish / layer
2. destroy / produce / generate
3. danger / method / risk
4. dispose of / throw away / dump / contaminate / discard

WB For focus on reading skills, go to Workbook page 55.

242 IELTS Target 5.0

IELTS Target 5.0 243

244 IELTS Target 5.0

IELTS Target 5.0 245

Objectives

- To show students the importance of understanding reference words in a text.

- To help students understand the references in a text more quickly.

- To learn and practise linking devices used in academic texts.

- To practise reading a typical text from the IELTS Academic exam Reading Module.

Reading 1

The aim of the first section is to engage students in the topic, to pre-teach some key vocabulary and to give them a small taste of the content of the text they will read.

A You could tell students to cover the pictures, but they can look at them if they want to, and get a general idea of what the unit focus is. You can either explain the highlighted words in the first sentence, or tell students to use dictionaries as they answer the questions. Work with words that you think students will already know, then explain the new words, such as 'throw away' for 'dispose of' and 'rubbish' for 'waste'. Point out that 'waste' is anything you don't use or need anymore. Make sure students understand that the dependent preposition 'of' always goes with 'dispose'. Give students a few minutes to discuss the questions in pairs, and then get some feedback from the class. If students lack ideas, avoid teaching them too much as the tasks that follow give them more guidance.

B Deal with the questions in the same way as you did in Exercise A. It is probably best to make sure students understand 'solid' and 'liquid', before teaching 'consistency'. Point out that 'consistency' is the noun of 'consist of', which students have met on the General Training course.

C Give students a minute to look at the pictures and match them with the words. They will need to use dictionaries, as most of the words will be completely new to them. Point out that the words themselves are not especially useful, but that they are core to the text students will read.

Students should work individually, and then compare with a partner. Note that students will find it difficult to distinguish between 'incineration' and 'waste injection' from the pictures, but the text will explain the difference. You might like to read through the text in advance, so that you can briefly explain the two processes during feedback. As you check answers, focus on the pronunciation of the key words, and deal with any related words that will be useful, such as 'compost', some people put it on their garden, 'incinerate' means burn to nothing, an 'injection' is what you have at hospital, and so on.

As an alternative, you could deal with this stage as a whole-class activity. Match the words and pictures together and clarify as you go.

Answers: 1. e   2. b   3. c   4. d   5. a

D You can conduct this as pairwork as suggested, or as a whole-class discussion. Make sure students know that they are not expected to know a lot about the issue, and they may not be able to say much. You might prefer to ask questions to guide them, such as 'Which method is very expensive?', 'Which method can be used only with some types of waste?', 'Which method causes the most pollution?', and so on. You could ask students if they would be happy to live near a landfill site or an incinerator.

E You can either give students five minutes to work individually to check all the words in dictionaries, or you can work through the words one at a time, giving students 20 or 30 seconds to check in their dictionaries. This would give them useful practice finding and checking words quickly. Pronounce the words for them, and make sure these are all clear before they go on to read the text.

Answers: 1. watch it and check it
2. throw it away   3. dangerous
4. could hurt you or kill you
5. allows water to escape   6. not good
7. harmful to   8. breaks down

Reading 2

Tell students that they will read the text later in the lesson, but for now they will focus on two other important aspects of reading. Note that the example sentences here are very much related to the text, and provide a further taste of what they can expect to read.

A Students worked with a similar task on the General Training course, and should see this as revision. You can do the first sentence with them as an example if you think it is necessary. They should work individually, and then compare with a partner. Students should read the full sentences as feedback, but make sure correct answers are clear. Note that students might use 'it' in the first sentence, but should change their answer once they have worked through the whole exercise.

Answers: 1. this   2. They / them / they
3. it / there   4. it / then

B Look at the linking words together, and check the pronunciation. Ask students if they are familiar with all of them, but don't explain any new ones yet as these are best learnt in context. Work through the task as you did with Exercise A. Check that students use capital letters where necessary. Tell students that they will do more work with linking in the Writing Module of this unit. 'Despite' may be new to some students, so explain that it works like 'but', except that it is a preposition and is usually used at the beginning of a sentence to be more emphatic. You could write a simple transformation on the board to clarify, such as 'It was raining, but we played football'. / 'Despite the rain, we played football'.

Answers: 1. also   2. because   3. however
4. Despite   5. In addition

Reading 3

Students have been well prepared for this text, and have been shown much of the content. They should be more familiar with these longer texts by now, as well as the skills they need to apply. They should be left on their own to complete the tasks.

Take a quick look at the tasks, and remind students that they have practised all of them before.

A Tell students to skim through the text and to read the parts that provide answers for each task in turn. Set a time limit of 20 minutes. Students should be applying the timing breakdown that they learnt on the General Training course.

B Give students sufficient time to check and think about why they may have answered incorrectly, before moving on to Exercise C. The answers are reproduced here, together with the lines that provide the answers.

Answers:
1. B   2. F   3. I   4. D   5. A   6. E
7. C (However, since then, our waste has become more complicated, and cannot simply be placed in a hole in the ground)
8. B (Sludge contains between 3 and 25% solids, and the rest of it is made up of water ...)
9. B (Examples of special waste would be radioactive and medical waste, and there are very clear rules about how this can be disposed of.)
10. A (It is the most cost-effective way of disposing of rubbish, as collection and transport represents 75% of the total cost involved)
11. WI (The wells are constantly monitored ...)
12. I (... incineration recovers energy in the waste, which can be used to generate electricity)
13. C (Organic material ... detoxified biologically... Hazardous waste must be detoxified because it can leak ... causing water contamination)
14. I (Older incinerators ... do not separate the material that is burnt ...)
15. WI (... it has caused ... earthquakes in the past)

C Students will be familiar with this type of reflective process by now. Remind them that identifying what they are doing well and not doing so well is a very good way of focusing on what they can do better next time. Note that the focus here is what was specifically practised in the unit. Allow students time to reflect and complete the task, and then ask them if they are happy with the number of correct answers. You may like to ask one student what he or she will do differently next time.

Read the exam tip slowly and carefully, giving students time to look back at the examples in the text.

The Workbook tasks give further practice with grammatical reference words, and extend the focus onto general nouns, which refer back to previously mentioned ideas in the text.

Key vocabulary in context

The aim here is to show students that texts on a particular theme usually contain a lot of synonyms, or at least near synonyms. Make sure students understand what synonyms are. If you want to, point out that one word rarely means exactly the same thing as another – there are often differences in usage and register, for example. Give students time to check the words in the text if they need to. They should work individually, and then compare with a partner. During feedback, clarify any subtle differences between words that you think will be useful.

Answers: 1. layer   2. destroy   3. method
4. contaminate

Writing

Objectives

- To familiarize students with flow charts and the type of information they show.

- To revise the present simple passive, and to show its typical use when describing flow charts.

- To present and practise typical ways of linking together a description of a flow chart.

- To practise writing a report based on information presented in a flow chart.

Writing 1

Students were introduced to flow charts as part of the General Training course, but then the focus was on listening. They have not yet practised writing a description of one. In many respects, describing a flow chart is the easiest of the Writing 1 tasks. It involves linking together the elements of the diagram that students are given. Some, however, may feel that understanding the process shown in the chart is difficult, and that using passive structures is challenging.

A The aim here is to re-establish the purpose of a flow chart in the form of a task. Start by asking students what they remember about the flow charts they saw previously (they showed what a patient should do if showing various symptoms of illness). Tell students to read the whole extract before attempting to fill the gaps. They should work individually, and then compare with a partner. One stronger student can read the extract aloud to check answers.

Answers:
stages / process / effect / event / arrows

B The lead-in stage revises what students talked about in the Reading Module, and adds further points. If all your students are from the same country, you might like to discuss the first question as a whole class. If they are from various different countries, there will be more to compare. Check the meaning of the highlighted words, and give examples of an 'appliance'. Students should work in pairs to answer questions 2 and 3, but make sure they understand that they are not supposed to know the correct answer to question 3.

C Make sure students cover the diagram before they look at the sentences. Put students into pairs or groups of three. You can either set a time limit of about six or seven minutes, or end the task when about half the class has finished. Tell students to check key words in dictionaries as they order the process, rather than check them all first. If you think it is necessary, you could establish which sentence comes first together as a class. There is no need to check answers, as students will now see the labelled diagram.

Answers:
3 glass crushed into small pieces called cullet / different colours of cullet made
6 molten glass moulded into new bottles and jars.
2 glass transported to processing plant / metal tops and plastic sleeves removed
7 new bottles and jars shipped to companies for filling and distribution
5 mixture heated to high temperatures in furnace
1 glass collected from bottle banks / clear, green and brown glass separated
4 cullet mixed with sand, limestone and soda ash

D As students look at the flow chart, you can clarify anything they don't understand. However, avoid explaining what students don't need to know – they will have to get used to describing processes that they don't fully understand by using the language they are given.

E Students are familiar with instructions for writing tasks. Give them a moment to read through, and think about what they would say. Then tell them to read the questions, and give them time to answer in pairs. Get some feedback from them, but make sure they understand what to do and what not to do when describing processes.

Answers:
1. No (the information and any technical language is given)

2. No (if they don't know much about the process, they can't add their own ideas. They can add small points to make the description more interesting, but not invent points that are not presented)

F Students are accustomed to assessing written compositions like this now. Give them a few minutes to read the report, and make some comments either to a partner or directly to you. They will probably say that it is much too short, and that sentences are too short and not linked. Don't worry about getting many comments now because the next task teaches them to look more closely.

G Make sure students understand that these are comments made by a teacher, but that some of them are unfair or not true. Students should do the task individually, so that they are able to think, and look up any words they need to. Tell them to compare ideas with a partner. Go over answers so that what is wrong with the report is clear, but don't go into too much detail about points 4 and 5, as that is the focus of the next stage of the lesson.

Answers: 1. F   2. T   3. T   4. T   5. T
6. F   7. T

Writing 2

Students will have studied passive structures at their level, and looked at various passive structures on the General Training course. Present simple passive should be manageable by now.

A   Students should work in pairs to find a couple of examples of each point. The best way to give feedback would be to reproduce the report on an OHP transparency, and make corrections on the board. If that is not possible, you will need to rewrite some of the structures shown in the model below.

Answers:
<u>They collect</u> the glass from bottle banks and <u>separate</u> the clear, green and brown glass. <u>They transport</u> the glass to a processing plant. Any metal tops and plastic sleeves are removed here. <u>They crush</u> the glass into small pieces what is called cullet. <u>They make</u> three different colours of cullet. The cullet is mixed with sand, limestone and soda ash. The mixture is heated to a very high temperature in a big furnace. The molten glass is made into new bottles and jars. The new bottles and jars are shipped to companies for filling and distribution.

Grammar check

Read through the grammar check with students slowly, one point at a time. Give them a couple of minutes to make the transformations and check them. Students can check the typical errors in their own time.

Answers:
1. The glass is transported to ...
2. The new bottles and jars are filled ...

Read the exam tip with students, and then tell them to cover it and tell you what it said. Ask them to give you some examples of irregular verbs that are typically used to describe a process, and check the past participles like 'made', 'take' and 'put', for example.

B   Point out that this is a grammatically correct version of the student's report, though it is still much too short and needs linking devices. Students should work individually, and then compare answers. Write the correct answers on the board for clarity.

Answers:
is collected / is separated (glass is uncountable, and the focus is on glass, not the three different colours) / is transported / are removed / is crushed / is made / is mixed / is heated / is made / are shipped

Grammar check

Rather than read through the grammar check here, write the two incorrect sentences on the board, and ask students to tell you what is wrong. You can cross out the unnecessary parts, that way clarifying the point. Once you have done that, give students time to read through the explanation.

Writing 3

Students have looked at linking words before, but not those especially used to describe a sequence.

A   Tell students to read the whole of the second version of the report, and ask them if they think it has improved. Look closely at the introductory line, and emphasize the importance of it. Tell students that this introductory line is more than 40 words, and that the report would be too short without it. Students can work individually, and then compare, or work in pairs if they prefer. To feed back, students can read the report to you, but make sure answers are clear, and that you write the correct option on the board. If you use an OHP transparency, you can delete the wrong option on it.

Answers:
1. First of all ('At the beginning' is used more in stories. Students may suggest 'To begin with', which is correct)
2. At this point
3. then ('after' is a preposition, and must come directly before a noun or pronoun)
4. where
5. Next ('Secondly' is wrong because there have been other stages since the first one)
6. such as (similar to 'for example')
7. When
8. which
9. Finally ('In the end' can mean exactly the same as 'finally' in a story when there is a consequence, but is not used simply to express sequence in a report)

B This task is designed to bring the two focus points together. Students are working with a new theme, so look at the picture first and establish that the extract is about recycling tins and cans. Make sure students read the whole extract before attempting to fill gaps. They should work individually, and then compare answers with a partner. To give feedback, either use an OHP transparency, or write the complete extract on the board as you elicit answers. This model is a guide, and alternative answers are possible in some cases.

Answers:

(1) First of all, aluminium tins and cans (2) are collected from recycling points. They are (3) then transported by truck, train or ship to smelting plants, (4) where they are unloaded and (5) tested for quality. (6) At this point, they are checked to see if they contain any liquid.

(7) Next, the tins and cans are shredded into small pieces and (8) placed in an oven to remove paint and labels. They (9) are heated to over 500 degrees in a furnace, (10) where they melt and mix together with other molten metal. Salt and other chemicals (11) are added to the mixture. (12) When the chemistry of the molten mixture has been checked, it (13) is removed from the furnace and (14) poured into moulds to be made into rectangular blocks. These blocks (15) are allowed to cool and are (16) then passed through huge rollers to become metal sheets. (17) Finally, these metal sheets are transported to a can manufacturer, where they (18) are made into new tin cans.

C In this unit, the writing task can be found in the exam practice section at the end of the Course Book unit. See instructions for that section below.

Consolidation

Consolidation

Reading

A Tick the option that is true for you in each pair of statements.

1. A I know immediately what reference words refer to in a longer text.
   B I sometimes have difficulty knowing what reference words refer to and it slows me down when I read.
2. A I recognize most linking words now and they help me make predictions about what will follow.
   B I still confuse some linking words and phrases when I read more challenging texts.

B Complete each of these definitions with a word from the Reading Module. The first letter is given.

1. If something l _ _ _ _ _ , it allows water in or water to escape.
2. If you d _ _ _ rubbish, you throw it away or leave it somewhere.
3. If something is h _ _ _ _ _ _ , it isn't good for you and it could hurt you.
4. If something is a r _ _ _ , it isn't safe and it could hurt you.
5. If material d _ _ _ _ _ _ _ _ , it breaks down and goes back into the earth.
6. If you m _ _ _ _ _ a situation, you watch it carefully and check that there is not a problem.
7. If something c _ _ _ _ _ _ _ _ _ water, you cannot drink it.
8. If power is g _ _ _ _ _ _ _ _ , it is produced from a process.
9. One way of defining consistency is to say if something is s _ _ _ _ or l _ _ _ _ .

Writing

A These verbs are typically used to describe a process. Write the correct past participle.

1. make _____   2. take _____   3. break _____
4. bring _____   5. build _____   6. give _____
7. leave _____   8. send _____   9. throw _____
10. hold _____   11. put _____   12. write _____

B Rewrite these descriptions using a passive structure. Only mention the agent if necessary.

1. Somebody breaks the glass into small pieces.
2. Robots build cars in most factories.
3. Secretaries send the parcels out to the various offices.
4. Workers package the drinks in plastic containers.
5. Ships transport the coal to North Africa.
6. An official writes a number on each envelope that he sends.

C Below is part of the report from the Writing Module. Find eight words that are spelt wrongly and correct them.

First of all, glass bottles and jars are collected from bottle banks all around the area. At this point, clear, green and brown glass is separated. The glass is then transported to a processing plant, where it is crushed into small pieces called cullet. This cullet is made in three different colours. Next, the cullet is mixed with other materials, such as sand, limestone and soda ash. The mixture is heated to a very high temperature in a huge furnace.

IELTS Target 5.0 249

Reading

A The aim is to give students the opportunity to talk about the reading skills that were the focus of the Reading Module, as well as express any further concerns they may have about the level of challenge in the Academic exam. Give students a moment to read the options and choose, then get some feedback from the class.

B You might like to make this into a competition. Put students into pairs or groups of three, and set a time limit of seven or eight minutes. See which team can get the most correct answers. Make sure spelling is emphasized. Either you or students can write the correct spellings on the board to round off.

Answers: 1. leaks   2. dump   3. harmful
4. risk   5. decomposes   6. monitor
7. contaminates   8. generated
9. solid / liquid

Writing

A This can be set either as individual or pairwork. Students might like to work together to check what they know. Make sure they know they are writing the past participle, and not the past simple form. Do the first one with them as an example. You can write the answers on the board, or refer students to a list of irregular verbs that they might have in a course book or dictionary.

Answers: 1. made   2. taken   3. broken
4. brought   5. built   6. given   7. left
8. sent   9. thrown   10. held   11. put
12. written

B This can be set either as individual or pairwork. Students might like to work together to check what they know. Either you or students can write the correct answers on the board. Explain that the agent is expressed when it provides information that is necessary or likely to be unknown.

Answers:
1. The glass is broken into small pieces.
2. Cars are built by robots in most factories.
3. The parcels are sent out to the various offices.
4. The drinks are packaged in plastic containers.
5. The coal is transported to North Africa by ship.
6. A number is written on each envelope.

C This can be set either for individual completion or as pairwork. Pairs could compete to see which finds the eight errors and corrects them first.

Answers:
First of all, glass bottles and jars are <u>collected</u> from bottle banks all around the area. At this point, clear, green and brown glass is <u>separated</u>. The glass is then transported to a <u>processing</u> plant, where it is crushed into small <u>pieces</u> called cullet. This cullet is made in three <u>different</u> colours. Next, the cullet is mixed with other <u>materials</u> such as sand, limestone and soda ash. The <u>mixture</u> is heated to a very high <u>temperature</u> in a huge furnace.

Exam Practice

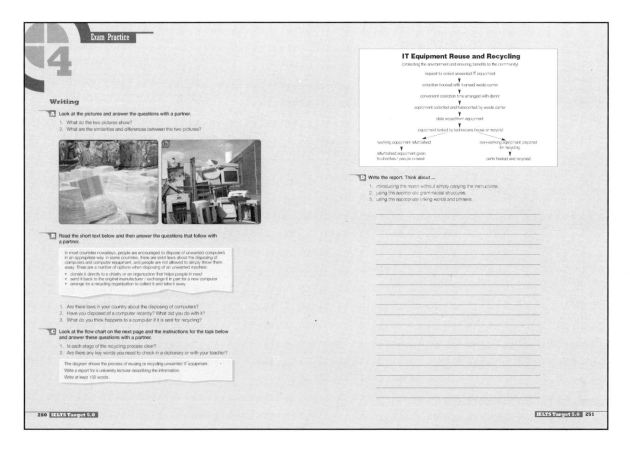

Writing

Students have not practised writing a report of a flow chart, and will need plenty of preparation and guidance.

A Students have been talking about recycling, and so should be focused on the topic. The task should get them thinking about this particular aspect of recycling, and provide some motivating speaking practice. Students should try to use some of the vocabulary they have learnt from the unit when talking about the pictures. Give them a few minutes to talk in pairs, and then get some ideas. You could write any key words that emerge on the board. If students don't see the connection between the pictures, open it up as a whole-class discussion, and ask questions to guide them, like 'Which picture shows computers that are being recycled?' and so on.

Answers:
1. old computers that have been thrown / discarded

2. they are similar because they show old computers / they are different because the second picture shows a landfill site and piles of computers that have been dumped, while the first shows computers that have been recycled.

B The aim here is to further guide students towards understanding the writing task, rather than giving them more reading practice. Don't worry about helping them with words and phrases in the text. Tell them to read through the first part of the text, and check that key words are understood, such as 'encouraged' and 'strict'. Then go on to the bullet points. Again, check key words like 'donate', 'charity', 'original manufacturer' and so on. Now allow students time to answer the questions in pairs or small groups. Get some ideas and add comments of your own. Avoid telling them about the recycling process, as they will see this in the flow chart.

C Give students the time they need to look at the flow chart and the instructions. They can answer the questions in pairs as suggested, or together as a class. Make sure, though, that anyone who doesn't understand speaks up. Tell students that 'refurbish' means something like 'make like new' – for example, you can 'refurbish' a kitchen.

D Remind students they are advised to spend about 20 minutes on this first writing task so that they have 40 minutes for the more challenging discursive composition. Students may feel that if they find this first task easier, they should spend a little longer on it, and gain as many marks as possible. Certainly for now, they should spend at least 30 minutes doing the task. Monitor as students work, but check more that they are organizing their reports, and using the appropriate structures and linking devices. When they have finished, allow them time to exchange and compare reports. If you collect students' reports to mark, get an idea of what they are capable of, and give constructive feedback rather than correct every mistake.

The model report is reproduced below, as well as at the back of the Course Book.

The flow chart shows what happens to unwanted IT equipment. It shows the various stages of how the equipment is collected and then prepared for either reuse or recycling. First of all, there is a request from a company or individual to collect some unwanted IT equipment. A collection is booked with a licensed waste carrier and a convenient time to collect the equipment is arranged with the donor. The equipment is then collected by the waste carrier and transported to a place where it can be prepared for reuse or recycling.

Next, any data is wiped from the equipment and it is tested by technicians. If the equipment is working properly, it can be refurbished and reused. If it is not working properly, the various parts are treated so that they are ready for recycling.

Finally, working equipment is distributed to charities or to individual people who are in need, while equipment that cannot be used is recycled.

Unit 4 Workbook answers

Reading

A   1. Text C   2. Text A   3. Text B

B   Text 1   it – their rubbish
             They – cats, seagulls and foxes
             there – all over the streets

   Text 2   It – waste
             Then – In pre-industrial times

   Text 3   these – Taking glass bottles to a bottle
             bank, giving unwanted clothes to a
             charity shop and using vegetable waste
             as compost in your garden

C   1. transition   2. measure   3. practice
      4. development   5. situation

Writing

A   1. To start with   2. This is when   3. After that
      4. like   5. Once   6. Lastly

5 Movement

Reading

Page 252

Reading

5 Movement

Reading 1: timing yourself

A Answer these questions with a partner.

1. How many texts will you have to read in the IELTS Academic Reading Module?
2. In what ways are the texts in the Academic exam more difficult than those in the General Training exam?
3. Are all the texts of equal difficulty?
4. Should you spend an equal amount of time on each text?

Exam tip: It is not easy to decide how long to spend on each part of the Reading Module. Most students plan to spend a little longer on the second text than the first, and a little longer on the third than the second. However, at your level, you may decide that you want to spend longer on the first part because you will have more chance of getting answers correct and scoring marks. Whatever you decide, it is very important that you try to improve your reading speed as much as you can.

B Read the sentence below and decide if it's true. Then answer the questions 1–6 with a partner.

Now that you have read lots of texts and know all the different types of reading task, you will know how long to spend on the various stages of the reading process for each part.

1. How long do you spend reading the heading and looking at any visual support?
2. How long do you spend skimming the text to get a general idea of what it's about?
3. How long do you spend reading the instructions and questions?
4. How long do you spend reading more carefully to complete the tasks?
5. Do you take more time to complete some types of tasks than others?
6. How long do you spend checking that your answers are spelt correctly and that you are happy with them?

Reading 2: checking answers

A Here are some possible mistakes you can make when you write your answers onto the answer sheet. Complete each with **one word only**.

1. You might _____ a word wrongly when copying it from the text.
2. You might not use a _____ letter for the name of a person, a place or a month.
3. You might use more _____ than the instructions say are allowed.
4. Your final answer might not be _____ to the examiner if you cross or rub out a previous answer.

Exam tip: Remember that in the reading exam, you do not have extra time to transfer answers. You write answers directly onto the answer sheet as you read. Nearly half of the tasks that can occur in the Reading Module involve writing words and phrases as answers. You MUST spell your answer correctly – the words that you need to use occur in the text or the summary box, so make sure you copy them correctly. You MUST NOT use more than the stated number of words. If you change an answer, rub it out or cross it out completely. Your final answer MUST be clear.

Page 253

Reading 3: preparing to read

A Answer these questions about tourism with a partner.

1. When do you think people first started travelling for pleasure?
2. When do you think tourism as we know it today really began?
3. When do you think mass tourism started to develop?

B Work in small groups. Think of examples of each of the following.

1. the benefits of tourism to tourists
2. the benefits of tourism to the people who live in the place that is visited
3. the negative impact of tourism

C Look at the pictures and answer these questions with a partner.

1. What negative effects of tourism do the pictures show?
2. Can anything be done to reduce these negative effects?

D Look at the three highlighted words in the text on the next page and the sentences in which they occur. Answer these questions.

1. Do the three words have a similar meaning, or do they all have different meanings?
2. Are the words more connected with people, or with organizations and systems?
3. What do you think the text will tell you about infrastructure, resources and facilities?

Reading 4: practise timing yourself and checking answers

A Skim the text quickly and match parts of it with some of the pictures.

B Read the text and answer the questions 1–13 that follow. Write your answers directly onto the answer sheet provided on page 255.

The Impact of Tourism

In recent years, any debate about the effect of increased travel on the environment has tended to focus mainly on issues of aviation, global warming and man-made climate change. Discussions about the negative impact of tourism in particular have centred on the issue of carbon emissions. The ever-growing number of flights that take people to more and more distant corners of the globe, and the resulting release of fossil carbon into the atmosphere is a concern, but it is certainly not the only concern.

In many parts of the world, the physical environment can be hugely affected by the passage of tourists, especially for popular destinations, where the sheer number of people visiting can simply prove too much.

Page 254

As a tourist destination becomes more popular, a period of construction frequently follows the expansion of the original settlement, usually to the detriment of the local environment. Since the beauty of the local environment is what attracted visitors in the first place, this can be disastrous. More hotels and restaurants put more strain on the local infrastructure, but they also mean more light pollution, and this can have a dramatic impact on nature. In the Greek islands, it is known that the light from the many restaurants along the coast confuses young turtles. Instead of heading for the natural light of the sea, they head inland towards the artificial light of the buildings, where there is no protection from cats and seagulls.

The seasonal invasion of tourists puts a huge additional demand on local resources, especially in more remote and poorer parts of the world. Water, energy and food, for example, are often used far less wastefully in those countries than in the west. The typical tourist generally requires far more than what locals would consider necessary by the standards of the region. Even where the infrastructure exists to meet this demand, in many places it simply does not, and the end result often leads to a gradual environmental deterioration, unless considerable new investment is made. It does not take too much additional water extraction from watercourses or groundwater to begin to see changes to rivers and wetlands. At the same time, hydroelectric schemes that aim to resolve the problem can in fact have an effect on aquatic habitats.

Tourism also increases the pressure on the arrangements for managing waste and wastewater. Even in the developed world, this can be a significant issue, especially if the resort has a small year-round local population. It is unlikely that the original facilities have been made large enough to cope with the additional load placed on them during the holiday season.

The problem of over-usage is not limited to seaside resorts. Many of the most popular national parks, mountain paths and forest walks show the signs of wear and tear, too – eroded paths, excessive litter and general damage. A growing number of people look to reduce the number of flights they take and reconnect with nature. They take their holidays in the country, closer to home, but while attempting to help resolve one problem, they unknowingly contribute to another.

The impact of tourism is far worse for many developing countries, where the existing infrastructure is basic and has difficulty coping with the demand of the local population alone. Resources can be significantly stretched by any additional visitors to the area. It is almost impossible for travellers to avoid having some kind of negative environmental impact when they travel. The very act of going on holiday inevitably means causing some kind of damage and making some demands, however unintentional.

For questions 1–7, complete these sentences with words from the text. Use **no more than three words** for each answer.

1. Most discussions about the impact of tourism focus on the number of ... that tourists make as they travel around the world.
2. When destinations become popular, the ... can be badly affected by increased building work.
3. ... , caused by an increase in buildings along the coast, sometimes results in local wildlife behaving unnaturally.
4. Western tourists often use resources more ... than people local to a poor area would.
5. Areas where infrastructure is poor need ... before they are able to cope with large numbers of visitors.
6. ... do not necessarily resolve the problem of water extraction from rivers and wetlands.
7. Even a ... in a developed part of the world will have difficulty coping with large numbers of tourists if the facilities were designed for fewer people.

Page 255

For questions 8–13, complete the summary below with words from the text. Use no more than three words for each answer.

Not only (8) ... are affected by an increase in the number of visitors. Many people choose to go on holiday closer to home and visit areas of natural beauty in the country, hoping (9) ... air pollution. However, although people do not mean to do harm, they drop (10) ... and cause (11) ... . Generally speaking, in (12) ... an increase in tourism has a more dramatic impact. Travellers do not wish to damage the environment, but it is almost impossible (13) ... doing so.

1		8	
2		9	
3		10	
4		11	
5		12	
6		13	
7			

C Check the key on page 276. How many questions did you answer correctly?

D Answer these questions about the reading task with a partner and think about how you can answer more questions correctly next time.

1. Did you answer the questions in the time that you had?
2. Did you get any answers wrong because they were not spelt correctly or transferred wrongly?
3. Did you use the correct number of words for each answer?
4. Are you happy with the number of questions you answered correctly?

Key vocabulary in context

A Find the nouns of these verbs in the text and write them in the spaces.

1. expand _____
2. settle _____
3. protect _____
4. invade _____
5. extract _____

B Now find the adjectives of these nouns in the text and write them in the spaces.

1. disaster _____
2. season _____
3. addition _____
4. excess _____

→ For focus on reading skills, go to Workbook page 57.

Objectives

- To emphasize the need for students to time themselves when they read under exam conditions.
- To practise and improve reading speed.
- To practise writing answers directly onto the answer sheet.
- To emphasize the need to check answers carefully at the end of each part.
- To practise reading a typical text from the IELTS Academic exam Reading Module.

Reading 1

At the end of the General Training course, students focused on timing themselves and checking answers. The aim here is to remind them of the difference between the two exams, which is the number of texts they will have to read as well as the additional challenge of the texts in the Academic exam.

A   This task can be conducted as pairwork as suggested, or as a whole-class discussion. Students should know the answers to the questions by now. Check answers with them.

Answers:
1. three
2. they are longer / more academic in style and in terms of grammatical structure / contain more advanced vocabulary
3. no (they get more difficult)
4. students' own answers (see exam tip)

Read the exam tip with students. They have read this advice before, and should have decided how they want to approach the Reading Module of the exam by now.

B   Give students time to read through the questions and calculate their timing. Then give them four or five minutes to compare with a partner. Monitor to check what students are saying. There are not really correct answers, so a more formal feedback phase would not be helpful here. Finish by emphasizing the need to spend at least a couple of minutes looking at headings, visual support and task instructions, as well as a minute or so checking answers at the end.

Reading 2

A   At the end of the General Training course, students looked at examples of the mistakes they might make when transferring answers or writing answers directly onto the answer sheet. This is revised with the task here. Students can work individually or with a partner. To feed back, write the answers on the board for clarity.

Answers:
1. copy   2. capital   3. words   4. clear

Read the exam tip slowly and carefully with students.

Reading 3

As students are moving from talking about exam technique straight into preparing to focus on a new topic, you might want to lead in, rather than going directly into the questions. Write 'tourism' on the board and ask students to define it. You could ask students if they think that everyone who travels is a tourist, and if not, why not.

A   It is important that students understand they are not supposed to know the correct answers to the questions. Read through the questions with them, explaining that 'mass tourism' means hundreds of thousands of people going on holiday every year. Students can talk in pairs or small groups. Get some ideas from the class to finish. Don't worry about giving long, detailed correct answers, as some information will be revealed in the unit.

Possible answers:
1. Wealthy Romans travelled for pleasure more than 2,000 years ago.
2. At the time of the Industrial Revolution in the middle of the 19th century, ordinary people had free time and money to spend for the first time.
3. Improved technology in aviation, and the affordability of flying saw an explosion in the number of people travelling abroad in the 1970s.

B The aim of this discussion is to prepare students directly for the first reading text, and also for the topic of the discursive writing later. Make sure students cover the pictures for now, and come up with their own ideas. Read through the questions, and explain any words that need checking. Set a time limit of five minutes, and then get some feedback. Write any useful key words and phrases that emerge on the board. There is no need to help with ideas for the third question, as the theme is developed in the task that follows.

Possible answers:

1. They see interesting places and learn about other cultures. / They get a break from routine.
2. They make money from tourism. / They learn about people from places they have never visited.
3. Damage to global and local environment / exploitation / dying out of traditions and customs.

C The aim now is to focus more directly on the negative impact of tourism. This is something that students might have thought less about. Give them a minute to look at the pictures, read the questions and think about what they want to say. Write any words they ask about at this stage on the board – 'coral reef' / 'litter', for example. Give students about five minutes to talk, and then get some feedback. Use the opportunity to pre-teach any key vocabulary in context – 'pollution', 'emissions', 'construction' and so on. The unit doesn't really focus on solutions to the issues, but you can ask students if they think there are any solutions, and about what happens in their own country to reduce the negative effects of mass tourism.

D The three highlighted words are near synonyms, and occur frequently in the text. Pronounce the words for students, and drill them if necessary. Tell students to read around the words in the text, but not to start reading the text from the beginning yet. Set a time limit of two minutes to stop students reading more than they should. Give them time to answer the questions in pairs, and then get some feedback.

Answers:

1. They have a very similar meaning

2. They are connected with organizations and systems.
3. that tourism puts a strain on them

Reading 4

A Although students have been well prepared for this text and should now be left on their own to complete the tasks, this matching task will give them the opportunity to relate the pictures they have been discussing directly to the text. Point out that this is not an exam task, but that doing it will give them more confidence when it comes to completing the exam tasks. Set a time limit of two minutes, and then quickly give the answers.

Answers:

Picture a matches the first paragraph.

Picture b matches the fifth paragraph.

Picture c matches the second paragraph (but also most of the text).

Picture d matches the second and third paragraphs.

Picture e matches the fifth paragraph.

Picture f is mentioned in the fifth paragraph.

B Now set a time limit of 20 minutes, and let students decide how they will time each stage of the reading and answering process. Make sure they know to use the answer sheet extract.

C Give students sufficient time to check and think about why they may have answered incorrectly, before moving on to Exercise C.

Answers: 1. flights   2. local environment
3. light pollution / artificial light   4. wastefully
5. (new) investment   6. hydroelectric schemes
7. resort   8. seaside resorts   9. to reduce
10. litter   11. damage
12. developing countries   13. to avoid

D Students will be familiar with this type of reflective process by now. Remind them that identifying what they are doing well and not doing so well is a very good way of focusing on what they can do better next time. Note that the focus here is what was specifically practised in the unit. Allow students time to reflect and complete the task, and then ask them if they are happy with the number of correct answers.

You may like to ask one student what he or she will do differently next time.

Answers:

A 1. expansion   2. settlement   3. protection
   4. invasion   5. extraction

B 1. disastrous   2. seasonal   3. additional
   4. excessive

The Workbook tasks provide further practice, with a focus on timing and checking answers.

Writing

Objectives

- To clarify the difference between the second writing tasks in the General Training and Academic exams.

- To revise the components of a good balanced discursive composition.

- To improve the all-round quality of students' discursive compositions.

- To plan and write a discursive composition suitable for the Academic exam.

Writing 1

Students had fairly rigorous practice writing compositions for the second writing task on the course for the General Training exam. They practised compositions that they would not expect to be given in the Academic exam, as well as some that are very similar to what they can expect. Students are certainly not unfamiliar with the type of composition they need to write now.

A Give students two or three minutes to answer the questions, and then ask one student to tell the class. There is no need to give an answer yourself, as the exam tip provides an answer.

Read the exam tip slowly and carefully with students. Explain that 'sophisticated' means more mature, more appropriately expressed, and with a greater range of vocabulary.

B The aim here is not necessarily to correctly identify in which exam each of the instructions would be given, but to give students a general idea of the difference between the task types. Give students time to think and individually mark each set of instructions, and then a couple of minutes to compare with a partner. Go through answers, but say that there are no set rules for this.

Answers: 1. GT   2. A   3. A   4. GT
5. A (possibly GT too)

Writing 2

A Students have previously discussed their strengths and weaknesses in writing, and this is a logical way of finishing the final Writing Module of the course. If students feel that they are confident with each of these aspects of composition writing, they will certainly be ready to tackle the Academic exam. Give them time to complete the task individually, and then a few minutes to compare. Monitor, and encourage students who have marked a lot of points with an X. You will know by now whether that is an accurate reflection of their ability.

You can finish by asking how many students have more ticks than question marks or crosses. Make sure they understand that if they wrote successful compositions for the General Training second tasks, it is only a small step now.

B Students have previously seen these instructions so should already have a clear idea of whether they think they could manage the composition or not. The text in the Reading Module provided a lot of arguments that students could use, and this should make them feel more confident.

C Read the rubric with students, briefly reminding them about the negative effects of tourism. Then give them a few minutes to list any positive effects they can think of. Don't ask them for

ideas now, as they will compare their points with the first composition.

D Tell students to read the composition, and look for the positive effects it mentions, making sure that they don't start criticizing it yet. Ask if anyone thought of the positive effects mentioned in the composition.

E Students have previously analyzed compositions and identified weaknesses, so they will know what to look for. Note here that this task guides students towards noticing elements of the writing. To avoid the two tasks becoming repetitive, set a time limit of about three minutes for the individual stage, and then about two minutes for comparing with partner. Move on to Writing 3 without asking for their ideas.

Writing 3

A If students have identified issues with the composition themselves, they should be able to go through this list of points quite quickly. If you are confident that students have discussed most of the points during the pairwork, you can go straight through the list together as a whole class. Give your own answer to clarify.

Answers: 1. No   2. Yes, generally
3. Not really   4. No   5. No
6. No, some points are made too strongly
7. No   8. No

B Give students time to read the second composition through properly. Tell them not to worry about the highlighted words for now. Note that in the task that follows, they use the list in Exercise A as a checklist, so for now tell them to sum up what they think is the biggest improvement. If you prefer, you can get students to work through this task and Exercise C as one analytical task.

C See above. Go through the answers with students to conclude that this second composition is indeed much better than the first. Almost all answers are yes (point 4 is debatable, as paragraphs are not set out clearly).

D Students have seen some of these linking devices previously, and some will be new. Don't pre-teach any of them, as the aim is for them to learn them in context by looking more carefully again at the composition. Emphasize the importance of linking words and phrases like this that introduce an opinion, and make sure students understand that using these will greatly improve their discursive compositions. Students should work individually, and then compare with a partner. End the activity when about half the class has finished. Write the answers on the board against the numbers, and deal with any queries. Remind students 'too' comes at the end of a sentence, while 'also' comes before the verb. Explain that 'all in all' is like saying 'taking everything into consideration', and is a very good way of summing up a balanced argument.

> **Answers:**   1. of course
> 2. in addition / too / also   3. all in all
> 4. though   5. personally   6. unfortunately

E If you think this will be difficult for students, and that they will struggle for ideas, work through as a whole class, adding points to the board. Start with a simple idea, such as 'Unfortunately, even the most careful travellers have some impact on the environment they visit'. Add a second point that continues the theme – 'In addition, the act of simply getting to their destination in the first place causes pollution', for example. Gradually, get more ideas from students, correcting them if their suggestions don't really work with the introductory device. Tell your students to work alone or in pairs if they need to, and monitor to check that they have understood how the linkers work.

Grammar check

Students have practised with passive forms previously, but here more advanced passive structures are the focus, and there is a definite contrast with active forms. Students may not see why an active or passive is used in some cases. Read through the two active examples, and write the passive alternatives on the board – 'more and more remote places are being visited by tourists' / 'the natural environment is spoilt'. Students should see that the first example sounds unnatural with the attention on the wrong thing. Explain that although the passive is possible in the second example, an active form is used with the pronoun 'this', which refers to the subjects that were the focus earlier in the paragraph.

Read through the passive examples, and again write the alternative active forms 'somebody needs to build an airport' / 'everywhere people feel the effects of tourism'. They should see here that the unnecessary agent is not natural.

Give students time to highlight further examples, and then to compare and discuss, but have a time limit in mind, as the aim of the module is not to make too much of the grammar point. Monitor as students work, and get them to explain why there are sometimes examples of active and passive within the same paragraph. Put a couple more examples of passive use on the board, and point out the structures – 'the south coast of Spain has been changed dramatically' (present perfect passive) / 'coral reefs are destroyed by too many people diving' (present simple). Students can check the typical errors in their own time.

F In this unit, the writing task can be found in the exam practice section at the end of the Course Book unit. See instructions for that section below.

Consolidation

Consolidation

Reading

A Mark each of these statements about your reading skills (T) true or (F) false.
   1. My reading speed is improving all the time.
   2. I feel more confident reading longer academic texts.
   3. I know how long I want to spend on each part of the Reading Module.
   4. I can usually complete the tasks in the time I have.
   5. I do not make mistakes when I write my answers onto the answer sheet.

B Correct the spelling mistakes in these words.
   1. resorces   2. facilities   3. infrastructure   4. invironment   5. preasure   6. skeme

C Fill the gaps with a word made from the root word in the box.
   1. There are arguments for and against the _____ of resorts.
   2. There is only a limited _____ demand for some products.
   3. _____ tourism is bound to have an impact on an area.
   4. Local people might see increased numbers of tourists as an _____.
   5. Travellers must try not to use local resources _____.
   6. Some events have a _____ effect on a country's economy.

   expand
   season
   excess
   invade
   waste
   disaster

Writing

A Answer these questions with a partner.
   1. Do you feel more confident about the first or second writing task in the Academic exam?
   2. What concerns do you have about the second writing task?
   3. What aspects of writing a discursive composition have you most improved?

B Without looking back to the Writing Module, complete each linking word or phrase.
   1. I think this is clear to everyone. of _____
   2. I want to add something to what I said before. a _____ / t _____ / in a _____
   3. I want to introduce a general conclusion. _____ in _____
   4. I want to make a point that is in slight contrast to something I said before. t _____
   5. This is something I know from my own experience. p _____
   6. I want to soften a negative point as I introduce it. unf _____

C Rewrite these sentences using a passive structure. Only mention the agent if necessary.
   1. People should not use water wastefully.
      Water _____
   2. Tourism has changed many small towns dramatically.
      Many _____
   3. Society can feel the effects of mass tourism across the globe.
      The effects _____

IELTS Target 5.0   259

Reading

A This is another opportunity for students to assess and discuss their reading skills, and any concerns they may have, especially about the increased challenge of the Academic exam. Once students have marked each point, they can either compare with a partner or tell you directly. Get a few students to tell you how they feel, and try to encourage anybody who is still apprehensive.

B Students can either work individually and then compare, or work with a partner. You may prefer to simply ask students to come up and write the correct spellings on the board.

Answers: 1. resources   2. facilities
3. infrastructure   4. environment   5. pressure
6. scheme

C Students have seen this type of task previously, and know that the aim is to check vocabulary retention and spelling. They should work individually, and then compare with a partner. Write the correct spellings on the board for clarity.

Answers: 1. expansion   2. seasonal
3. excessive   4. invasion   5. wastefully
6. disastrous

Writing

A This is the final opportunity for students to discuss whether or not their writing has improved, and to express any concerns, especially in terms of tackling the Academic exam. Students should talk in pairs so that everyone has the chance to express a view. Finish by asking if anyone has any particular worry that he/she wants to talk about.

B Make sure students do this without looking back at the Writing Module. They should work individually, and then compare with a partner. Either write the correct spellings on the board, or tell students to check in the Writing Module when they have finished.

Answers: 1. of course
2. also / too / in addition   3. all in all
4. though   5. personally   6. unfortunately

C Read through the instructions with students so that they are clear. They should work individually, and then compare with a partner if necessary. Either you or they can write the passive structures on the board to check.

Answers:
1. Water should not be used wastefully.
2. Many small towns have been changed dramatically by tourism.
3. The effects of mass tourism can be felt across the globe.

Exam Practice

5

Reading

A Earlier in this unit, you talked about how tourism started. Can you remember what you said?

B Now answer these questions with a partner.
1. Why did tourism develop more quickly in Britain than anywhere else?
2. Why didn't British people travel abroad until much later?
3. Do you know the names of any famous British tour operators?

C Read the text and answer questions 1–14 that follow. Write your answer directly onto the answer sheet at the bottom of the next page.

The Origins of Mass Tourism

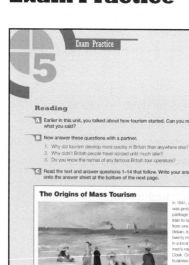

In 1841, a man organized what was probably the world's first package tour. He chartered a train to take a group of people from one town in the middle of Britain, to another town just twenty miles away, to take part in a local political event. The man's name was Thomas Cook. On that day, he saw the business potential of his idea, and he soon became a tour operator. Today, Thomas Cook is regarded as 'The father of mass tourism', and the company he founded is known throughout the world.

Other entrepreneurs followed Cook's lead, and the tourist industry grew rapidly in early Victorian Britain. At first, it was the growing numbers of wealthy middle-class people who supported it. They could afford the luxury of travel and they had the time on their hands to enjoy it. However, for mass tourism to really explode, two things needed to happen. Firstly, an improvement in transport that meant large numbers of people could quickly be taken to places of interest, and secondly, an increase in leisure time for ordinary working people, so that they, too, could enjoy the benefits of travel.

The invention of the railway was a significant development. Suddenly, the coast was in easy reach of Britain's largest industrial cities. At the same time, as the Industrial Revolution was having an impact and working conditions were improving, hundreds of thousands of people were given free days and short holiday breaks. As a result, the first holiday resorts developed in seaside towns all over the country. In the north, Blackpool and Scarborough were very popular, and in the south, Brighton, Eastbourne and Southend became frequent visiting spots for Londoners. Some resorts became known throughout Europe as the most fashionable destinations of the time.

In the 19th century, health tourism began to develop. Wealthier British holidaymakers would visit resorts in Southern Europe, and on finding the higher temperatures favourable, would decide to stay for the winter months, and in some cases forever. Some tourists began to visit places that were supposed to have health-preserving mineral waters, in the hope of treating a range of illnesses and conditions. King George III was known to have regularly visited the sea whenever he was feeling unwell.

For nearly a hundred years, however, the majority of tourism was domestic. Only the very wealthy or those who travelled for educational purposes ventured to foreign destinations. In Britain, holiday villages, like Butlins, became popular. Here, families could be beside the sea in cheap accommodation and enjoy a range of entertainment organized by the tour provider. These establishments only went into decline when the option of flying became accessible to ordinary people, and when people became confident that they could enjoy the same comforts abroad as they could closer to home.

Some of these early developments in tourism were seen in other parts of Europe, like France, Belgium and Holland, but it was in Britain that industrialization occurred more quickly, and that allowed tourism to grow in a way that was not possible elsewhere. It also allowed a greater number of wealthier people to experience overseas travel. This is reflected in the fact that all over Europe, hotels bear the names of British cities, and British kings and queens. In Nice, one of the most famous resorts on the French Riviera, the long walkway to the sea, is known to this day as the Promenade des Anglais.

For questions 1–3, decide if the information given below agrees with the information given in the passage. Write (T) true, (F) false or (NG) not given.

1. Thomas Cook discovered the business potential of tourism by chance.
2. There were several well-known tour operators in Victorian Britain.
3. Mass tourism grew because there were so many rich people in Britain.

For questions 4–6, answer these questions with words from the text. Use no more than three words for each answer.

4. Which method of transport had most impact on early tourism?
5. Which historical event allowed mass tourism to develop in Britain?
6. Which people typically visited holiday resorts in the South of England?

For questions 7–8, choose two of the following statements that are true according to the text. Write the letters on the answer sheet below.

A. Some British holidaymakers moved permanently to warmer places.
B. Some British tourists became ill when they travelled outside Britain.
C. Some people believed that a certain type of water was good for their health.
D. King George III was not a very healthy man.

For questions 9–14, complete this summary with some of the words and phrases from the box.

in Britain	escape	to see	alone	visit	afford	to fly
	abroad	in France	to learn			

For almost a century, most British people holidayed (9) ... Wealthy people or people who wanted (10) ... about foreign countries travelled (11) ... but it was not common. Holiday villages near the sea that ordinary people could (12) ... were very popular until quite recently. More people began to travel overseas when it was possible (13) ... more cheaply and travel more comfortably. The fact that early tourism developed most quickly in Britain is plain (14) ... all over Europe. Hotels and tourist attractions in many places are named after British institutions.

1		8	
2		9	
3		10	
4		11	
5		12	
6		13	
7		14	

Writing

A Look at the pictures and think about the cultural effects of tourism. Do the images show a positive or negative effect?

B Look at these instructions for a typical writing task and think about how you would answer it.

As part of a class assignment, you have been asked to write about the following topic:

A lot of people feel that increased tourism has a negative effect on the traditional lifestyles and culture of people in developing countries.

Do you agree, or do you feel that tourism benefits the way of life in those places?

Give reasons for your answer and include any relevant examples from your experience.

Write at least 250 words.

C Read these extracts from a conversation between two friends. Who do you agree more with? Compare with a partner.

Tony: Tourists bring a huge amount of money into developing countries.
Lisa: Yes, but many hotels and tourist-related businesses are run by Western companies. The money doesn't always go to the local community.

Tony: Yes, but tourists buy products that are made by local people.
Lisa: Once the local people know that tourists will buy those products, they mass produce them and gradually commercialize what was traditional art and craft.

Tony: Tourism creates a lot of jobs for local people.
Lisa: Not always. Managerial jobs often go to Westerners, while local people are given jobs serving guests or cleaning. Local people can feel exploited by tourism.

Tony: The more tourists travel, the more they learn about traditional cultures and learn to respect lifestyles that are different from their own.
Lisa: Maybe, but wealthy tourists often just want to take what a country has to offer and not learn about the local way of life. The local people actually learn more about the visitors' culture and sometimes want what wealthy tourists appear to have.

Tony: Don't you think that tourism helps people to be tolerant about the way people live in other countries?
Lisa: Not necessarily. Holidaymakers don't always respect local customs. They sometimes behave in a way that is inappropriate or even offensive to local people.

D Talk in small groups. Are there any other points you want to make about this issue?

E Decide which points from the conversation and which points of your own you want to use. Then write the composition.

_____
_____
_____
_____
_____
_____
_____
_____
_____
_____
_____
_____
_____
_____
_____
_____
_____
_____
_____
_____
_____
_____
_____
_____
_____
_____
_____
_____
_____

As this is the final unit of this short course, the exam practice section includes both reading and writing practice. Although the aim is to give students something approaching authentic exam practice, both parts have preparation stages that will boost their confidence, and make reading more enjoyable. Both parts revisit themes that students have been focusing on in the unit.

Reading

A The aim here is to remind students about the topic they started discussing at the beginning of this unit. The question can either be answered in pairs, or quickly as a whole class. Elicit some of what you told students about the Industrial Revolution, and about flights becoming cheaper in the 1970s. Avoid too lengthy a discussion or providing too many answers yourself, though, as you will teach too much of what is in the text.

B Read the questions with students, and make sure they understand that they are not expected to know the answers. Students can either answer the questions in pairs as suggested, or as a whole class. There is no need to provide answers as information is given in the text. If you think students will benefit from skimming the text to find the answers, you can allow them a couple of minutes to do so, but it would probably be better to get on with the exam practice and let them find the answers to these discussion points later.

C Students should now be left to work on their own. Set a time limit of 20 minutes, and monitor for the first couple of minutes to check that they are skimming, and then looking at the instructions and questions.

Answers: 1. T   2. NG   3. F   4. the railway
5. the Industrial Revolution   6. Londoners
7. A
8. C (the order of the letters in 7 and 8 is not important)
9. in Britain   10. to learn   11. abroad
12. afford   13. to fly   14. to see

Writing

Remind students that they previously read and talked about the environmental impact of tourism (the physical effects). Tell them they are now going to focus on the cultural impact of tourism – for example, how tourism affects people's way of life and how they think.

A Read the questions, and allow students to look at the pictures and think. Tell them that the pictures don't necessarily show a negative or a positive effect, and that they may show some aspects of both. Put them into pairs to talk or develop a class discussion. Remember that pairwork allows more students the opportunity to say something. Get a few ideas from the class to finish. You might like to ask if students think that tourists learn more from the local people in the places they visit, or if the locals learn more from the tourists.

B Students are accustomed to looking at instructions for writing tasks and asking questions. Give them time to absorb the task, and then get a general consensus as to whether it's a composition they would enjoy writing, or one they would find too challenging. Ask students if they would agree or disagree, or try to balance their argument.

C The aim of the conversation extracts is to provide students with some ideas for the composition. Although students should understand that getting ideas together and deciding what to say is an essential part of the task, some guidance with content will help them tackle this more academic, discursive composition for the first time. Tell students that the conversation is not complete, as it is more a series of short exchanges. Give them five or six minutes to read it through, and highlight points they agree or disagree with. Then give them a minute or two to compare, before getting some feedback.

An alternative approach here would be to reproduce the conversation extracts on an OHP transparency, and tell students to close their books. Make sure students know that Tony is enthusiastic about the benefits of tourism, and that Lisa is very cynical. Show Tony's comments one at a time, keeping Lisa's responses covered.

Ask students what they think Lisa will say in response to each of Tony's points, and then show them for confirmation.

D This can be a small-group discussion as suggested, or a whole-class discussion. At this point, students may not have much more to add to the argument.

E Remind students that they are advised to spend about 40 minutes on the second writing task, but that that will depend on how long they spend on the first. For now, set a time limit of 30 or 35 minutes, reminding students that much of the preparation stage has already been done.

Monitor as students work, and above all check that they are organizing their compositions and using paragraphs appropriately. Make suggestions as they work, so that their work is as successful as possible by the time they hand it in. When they have finished, allow them time to exchange and compare their work if they want to. If you collect students' compositions to mark, focus on the bigger issues that will determine the examiner's mark, rather than correct every mistake.

The model composition is reproduced below, as well as at the back of the Course Book.

The world is getting smaller, and more and more tourists are visiting developing parts of the world, as well as the more typical holiday resorts. Travellers usually visit these countries because they want to see a traditional way of life and a culture that is very different from their own. However, it could be that by visiting these places, they have more of a negative impact than a positive one.

Of course, tourists bring a lot of money into countries that are often very poor, but the hotels that they stay in are often run by Western companies and not much of the money goes to the local community. Although local people are employed in hotels, restaurants and other tourist-related businesses, managerial jobs go to Westerners. Travellers buy traditional products and souvenirs, but quickly these are mass-produced. This commercialization destroys traditional art and craft.

Many people believe that tourists try to learn something about local customs and lifestyles,

but it might be that local people actually end up learning more about Western culture. They see wealthy visitors who seem to have every material possession and they want the same. We have all seen pictures of children in poor African villages wearing Manchester United shirts and holding mobile phones. Tourists do not always respect local customs, and they sometimes behave in a way that is inappropriate or even offensive to local people. When I was on holiday in Greece, I was shocked to see how some young travellers behaved at night.

All in all, I would like to believe that tourism is of cultural benefit to both people travelling and the people in the country that is being visited. However, I am not sure that that is really the case, and I am worried that traditional lifestyles are being changed by the increased number of visitors.

Unit 5 Workbook answers

Reading

A 1. F 2. NG 3. T 4. dive shops
5. sludge 6. scuba divers
7. neighbouring coastal areas

Writing

A and B Students' own answers (they should
use the Course Book model to compare)

Mock tests

How to use these tests

There are three tests, one for each of the three sections of the course. The tests include a full Listening, Reading and Writing Module, but not a Speaking Module. It would be useful for the students if you could arrange your own Speaking Modules to complement the tests provided here.

The first and second tests are designed to be slightly more challenging than the content of the course, but not as challenging as an authentic exam. For this reason, it is best to complete the texts at the end of each section, rather than all together at the end of the course. The third test is designed to be at the level of an authentic IELTS General Training test, and should be completed at the end of the third section, i.e., at the end of the course.

It would be helpful for the students to set the tests under exam conditions, although it might be difficult to set the Listening, Reading and Writing in one day. Irrespective of other test conditions, each module should be timed strictly and students should not be allowed to use dictionaries or other resources. If you do not want to use classroom time for all three tests, they could be set as homework tasks. If you choose this option, students should be encouraged to time themselves properly.

Marking mock tests can be time-consuming. For example, several parts of the test involve writing words and phrases, and spelling needs to be correct. If an accurate assessment of the students' progress and potential to pass the exam is required, you should collect and mark the tests yourself. If, however, you are using the tests to get a rough idea of how well students are doing, they could be given a key to mark the test themselves.

A breakdown of how marks for each module are added up, the weighting of each module and how a total mark is calculated will be available on the IELTS web page, as will the IELTS band that a total mark corresponds to.

Marking

Listening

Each of the 40 questions is given one mark, and this is converted into a score on the IELTS nine-band scale.

Reading

Each of the 40 questions is given one mark, and this is converted into a score on the IELTS nine-band scale.

Writing

The Writing Module is graded according to the following four criteria:

- **Task achievement (Task 1 only):** Satisfying all the requirements of the task; presenting a clear overview of the key features

- **Task Response (Task 2 only):** Dealing with all the issues relevant to the task; taking a clear personal position, and supporting with relevant ideas and arguments

- **Coherence and Cohesion (Tasks 1 & 2):** Organization of writing; progression of information and ideas; logical linking of sentences and paragraphs

- **Grammatical Range and Accuracy (Tasks 1 & 2):** Variation in use of language; accuracy of grammar and pronunciation

The overall result is translated into a score on the IELTS nine-band scale.

Speaking

The Speaking Module is graded according to the following four criteria:

- **Fluency and Coherence:** Clarity and coherence, and fluency in expressing ideas and opinions
- **Lexical Resource:** Range of vocabulary
- **Grammatical Range and Accuracy:** Range of structures and accuracy of use
- **Pronunciation:** Ability to be understood; natural use of English pronunciation features

The overall result is translated into a score on the IELTS nine-band scale; see below.

The IELTS nine-band scale

Band 9 – Expert User

Has fully operational command of the language: appropriate, accurate and fluent, with complete understanding.

Band 8 – Very Good User

Has fully operational command of the language, with only occasional unsystematic inaccuracies and inappropriacies. Misunderstandings may occur in unfamiliar situations. Handles complex detailed argumentation well.

Band 7 – Good User

Has operational command of the language, though with occasional inaccuracies, inappropriacies and misunderstandings in some situations. Generally handles complex language well and understands detailed reasoning.

Band 6 – Competent User

Has generally effective command of the language, despite some inaccuracies, inappropriacies and misunderstandings. Can use and understand fairly complex language, particularly in familiar situations.

Band 5 – Modest User

Has partial command of the language, coping with overall meaning in most situations, though is likely to make many mistakes. Should be able to handle basic communication in own field.

Band 4 – Limited User

Basic competence is limited to familiar situations. Has frequent problems in understanding and expression. Is not able to use complex language.

Band 3 – Extremely Limited User

Conveys and understands only general meaning in very familiar situations. Frequent breakdowns in communication occur.

Band 2 – Intermittent User

No real communication is possible, except of the most basic information, using isolated words or short formulae in familiar situations and to meet immediate needs. Has great difficulty in understanding spoken and written English.

Band 1 – Non User

Essentially has no ability to use the language beyond possibly a few isolated words.

Band 0 – Did not attempt the test

No assessable information provided.

Tapescripts

Listening

Tapescript 🎧 162 (8 mins, 44 secs)

TEST 1

You will hear a number of different recordings and you will have to answer questions on what you hear. There will be time for you to read the instructions and questions and you will have a chance to check your work.

All the recordings will be played once only. The test is in four sections.

SECTION 1

Now turn to section one.
(four-second pause)

Section one. You will hear a conversation about a language course. First, you have some time to look at questions 1–5.
(fifteen-second pause)

You will see that there is an example that has been done for you. On this occasion only, the conversation relating to this will be played first.

Receptionist: Good morning, Borgheimer Language Courses. How may I help you?

Customer: Oh, yes. I contacted you some time ago about following a German course in Germany, and you advised me to take your placement test before we go any further. Well, I've done that now, so I'd like to go ahead with booking the course for this summer, if that's possible.

Receptionist: Certainly, sir. You said you took the placement test. What was the result?

Customer: I was placed at the 03 level.

Receptionist: 03. Right, that's Lower Intermediate. Fine, Mr ...?

The answer is 'Level Three or Lower Intermediate', so the course level has been filled in for you. Now we shall begin. You should answer the questions as you listen because you will not hear the recording a second time. Listen carefully and answer questions 1–5.
(four-second pause)

Customer: Pettersson. John Pettersson.

Receptionist: Could you spell that for me please, Mr Pettersson?

Customer: P, E, double T, E, R, double S, O, N.

Receptionist: That's a double T and a double S, am I right?

Customer: That's right. Now, could I ask you where the course takes place?

Receptionist: Well, we offer courses in Hamburg and Berlin. For your level, there's never a problem. There are always plenty of people for the intermediate classes.

Customer: Oh, dear. Does that mean that there might be a lot of students in my class? I wouldn't be very happy about that.

Receptionist: No, don't worry, Mr Pettersson. The maximum class size is 12, but I've never known there to be more than nine or ten in a class. It could even be five or six.

Customer: Good. Actually, I'd prefer to study in Berlin. And how long is the course?

Receptionist: Three weeks, five hours a day. Two hours only on Saturday. Sundays free.

Customer: I see, and what about accommodation?

Receptionist: There you have a choice, Mr Pettersson. You can either stay with a German family, who are used to having such guests, or you can stay on the university campus, or we can book you into a nearby bed and breakfast.

Customer: Is there a big difference in price?

Receptionist: Not really. Staying with the family works out the cheapest, and the bed and breakfast is a bit more money. Staying on the university campus comes somewhere between the two, price wise. But Berlin is not too expensive anyway.

Customer: Which do you recommend?

Receptionist: Well, if you want to practise your German and be part of a German family, I would recommend staying with a family. Our families are all hand-picked, and we've never had any sort of complaint.

Customer: Yes, I'll probably do that then. What are the dates of the course?

Receptionist: The first summer course starts on the first of June in Hamburg, and a week later in Berlin, which is what would concern you as you have chosen the Berlin course. That's the 8th of June. The next course would begin on the 2nd of July, and then ...

Customer: The second of July course would be perfect for me. Can you put me down for it now?

Receptionist: Certainly, Mr Pettersson. Can I have your address, please?

Customer: 26, Mayfield Drive, Orpington, Kent. I'm afraid I can't remember the postal code.

Receptionist: Don't worry, Mr Pettersson. I'll check on it.

(four-second pause)

Before you hear the rest of the conversation, you have some time to look at questions 6–10.
(fifteen-second pause)

Now listen and answer questions 6–10.

Customer: There are a couple of other things I'd like to ask.

Receptionist: Certainly.

Customer: What do I need to bring on the course?

Receptionist: Well, apart from the obvious, you'll need our textbooks. I'll e-mail you the name and publisher. You should be able to find it in your local bookstore. If you do have problems, call me or e-mail me, and I'll see what I can do. We provide the computers, computer disks, translation exercises and all that sort of thing, but you will need a good dictionary. We recommend Langenscheidt, which is more than adequate for your level. You don't have to go and spend a lot of money on an expensive dictionary – not yet, anyway! Maybe you will when your German reaches a very high standard.

Customer: That would be very nice. Now, finally, what about the cost of the course, and how do I pay?

Receptionist: Would you like to pay that in pounds or in euros?

Customer: Euros would be fine.

Receptionist: In that case, it's 550 euros. You can pay by credit card, if you like.

Customer: Oh, dear. I'm afraid I haven't got a credit card. How else can I pay?

Receptionist: That's not a problem, Mr Pettersson. You can pay by bank transfer.

Customer: Fine. By the way, I forgot to mention I am a full-time student.

Receptionist: Have you got a student card?

Customer: Oh, yes.

Receptionist: Then that does make a difference, you'll be pleased to hear. You are entitled to 35% off the full price. And if you can persuade a few people to join you, it would work out even cheaper.

Customer: How do you mean, exactly?

Receptionist: Well, for every five people you find, one goes free. In other words, if there are six of you, you get one free course. Of course, in reality, you would divide up the savings amongst you, presumably.

Customer: Right, well, I'll see what I can do. Thank you.

Receptionist: Not at all, Mr Pettersson, and I'm sure you'll enjoy the course. There are, of course, sightseeing possibilities. Would you like me to send you our brochure describing them?

Customer: Yes, thank you. I'd appreciate that. Anyway, thanks for your help. If I want to call back, who do I ask for?

Receptionist: Susanna. I'm here most of the time.

That is the end of section one. You now have half a minute to check your answers.
(thirty-second pause)

Now turn to section two.
(four-second pause)

Answers:
1. John Petterson
2. 12 / twelve
3. 5 / five
4. bed and breakfast
5. 8th June
6/7. C and E
8. 550
9. bank transfer
10. five

Listening

Tapescript 🎧 163 (5 mins, 19 secs)

SECTION 2

You will now hear a radio talk on agricultural regulations. First, you have some time to look at questions 11–15.
(fifteen-second pause)

Now listen carefully and answer questions 11–15.

Could there be clearer proof of the arrogance and indifference of those who are supposed to keep our food safe, than the muzzling of John Verrall? Agriculture is a business, true, and businesses have to make money, but this shows how ministers and officials put the profits of the agriculture business before the well-being of the British people.

Mr Verrall, a pharmaceutical chemist, was appointed to represent consumers on one of the many committees that advise the government on food safety. When he tried to do his job, though, and wanted to warn ministers of a danger to children's health, he was refused permission to do so.

The danger comes from hormones given to cattle in the USA, and some other countries, to make them grow faster. They speed up the animals' development to maturity, thus making meat production more profitable.

There have, however, long been fears that the hormones have horrendous effects on the people who eat them, causing diseases as serious as cancer. Once, these hormones were used on British cattle, too, but over twenty years ago, they were banned in Europe for being too dangerous.

Indeed, so concerned is the European Union that it banned imports of hormone-fed beef years ago, much to the fury of the US government, which wants to sell it all over the world.

Several years ago, the USA and Canada asked the World Trade Organization to declare the ban illegal and to punish Europe for failing to lift it. The WTO, with its long record of refusing to let environmental or safety concerns interfere with trade, agreed, imposing fines of more than $120 million a year on the EU for its refusal to back down. The British government now backs the Americans, claiming that there is no proof that hormone-fed beef does any harm.

This is where Mr Verrall comes in. He is very angry with the government, especially as their claim comes out just after a Danish study shows that growth hormones are 200 times more dangerous than was previously thought. Worried by these findings, Mr Verrall spoke to government representatives, who did nothing.
(four-second pause)

Before you hear the rest of the talk, you have some time to look at questions 16–20.
(fifteen-second pause)

Now listen and answer questions 16–20.

Not only that, but they have not been testing beef which is imported, which by law they are required to do. This directly affects the British public as about 40% of the beef British people eat comes from abroad, supposedly from countries like Brazil, which does not allow the use of growth hormones. Brazilian beef is stocked by some British supermarkets and widely used in catering. Yet when a Brazilian farm was recently visited by EU inspectors, a large stockpile of this banned substance was found.

This is not the first food scandal we have had in our country. Take the present concern over a well-known chocolate company. Several months ago, the company found out that its sweets were contaminated with a rare form of salmonella, but they did nothing about it, leaving their sweets in the shops to be bought by the unsuspecting public. It was not until five months later, when several children had suffered food poisoning, that the chocolate bars were removed from the shelves. It makes you wonder how many other dangerous foods have been allowed onto our plates.

That is the end of section two. You now have half a minute to check your answers.
(thirty-second pause)

Now turn to section three.
(four-second pause)

Answers:
11. profits
12. grow faster
13. 20 / twenty years
14. illegal
15. 200 / two hundred times
16. imported
17. 40% / forty per cent
18. (growth) hormones
19. large stockpile / quantity
20. a rare form

Listening

Tapescript 🎧 **164** (7 mins, 0 secs)

SECTION 3

You will hear a conversation between a tutor and two students, Amanda and Jake. First, you have some time to look at questions 21–25.
(fifteen-second pause)

Now listen carefully and answer questions 21–25.

Tutor: So, Jake and Amanda, how did the project go?

Amanda: Very well, I think, Dr Hinton. I certainly learnt a lot and enjoyed myself at the same time.

Jake: Me too.

Tutor: So, remind me. What was your project about?

Jake: Basically, what makes successful people – let's call them 'top achievers' – successful.

Amanda: Yes, how are they different from us? What do they do that other, less successful people, don't do?

Tutor: Interesting, and did you come to any conclusions?

Amanda: Quite a few, actually.

Tutor: Good. Share some with me, then.

Jake: Well, I'd always thought that a top achiever would be the sort of person who would bring work home every night and slave over it, but it appears not. Those types tend to peak early and then go into decline. They become addicted to work itself, with much less concern for results. We found that high achievers were certainly ready to work hard, but within strict limits. They knew how to relax, could leave their work at the office, prized close friends and family life, and spent a healthy amount of time with their children and friends.

Tutor: There's a lesson for us all there. Anyway, go on.

Amanda: It's also very important to choose a career which you enjoy, not just one that pays well, or which assures you of a pension many years down the line.

Tutor: Surely that's important though, Amanda?

Amanda: Yes, I agree, but being happy in your work is far more important than anything else. Top achievers spend over two-thirds of their working hours on doing work they truly prefer, and only one-third on disliked chores. They want internal satisfaction, not just external rewards, such as pay rises and promotions.

(four-second pause)

Before you hear the rest of the conversation, you have some time to look at questions 26–30.

(fifteen-second pause)

Now listen and answer questions 26–30.

Jake: Actually, in the end they often have both because they enjoy what they are doing, so their work is better and their rewards higher.

Tutor: Yes, Jake, that certainly makes sense. Now, can I ask you something? Do high achievers, as you call them, take many risks?

Jake: Yes and no. I interviewed one business executive who told me he was able to take risks because he carefully considered how he could salvage the situation if it all went wrong. He imagined the worst that could happen, and if he could live with that, he went ahead. If not, he didn't take the chance. Other people prefer to stay in what I heard described as the 'comfort zone'-setting for security, even if it means settling for mediocrity and boredom, too.

Tutor: Would you call top achievers 'perfectionists'?

Amanda: Contrary to what I expected, no, I wouldn't. We came to the conclusion that a lot of ambitious and hard-working people are so obsessed with perfection that they actually turn out very little work.

I happen to know a university teacher, a friend of my mother's, who has spent over ten years preparing a study about a playwright. She is so worried that she has missed something, she still hasn't sent the manuscript to a publisher. Meanwhile, the playwright, who was at the height of his fame when the project began, has faded from public view. The woman's study, even if finally published, will interest few people.

Tutor: So, what has this got to do with top achievers?

Amanda: Well, top achievers are almost always free of the compulsion to be perfect. They don't think of their mistakes as failures. Instead, they learn from them, so they can do better next time.

Tutor: Hmm ..., well, would you call them competitive?

Jake: High performers focus more on bettering their own previous efforts than on beating competitors. In fact, I, or we, came to the conclusion that worrying too much about a competitor's abilities – and possible superiority – can be self-defeating.

Amanda: Yes, and we found that top achievers tend to be team players, rather than loners. They recognize that groups can solve certain complicated problems better than individuals and are eager to let other people do part of the work.

Jake: Yes. Loners, who are often over-concerned about rivals, can't delegate important work or decision-making. Their performance is limited because they must do everything themselves.

Tutor: Well, it looks as if you two have done a thorough job, and learnt something into the bargain, too. Now, there are just a couple of points I'd like to clarify with you ...

That is the end of section three. You now have half a minute to check your answers.

(thirty-second pause)

Now turn to section four.

(four-second pause)

Listening

Tapescript 🎧 **165** (5 mins, 21 secs)

SECTION 4

You will hear a talk on Seasonal Affective Disorder. First, you have some time to look at questions 31–40.
(fifteen-second pause)

Now listen carefully and answer questions 31–40.

In the past few years a new condition has been identified and given a name – SAD, short for Seasonal Affective Disorder. This is now recognized as a distinct kind of clinical depression, where people become depressed at the onset of winter, accompanied by a craving for sweet things, causing weight gain. Each spring and summer would then bring on almost maniacal highs, and feelings of boundless energy and happiness.

Experiments to combat this depression showed that increased exposure to bright light in humans could suppress their production of a darkness-related hormone called melatonin. The light needed to induce this change was about 2,000 lux, or about four times brighter than ordinary household lighting.

It was then calculated that if bright light could suppress melatonin secretion, then it might have other effects on the brain, including the reversal of symptoms of depression. While melatonin's precise role in SAD has not been pinned down, the theory led to effective treatment.

Not surprisingly, SAD affects more people where winter nights are longer and days shorter. In the UK, an estimated half a million adults develop full-blown SAD in winter, and twice this number suffer the milder condition called sub-syndromal SAD. About 80% of sufferers improve when given light therapy, and improvement usually comes within two to four days. Scientists are still unsure why winter depression happens, but more than a decade of research has turned up some surprising findings.

Nearly 80% of SAD victims are women. Researchers are uncertain why this is so. SAD can affect people at any age, but typically it begins around the age of twenty and becomes less common between 40 and 50. SAD is comparatively rare in children and adolescents, but so far researchers have been unable to come up with a logical reason for this. As many as half of SAD sufferers have at least one family member with depressive illness, suggesting that the depression has a genetic component.

Some patients experience shifts in their body clocks when they're depressed in winter. They are 'morning people' at one time of the year, and become 'evening people' at another. What is the underlying difference between SAD sufferers and others? A clue can be found in carbohydrate craving, a common symptom. People often become obsessed with chocolate, for example. Carbohydrates alter brain chemistry by increasing the level of a soothing chemical called serotonin, a neurotransmitter that carries signals between brain cells. SAD sufferers crave carbohydrates because they may need serotonin to lift their mood. This craving can be intense – in fact, an addiction.

It may be that the serotonin system of the brain has problems regulating itself during the winter. Some SAD sufferers respond well to the drug Prozac, thought to influence the brain's serotonin-using system.

Other brain chemicals and hormones probably play a role in winter depression. Another neurotransmitter, dopamine, for example, may be inadequate in certain cases. Researchers hope to uncover clues to SAD's secret by probing similarities between SAD and hibernation. Though no valid link between the two has been established, some SAD patients say they feel like hibernating animals. SAD sufferers tend to put on fat in autumn and early winter, roughly the time when such hibernators as bears and squirrels do.

That is the end of section four. You now have half a minute to check your answers.
(thirty-second pause)

That is the end of the listening test. In the IELTS test, you would now have ten minutes to transfer your answers to the listening answer sheet.

Answers
31. A
32. C
33. A
34. C
35. genetic component
36. carbohydrate / chocolate
37. soothing
38. (the) winter
39. inadequate
40. hibernators

Reading

Part 1
1. E   2. A   3. H   4. F   5. standing time
6. hot spots   7. bacteria   8. microwave safe
9. T   10. F   11. F   12. NG   13. T   14. ID
15. date of birth   16. performances

Part 2
17. Section A: iii
18. Section B: viii
19. Section C: i
20. Section D: ii
21. Section E: vi
22. Section F: v
23. C   24. B   25. A   26. B   27. C   28. B
29. C   30. B

Part 3
31. G   32. D   33. H   34. E
35. fixed focus   36. (about) two feet   37. smile
38. face   39. an adult   40. clearly

Listening

Tapescript 🎧 **166** (6 mins, 40 secs)

TEST 2

You will hear a number of different recordings and you will have to answer questions on what you hear. There will be time for you to read the instructions and questions and you will have a chance to check your work.

All the recordings will be played once only. The test is in four sections.

SECTION 1

Now turn to section one.
(four-second pause)

Section one. You will hear a conversation between a university counsellor and two students, Joseph and Kara. First, you have some time to look at questions 1–5.
(fifteen-second pause)

Now we shall begin. You should answer the questions as you listen because you will not hear the recording a second time. Listen carefully and answer questions 1–5.
(four-second pause)

Counsellor: Hi, Joseph, how are you today?

Joseph: Fine, thanks.

Counsellor: And Kara, how are you?

Kara: Good.

Counsellor: As we discussed on the phone earlier, I wanted to speak with both of you about the subjects you have chosen to study, and how you are managing your time. OK?

Joseph: Yes.

Kara: I think so.

Counsellor: OK, so I'll start with Kara. You've been here for how many months now?

Kara: I've been here for six months.

Counsellor: How are you finding it?

Kara: It's good. I'm enjoying the course.

Counsellor: And what about life outside? Are you making friends and socializing?

Kara: Not really. People here are quite closed. They don't talk to you.

Counsellor: I see. So, what do you do after classes?

Kara: I usually go home and study, and I might go out for a walk, but never really with anyone. Sometimes my roommate, Louisa, comes with me, but she always seems to be busy.

Counsellor: How is this affecting your schoolwork?

Kara: I don't think it is, but I miss home.

Counsellor: Kara, what I suggest for now is that you look into joining one of the social clubs on campus. There are a variety of them. You can go camping, skiing, snorkelling, painting, dancing, reading, horse riding, rowing. There's a list on the school website. Have a look and work out which one you're interested in, and which suits your timetable. You'll meet friends that way, and people who have the same career interests as you. As for the subjects you've chosen for a career in microbiology, I think you should look into dropping one of your subjects and picking it up again next year as a minor. You have a lot on your plate and this will just cause great pressure. It doesn't mean that you aren't coping, but you're doing about ten hours more than the average student a week. Think about it and we can make another appointment to discuss it. When are you free?

Kara: I have an hour free usually on Wednesdays at 11.30.

Counsellor: OK. Good. Come to my office at 11.45 and wait in reception. OK?

Kara: OK. I'll see you then.

(four-second pause)

Before you hear the rest of the conversation, you have some time to look at questions 6–10.
(fifteen-second pause)

Now listen and answer questions 6–10.

Counsellor: Joseph, how are you finding the university?

Joseph: I love it. It's very different from home. Life here is very much focused on study and also socializing through sport. People have been very friendly and curious about my culture.

Counsellor: So, you've managed to integrate well?

Joseph: I think so. I've joined the rugby team – something I'd never thought I'd be interested in.

Counsellor: And how are your studies going?

Joseph: I think I'm doing well. I have a few assignments that need some work, but overall I'm coping.

Counsellor: That's good. I'm happy that you're enjoying the university, but remember, don't let your schoolwork get too far behind, because it will pile up, and before you know it, you will be late handing in work. You know that there's a penalty for handing in work late?

Joseph: No, I didn't.

Counsellor: You would have been told at the start of the course, during orientation.

Joseph: I don't remember.

Counsellor: You need to remember these things. They are very important. You might be an excellent student, but if you consistently hand in work late, you'll be penalized and you might end up losing your degree over it. That's a lot of years of work, OK?

Joseph: Yes, I'll remember that.

Counsellor: And also remember that you have to attend 90% of your classes. So far, you have missed five tutorials. Be careful here. These could also cost you your degree. Is there any particular reason you missed these classes?

Joseph: I'd been training for our rugby match the night before and well, we went out afterwards, and I slept past my alarm clock.

Counsellor: Joseph. I know this culture must be very different from where you come from, but please try and be a little more conservative with your time.

I think maybe you should spend more time on your studies and less time on socializing. The subjects you've chosen are intensive. I want you to spend three hours a night studying before you decide to do anything else. I'll make an appointment to see you in a month, and we can assess your progress. I'll give you my business card. All my contact details are there. Call me in three weeks to organize another meeting. Do you have any questions for me?

Joseph: No, none.

Counsellor: OK, I'll see you in a month.

That is the end of section one. You now have half a minute to check your answers.
(thirty-second pause)

Now turn to section two.
(four-second pause)

Answers:
1. six / 6 months
2. (quite) closed
3. Louisa
4. campus
5. great pressure
6. through sport
7. the rugby team
8. a penalty
9. five / 5 tutorials
10. intensive

Listening

Tapescript 🎧 **167** (4 mins, 21 secs)

SECTION 2

You will now listen to a talk on bicycles. First, you have some time to look at questions 11–20.
(fifteen-second pause)

Now listen carefully and answer questions 11–20.

Today, we're going to talk about the latest bikes for professionals and novices. There's something to suit everyone from price to function.

The Atlantis is a touring frame. It's also perfect for commuting and trail riding, and anything short of super-fast road riding. The tubes are stout, to take touring loads and trail abuses. The tyre clearances are majestic, so you can fit tires up to 2.35 inches. It's designed for cantilevers or V-brakes. If you have to limit yourself to just one bike, and you want to be able to ride just about anywhere, this is the bike to be on. It is our most popular model for just that reason, and there isn't an unhappy Atlantis owner in the land.

The Rambouillet, our all-around road bike, is available either as a frame with fork and headset for $1,400, or as a complete bike, for $2,300. Compared to the Atlantis it is a lighter frame, not intended for loaded touring or rough trail riding. As a road bike, it has sidepull brakes.

The Quickbeam is our version of the single-speed bike. We've done it a little better, though. The crankset has a 42/34 combination, running an 18-toothed freewheel cog in the rear. And the rear hub is threaded opposite the driveside, so you can install a fixed cog of your own choice. In essence, you can have four speeds on the Quickbeam, if you choose. The Quickbeam is available as a frame with fork and headset, for $900, or as a complete bike, for $1,300. This is a rugged, versatile bike that you can ride on the road, as well as on rough trail.

The Saluki is our roadish, light-touring/randonneuring frame. It's designed for 650B wheels. If '650B' means anything to you, you'll either love it or think it's marketing suicide. If you're new to 650B and a follower, you won't want it. If you're new and a rebel, you will.

Now, I'll just talk a little about saddle comfort. The road bike, for the most part, has turned into a high-tech, uncomfortable machine, and the proof is all around us. Look through any bike magazine or catalogue and you'll see the saddle up to six inches higher than the handlebars. It is impossible to be comfortable on such a bike. It forces you to lean forward, putting more weight on your groin, hands and arms. People ride these bikes with straight, locked-out arms, and wake up with aching backs. They endure it, get used to it or buy recumbents.

When we custom-design a bike for you, you'll be able to get a comfortable position. Your back will be between 45 and 50 degrees and there will be a noticeable bend in the arms, and most importantly, your arms won't be supporting your body weight. You won't have to look up to look ahead, because you won't be hunched over and low. That means our bikes are more accessible for riding on the flats, or even for short climbs. We consider this when we design and build your custom frame.

That is the end of section two. You now have half a minute to check your answers.
(thirty-second pause)

Now turn to section three.
(four-second pause)

Answers:
11. function
12. $2,300
13. single-speed
14. 42/34 or 42:34
15. rough trail
16. 650B
17. rebel
18. saddle
19. aching
20. custom design

Listening

Tapescript 🎧 **168** (7 mins, 40 secs)

SECTION 3

You will hear a conversation between two students, David and Claire. First, you have some time to look at questions 21–24.
(fifteen-second pause)

Now listen carefully and answer questions 21–24.

Claire: Hi, David. How are you going with your History studies?

David: Very well. I've actually finished it.

Claire: That's great. What era did you write on?

David: I researched Roman London, something I never thought I'd be interested in.

Claire: That sounds interesting.

David: I wanted to tie it in to the work I've been doing on engineering, and I found it fascinating, and learnt many things along the way.

Claire: Such as?

David: Well, although there were prehistoric settlements throughout the vast area now called London, strangely enough no evidence has yet been found for any such community at the northern end of London Bridge, where the present city grew up.

Claire: The origins of London lie in Roman times, right?

David: Right. When the Romans invaded Britain in 43 AD, they moved north from the Kentish coast and traversed the Thames in the London region, clashing with the local tribesmen just to the north. It has been suggested that the soldiers crossed the river at Lambeth, but it was further downstream that they built a permanent wooden bridge, just east of the present London Bridge, in more settled times some seven years later. As a focal point of the Roman road system, it was the bridge which attracted settlers and led to London's inevitable growth.

Claire: So, London Bridge has been there for hundreds of years?

David: Yes, and though the regularity of London's original street grid may indicate that the initial inhabitants were the military, trade and commerce soon followed. The London Thames was deep and still within the tidal zone – an ideal place for the berthing of ships.

Claire: What other industry did they have?

David: Well, as the area was also well-drained and low-lying, it was geologically suitable for brickmaking. There was soon a flourishing city called Londinium in the area where the Monument now stands.

Claire: Londinium? That's Latin.

David: That's what I thought, too, but the name itself is Celtic, not Latin, and may originally have referred merely to a previous farmstead on the site.

(four-second pause)

Before you hear the rest of the conversation, you have some time to look at questions 25–32.

(fifteen-second pause)

Now listen and answer questions 25–32.

Claire: Wasn't London burnt to the ground at some stage?

David: It happened in AD 60, by the forces of Queen Boudicca of the Iceni tribe, from modern Norfolk, when she led a major revolt against Roman rule. The governor, Suetonius Paulinus, who was busy exterminating the Druids in north Wales, marched his troops south in an attempt to save London but, seeing the size of Boudicca's approaching army, decided he could not mount an adequate defence and evacuated the city instead. Not everyone managed to escape though, and many were massacred.

Claire: What about the beautiful old architecture? Did you research that, too?

David: I sure did. The major symbol of Roman rule was the Temple of the Imperial Cult. Emperor worship was administered by the Provincial Council, whose headquarters appear to have been in London by AD 100. A member of its staff, named Anencletus, buried his wife on Ludgate Hill around this time. Pagan worship flourished within the cosmopolitan city. A temple to the mysterious Eastern god, Mithras, was found at Bucklersbury House and is displayed nearby.

Claire: I quite like St Paul's.

David: Traditionally, St Paul's cathedral stands on the site of a Temple of Diana. Other significant buildings also began to appear in the late 1st century, at a time when the city was expanding rapidly. The forum, a marketplace and basilica, which housed the law-courts complex at Leadenhall Market, was erected, and then quickly replanned as the largest such complex north of the Alps. The forum was much bigger than today's Trafalgar Square.

Claire: Who was in charge of all the town planning at the time?

David: Procurator Agricola. He encouraged the use of bath houses and had a grand public suite made, which has now been excavated in Upper Thames Street. They were as much a social venue as a place to bathe. There was a smaller version at Cheapside and, in later centuries, private bath houses were also built. Another popular attraction was the wooden amphitheatre erected on the north-western outskirts of the city. It's possible that gladiatorial shows were put on here, though lesser public sports, like bear-baiting, may have been more regular.

Claire: I thought that happened mainly in the Colisseum in Rome, but I guess London being settled by the Romans explains their lust for blood.

David: By about AD 200, the administration of Britain was divided in two. York became the capital of Britannia Inferior and London of Britannia Superior. Around the same time, the city also acquired its famous walls, probably about 20ft high.

Claire: Why did they build such high walls?

David: It was a protective measure which may have been due to civil war, initiated when Governor Clodius Albinus tried to claim the Imperial Crown in Rome.

Claire: Was Paganism still predominant then?

David: Yes, but Christianity appears to have reached the province at an early date and, only a year after the religion became officially tolerated in the Empire, London had its own Bishop, Restitutus, who is known to have attended the Imperial Council of Arles.

Claire: You really delved deep. I think you'll do well on your tutorial paper. Good luck, David.

David: Thanks.

That is the end of section three. You now have half a minute to check your answers.
(thirty-second pause)

Now turn to section four.
(four-second pause)

Answers:
21. B
22. B
23. C
24. C
25. Norfolk
26. evacuated
27. Pagan
28. Trafalgar Square
29. A social venue
30. Bear-baiting
31/32. A and D

Listening

Tapescript 🎧 **169** (5 mins, 19 secs)

SECTION 4

You will hear a lecture about staying healthy in university. First, you have some time to look at questions 33–40.
(fifteen-second pause)

Now listen carefully and answer questions 33–40.

Peter: Good morning, all. Welcome to our regular lecture on health issues. This series of lectures is organized by the Students' Union, and is part of an attempt to help you stay healthy while coping with study and social life at the same time. It's a great pleasure to welcome back Ms Mary Kirk, who is a professional health advisor and physical education officer.

Mary Kirk: Thank you, Peter, for the introduction. It's a pleasure to be back. Today we're going to discuss the benefits of exercise. University life is hectic and stressful. It also involves a lot of sedentary work, that is, sitting for many hours at a time. What I'd like to focus on is how to approach exercise, not only from the aspect of health benefits, but also as a form of stress relief. I know it's hard to organize your time around studies and socializing, but you can socialize while exercising. If you have an hour free in the morning, afternoon or evening, it would be a good idea to get together with your friends and create a sports team. The grounds of the university are ample enough to support every student's need to become active. There are also readily available facilities at your disposal, such as a football field, tennis and badminton courts. There's also a swimming centre, and within that building is a gymnasium with a variety of programmes, such as aerobics and weight training. If the idea of attending one of these facilities seems daunting, then you can walk along the river. Oh, and that reminds me, the university also offers rowing. If there is a sport that you're interested in that's not on offer, you can approach either your Student Union representative or speak with Sports Administration Manager, Mr Lawrence Cavendish. Now, I want to talk about why exercise is beneficial physically and emotionally. The obvious results are physical. You can keep fit by using muscles that ordinarily don't get used in the classroom. The health benefits are astronomical. You'll live longer, be happier and look good. By building muscle, you strengthen your bones – a definite advantage for women in their later stages of life, as women are prone to osteoporosis. It also strengthens your heart. Yes, don't forget your heart is a muscle, and the more exercise you do and the harder you work, the more blood is pumped from your heart to your brain. Now, this brings me to the psychological advantages of exercise. When we are active, endorphins are released into our brain. An endorphin is a chemical that is released when your heart rate is pumping beyond its normal capacity. It's the same as adrenaline. You can actually feel when endorphins kick in. You feel a rush, almost a high. The benefits of this are numerous.

Your brain works at peak capacity for a longer period of time, your awareness is maximized and the fatigue you usually feel at 4 o'clock in the afternoon are non-existent. In one word, exercise makes you 'sharp'. Now, I'm not saying you should overdo exercise, because too much of anything can be dangerous, but if you think about your daily routine, you spend about six hours a day in lectures and another two or more hours studying. That's a long time to be sitting. And that is a long time for your body not to be moving around, so try and find at least one hour a day to get some exercise. If you can't fit in one hour a day, try one hour every second day or half an hour a day. You will see rewards instantly. You'll feel great and look great. This I can promise you.

That is the end of section four. You now have half a minute to check your answers.
(thirty-second pause)

That is the end of the listening test. In the IELTS test, you would now have ten minutes to transfer your answers to the listening answer sheet.

Answers:
33. B
34. C
35. C
36. Sports Administration
37. strengthen your bones
38. at peak capacity
39. C
40. B

Reading

Part 1
1. A   2. C   3. B   4. A   5. C   6. E   7. C
8. A   9. G   10. D   11. sell food   12. fresher
13. pick   14. likely   15. visited   16. quality

Part 2
17. T   18. F   19. NG   20. F   21. NG   22. T
23. F   24. opportunity   25. information
26. successful   27. general public
28. qualities and skills
29. confirm the appointment   30. Appearance
31. body language

Part 3
32. C   33. A   34. C   35. B   36. valuable time
37. too expensive   38. follow   39. destroy
40. benefit

Listening

Tapescript 🎧 **170** (7 mins, 7 secs)

TEST 3

You will hear a number of different recordings and you will have to answer questions on what you hear. There will be time for you to read the instructions and questions and you will have a chance to check your work.

All the recordings will be played once only. The test is in four sections.

SECTION 1

Now turn to section one.
(four-second pause)

Section one. You will hear three conversations. The first and the third between two students, and the second between a student and a clerk. First, you have some time to look at questions 1–5.
(fifteen-second pause)

Now we shall begin. You should answer the questions as you listen because you will not hear the recording a second time. Listen carefully and answer questions 1–5.
(four-second pause)

Phoebe: Hi. It's Mike, isn't it?
Mike: Yes, and you're …
Phoebe: Phoebe.

Mike: Phoebe. Right. Where are you headed?

Phoebe: I'm looking for the Main Hall.

Mike: So am I. Are you going there to register for next year?

Phoebe: Yes. I was told to go to Administrations and fill in an application form.

Mike: That's what I'm about to do. I went to Information and they told me it was at the end of this corridor. Then we have to turn left, and immediately right. That should lead us to the exit, where opposite we should find the entrance to ground level, Main Hall. It's a big old red building. From there, we need to go to the first level, and then follow the signs. Apparently, it's the second office opposite the foyer. It would be pretty hard to miss.

Phoebe: That sounds easy. It shouldn't be too hard to find. Well, since we're both heading in that direction, let's go together.

Mike: Hopefully it won't take too long. I haven't had anything to eat and I'm starving.

Phoebe: Me too.

Mike: Well, how about I go to the canteen and get us something while you make your way to the Main Hall? I'm sure there's going to be quite a wait. There always is. I can meet you there.

Phoebe: Sounds like a good plan.

Mike: What do you want me to get you?

Phoebe: Um, how about a chicken and salad roll and a drink?

Mike: OK. What if they don't have a chicken and salad roll?

Phoebe: Anything similar, like ham and salad, or just plain salad and cheese. Oh, and don't forget the drink. I feel so dehydrated.

Mike: No problem. What type of drink?

Phoebe: I don't know. Um …

Mike: How about a Coke?

Phoebe: No, nothing like that. Something healthier.

Mike: An orange juice.

Phoebe: They're usually full of sugar, unless you get it freshly squeezed.

Mike: Water?

Phoebe: Yes. That's perfect. Here, take two pounds. That should cover it. If it's more, I'll give it to you when you get back. I only have a twenty, and you know that they get cranky if you give them large notes.

Mike: OK. See you in five minutes.

(four-second pause)

Before you hear the second conversation, you have some time to look at questions 6–10.
(fifteen-second pause)

Now listen and answer questions 6–10.

Phoebe: Hi, I'm here to register for first-year Economics.

Clerk: I'll just have to fill out this form for our records. What's your name?

Phoebe: Phoebe Payne.

Clerk: Can you spell that for me?

Phoebe: Sure. P-H-O-E-B-E P-A-Y-N-E.

Clerk: Your address?

Phoebe: 6 Wainright Avenue, that's W-A-I-N-R-I-G-H-T, Nottingham.

Clerk: Nottingham. And your phone number?

Phoebe: It's not connected yet. I've just moved in.

Clerk: OK, when you get your phone connected, contact us. I'll just make a note that your phone number is to be advised.

Phoebe: I'll do that.

Clerk: What course were you doing? Law?

Phoebe: No, Economics. First-year.

Clerk: First-year Economics.

Phoebe: Yes, that's right.

Clerk: OK. Take this card across to the Economics Department and get it stamped, and then you need to come back here to pay your fees.

Phoebe: I've made an arrangement to pay in instalments.

Clerk: Do you have any documentation verifying that?

Phoebe: Yes, I have a statement from Administration.

Clerk: OK, when you return, we'll have a look at it.

Phoebe: Thank you very much.

(four-second pause)

Before you hear the next conversation, you have some time to look at questions 11 and 12.
(fifteen-second pause)

Mike: Here you are.

Phoebe: It was quicker than I thought, but I have to get this card stamped and return here to organize my fees.

Mike: That's good. It means that I won't have to wait long, either.

Phoebe: How did you get on?

Mike: What with? Oh, the food. Well, there wasn't much left so I got you a cheese and tomato sandwich and water.

Phoebe: That's fine. Do I owe you any more?

Mike: No, I need to give you back three pounds.

Phoebe: But I only gave you two.

Mike: Oh, yeah. I thought you gave me a fiver. OK, so we're square. So, what do I have to do?

Phoebe: Go to the desk and give your personal details. Then, they'll give you a card that you need to take to your faculty. What's your major?

Mike: Environmental Science.

Phoebe: OK, so you'll have to take the card to the Environmental Science Faculty and get the card stamped, return to Administration in the Main Hall and organize your fees.

Mike: And that's it?

Phoebe: Yes, that means you're registered. Then we receive a letter with the details of our course, where we'll be informed to go to the notice board, or online to find out when and where our lectures are.

Mike: OK. Let's have this bite to eat first.

That is the end of section one. You now have half a minute to check your answers.
(thirty-second pause)

Now turn to section two.
(four-second pause)

Answers:
1. C
2. B
3. A
4. C
5. C

6. Phoebe Payne
7. 6 Wainwright Avenue
8. Nottingham
9. not connected (yet)
10. (first-year) Economics
11. C
12. A

Listening

Tapescript 🎧 171 (5 mins, 2 secs)

SECTION 2

You will now hear a speaker talking about student loans. First, you have some time to look at questions 13–21.
(fifteen-second pause)

Now listen carefully and answer questions 13–21.

Thanks for turning up today, and welcome to this short talk on student loans. What you'll hear from me today are a few starting points, which should guide you in the right direction for what is suited for you. I'm assuming that most of you have an account at a bank or building society that you can draw funds from. These funds will either be your own or through a loan you may have with the bank. You may even have a credit card you can use. If you don't have a bank account, I suggest you open one with one of the major banks. It's the best option, as you will find major banks have more outlets. Within the city and in close proximity to the university, are HSBC in City Plaza, Barclays in Ragdale Square, National Westminster in Preston Park and Halifax in Hope Street. At this stage, I just want to inform international students that not all the services available for resident students will be available to you. As international students, you need to provide documentation stating that you have funds available to see you through the duration of your study. Different banks have different policies, so search out the one that will benefit you the most. You will also need to provide a photocopy of your passport and certification of your enrolment in the university.

The most common way of taking out a student loan is either through the university or through a banking institution. If you decide to go with the university, again, you need to supply certification of enrolment and passport if you're an international student, or if you're a resident, you will only need the enrolment details. One word of warning is that you need to be clear on the interest you will be paying on your loan. The interest level through some universities is almost as much as the loan itself, so if you borrow ten thousand pounds you might have to pay back close to twenty. Also, with student loans through the university, you have a limited time to pay them back and this time is not flexible. You might have only one year, you might have five. As I said, different universities have different policies. This university, for example, has an interest rate of 23.5%. It's quite high, but not as high as many of the other larger universities. The other option is to take out a loan through your bank. You will find that most banks will have lower interest rates than the university. They average roughly between 14.5–18.5%. Banks also give you an option of over how many years you want to make repayments. You can basically choose to pay it back in a year or in ten – even more if you are finding it difficult. Make sure you have an account with the bank you decide to go with. Either a current account or a savings account is enough. With either of these accounts, you can use your card to make withdrawals and deposits from automatic teller machines at any time, and make payments over the Internet if you choose. You can also use Maestro, one of the systems which automatically take the money from your account at a time that you have specifically stated, and deposits it into a nominated account of your choice. You might decide to have 150 pounds taken out each month, and each month this is what will happen. Also, check what fees apply with what services. Some services are free of charge, but they are few and far between. OK, so that's all from me. If there are any questions related to what I've covered today, please raise your hand.

That is the end of section two. You now have half a minute to check your answers.
(thirty-second pause)

Now turn to section three.
(four-second pause)

Answers:
13. Hope Street
14. documentation
15. certification
16. limited / not flexible
17. 23.5%
18. current account
19. savings account
20. withdrawals and deposits
21. automatically take

Listening

Tapescript 🎧 **172** (5 mins, 42 secs)
SECTION 3

You will hear a dialogue between two students, David and Jim. First, you have some time to look at questions 22–25.
(fifteen-second pause)

Now listen carefully and answer questions 22–25.

David: Hi, Jim.

Jim: Hi, David! I'm glad I found you. I've got a topic for our presentation next month.

David: What is it?

Jim: I thought it would be a good idea to talk about glass and how it's recycled.

David: That doesn't sound very interesting.

Jim: That's what I thought, but it is. Did you know that glass has been around since as early as 4000 BC, when glass was used in the Middle East as a glaze to decorate beads?

David: Is it really that old?

Jim: Yes, and by 1550 BC, coloured glass vessels were widespread and used for cooking and drinking. The earliest-known clear glass is a vase found in Nineveh in Assyria, dating from around 800 BC, which is now in the British Museum here in London.

David: You know, I think I've seen that. I was at the British Museum a couple of months ago with Lisa.

Jim: We don't realize how valuable glass was.

It wasn't used widely back then. Until the 18th and 19th centuries, glass was very expensive and was used for limited applications, such as stained glass windows for churches. Large-scale glass manufacturing began with the Industrial Revolution, with the mass production of glass containers beginning at the onset of the 20th century, and glass light bulb production automated in 1926.

David: How expensive?

Jim: I don't know, but nowadays glass is much less expensive, and is taken for granted as a packaging material, in addition to its use in windows and other applications.

David: Do you know what glass is made from?

Jim: New glass is made from a mixture of four main ingredients: sand, soda ash, limestone and other additives. These additives include iron for colour (brown or green), chromium and cobalt for colour (green and blue respectively), lead to alter the refractive index, alumina for durability and boron to improve the thermal options. Annually, total glass use in the UK is estimated at around 3.6 million tonnes.

(four-second pause)

Before you hear the rest of the conversation, you have some time to look at questions 26–31.
(fifteen-second pause)

Now listen and answer questions 26–31.

David: You're kidding. That's phenomenal. What do we do with all that glass? Where does it go?

Jim: Using present technology, the UK glass industry has the capacity to recycle over one million tonnes of glass each year and this, coupled with the material's unique ability to be infinitely recycled without compromising its quality, creates a compelling case for the recycling of glass. Despite this, glass makes up around 7% of the average household dustbin and last year, over 2.5 million tonnes of this material was landfill.

David: How can glass be recycled?

Jim: It can be recycled indefinitely as part of a simple but hugely beneficial process, as its structure does not deteriorate when reprocessed. In the case of bottles and jars, up to 80% of the total mixture can be made from reclaimed scrap glass, called cullet.

David: What's it called?

Jim: Cullet. C-U-L-L-E-T. Cullet from a factory has a known composition and is recognized as 'domestic cullet'. From bottle banks it is known as 'foreign' and its actual properties will not be known. Recycling two bottles saves enough energy to boil water for five cups of tea.

David: You know, I wouldn't mind a cuppa now.

Jim: Did you know that recycling reduces the demand for raw materials? There is no shortage of the materials used, but they do have to be quarried from our landscape, so from this point of view, there are environmental advantages to recovering and recycling glass. For every tonne of recycled glass used, 1.2 tonnes of raw materials are preserved. Recycling also reduces the amount of waste glass which needs to be used as landfill.

David: I know. It's a social conscience we all need to have.

Jim: Taking part in recycling the waste we produce makes us think about the effect we are having on our environment and enables us to contribute towards a greater level of sustainability. It's not all about economics, you know.

David: I'm sure you're right, Jim.

That is the end of section three. You now have half a minute to check your answers.
(thirty-second pause)

Now turn to section four.
(four-second pause)

Answers:
22. glaze
23. 20th century
24. sand, soda ash
25. 3.6 million tonnes
26. B

27. B
28. C
29. C
30. A
31. C

Listening

Tapescript 🎧 **173** (5 mins, 40 secs)

SECTION 4

You will hear an orientation lecture on sports therapy. First, you have some time to look at questions 32–40.

(fifteen-second pause)

Now listen carefully and answer questions 32–40.

Good morning, and welcome to the university's Open Day and to our lecture on Sports Therapy. There are two good reasons to be here. Firstly, you will experience what a university lecture is like – so take out your notebook and pen – and secondly, you will find out about the Sports Therapy programme. OK, so what does a Sports Therapy programme involve? Everybody in today's society knows the impact sport, health and fitness makes on the population's physical and mental health. Studying at Kent will develop your understanding of the ideas and issues within the sports therapy, health and fitness industries. Sports therapy is one of the fastest-growing careers within the sports sector. The programme teaches you all the specialist knowledge you need in order to work within these industries. This includes scientific aspects, such as anatomy and physiology and sports psychology. You learn how to design training programmes and lifestyle profiles for a range of clients, and to understand the role of sports promotion and event management. The degree also covers the treatment and prevention of sporting injuries and the importance of referral programmes. There will be a full description of these subjects for you available at the door when you leave this lecture. Now, just to talk a little about teaching and

assessment. The programme involves taking part in and designing practical sports sessions, lectures, small-group seminars and private study. On average, you have six lectures, three practical sessions and a one hour-long seminar per week, and you also spend additional time developing your coaching and theoretical knowledge in real-life situations. At Stage 1, the first half of the year is assessed by 100% coursework and observed assessments. A majority of the modules also have written exams within the final half of the year, with the rest practically assessed. Stage 2 and 3 assessment varies, from 100% coursework to a combination of examination and coursework, usually in the ratio 50:50, 60:40 or 80:20. You're probably wondering what career paths you can take once you've completed this degree. Well, careers can vary from employment in health and fitness clubs, sports injury clinics, sports development within local authorities, or with national governing bodies of sport, working in community leisure or sports attractions, self-employed personal trainer or sports therapist. There are some requirements you need to fulfil to enter this course. International students can qualify with the following: School Certificates and Higher School Certificates awarded by a body approved by the university; matriculation from an approved university, with a pass in English Language at GCSE O level, or an equivalent level in an approved English language test, passing one of Kent's foundation programmes, provided that you meet the subject requirements for the degree course you intend to study; or an examination pass accepted as equivalent to any of the above. In order to enter directly onto a degree course, you also need to prove your proficiency in English, and we ask for one of the following: average 6.5 in IELTS test, minimum 6.0 in Reading and Writing; grade B in Cambridge Certificate of Proficiency in English; grade A in Cambridge Advanced Certificate in English; a pass overall in the JMB/NEAB Test in English for Overseas Students, with at least B in Writing, Reading and Speaking Modules; a TOEFL score of at least 580 (written test) or 237 (computer test). If you haven't yet reached those standards, Kent runs a foundation course for international students which gives you a year's academic and language training before you begin on your degree. Right, that's about it. Any questions?

That is the end of section four. You now have half a minute to check your answers.
(thirty-second pause)

That is the end of the listening test. In the IELTS test, you would now have ten minutes to transfer your answers to the listening answer sheet.

Answers:
32. Sports Therapy programme
33. ideas and issues
34. anatomy
35. sports psychology
36. one hour-long
37. written exams
38. trainer
39. an equivalent
40. foundation course

Reading

Part 1
1. C   2. D   3. E   4. D   5. B   6. A
7. E   8. B   9. G   10. K   11. F   12. H
13. D   14. J

Part 2
15. B   16. C   17. E   18. H   (in any order)
19. tips   20. relate to   21. interviews
22. go online   23. C   24. A   25. B   26. B
27. C   28. A   29. A   30. B

Part 3
31. best-sellers   32. outline or sample
33. main characters   34. coincidences
35. new character   36. cut
37. use their imagination   38. dramatic verbs
39. background   40. climax